Protestants on Screen

Protestants on Screen

Religion, Politics, and Aesthetics in European and American Movies

Edited by
GASTÓN ESPINOSA, ERIK REDLING,
JASON STEVENS

OXFORD
UNIVERSITY PRESS

OXFORD
UNIVERSITY PRESS

Oxford University Press is a department of the University of Oxford. It furthers the University's objective of excellence in research, scholarship, and education by publishing worldwide. Oxford is a registered trade mark of Oxford University Press in the UK and certain other countries.

Published in the United States of America by Oxford University Press
198 Madison Avenue, New York, NY 10016, United States of America.

CIP data is on file at the Library of Congress
ISBN 978–0–19–005891–3 (pbk.)
ISBN 978–0–19–005890–6 (hbk.)

DOI: 10.1093/oso/9780190058906.001.0001

Paperback printed by Marquis Book Printing, Canada
Hardback printed by Bridgeport National Bindery, Inc., United States of America

This book is dedicated with much love to my three children, Rafael, Maria, and Carina, for all the countless hours over the years they've talked with Dad about his crazy book and film ideas and to my late great-uncle Frank Espinosa, who spent many years acting in Spanish-language films in the United States and Mexico.
—Gastón Espinosa

This book is dedicated to my parents, for always loving and supporting me, and to my wife, Kathrin, and my two boys, Lennart and Henri, for making me see the beauty of life—every day.
—Erik Redling

This book is dedicated to my brother Justin, who is always ready to talk about movies; my friend Michelle, who helped me when I most I needed support; and Rita, who was by my side for so much of the journey.
—Jason Stevens

Contents

Acknowledgments xi
List of Contributors xiii

Introduction, by Gastón Espinosa, Erik Redling, and Jason Stevens 1
Introduction Part I: Why Protestants and Film 1
Introduction Part II: What Is Religion and Why Is It Important in Film? 5
Introduction Part III: What Is Protestantism? 10
Introduction Part IV: Protestantism and Film—Historical Overview 19
Introduction Part V: Protestant Film Aesthetics 41
Introduction Part VI: Chapter Overview 48

PART I HISTORY AND THEORY OF PROTESTANTISM IN RELIGION AND FILM STUDIES

1. Protestant Responses to Hollywood, Censorship, and Art Cinema, by William D. Romanowski 57
2. Independent Protestant Film, from the Silent Era to Its Resurgence, by Andrew Quicke 71
3. Protestant Themes Within Secular Models of Salvation—"Redeemed" or Just "a Bit Happier"? The Example of *Crazy Heart*, by Clive Marsh 83

PART II THE PROTESTANT REFORMATION ON SCREEN

4. "Here I Stand I Can Do No Other": Martin Luther in German and American Biopics, by Esther P. Wipfler 97
5. The Vexed Man: Oliver Cromwell and the English Reformation and Civil War on Screen, by Gastón Espinosa 109
6. Propaganda, Blasphemy, and the Savage God in *Witchfinder General* and *The Wicker Man*, by Victor Sage 127

PART III PROTESTANT INFLUENCES IN EUROPEAN ART FILMS

7. Words Versus "the Word": Language and Scripture in Ingmar Bergman's Films and Writings, by Maaret Koskinen 141

8. Protestant Miracle in Dreyer's *Ordet*, by Mark Le Fanu 155

9. Babette's Feast: Protestant Pietism, the Conflict of Spirit and Flesh, and Reconciliatory Grace in the Danish *Babette's Feast*, by Kjell O. Lejon 167

10. Protestant Ambivalence Toward Allegory in Wim Wenders's *The Scarlet Letter*, by Erik Redling 179

PART IV PROTESTANT EXPERIENCE IN AMERICAN MOVIES

11. "Where Were You?" The Problem of Evil in Terrence Malick's *The Tree of Life*, by Mark S. M. Scott 193

12. "Holy Ghost Power!" in Robert Duvall's *The Apostle*, by Gastón Espinosa and Jason Stevens 203

13. Sinner or Saint? Martin Luther King Jr. and the Civil Rights Movement in *Selma*, by Julius H. Bailey 221

14. The Religious Motif of Mountains in Tyler Perry's *Why Did I Get Married?*, by Melanie Johnson 239

15. A Tender View of Conservative Evangelicalism in *Higher Ground*, by Paula M. Kane 253

16. Evangelicals and *Star Wars*: Appropriating a Culture from a Galaxy Far, Far Away, by Alex Wainer 267

PART V PROTESTANT THEMES IN FILM GENRES

17. The Rise and Fall of Evangelical Protestant Apocalyptic Horror: From *A Thief in the Night* to *Left Behind* and Beyond, by Timothy Beal 281

18. The Western: Radical Forgiveness in *Unforgiven*, by Sara Anson Vaux 293

19. Protestant Pacifist: War and Pacifism in Mel Gibson's *Hacksaw Ridge*, by Matthew S. Rindge 307

20. Film Noir, Calvinism, and Self-Surveillance in Paul Schrader's *Hardcore*, by Jason Stevens 321

21. Lost in Adaptation: Aslan's Divinity and the Purpose of Real Pain in *Narnia* Versus Fantasy Film, by Devin Brown 335

Notes 345
Index 389

Acknowledgments

There have been a number of sponsors that helped give birth to this book.

The idea for this book was birthed by Gastón Espinosa, Erik Redling, and Jason Stevens over lunch one day while we were on sabbatical at the National Humanities Center Institute for Advanced Studies, in North Carolina. We swapped stories about our love for religion, race, and film and the classes we taught at our respective institutions. This conversation gave birth to a conference that was co-sponsored by the Martin Luther University Halle-Wittenberg; the Leucorea Foundation, located in the historic birthplace of the Protestant Reformation, Wittenberg, Germany; and Claremont McKenna College, in California. This conference generated a number of outstanding papers that were augmented by equally creative commissioned papers that have been transformed into this present book.

This book received generous support from sponsors in Germany. In Germany, we wish to thank Martin Luther University Halle-Wittenberg, the Muhlenberg Center for American Studies (MCAS), the US Embassy in Berlin and the US Consulate in Leipzig, the German Association of American Studies (GAAS/DGfA), the Leucorea Foundation in Wittenberg, the city of Lutherstadt Wittenberg, and especially the Fritz Thyssen Stiftung.

Our sponsors in the United States were equally helpful. We wish to thank Claremont McKenna College president Hiram Chodosh, deans Peter Uvin and Heather Antecol, associate dean Shana Levin, and director Amy Kind of the Gould Center for Humanistic Studies; the National Humanities Center Institute for Advanced Studies, in Research Triangle Park, North Carolina; and the Humanities Center at the University of Pittsburgh for their generous financial support for sabbaticals/leaves, the conference, and/or the book.

All of us wish to thank our families, for their patience and encouragement throughout this process, and our religion and film students, who continue to inspire in us a passion for analyzing the creative intersections of religion, race, and film studies.

Finally, we are deeply grateful to all of our incredible contributors, Oxford University Press, and fellow colleagues and editors for all of their patience and generous spirits.

List of Contributors

Julius H. Bailey, University of Redlands, USA.
Dr. Julius H. Bailey is a Professor of Religious Studies at the University of Redlands. He received his M.A. and Ph.D. in Religious Studies from the University of North Carolina at Chapel Hill. He has written three books, including *Down in the Valley: An Introduction to African American Religious History* (Fortress Press, 2016) and has written numerous articles and book chapters on Black religion, culture, and society. He has also given lectures on African mythology entitled "The Great Mythologies of the World: Africa" produced by the Great Courses series.

Timothy Beal, Case Western University, USA.
Timothy Beal is Distinguished University Professor, Florence Harkness Professor of Religion, and director of h.lab at Case Western Reserve University. His extensive bibliography includes *Religion in America: A Very Short Introduction* (Oxford University Press, 2008), *Mel Gibson's Bible: Religion, Popular Culture, and The Passion of the Christ*, of which he is co-author (University of Chicago Press, 2006), and "Behold Thou the Behemoth: Imagining the Unimaginable in Monster Movies" in *Imag(in)ing Otherness: Filmic Visions of Living Together* (American Academy of Religion and Oxford University Press, 1999).

Devin Brown, Asbury University, USA.
Dr. Devin Brown is Lilly Scholar and Professor of English at Asbury University and specializes in Tolkien and C.S. Lewis. He is author of *Discussing Mere Christianity* (Zondervan, 2015), *A Life Observed: A Spiritual Biography of C. S. Lewis* (Brazos, 2013), and *The Christian World of The Hobbit* (Abingdon, 2012).

Gastón Espinosa, Claremont McKenna College, USA.
Gastón Espinosa is the Arthur V. Stoughton Professor of Religious Studies at Claremont Mckenna College, and author or editor of eight books, including *Religion, Race and Barack Obama's New Democratic Pluralism* (Routledge, 2012), *Mexican American Religions: Spirituality, Activism and Culture* (Duke University Press, 2008), and *Latino Pentecostals in America: Faith and Politics in Action* (Harvard University Press, 2014). After receiving his Ph.D., Espinosa studied at the UCLA School of Theater, Film and Television and worked with Lawrence Bender and Luis Mandoki on screening *Innocent Voices (Voces Innocentes)* and preparing a marketing schematic for religious audiences for *An Inconvenient Truth*. He teaches courses on religion and film annually.

Melanie Johnson, Claremont Graduate University, USA.
Melanie Johnson is a freelance writer for various faith-based and non-profit organizations and for artistic projects. She received her Ph.D. in Religion with a concentration in

Media Studies from Claremont Graduate University and taught as an adjunct professor in the Religious Studies Department at Mount Saint Mary's University in Los Angeles. She received her M.Div. from Columbia Theological Seminary. While studying Television Writing and Producing at Columbia College Chicago, she co-taught the course, "Race, Culture, and Media." Her dissertation on African American filmmaker Tyler Perry is a transdisciplinary project examining the religious motifs and symbolism in Perry's movies. She has published one children's book, *Benjamin the Wise Bee* (2009).

Paula M. Kane, University of Pittsburgh, USA.
Paula Kane is the John and Lucine O'Brien Marous Chair of Contemporary Catholic Studies and Professor of Religious Studies at the University of Pittsburgh. She teaches courses on American religious history, global Christianity, Catholicism, and religion and media. Among her publications are "Jews and Catholics Converge: *Song of Bernadette*" in *Catholics in the Movies* (Oxford University Press, 2007) and *Sister Thorn and Catholic Mysticism in Modern America* (University of North Carolina Press, 2013). She received her Ph.D. in American Studies from Yale University.

Maaret Koskinen, Stockholm University, Sweden.
Maaret Koskinen is Emeritus Professor of Cinema Studies at Stockholm University. She was the first scholar given access to Ingmar Bergman's private papers, which led to the formation of the Bergman Foundation. Books in English include *Ingmar Bergman Revisited: Cinema, Performance and the Arts* (Wallflower Press, 2008), *Ingmar Bergman's The Silence: Pictures in the Typewriter, Writings on the Screen* (University of Washington Press, 2010), and *Ingmar Bergman at the Crossroads: Between Theory and Practice* (ed. with Louise Wallenberg, Bloomsbury Academic, 2022). Her Swedish-language *I begynnelsen var ordet,* on Bergman as writer, was published in Spanish in 2018 as *Ingmar Bergman y sus primeros escritos. En el principio era la palabra* (Shangrila).

Mark Le Fanu, University College London, UK.
Mark Le Fanu lectures at University College London. A film academic and writer, he focuses on documentary film and world cinema. His most recent book is *Believing in Film: Christianity and Classic European Cinema* (Bloomsbury, 2019). He has also written extensively on the film culture of Russia and Japan, notably in *Mizoguchi and Japan* (BFI Books, 2005 [re-issued by Bloomsbury, 2020]) and *The Cinema of Andrei Tarkovsky* (BFI Books, 1987). His film essays appear in *Sight & Sound* and *Positif*, and as liner notes for the Criterion DVD label.

Kjell O. Lejon, Linköping University, Sweden.
Kjell O. Lejon is Professor of Religious Studies, Head of Division, and Director of Studies at the University of Linköping. His two interest areas are religion and politics in the modern United States and Swedish church history and has published 25 books, including works in English, such as *George H. W. Bush: Faith, Presidency and Public Theology* (Peter Lang, 2014). *Linköping – an Introduction to the Diocesan History* (Artos, 2012), and *Reagan, Religion and Politics* (Lund UP/Chartwell-Bratt, 1988).

Clive Marsh, University of Leicester, UK.
Clive Marsh is Principal of the Queen's Foundation for Ecumenical Theological Education, Birmingham, UK. A specialist in theology and culture (pop culture & arts), his most relevant works within the area of film and religion include *Explorations in Theology and Film* (with G. Ortiz, Blackwell, 1997), *Cinema and Sentiment: Film's Challenge to Theology* (Paternoster Press/Authentic Media, 2004), and *Theology Goes to the Movies: An Introduction to Critical Christian Thinking* (Routledge, 2007). His most recent major work is *A Cultural Theology of Salvation* (Oxford University Press 2018).

Andrew Quicke, Regent University, USA.
Professor Andrew Quicke teaches at Regent University in the Department of Film & Television. His interests include redemptive cinema, the history of contemporary American cinema, and foreign cinema. In addition to his production experience, he has published *The Age of Censorship 1930-1966* (Routledge 2009), and *The Emergence of the Christian Film Industry 1930-1986* (New York University Press, 2011), co-authored with Terence Lindvall.

Erik Redling, Martin Luther University Halle-Wittenberg, Germany.
Erik Redling is Professor of American Literature at Martin Luther University Halle-Wittenberg, Germany. He is the author of *"Speaking of Dialect": Translating Charles W. Chesnutt's Conjure Tales into Postmodern Systems of Signification* (Königshausen & Neumann, 2006) and *Translating Jazz into Poetry: From Mimesis to Metaphor* (De Gruyter, 2017). He has (co-)edited several books, including *The Handbook of the American Short Story* (with Oliver Scheiding, De Gruyter, 2022), and published in the fields of visual culture, cognitive theories, and intermedial translations. He has co-taught courses on religion and film and co-organized two international conferences on Protestantism and popular culture.

Matthew S. Rindge, Gonzaga University, USA.
Matthew S. Rindge is Professor of Religious Studies at Gonzaga University, where he teaches "Bible and Film," "Religion and Film," "Religion and Horror," and related courses. He is the author of *Bible and Film: The Basics* (Routledge, 2021), *Profane Parables: Film and the American Dream* (Baylor University Press, 2016), and *Jesus' Parable of the Rich Fool: Luke 12:13-34 among Ancient Conversations on Death and Possessions* (Society of Biblical Literature, 2011). For six years he chaired the Bible and Film section in the Society of Biblical Literature, and he continues to serve on their steering committee.

William D. Romanowski, Calvin College, USA.
William D. Romanowski is Emeritus Professor at Calvin University in the Department of Communication. His books on religion and film include *Cinematic Faith: A Christian Perspective on Movies and Meaning* (Baker Academic, 2019), *Reforming Hollywood: How American Protestants Fought for Freedom at the Movies* (Oxford University Press, 2012), *Eyes Wide Open: Looking for God in Popular Culture* (Brazos Press, 2001, rev. and exp. ed., 2007), and *Pop Culture Wars: Religion and the Role of Entertainment in American Life* (InterVarsity Press, 1997).

Victor Sage, East Anglia University, UK.
Victor Sage is an Emeritus Professor of English Literature in the School of Literature, Drama and Creative Writing at the University of East Anglia, Norwich, England. He is the author of *Horror Fiction in the Protestant Tradition* (St. Martin's Press, 1988) and *Le Fanu's Gothic: The Rhetoric of Darkness* (Palgrave Macmillan, 2007). He is also the editor for Charles Maturin's *Melmoth the Wanderer* (Penguin Classics, 2001) and Sheridan Le Fanu's *Uncle Silas* (Penguin Classics, 2001). With a piece on Sir Walter Scott and E. T. A. Hoffmann, he participated in the first research collection on German Gothic for thirty years, *Popular Revenants: The German Gothic and its International Reception, 1800–2000*, eds. Cusack and Murnane (Boydell and Brewer, 2012). Later publications include an essay on the Elementary Spirits as a vehicle for the Gothic in *Romantic Gothic: an Edinburgh Companion*, eds. Wright and Townsend (2016). More recently, he has been working on the theme of cultural cross-currents in the French *fantastique*, and he has a piece on forbidden spaces in George Sand, Hoffmann, and Scott in the forthcoming *Europe in British Literature and Culture*, eds., William Rossiter and Petra Rau.

Mark S. M. Scott, Thorneloe University, Canada.
Dr. Mark Scott is an Associate Professor in the Department of Religious Studies and Theology at Stonehill College. He received his Ph.D. and A.M. (Religion) from Harvard University, his M.A.R. (Theology) from Yale Divinity School, and his B.A. (Honours) in Religious Studies from McMaster University. He has published two academic monographs: *Pathways in Theodicy: An Introduction to the Problem of Evil* (Fortress Press, 2015) and *Journey Back to God: Origen on the Problem of Evil* (OUP, 2012 [paperback: 2015]). His essays have appeared in numerous scholarly venues, including *Harvard Theological Review*, *Journal of Early Christian Studies*, *Religious Studies*, *Open Theology*, and elsewhere. His research interests include theology, philosophy of religion, early Christianity, and religion and literature.

Jason Stevens, Independent Scholar, USA.
Jason Stevens is the author of God-Fearing and Free: A Spiritual History of America's Cold War (Harvard University Press, 2010) and the editor of This Life, This World: New Chapters on Marilynne Robinson's Housekeeping, Gilead, and Home (Brill, 2015). He contributed three essays, "Secularism," "Christianity," and "Religion," to the series American Literature in Transition (Cambridge University Press, 2018-19). His writings have also appeared in Literature/Film Quarterly, American Literature, and Boundary 2. He has taught at Harvard University and the University of Maryland, Baltimore County, and held fellowships at National Humanities Center (Durham, NC) and the University of Pittsburgh.

Sara Anson Vaux, Northwestern University, USA.
Sara Anson Vaux is Emeritus Lecturer in the Department of Religious Studies at Northwestern University, Evanston, Illinois. She has published *Finding Meaning at the Movies* (Abingdon, 1999), *The Ethical Vision of Clint Eastwood* (Eerdmans, 2011), and *Eastwood: A Biography* (Greenwood Biographies, 2014). She taught courses and lectured (among others) on Robert Bresson, Andrei Tarkovsky, Carl-Theodore Dreyer, and the

Dardennes Brothers, with an emphasis on social justice and the search for the beloved community. She received her Ph.D. from Rice University and served as an administrator at University of Chicago before her tenure at Northwestern.

Alex Wainer, Palm Beach Atlantic University, USA.
Alex Wainer is Professor Emeritus of Communication and Media Studies at Palm Beach Atlantic University. He has published a book entitled *Soul of the Dark Knight: Batman as Mythic Hero in Comics and Film* (McFarland, 2014) and numerous articles, including "Faith, Hope and Pixie Dust" (*World Magazine*, Jan. 26, 2008), "Willing Suspension of Belief: Faith and Unbelief in Classic Horror Films" (*The McNeese Review*, 1996), and two sidebar essays, "Tyler Perry's Redemptive Stories in Drag" and "Is Disney's Magic Family Friendly?" in *Understanding Evangelical Media* (IVP academic, 2008).

Esther P. Wipfler Zentralinstitut für Kunstgeschichte, Munich, Germany.
Esther P. Wipfler, Ph.D., M.A. is a researcher and editor at the Zentralinstitut für Kunstgeschichte in Munich since 2001. Her publications include the monograph *The Image of Martin Luther in Motion Pictures: A History of a Metamorphosis* (Göttingen: Vandenhoeck & Ruprecht, 2011) and the papers "Luthers 95 Thesen im bewegten Bild" in *Faszination Thesenanschlag — Faktum oder Fiktion*, eds. Joachim Ott and Martin Treu (Leipzig: EVA, 2008) and „Katharina Luther" oder die Emanzipation einer Filmfigur, in: Die Luthers medial: Nachklänge zu einem Jahrhundert-Jubiläum, eds. Sabine Kramer (Lutherstadt Wittenberg: Drei Kastanien Verlag 2018). Recently she edited *Das Gesangbuch und seine Bilder. Voraussetzungen, Gestaltung, Wirkung* (Köln: Böhlau 2020) and co-edited with Andrea Hofmann the proceedings of the international conference *500 Jahre Evangelisches Gesangbuch: Musik, Theologie, Kulturgeschichte* (Regensburg: Schnell&Steiner 2024).

Introduction

Gastón Espinosa, Erik Redling, and Jason Stevens

Introduction Part I: Why Protestants and Film

This book explores the Protestant contributions to American and European film over the past hundred years, with emphasis on the post-1960 period. It analyzes the various ways Protestant beliefs, theology, symbols, sensibilities, and cultural patterns have shaped film in the United States and western Europe. While Colleen McDannell's *Catholics in the Movies* has underscored the Catholic contributions to film, this is the first book to explore the critical role of Protestantism.[1]

After laying out our book's multitiered, diverse, and mutually reinforcing arguments about Protestantism and film, this Introduction proceeds in sequence to provide necessary contexts and definitions. In Part II, we will define religion, discuss why it is potentially important to filmmakers and studio marketing, and how religious traditions, symbols, and archetypes can add depth and meaning to characters and storytelling. In Part III, we will provide a brief history of Protestantism and its beliefs, and then, in Parts VI and V, we will explore its expression in film aesthetics and contributions to the history of Hollywood and European films. Part VI provides a structural overview of the book's chapters, organized by topic.

Protestantism on Screen makes several historical claims, each of which is elaborated in Part IV of this Introduction. Protestants helped birth cinema in the United States. From its inception, Protestants helped create and harness the power of motion pictures for spiritual instruction, edification, and cultural influence. Moreover, Protestants influenced filmmaking in the United States in three distinct but at times overlapping ways from the 1920s to the present.

First, mainline Protestants contributed to nonsectarian approaches to filmmaking in Hollywood and often protested the Catholic Legion of Decency film censorship. Additionally, in the post–World War II era, theologically liberal Protestants helped create a space for increasingly secular stories, meaning stories with religious subtexts or values that correlate with Christianity but do not necessarily display overt religiosity. Though their influence has waned since the 1970s because of cultural shifts and Reagan-era media consolidation that we detail in Part IV of this Introduction and Chapter 1, mainline Protestants contributed to

Gastón Espinosa, Erik Redling, and Jason Stevens, *Introduction* In: *Protestants on Screen*.
Edited by: Gastón Espinosa, Erik Redling and Jason Stevens, Oxford University Press. © Oxford University Press 2023.
DOI: 10.1093/oso/9780190058906.003.0001

making Hollywood a secular industry. By secular, we do not mean anti-religious because liberal Protestant agencies also instrumentally cooperated with liberal Catholic agencies in the 1960s to support the invention of the movie ratings system (see Chapter 1). Additionally, mainline Protestant nonsectarian and pluralistic values have persisted in Hollywood's secular openness to films that demythologize and psychologize biblical stories (Richard Fleischer's *Barabbas*, Martin Scorsese's *The Last Temptation of Christ*, Darren Aronofsky's *Noah*, Ridley Scott's *Exodus*) and to movies that have spiritual or religious themes, but are made by religious and non-religious filmmakers.

For this reason, we cover several films by Hollywood producers, directors, and actors who are not avowedly Protestant, though most have been shaped by larger Protestant sensibilities and religio-cultural frameworks . Recent examples that we cover include Robert Duvall (*The Apostle*), Vera Farmiga (*Higher Ground*), and Ava DuVernay (*Selma*), each of whom has searchingly portrayed race and gender in religiously imbued social movements.[2] Since the silent era, moreover, Hollywood has made movies with Protestant themes and characters appearing in popular film genres that, in contrast to biblical epics (or "Bible and sandals" movies), are not branded as "religious films." Therefore, we consider how three non-Protestant filmmakers—Clint Eastwood, Mel Gibson, and Paul Schrader—have each worked in a distinct genre: Western (*Unforgiven*), war movie (*Hacksaw Ridge*), and film noir (*Hardcore*), to provide commentary on Protestantism.[3]

Second, Protestants have served as major catalysts for an independent "faith-based" Christian film industry, which evangelicals now largely lead. In the silent era, with mainline and evangelical support, Protestants made and distributed nontheatrical movies for church audiences, with production peaking in the mid-1920s. Increasingly marginalized by the success of Hollywood religious spectacles like *King of Kings* (1927), this emergent industry was almost put out of business, but black-and-white Protestant films continued to be made in the sound era. With considerable help from evangelical leader Billy Graham, the independent Protestant film industry began to recover artistically and financially in the post–World War II era, and by the 1970s it had laid the groundwork for an evangelical film resurgence and renaissance beginning in the late 1990s and proceeding through the 2000s. As underscored in the messaging of 1970s evangelical apocalyptic horror movies, launched by Donald Thompson's widely screened *A Thief in the Night* (1972), the resurgence had its roots in midcentury evangelicalism's desire to lure youth from the counterculture, resist certain Hollywood religious stereotypes, and protest declamations of "the death of God."[4] In the 2000s, the profitability of Christian filmmaking (Protestant and Catholic) has persuaded major entertainment conglomerates to launch their own slates of "faith-friendly" movies, many of them targeting evangelical and traditional Catholic audiences. Those scholars who argue that "the political reality of evangelicals" far outstrips their "representative power" on the screen compared to Catholics have failed to take adequate account of this upsurge in the number, quality, and financial success of evangelical filmmaking or its impact on the larger film industry (see Part IV of this Introduction).[5]

An important feature of this resurgence and a third way that Protestants have influenced U.S. filmmaking is that evangelicals in Hollywood—producers, directors, writers, actors—themselves began creating films that portrayed Protestant and Christian values and characters in sympathetic and respectful, but at times critical, ways. There are earlier precedents, of course; Protestants like D. W. Griffith, Cecil B. DeMille, and Lois Weber (see Part IV) each made explicitly Christian films for secular studios. However, in contrast to these pioneers who were operating in a post-Victorian age, recent filmmakers like Tyler Perry, actors like Denzel Washington and David Oyelowo, and studios like Walden Media, famous for the Narnia fantasy-film series and owned by conservative Protestant Philip Anschutz, are putting faith perspectives into movies to resist, as they see it, a rising secular tide in contemporary culture.[6]

The rise of high-profile Black Protestant filmmakers and actors in Hollywood and in independent faith-based films (T. D. Jakes, for example) has called attention to the growing racial-ethnic diversity of American evangelicalism, a consequence due largely to growth of the evangelical and largely Holiness-Pentecostal movement among African Americans and Latinos. While Golden Age Hollywood films about Protestants might lack the rich evocation of urban ethnic ghettoes that appear in classic films about Catholics, modern Protestant films are not confined to "a rural hinterland" and represent ethnic-racial minorities, often in gritty settings (e.g., movies by Tyler Perry and T.D. Jakes), as we shall see in Part IV and the chapters that follow.[7]

Parallel to developments in U.S. cinema, we track several European trends, focusing primarily on the United Kingdom, Germany, and Scandinavia. These trends include Luther biopics, pastor-focused psychological dramas, period films about the Reformation, and British historical folk horror about Puritanism. The influence of Lutheranism looms large in European art cinema, to which we give special attention. Figures like Carl Dreyer, Ingmar Bergman, and Wim Wenders reacted against Hollywood religious films as well as conventional European religious cinema and forged new ways to explore Protestantism on-screen, including personal critique. In the late 1960s and 1970s, European art cinema helped give rise to the New Hollywood, in which aspiring American auteurs like Paul Schrader, an ex-Calvinist, experimented with more daring treatments of spiritual themes than had been possible in classic American film, which, while beloved, had been constrained by Hollywood's Production Code. Beyond their contributions to the New Hollywood, European films—as we see in Part IV—have remained a vital source of reflection on Protestantism, with contributions by Wenders, Gabriel Axel, Michael Haneke, Mirjam von Arx, and the Dogme 95 movement, among others. Overall, we show that, as in U.S. cinema, even filmmakers who have left the Protestant fold can continue to make films that reflect a Protestant sensibility and worldview.

Our book's uniquely transatlantic perspective allows us to track common Protestant themes across American and European films: faith and doubt, sin and depravity, biblical literalism, personal conversion and personal redemption, holiness and sanctification, moralism/pietism, Providence and secularism, apocalypticism and the end of the world as the individuals know it, righteousness and justice and the political quest for these values (reform, revolution, civil rights), the priesthood of all believers and its offshoots—democratization, individualism, manifest destiny.[8] The ubiquity of these themes across nationalities, periods, and genres contradicts the claim that "in the world of the movies, religion is Catholic."[9]

Through its comparative approach, this book tackles two major assumptions in the fields of religious studies and film studies. First, the transatlantic perspective of this volume qualifies one of the ascendant theories of religious studies: that is, not only did Protestantism perform the demolition work for secularism to emerge in the West, but some forms of liberal Protestantism are particularly agreeable with secularism because the latter derived its foundational notions of selfhood, conscience, history, reason and knowledge, poetics, and "good" and "bad" forms of religion from pervasive liberal Protestant attitudes, beliefs, and practices.[10] Immediate questions have followed from this theory—namely, does it hold for both Europe and America, given the differences in their histories and in the ways that they institutionalize secularism? We find that while American and European films reflect these historical differences depending on how secularism emerged in their respective societies, they nonetheless share a common focus on this-worldly pursuits within a Protestant framework. Mainline Protestants in the United States and the United Kingdom, for example, tended to favor a form of secularism that freed industry from religious oversight, regulations, and censorship, while still promoting religious values—a project that proved difficult for them to sustain. The films we cover portray characters not entirely at home with secularism, if we mean by secularism the privatization of religion (and consequent withdrawal from the public sphere), the hyperrationalization of life, or an easeful adaptation of Christianity to secular culture. In his *Christ and Culture* (1951), H. Richard Niebuhr discusses five different ways Christians have related to culture: Christ against culture (separatism), Christ of culture (accommodation), Christ above culture (medieval synthesis), Christ and culture in paradox (dualism), and Christ transforming culture (dynamic interaction). He argues that most Protestant churches neither withdrew from secular culture nor thoroughly accommodated to it, but instead strove to instruct and transform secular culture to be more Christian in its norms, while still respecting the differences between church and state.[11] This dynamic tension is sustained in the work and thought of filmmakers (producers, writers, directors), film industry reformers, film critics (lay and professional), and theologians of film, and in the struggles of characters in films as varied as *Selma*, *Higher Ground*, and Luther biopics with their mutating iconography of the hero.

Second, *Protestantism on Screen* problematizes the assumption in film studies of Protestant thematic and aesthetic Puritanism, an image forged in Counter-Reformation polemics and given support by Weber's theory of disenchantment.[12] We reject the stereotype of Protestants as world-denouncing and -defying Puritans and iconoclasts who stood in the way of film's maturation as an art.[13] Instead, we argue that Protestant films have identifiable aesthetic impulses: reform, embodiment of the biblical Word, a reenchantment of the mundane, reduction (or "decluttering"), and the interplay of the literal and the symbolic. With reference to our case studies, Part V of the Introduction explores these impulses and connects them to Protestantism's ongoing effort since the Reformation to define the relationship between the sacred and profane, saint and sinner, and religion and art. In some of these impulses, such as embodiment of the biblical Word, we see contrasts with Catholic aesthetic practices that traditionally materialize the sacred in three-dimensional objects rather than emphasize the spoken, written, and enacted (lived-out) scripture. In capturing these impulses, however, filmmakers must look for solutions that work cinematically. David Morgan's case that Protestants use lighting and space in their churches to highlight the iconicity of biblical texts is well taken, but as a strategy for film, which is a sensory-rich medium, an aesthetic driven toward "pure white walls" and "clean, well-lit, and sound-swept interiors" would be unduly limiting.[14] Even when a filmmaker like Ingmar Bergman attempts this degree of reduction, indeed radicalizes it, he does not push space, imagery, bodies, faces, and action into the background, mute secular music, or utterly dispense with conversational dialogue. The interaction of Protestantism and film is fascinating because there is no single aesthetic solution—and there cannot be, given the rich diversity within the Protestant tradition, the variety of filmmakers' attitudes toward Protestants, and the many creative potentials of film.

Introduction Part II: What Is Religion and Why Is It Important in Film?

What is religion? The Merriam-Webster dictionary defines religion as "a personal set or institutionalized system of religious attitudes, beliefs, and practices" and "a cause, principle, or system of beliefs held with ardor and faith."[15]

Figure 1 George Lucas (1944–) directing *Star Wars III – Revenge of the Sith* in 2005.
Lucasfilm / Morton, Merrick Album / Alamy Stock Photo

Religion is thus a personal or institutional (or both) belief in a cause or principle (God, the Tao, Brahman, all-pervading life force, etc.) held with conviction and faith, the latter of which is defined as a belief and firm trust in something one cannot concretely prove. What sets religion apart from other cultural institutions and phenomena is that it is often ancient, mysterious, all-encompassing, experiential, deeply personal, nonrational, and/or the bedrock of many cultural ideas and values. Despite the decline of institutional religion in some countries (e.g., western European countries and Marxist countries elsewhere), in many other areas around the world religion is resurging, especially in post-Marxist societies.[16]

In addition to personal and institutional religion, there is also popular religion, or those expressions of religion that overlap with and/or exist alongside institutional forms. We see popular religious expressions not only in the song lyrics of Bob Dylan, Johnny Cash, Carlos Santana, U2, Madonna, Kanye West, and Kendrick Lamar but also in movies like *Star Wars*, *Raiders of the Lost Ark*, *The Matrix*, *Malcolm X*, *The Da Vinci Code*, and *Avatar*. Since popular religion is not dependent on institutional religion to survive, at the same time as some institutional forms of religion may be declining, various forms of popular religiosity may also be growing and thriving.

Religion is important to filmmakers for many reasons. First, most of the world has been and remains religious. Almost 7 of the 7.8 billion people around the world are religious, which is important for marketing films in countries where religion plays a robust role in society. The seven largest religious traditions make up over 90 percent of all religious practitioners: Christianity (31.2 percent of the world's population), Islam (24.1 percent), Hinduism (15.1 percent), Buddhism (6.9 percent), folk religions (5.7 percent), Judaism (0.2 percent), and all other religions (0.8 percent), each having smaller denominations and traditions. Approximately 16 percent are unaffiliated, of which about 5-6 percent are agnostics or atheists.[17] Filmmakers can tap into world religions for stories, for characters, and as a vehicle for marketing films overseas. Religious ideas from around the world are evident in *Star Wars*, *The Matrix*, *The Apostle*, *Chronicles of Narnia*, *The Life of Pi*, and *Avatar*.

Second, the vast majority of Americans are religious, spiritual, or open to the supernatural, which can be important for marketing films in the United States. According to the Gallup Poll, at least 76 percent of Americans self-identify as religious: 69 percent report being Christian (46 percent Protestant/Other Christian, 22 percent Catholic), 7 percent other world religion (Jews, Muslims, Hindus, Buddhists, others), 21 percent no religious preference (some of which are religious), no religion, or agnostic, or atheist; 3 percent gave no answer. Depending on the survey, about 32-35 percent of Americans report being a "born-again" or evangelical—that is, someone who has had a personal conversion experience with Jesus Christ. Racial-ethnic minorities, women, immigrants, the working class, and the disabled tend to be significantly more likely to be religious than whites and elites, perhaps because religion provides them with a greater sense of love, community, purpose, power, hope, and personal agency.[18]

Third, religion in important as a potential avenue for marketing film. An understanding of religion can help writers, producers, and directors tap into U.S. and global markets and avoid unnecessarily offending movie-goers. For example, *Indiana Jones and the Temple of Doom* was banned in India because of its racist and orientalist portrayals of Indians and Hinduism. Similarly, Disney's animated *Hunchback of Notre Dame* was heavily criticized for its blatant anti-Catholic bias. Hindus and Christians called for boycotts of both films, thus undercutting the filmmakers' marketing efforts and global markets in Hindu- and Catholic-majority countries. Given that the average Hollywood blockbuster film costs over $100 million to get to the big screen (about $100,000 per page of screenplay) and that producers are always seeking new overseas markets, it's not surprising that some might pay increasing attention to religion and spirituality.[19]

Fourth, religious traditions, leaders, and archetypes have shaped countless stories in film. They have had a profound impact on traditions, morals, taboos, and social views on family, gender, race, class, sexuality, politics, and social change—all things that shape stories. Religion often provides the larger backdrop for film stories and shapes the personality and worldviews of protagonists (e.g., *Luther*, *Cromwell*, *The Apostle*, *Left Behind*, *Selma*), antagonists (e.g., *Witchfinder General*, *Cape Fear*), and the quasi-religious archetypes that ordinary people can recognize regardless of the film. Many films can also conjure up religious archetypal heroes (gods, angels, Moses, Jesus Christ, the Virgin Mary) and villains (Satan, demons, Judas, Jezebel), though these character types are normally cast in a more nonsectarian and secularized form. For all of the above reasons, religion is important to filmmakers in the United States and around the world.

The Role of Religious Archetypes in Films

A growing number of filmmakers (religious and nonreligious) draw on religious traditions, symbols, and beliefs as a way to deepen their story and its appeal. One way they do so is by tapping into religious archetypes and monomyths. In his book *The Hero with A Thousand Faces*, Joseph Campbell argues that most religions have divine and/or human heroes that undergo journeys. These quests follow a similar pattern that seems to "underlie a number of . . . different myths" around the world. The pattern, which he calls the "monomyth," parallels the life paths taken by many religious founders, saints, and leaders. In films, the monomyth is often secularized and stripped of the obvious religious references—but with the deeper archetypal characters and struggles intact.[20] George Lucas drew on Campbell's monomyth framework of the hero's journey to help create the story arc for Luke Skywalker in *Star Wars*.[21] The monomyth concept could help to explain why the series' concept of the Force was so well received around the world: it resonates with the Christian concept of God as the creative force of the universe, the Taoist notion of the Tao as an impartial force that does not take sides, and the Hindu notion of Brahman as an all-pervading life force that ties the universe together. We see the archetypal characters: Obi-Wan Kenobi as the threshold guardian and quasi-spiritual mentor and Darth Vader as the embodiment of evil.

Christopher Vogler translated Campbell's insights into a popular and influential book for screenwriters called *The Writer's Journey: Mythic Structure for Writers*. In it, he identifies a number of archetypal characters found across traditions: the hero (savior), antagonist (devil/evil/opponent), mentor, threshold guardian, herald, shape-shifter, shadow, ally, and trickster. Following Aristotle's teachings on plot, Vogler breaks the hero's journey down into three acts: beginning, middle, and end. In Act I, we encounter the hero in an ordinary and idyllic world, just before it is disrupted (the inciting incident). Once the hero receives the call to adventure, they initially refuse it (usually due to fear or a lack of self-confidence or faith), but eventually they meet a mentor who helps them overcome external and internal fears. The hero and mentor then cross the first threshold. In Act II, there are rising conflicts/tensions/stakes as the hero faces tests, makes allies, and battles against enemies. The hero faces personal doubts as well and, journeying to the innermost cave (normally a physical location of some kind and/or in their mind), undergoes a major ordeal that externalizes their fears. The plot reaches a point of no return wherein the hero can never go back to the world from which they came and they must face their greatest challenge and fear alone—without their mentor or any external aids. In Act III, the hero faces a crisis where they appear to overcome the dragon or main antagonist and save the world, but then suffers a reversal that puts them in mortal danger, sometimes ending in their apparent loss, death, or sacrifice, and leaving the impression that all hope is lost. At the film's climax, the protagonist is resurrected (physically and/or emotionally/psychologically/spriritually) and musters the inner strength to overcome their fears to slay the dragon. The resolution is reached when the hero returns home and brings healing and peace to the new world order (elixir).[22]

According to screenwriters who follow Vogler's model, the plot points of the hero's journey create a rising tension of "hope versus fear," which is a writing device that drives many good stories. In *Jurassic Park*, for example, we hope the hero will overcome the various obstacles to escape the island before they are discovered, but we fear that before this happens they will be eaten by the raptors or *T. rex*. Most classical stories are built around the protagonist having to overcome five to seven increasingly dangerous obstacles (aka plot points), which may keep the hero from reaching their goal. The antagonist can be a personal villain, a monster, a cosmic being, a society, and/or a structure. Regardless of whether the protagonist is religious, many of the mentors, threshold guardians, and people (or beings) that help the protagonist overcome their inner doubts and fears are often people who have supernatural or quasi-spiritual powers and/or insights (e.g., Obi-Wan Kenobi). Their purpose is to help the protagonist engage in self-reflection in order to muster up the inner courage to overcome their inner and external obstacles and reach their goals. These quasi-spiritual mentors and supernatural forces (good and bad) add depth, mystery, hope, and fear to the protagonist's story arc. How would *Star Wars* reach its resolution without Yoda and Obi-Wan Kenobi (quasi-spiritual Jedi masters in touch with the all-pervading Force) helping Luke Skywalker to harness the power of the Force? How would Neo overcome the Matrix without Morpheus, the Oracle, and Trinity to guide and protect him? What would Pocahontas do without Willow's advice and comfort, and how would Jake Sully garner the inner strength to defeat the Sky People without first praying to Eywa through the Tree of Souls in *Avatar*?

These quasi-spiritual guides enable the protagonist to overcome their doubts, slay the dragon, and save the world.

These venerable story types and structures, which gird classical film narratives and blockbusters, are not definitive of screen storytelling and some films don't follow them at all. Throughout the history of narrative film, moviemakers have adventurously departed from these formulas. The patterns that Campbell and Vogler have highlighted are important as models that filmmakers not only rediscover and adopt but also revise and overturn as they grapple with the continuing presence of religion in their environment. Vogler has had a significant influence in Hollywood, having worked in the development departments for Disney, Warner Brothers, and Fox 2000.

Introduction Part III: What Is Protestantism?

Historical Origins

Protestants are Christians who trace their religious roots back to Martin Luther's "protest" against spiritual abuses in the Catholic Church first layed out in Luther's *95 Theses* in 1517 in Wittenberg, Germany. Protestants deny the universal authority of the Pope and affirm the Protestant Reformation principles of justification by faith in Jesus Christ alone for salvation and the primacy of the Bible as the only infallible source of revealed truth. Today most Protestants no longer protest against the Catholic Church because the latter has undergone major reforms to address past abuses and problems and because today Protestants and Catholics often work cooperatively on social issues.[23]

Protestantism is the largest Christian tradition in western Europe, Scandinavia, Australia, New Zealand, South Africa, and the United States. It can be broken down into two main groupings: mainline/historic Protestants and Evangelical Protestants. Evangelicals can further be broken down into four overlapping (at times) subgroups: Evangelical non-Pentecostal, Pentecostal, independent/nondenominational, and fundamentalist. The two most important characteristics that most Protestants tend to share in common are the convictions that the Bible is the Word of God and one must believe in Jesus to go to heaven. Evangelicals stress that to go to heaven one must repent of their sins and have a personal conversion experience with Jesus Christ. They base this on John 3:3, where Jesus said one must be "born again" to enter heaven, though liberal Protestants do not stress this and instead focus on being a good, moral person.

Most Protestants trace their theological roots back to the Protestant Reformation in Europe led by Martin Luther (d. 1546), John Calvin (d. 1564), and Anabaptist leaders like Menno Simons (d. 1561). Considered the father

IN SILENTIO FORTITVDO
ET SPE ERIT VESTRA

Figure 2 Martin Luther (1483-1546) is considered the main founder of the Protestant Reformation and Protestant Christian tradition. He influenced future Protestant leaders like John Calvin and and later Billy Graham, and William J. Seymour.

Engraving by Theodor Knesing from the picture of Lucas Cranach. Source: Courtesy Library of Congress Prints/Photographs Division, LD-USZ62-106322.

of Protestantism, Luther was originally a Catholic Augustinian monk, priest, and Bible professor at Wittenberg University, near Berlin, Germany. A good Catholic, he believed in the four-stage process of penance: sincere contrition for one's sins, confession of one's sins to a priest, satisfaction or restitution for one's bad actions, and, after these three stages were completed, absolution and forgiveness by a priest on God's behalf. However, Luther had a problem with Dominican friar Johann Tetzel abusing the penitential system by calling on the poor to buy indulgences to fulfill the requirement of restitution and satisfaction for sins in purgatory. Luther argued that the mechanical act of buying an indulgence did not take the place of sincere contrition and genuine sorrow before God for one's sins (a sin being any act of willful disobedience against God's known biblical statutes, such as the Ten Commandments).

Luther's frustration with these abuses and many others came to a head when he nailed his Ninety-five Theses to the cathedral door in Wittenberg on All Saints' Day, October 31, 1517. This event ignited the Protestant Reformation and gave birth to Protestantism. His Ninety-five Theses not only listed all of the popular abuses in the Catholic Church but also called on the Pope to reform the church and put an end to them. To Luther's surprise, the Pope branded him a heretic. Under the protection of Duke Frederick III of Saxony, Luther used the printing press to publish and spread his theses across Europe. He translated the Bible into German for the first time and published more than fifty-five other books and commentaries on the Bible, theology, and social issues, all of which laid the foundation for the Protestant tradition. Since Luther and Protestants believed that superstitions and extrabiblical traditions arose when people could not read the Bible for themselves, he promoted public education and the mass distribution of the Bible in the language of the people, not just Latin.

Luther and the Protestant Reformation stressed ten principles that still govern how many Protestants think to this day: salvation is by the grace of God alone (not God's grace plus a person's good works); human nature (mind, will, affections) and reason are corrupt and imperfect and therefore cannot contribute anything to one's salvation; the saving grace of God comes only through repenting of one's sins and asking Jesus Christ to be one's Savior and Lord; salvation is by faith in Jesus Christ alone (not faith plus Catholic tradition); certainty of salvation (one can know one is saved—by contrast, the Catholic Church teaches that can never presume know for certain if they are saved); reduction of the sacraments from seven to two (baptism and communion); the understanding that the church is an association of believers and not, as in Catholicism, the only intermediary between God and human beings for salvation; being saved leads to being virtuous as a natural consequence; the elimination of prayers for the dead, prayers to saints and the Virgin Mary, indulgences, and purgatory; and, finally, the priesthood of all believers (everyone should have the right and ability to read the Bible in their own vernacular language and serve as godly leaders in their families and societies). Luther and the Protestant Reformation's teachings can be summed up in the five solas: *sola scriptura*, *sola gratia*, *sola fide*, *solo Christo*, and *soli Deo gloria*.

The French Reformer John Calvin took Luther's ideas and wrote the first great systematic theology of the Protestant movement, *The Institutes of the Christian Religion* (1536, 1559). While Luther's ideas spread primarily to northern Europe and some English colonies in America, Calvin's version of Protestantism (called Calvinism or the Reformed tradition) spread around the world but had a greater impact in Switzerland, Holland, England, and the American colonies through the preaching and teaching of Theodore Beza in Switzerland, John Knox and the Presbyterians in Scotland, the Baptists in England, and the Pilgrims, the Puritans, the Dutch Reformed Church, Presbyterians, and early Baptists across the American colonies. The Calvinist brand of Protestantism dominated colonial America from the 1620s to the 1760s and spread via evangelistic revivals in the First Great Awakening of religion in the 1730s and 1740s.

Calvin taught that until a person's mind is spiritually regenerated by the Holy Spirit, they cannot be saved because the Bible teaches that they are spiritually dead to the things of God prior to God regenerating their minds and hearts (Ephesians 2:1, 5). People are completely dependent upon the grace and sovereignty of God to initiate and confirm their salvation. Calvin's views were crystallized by his followers in the five points of Calvinism (TULIP): total depravity (a person's mind, will, and affections are tainted by sinful and selfish desires), unconditional election to salvation (God's decision to save a person was not based on foreknowledge of that person's good works), limited atonement (while Christ died for the whole world in a general sense, his sacrifice is applied in practice only for the sins of the predestined elect), irresistible grace (God's love, grace, and salvation are irresistible), and the perseverance of the saints (God will enable true believers to persevere in their faith until the end of their lives).

The Calvinist notion of predestination, election, and limited atonement was too restrictive for some Protestants. This led Jacob Arminius (d. 1609) to create a theological system called Arminianism. His views were outlined by his followers in the *Remonstrance* (1610), or protest against classical Calvinism. Arminius stressed free will, conditional election, universal redemption or general atonement (God's offer of salvation is for anyone in the world who confesses their sins and believes in Jesus Christ—not just the predestined elect), and the conviction that Christians can lose their salvation by walking away from God and their faith. This system became widespread through the preaching of John and Charles Wesley and white and Black evangelists in the Second Great Awakening (c. 1790s–1840s). While many Presbyterians and Dutch Reformed traditions are Calvinist in origin, most Baptists, Pentecostals, Methodists, and independent Protestants are Arminian. Today, the vast majority of American Protestants embrace what amounts to an Arminian theological worldview, though some blend aspects of both in a "Calminian" (Calvinist-Arminian) outlook.

Protestants with an Arminian outlook argue that human beings are not simply predestined to heaven or hell, because this would remove a person's free will and human responsibility. For this reason, Arminians tend to place a greater premium on evangelism, conversion, and holy living. Thus evangelical and Pentecostal Protestants stress living a sanctified life, based on commonsense literal interpretation of the Bible's teaching on moral and ethical issues. They also believe that if a person falls away from their faith, or "backslides," they can regain their salvation by rededicating their life to Jesus Christ. Hence, they promote evangelistic crusades to convert the spiritually lost and revivals to recommit the spiritually backslidden.

Mainline Protestants

Most mainline Protestants are moderate-liberal Christians. They were all once evangelical in their theological orientation, stressing the need for a personal born-again relationship with Jesus Christ and the Bible as the infallible Word of God. They began to change their views in the late nineteenth and early twentieth centuries, after coming under the influence of higher criticism of the Bible, theological modernism, and scientists who questioned creation and the historicity of other biblical stories. The Scopes "Monkey Trial" of the 1920s marks a watershed moment: the crystallization and breaking away of a liberal branch of Protestantism that denied the inerrancy and infallibility of the Bible, the virgin birth of Jesus Christ, and the belief that Jesus is the only way to heaven. Although many mainline Protestant denominational and seminary elites embraced some of these views, the vast majority of ordinary parishioners and many leaders still maintained their conservative-moderate roots throughout much of the twentieth century. Some still do to this day. In general, mainline Protestants—Episcopalians, United Methodists, Presbyterians (Presbyterian Church USA), and Lutherans (Evangelical Lutheran Church in America)—tend to be highly rationalistic in outlook, creedal, theologically moderate-liberal, morally progressive, and liturgical. They joined together in 1950 to form the ecumenical National Council of the Churches of Christ in the USA.

Mainline Protestants are much more likely than evangelicals to hold liberal views on theological doctrine (universal salvation of all people) and on social and moral issues such as abortion, same-sex marriage, the ordination of gays and lesbians, and the death penalty. While they normally reject the inerrancy of the Bible, they are strongly committed to intellectual life and progressive social causes. They tend to have much higher income and educational levels than evangelicals and Pentecostals and, as a result, have been America's political, intellectual, and social elites. For reasons that are not entirely clear, they are less likely to be depicted in film than their evangelical and Pentecostal counterparts, though possibly it is because of their highly rationalistic and scientific approach to faith and reason. They tend to place less emphasis on the supernatural, divine healing, miracles, revivals, evangelism, and conversion—which are highly cinematic subjects.

Figure 3 John Calvin (1509-1564) the second most important Protestant leader and founder of the Calvinist / Reformed tradition, which spread to the U.S. and around the world to English-speaking colonies.

Engraving by John Sartain (?). Source: Courtesy Library of Congress Prints/Photographs Division LC-USZ62ll-72002.

Evangelicals, Pentecostals, and Fundamentalists

Evangelicals are conservative Protestant Christians who trace their roots directly back to Martin Luther, John Calvin, the Anabaptists, and the Protestant Reformation. The word "evangelical" is not new; Luther preferred it to the label "Protestant." The English word "evangelical" comes from the Greek *evangelion*, which means "good news." An evangelical is therefore someone who preaches the Good News about Jesus's life, death, and resurrection from the dead and the need for people to repent of their sins and have a personal born-again conversion experience with Jesus Christ (John 3:3; Romans 3:23, 6:23, 10:9–10). Although born-again Christians can be found in every denomination, in the United States the term "evangelical" is largely applied to politically, theologically, and morally conservative Protestants.

While almost all Pentecostals are born-again and thus evangelical, not all evangelicals are Pentecostals. Pentecostals affirm the validity and practice of tongues and the spiritual sign gifts (e.g., miracles, healings, speaking in tongues, prophecy) in the church today.[24] Overall, evangelicals can be classified into three groups: evangelical non-Pentecostals, Pentecostals and charismatics, and independents and nondenominationals. They all stress the Bible and having a born-again conversion experience with Jesus Christ.

The National Association of Evangelicals (NAE) in the United States was formed in 1942 to unite all conservative Protestant denominations and to create a national voice in American politics. Today the NAE represents sixty Protestant denominations and forty-five thousand churches—a group much larger than their liberal Protestant counterparts. The most prominent evangelical leaders in the United States over the past twenty years include Billy Graham, James Dobson, Rick Warren, Tony Campolo, Jim Wallis, Pat Robertson, T. D. Jakes, and Wayne Grudem. Evangelical churches are racially and ethnically diverse, and a growing number of younger and racial-ethnic evangelicals hold to progressive social views on race relations, civil rights, women in ministry, and social justice.

Fundamentalists are a much smaller segment of Protestantism—about 3 percent of all Protestants. Socially conservative and theologically antimodernist, they militantly fight to preserve the fundamentals of the faith from skeptics and liberal Protestants. Fundamentalists generally hold to an evangelical worldview, but tend to affirm dispensational premillennialism and/or a cessationist position of the spiritual sign gifts, the latter of which teaches the sign gifts—e.g., miracles, healings, speaking in tongues, prophecy—of the Holy Spirit ceased with the death of the Apostles in the New Testament and therefore are no longer needed in the church today. In 1928, the World's Christian Fundamentals Association rejected Pentecostals as a "fanatical" "menace" to Christians for promoting the sign gifts and the ordination of women.[25] For these reasons and others, Pentecostals/charismatics are not normally classified as fundamentalists, even though they affirm the core historic doctrines of Christianity. The vast majority of conservative Protestants today are evangelicals or Pentecostal/charismatics rather than fundamentalists. In fact, the term "fundamentalist" has fallen out of popular usage for most conservative Protestants because of the pejorative social, theological, and political stigma attached to the word and because most evangelicals and Pentecostals/charismatics are open to social and racial justice, the spiritual gifts, and in many cases women in ministry.

Pentecostals and Charismatics

Pentecostals take their name from Acts 2:4, where on the Day of Pentecost the Holy Spirit reportedly fell on the Apostles, causing them to speak in unknown tongues. Pentecostals today teach two types of tongues signifying baptism in the Holy Spirit: a human language one has never studied (xenolalia; Acts 2) and a divinely given speech known only to God (glossolalia; Acts 8:17–19, 10:44–46, 19:1–6). Additionally, they affirm all of the other spiritual gifts listed in the New Testament, including apostleship, evangelism, pastoring, service, healing, working miracles, prophecy, distinguishing/discerning spirits, casting out evil spirits, and interpretation of tongues (1 Corinthians 12:8–10, 28–30; Ephesians 4:11; Romans 12:6–8; 1 Peter 4:11; Mark 16:17).

The classical Pentecostal movement in the United States grew out of the nineteenth-century Protestant evangelical revival tradition and was born in the wake of Charles Fox Parham's Topeka Bible School revival in 1901 and William J. Seymour's Azusa Street revival in Los Angeles from 1906 to 1909.[26] The revival run by Seymour, who was African American, attracted twenty nationalities, held integrated services, allowed women in ministry, and crossed racial-ethnic and class barriers in an age when white supremacy and segregation were the norm in many parts of America. Parham and Seymour originally held that the baptism in the Holy Spirit *must* be evidenced by speaking in unknown tongues (xenolalia), but by October 1906 Seymour changed his mind. He and most global Pentecostals today teach that speaking in tongues is just one of the evidences of the Spirit baptism and that it could manifest itself as either xenolalia or glossolalia, though normally it is glossolalia. Parham never changed his view.[27]

The main purpose of tongues (xenolalia and glossolalia) was to empower people to carry out cross-cultural missionary work and/or other forms of service in the church. Pentecostalism has spread rapidly among racial-ethnic minorities, women, poor whites, the working class, and immigrants, and more recently it has moved into the middle class. In fact, the largest Pentecostal denominations in the United States today are the predominantly African American Church of God in Christ, the white Assemblies of God, the Church of God (Cleveland, Tennessee), and the Foursquare Church; the largest Latino-serving Protestant tradition is the Latin Districts of the Assemblies of God.

Charismatics are Christians in non-Pentecostal/charismatic denominations who believe most of the spiritual gifts are available to Christians today, though some exclude apostleship and/or prophecy. They affirm a born-again,

Figure 4 William J. Seymour and the Azusa Street Revival (1906-1909) Leadership Team, ca. 1907. He helped to found and spread the Pentecostal movement around the world. Today it is one of the largest Protestant traditions among Blacks and Latinos.
Flower Pentecostal Heritage Center

Spirit-filled life but normally do not mandate that a person must speak in tongues after conversion. The modern charismatic movement began in 1967 after Episcopalian Dennis Bennett, Lutheran Larry Christenson, Catholics Kilian McDonnell, Francis MacNutt, and Edward O'Connor, and others promoted the spiritual gifts within their traditions. Today there are charismatics in the Presbyterian, Baptist, Episcopalian, Methodist, and Catholic churches, and in almost all other Christian denominations and most independent churches.

Neo-charismatics in the United States grew out of classical Pentecostal bodies but left in the 1960s and 1970s to form their own independent churches and denominations that targeted youth during the countercultural movement. Some led the Jesus movement of the 1960s and 1970s and emphasized evangelism, expository Bible teaching, guitar- and band-led worship services, and a relaxed, laid-back, and "come as you are" style and atmosphere, which has appealed to young adults and families. The most popular neo-charismatic leaders and traditions include Chuck Smith and Calvary Chapel (Costa Mesa, California), John Wimber and the Vineyard Christian Fellowship, Hope Chapel, and Sonny Arguinzoni and Victory Outreach International (La Puente, California), among others. Many were birthed in Southern California and have spread globally. There are other neo-charismatic movements in Latin America, Africa, and Asia with no ties to the U.S. charismatic or neo-charismatic movements, but those emerged out of indigenous Pentecostal/charismatic traditions in their own countries.

Neo-charismatics have contributed to the evangelical pop subculture with evangelistically oriented Christian rock, rap, R&B, hip-hop, and pop bands, as well as clothing, videos, books, tattoos, magazines, art, and musicals/plays. They attract large numbers of racial-ethnic minorities and urban youth via evangelistic campaigns like Greg Laurie's Harvest crusades at Anaheim Stadium in California. The thread binding Pentecostals, charismatics, and neo-charismatics together is their born-again, Spirit-filled experience and affirmation of the gifts of the Holy Spirit.

Introduction Part IV: Protestantism and Film—Historical Overview

Protestant Influences on American Films

In the United States, the first films were produced by Protestants. They were East Coast entrepreneurs who became members of the monopolistic Edison Trust, formed in 1908, or else competed with the trust.[28] By the early twentieth century, Protestants had already developed a culture of "visual piety" receptive to movies. For edification and devotion, they had embraced commodified, technologically produced, and mass-disseminated images: lithographs, engravings, illustrated school primers, scriptural scenes, and picture lesson cards.[29] These "visual religious instructional materials" provided "film boosters" with cases to defend the spiritual use of motion pictures. Evangelists like Billy Sunday, defenders of the Bible like William Jennings Bryan, and ministers of Protestant churches like the Congregationalist Herbert Jump, who published the vigorous apologetic *The Religious Possibilities of the Motion Picture* (1911), were fervid proponents of early cinema.[30] Along with Protestant civic leaders, they were also leading reformers of the new medium. Early short films playing at nickelodeons were often targets of vice crusaders, but the rise of narrative cinema promised to make movies fit for highbrow and morally edifying entertainment, with proper guidance. Charles Parkhurst, the head of the Madison Avenue Presbyterian Church, became an avid movie critic and joined the National Board Review (founded in

1909), an agency designed to weed out objectionable films and promote uplifting ones and whose members were mostly well-to-do Protestants.[31]

Feature filmmaking also arrived against the background of a liberal mainline Protestant progressive movement to revitalize secular amusements. Leisure pastimes represented an opportunity to develop individuals' character (moral sense) and personality (the dynamic self).[32] The frivolous or immoral content of movies often disappointed reformers' high aspirations, and ministers themselves could be butts of ridicule.[33] Nonetheless, the tastes of the largely Protestant middle class remained an influential gauge of film content as producers strove for both respectability and profits. As a result, many silent-era films, especially Westerns and melodramas, reflected a Protestant sensibility mixing Puritanism and a softer Victorian piety.[34]

Writer-director D. W. Griffith, a mainline Protestant Southern Methodist with a genteel upbringing, conceived of cinema as an instrument of reform. In melodramas such as *One Is Business, the Other Crime* (1912), *Intolerance* (1916), and *Way Down East* (1923), the rich and well-off tend to be either knavish or benighted, and humankind in general is burdened by sclerotic institutions and self-righteous reformers who lack his heroines' capacity for Christian charity. Griffith framed his social criticism within a millennial vision of the Kingdom of God.[35] This vision, disturbingly, was a contradictory mix of WASP nationalism and the Social Gospel. On the one hand, the kingdom called for greater compassion for the poor and the downtrodden; on the other hand, it sanctified ethno-religious purity and violence, as in *The Birth of a Nation* (1915).

With its vicious racial stereotyping of Blacks as rapacious villains or pawns of unscrupulous northern carpetbaggers, *Birth of a Nation* became one of the KKK's sacramental texts. Spike Lee's *BlacKkKlansman* (2018) has recently called attention to the role that *Birth of a Nation* played in sanctifying the KKK. However, most have forgotten that nearly a century ago Oscar Micheaux—an independent secular Black filmmaker—wrote and directed a powerful rejoinder to Griffith's virulent epic. Micheaux's anti-lynching movie, *Within Our Gates* (1922), uses *The Birth of a Nation*'s own rhetorical devices, melodrama and sentiment, to portray Blacks as true Christians traduced and crucified by white Protestant racists. In response, Anne Morey has noted that Griffith's *The White Rose* (1923) employs a Black Christian character whose sympathetic portrayal seems designed to temper the criticism that the director was continuing to receive for *Birth of a Nation*.[36]

Writer-director Lois Weber, like Griffith, believed that movies were instruments of religious and social reform. She had served for two years in the mainline Protestant Anglican evangelistic Church Army, morally rehabilitating "gang members, alcoholics, drug addicts, and prostitutes."[37] Joining the American Gaumont film company in 1908, she saw movies as an extension of her former missionary work.[38] Of the hundreds of films she is estimated to have made, sadly only a few have survived, with *Hypocrites* (1915) being the best known. Taking as its prefatory texts Matthew 23:13–29 and the poetry and prose of the Puritan John Milton (*Paradise Lost*, *Areopagitica*), which are all quoted on-screen, the narrative of *Hypocrites* is presented as a Protestant minister's allegorical dream. Controversially for her time period, Weber represents the "nakedness of Truth" as a fully nude woman—as Milton describes Truth originally "com[ing] into the world with her Divine Master and . . . [having] a perfect shape glorious to look upon." In a recurring irony, no one shown in the dream except for Gabriel the Ascetic can look upon Truth because they live in deception. Even church-going Christians have "motes" in their eyes. In this blindness, Weber shows, humankind and society suffer the woes that Christ meted out to the Scribes and Pharisees.

Figure 5 Lois Weber (1879-1939) pictured in the advertising for one of her most famous films, *What do Men Want?* (1921).
Phoenix / Alamy Stock Photo

Along with Griffith and Weber, Cecil B. DeMille was the most significant director of religious films in the silent era. The son of a mainline Protestant Episcopalian minister and a Jewish mother who converted, DeMille, like Griffith, saw movies as visual sermons in a universal language. His most lasting contribution was in a genre that Griffith largely neglected: the biblical epic.[39] DeMille's approach to *King of Kings* (1927), a lavish life of Christ, universalized Jesus: an inclusive strategy that enhanced the film's commercial potential but also agreed with DeMille's broadly liberal Protestant leanings. For example, he strove to make his film ecumenical, consulting with Jewish as well as Christian advisors and drawing visually on nineteenth-century art beloved by both Protestants and Catholics (most especially works by Rembrandt, Tissot, and Doré). He and his scenarist, Jeanie MacPherson, also used multiple translations of the Gospels for the intertitles, whereas in *The Ten Commandments* (1923) they had relied solely on the King James Version.[40] Additionally, while the film is orthodox in its Christology in many respects (Jesus is the Son of God; atonement requires the Crucifixion; resurrection is physical), it emphasizes Jesus's good works rather than his miracles. DeMille and MacPherson, however, were less sensitive in their handling of the Jewish high priest Caiaphas and Jews featured during the Passion segments. When the Jewish Anti-Defamation League and B'nai B'rith accused the film of fanning bigotry, Griffith authorized significant reedits to the film, which enjoyed multiple reissues and church screenings and became an industry classic.[41]

DeMille's artistry and showmanship in *King of Kings* had the unintended consequence of helping to bring about the near demise of a parallel film industry for Christians. In the silent era, Protestant companies, such as Sacred Films, Herald Non-Theatrical Pictures, Plymouth Pictures, the International Church Film Corporation, the Film Library of Associated Churches, New Era Films, and the Religious Motion Picture Foundation (RMPF), were started to provide godly alternatives to secular entertainment. Terry Lindvall, the chief historian of this "sanctuary cinema," traces the origins to 1898, when evangelist Colonel Henry H. Hadley decided to add a photoplay version of a Passion play to his camp meetings in New Jersey. Combined with live music and preaching, the spectacular presentation drew thousands, inspiring him to take the film on the revival circuit. Mainline and Evangelical Protestant churches (Congregationalists, Methodists, Presbyterians, Northern Baptists, and some Southern Baptists) were among the earliest venues to exhibit films for educational and religious purposes. After World War I, clergymen and lay church leaders began financing, producing, and exhibiting their own nontheatrical films, for use in church services or in road shows run by itinerant preachers. Some of these films were sectarian in subject; others, like the RMPF's productions, were nondenominational. They ranged in genre from adaptations of Bible stories to missionary docudramas to morality tales in contemporary settings.

Between 1914 and 1920, major studio production shifted from the East Coast to the West Coast, giving birth to Hollywood and an extremely efficient machine for filling film markets. Larry May's *Screening Out the Past* and Neal Gabler's *An Empire of Their Own* argue that it was during this transitional period that films begin to pass from Christian Protestant control on the East Coast to a strong Jewish influence on the West Coast, where regulatory laws, religious leaders, and the general population were less stringent.[42] Early Hollywood's moral melodramas, Westerns, and Bible epics inspired the makers of church films, whose products were specifically designed for Christian audiences. This independent film industry and Protestant enthusiasm for it helped to highlight the vast market for religious entertainment—and the movie capital took notice. By the end of the twenties, competition with Hollywood's own religious products, especially lavish and effects-laden spectacles such as *Noah's Ark* (1928), DeMille's *The Ten Commandments*, and, most of all, *King of Kings* (1927), had largely eclipsed this independent Protestant film industry. The birth of "talkie" cinema with the premiere of *The Jazz Singer* (1927), which used expensive sound-recording technology, added an insuperable economic barrier.

African American church films and religiously themed Black films (genre movies designed for limited distribution to exclusively Black audiences) survived, despite the technical and budgetary limitations common to independent productions in this era, because Hollywood had no product that represented their audiences. Though 20th Century Fox produced films that cast Blacks in the roles of ministers, Sunday school teachers, biblical characters, seraphim, and even God Himself, including *Hallelujah!* (1929), *The Green Pastures* (1936), and *Cabin in the Sky* (1943), these were films addressed to white spectators. They lacked the theological and cultural specificity, for example, of James and Eloyce Gist's church film *Hell-Bound Train* (1930) or Spencer Williams's race film *The Blood of Jesus* (1941): "the structure of a sermonic form" (a spiritual journey likened to a journey by train), scenes of Southern Baptist worship, stark and direct imagery (blood dripping from a crucifix onto a penitent's face), or symbolism blending African and Christian motifs ("the cross-roads" as space of choice and occasion for grace).[43] Meanwhile, the sanctuary cinema that Protestants had produced in the silent era percolated in memory, reemerging on a small scale with 16 mm productions during the 1940s and beginning its resurgence in 1951 when the Billy Graham Evangelistic Association's World Wide Pictures was incorporated, preparing the way for new Protestant movie companies much larger than those of the silent era.

Figure 6 Cecil B. DeMille directing the *Greatest Show on Earth* in 1921. He was arguably the most important Protestant director in Hollywood history because he influenced a religious impulse in Hollywood films for generations.
Walter Oleksy / Alamy Stock Photo

Figure 7 *Samson and Delilah* poster (1949). The period from the late 1940s through the mid-1960s was the high point for Bible and Sandal films.
TCD/Prod.DB / Alamy Stock Photo

As Hollywood moved into the sound era, its occasional religious messaging could not stave off local censorship and increasing criticism of its overall output. The major studios consented to the creation of the Production Code. The story of the code's formulation and the forces that compelled Hollywood to invent its own regulatory agency for enforcing the code, the Breen Office, has been told in many histories. Looming large in these accounts are the Catholic Legion of Decency; the Jesuit priest Daniel Lord; Will Hays, the Presbyterian public relations man who touted the 1930 version of the code; and Joseph Breen, the Catholic layman who headed the Production Code Administration (PCA) from 1934 to 1954. What have received much less attention are Protestant efforts to develop a more democratic means of movie reform.

Liberal Protestants, influenced by modernist theology and Progressivism, sought structural remedies to reform Hollywood through voluntary regulation rather than censorship. In 1950, the National Council of the Churches of Christ in the USA (a national organization of mainline denominations created in 1908 as the Federal Council of Church of Christ in America), merged the Protestant Film and Radio commissions into the Broadcasting and Film Commission (BFC). Its main headquarters, in New York, rejected the model of the Legion of Decency, which sought to certify films as to their moral and religious fitness before they were released to the public, and instead focused on changing public taste in order to encourage Hollywood to change its product. This would involve developing a "theology of the arts" that treated film as a potentially religious medium while, in the spirit of secularism, criticizing the Legion of Decency's prior censorship as an establishment of religious authority. As William Romanowski has demonstrated in an eye-opening book and a subsequent essay in this book, this long-overlooked chapter in film and religious history is important because it envisioned an approach to movie regulation that did not rely on pietistic censorship or hegemonic control, even though it was deeply influenced by Protestant values and sensibilities.[44]

Hollywood's portrayal of Protestantism in the postwar era, as in the silent and early sound eras, "rooted that faith in an ideal rural past."[45] Metro-Goldwyn-Mayer's *Big City* (1948), a Manhattan-set comedy-drama in which a Protestant minister shares custody of an orphan with a rabbi and a Catholic police officer is the rare exception that proves the rule. In the biopic *A Man Called Peter* (1955), the Presbyterian pastor Peter Marshall's career takes him to the U.S. Capitol, but the movie opens with a long prologue in the Scottish countryside, amid sublime mountains, that link Marshall's religious sensibility and experience of God to an old rural order. The net effect of Hollywood portrayals was to throw a halo of nostalgia around Protestantism that seemed to cut it off from modernity, thus contradicting the objectives of the BFC's New York office, which sought to cultivate spiritually deep movies that would move contemporary audiences schooled in the best of twentieth-century literature and art. Their definition of "the best" reflected what Sally Promey has called the "taste culture" of postwar liberal Protestantism: it strongly preferred ironic, ambiguous, and abstract modernist literature and visual art, which the neo-orthodox Lutheran Paul Tillich (a German émigré to the United States) championed in such books as his bestselling *The Courage to Be* (1952).[46]

While the 1950s were a period of increased religious observance in America, there were changes in the offing that presaged greater artistic latitude and cultural shifts that would affect Protestantism both on- and off-screen. The Paramount Decree (1948), a legal ruling which forced major studios to divest their theater holdings, encouraged independent production. The 1952 Supreme Court case *Burstyn v. Wilson*, which concerned New York State's attempt to censor the Roberto Rossellini film *The Miracle*, reversed the Court's decision in the 1915 case *Mutual v. Ohio* and weakened the Production Code by removing the justification for prior censorship.[47] *The Night of the Hunter* (1955), *Elmer Gantry* (1960), and *Inherit the Wind* (1960)—each distributed by United Artists, which was dominated by independent producers—would test the boundaries of permissibility under these looser, more competitive conditions.

Hollywood's Production Code forbade "throw[ing] ridicule on any religious faith" or "us[ing] ministers as comic characters or as villains," and mandated that "ceremonies of any definite religion should be carefully and respectfully handled."[48] Its strictures temporarily put an end in Hollywood to pointed films like Frank Capra's *The Miracle Woman* (1931), which satirizes Pentecostal leader Aimee Semple McPherson.[49] *The Night of the Hunter* seemed likely to elicit a host of objections from the PCA: it has as its villain a psychopathic evangelist named Harry Powell (often referred to only as "Preacher") who believes that "the Lord" gives him murderous commands. Yet the film was passed with a PCA seal of approval on the grounds that it was technically not in violation of the code because Harry Powell is not a true man of God. Yet the film remains subversive for spreading Powell's psychopathology to the rural religious community that gives him shelter.[50] The Protestant small town—an image of nostalgia in other movies—is here repressed and self-deceived to the point of madness.

Elmer Gantry and *Inherit the Wind* were also passed with a PCA seal after intense negotiations and protests during production. *Elmer Gantry* took a sweeping view of the 1920s with an eye to the 1950s; writer-director Richard Brooks had

Figure 8 Richard Brooks's Oscar-winning *Elmer Gantry* (United Artists, 1959) was a key film in Hollywood's shift toward a more critical representation of evangelicals.
PictureLux/The Hollywood Archive/Alamy Stock Photo

studied news clippings of the era's best-known evangelist, Billy Graham. Beyond the title character's glib hypocrisy, the film broadens its critique to fundamentalism and the business side of revivalism, and it links both to conservative politics and WASP privilege. Director Stanley Kramer's *Inherit the Wind* (1960) returned to the Scopes "Monkey Trial" of 1925 to make an impassioned argument for free thought. The defender of the Bible, Matthew Harrison Brady, is portrayed as a bumptious enemy of progress, and the fundamentalists who salute him are depicted as authoritarian in mentality, intolerant of dissent, and hostile to outsiders.[51] *Elmer Gantry* and *Inherit the Wind* were Oscar-nominated and Oscar-winning movies from acclaimed source material and helmed by distinguished directors.[52] Subsequent films fused elements from both and moved the image of the religious huckster from Elmer Gantry's Midwest to the South. In the hit comedy *Oh, God!* (1977), God (George Burns) shows up to tell a blowhard southern televangelist, Reverend Willie Williams, that he doesn't know a thing about Him.[53]

One can point to several motivations for the turn to these critical and parodic versions of Protestantism. Not least is the violence and white backlash of the civil rights era, which morally darkened the image of the South. However, there is also the ground-shifting of the sixties and early seventies, which saw countercultural movements toward postmodern spirituality and, within Christianity, a thrust away from traditional religious observance and toward secular activism or to hippie-influenced, Jesus movement–style religion, as captured in the rock musical *Jesus Christ, Superstar* (1973). In this atmosphere, where the profane became sacred, Americans were questioning old pieties, and these included cinematic images of faith through which Hollywood, for decades, had pictured the soul of the nation.[54]

On-screen, *Easy Rider* (1969) helped to usher in the New Hollywood cinema. The film gave vent to oppositional, anti-establishment values in a narrative punctuated with unconventional spiritual imagery.[55] A tongue-in-cheek *Esquire* cover (August 1, 1970), designed by George Lois, pictured St. Patrick's Cathedral with a marquee advertising *Easy Rider* and captioned with the title of the issue's cover story, "The New Movies: Faith of Our Children." *Esquire*'s none-too-subtle but provocative point was that religious energies were shifting from traditional houses of worship to movie culture. Two years later at the Oscars, the Academy of Motion Picture Arts and Sciences seemed to confirm *Esquire*'s perception of the zeitgeist when it awarded Best Documentary Feature to *Marjoe* (1972), an exposé made with the cooperation of its subject, Marjoe Gortner, a Pentecostal evangelist who modeled his style on rock musicians and who was defecting from the revival circuit in hopes of parlaying his charisma and entertainment gifts into a career as a movie star. Evangelicals answered by vowing to harness the religious power of the medium. The *Esquire* cover solicited a challenge from one of the evangelical co-producers of *The Cross and the Switchblade* (1970), an unexpected box office success about the life of inner-city Pentecostal youth minister

Figure 9 *Esquire*'s cover story, "The New Movies: Faith of Our Children" (August 1970), equated the New Hollywood and the counterculture.
Permission to use full page image FREE of charge; granted by copyright owner George Lois, designer of the cover, who confirmed permission via email on July 18, 2022.

David Wilkerson: "The motion picture theater is a central place where the values and views of life of young Americans are shaped, and we think that we ought to be in that arena."[56] Evangelicals, energized by the success of *The Cross and the Switchblade*, had come to see films as a front line in the battle for the nation's youth, a battle between themselves and a permissive secular culture.

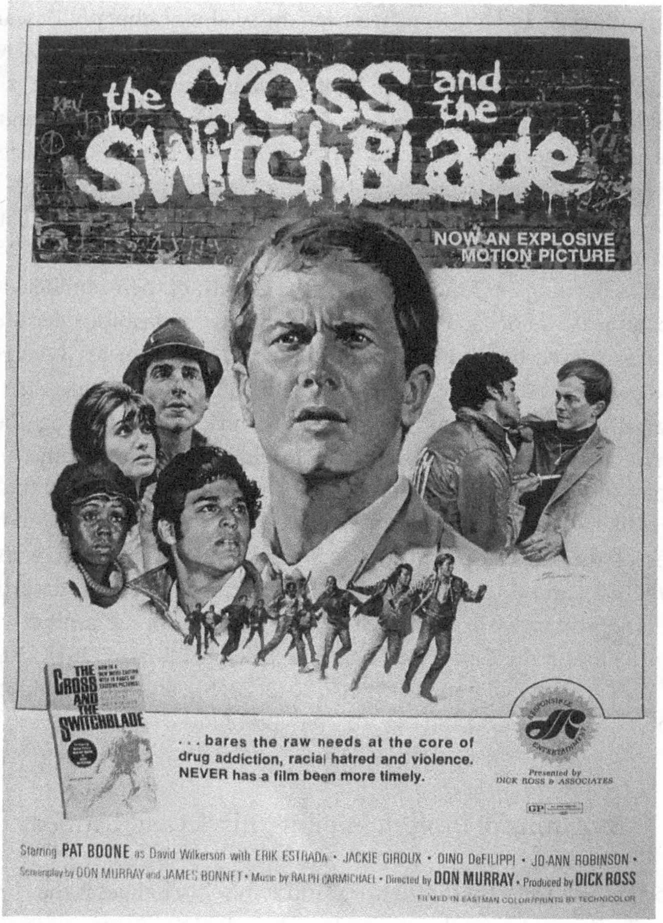

Figure 10 Poster Advertising *The Cross and The Switchblade*, emphasizing redemption from drugs, gangs, violence, and racial hatred, though with strong overtones of white saviorism.
Everett Collection, Inc. / Alamy Stock Photo

Rebounding from the counterculture, the New Hollywood, and the controversial release of Martin Scorsese's *The Last Temptation of Christ* (1988), evangelicals helped to grow the Protestant Christian film industry, which had been recovering steam since the fifties.[57] This evangelical cultural effervescence of cinema was assisted by two shifts. One is the decentralization of Hollywood's grip on the film industry and the decreasing costs of film technology and equipment needed to produce high-quality films. The second is a shift of the evangelical population into the middle class and higher echelons of the academy, film, politics, and other culturally elite circles. Jimmy Carter's successful bid for the presidency was a watershed moment. He was a Southern Baptist Evangelical and Democrat. Though the Moral Majority would reject him in 1980, Carter's election campaign helped to mainstream the term "evangelical" on both sides of the political aisle and led both *Time* and *Newsweek* to proclaim 1976 the "Year of the Evangelical."[58]

By 2004, national surveys reported that 80 percent of the U.S. population self-identified as Christian (60 percent Protestant and 20 percent Catholic) and 35–40 percent as born-again. Emboldened by the growth of their numbers as well as the increase in their social and political clout over the past four decades, evangelical voices started becoming increasingly heard and seen on the screen, and promoted greater film literacy and engagement with movie culture than ever before. Evangelicals' organized support mightily contributed to making *The Passion of the Christ* (2004), one of the most profitable religious films of all time, and awakening Hollywood to a vast potential market. This resurgence created the aegis for companies like Walden Media (of the Narnia series) as well as Sherwood Pictures (producer of the Kendrick brothers' box office hits *Facing the Giants* [2006], *Fireproof* [2008], and *Courageous* [2011], Sony's Provident Films (co-producer of the Kendrick brothers' *War Room* [2015] and marketer of the brothers' previous films), Pure Flix (of the *God's Not Dead* franchise [2014, 2016, 2018, 2021]), Fox Faith (of *The Ultimate Gift* franchise [2007, 2013, 2015]), and MGM's LightWorkers Media (of 2014's *Son of God* and the 2016 remake of *Ben-Hur*).

Browning of Protestant Films: Blacks and Latinos

An important feature of these structural and symbolic changes is the "browning" of evangelicalism, shaped by postcolonial and civil rights aspirations and struggles but carried over into the religious sphere. Robert Duvall's *The Apostle* (1997) was a breakthrough film for highlighting the multiracial and multiethnic character of the evangelical and especially Pentecostal movements in the United States, with intense depictions of interactions with Black and Latino (briefly) characters. Earlier, nonwhite evangelicals had been spotlighted by Sidney Poitier's Oscar-winning turn as a Black Baptist in the popular *Lilies of the Field* (1963), the conversion narrative of *The Cross and the Switchblade* (1970), the multiracial casts of *Jesus Christ Superstar* (1973) and *Godspell* (1973), and the four-minute Pentecostal revival segment of Robert M. Young's *Alambrista!* (1977). The dramatic turning point of *The Cross and the Switchblade*, a film influenced, like *Jesus Christ Superstar* and *Godspell*, by the burgeoning Jesus movement, is the conversion of Puerto Rican gang leader Nicky Cruz, who went on to be one of the most famous Latino evangelists of the 1960s and 1970s.[59]

Black Protestant writers, directors, and producers like T. D. Jakes and Tyler Perry have become household names in Hollywood and the evangelical Protestant subculture. Jakes, Pentecostal pastor of the Potter's House Church in Dallas, Texas, has co-produced films in multiple genres, including the romantic comedies *Not Easily Broken* (2009), based on his 2006 novel, and *Jumping the Broom* (2011); the musical *Sparkle* (2012), and dramas expressly marketed to Christian audiences, *Heaven Is for Real* (2014) and *Miracles from Heaven* (2016). Both of the latter were box office hits, and *Heaven Is for Real* exceeded

Figure 11 T.D. Jakes (1957 -) is here depicted at the 2016 world premiere of his Columbia Pictures' movie *Miracles from Heaven*, one of his most popular and profitable films.
Wenn Rights Ltd / Alamy Stock Photo

$100 million in worldwide ticket sales.[60] It is not a coincidence that Jakes's first film project, *Woman Thou Art Loosed*, appeared the same year, 2004, as Mel Gibson's *The Passion of the Christ*. Both were powered by their audiences' desires for alternatives to Hollywood's seemingly nontraditional values and spirit. Given his limited budget and promotion, Jakes's film performed surprisingly well, "debut[ing] in the top ten on less than five hundred screens with little to no major publicity."[61]

Tyler Perry, an ordained Pentecostal minister who attended Bible school, has reported that he felt called by God to produce films that were not afraid to "name the name of Jesus" as a "hope and resource" for inner-city and urban Blacks.[62] His comedy-dramas, such as *Why Did I Get Married?* (2007) and *The Family That Preys* (2008), convey the message of a Jesus whose grace is manifested amid gritty portrayals of the human condition, with Black Protestant churches and clergy often shown as less than perfect, but still key resources and bedrocks of support in times of need. Some of the ministers in Perry's films are actually pastors and co-pastors, including Marvin Winans (*I Can Do Bad All by Myself*, 2009) and Bishop Eddie Long (*Daddy's Little Girls*, 2007).

Black stars like Denzel Washington and David Oyelowo have also brought their Protestant evangelical heritage to bear in their acting and movies, and have openly signaled those commitments to Christian audiences. Washington, the son of a Pentecostal minister and a parishioner of the West

Figure 12 Denzel Washington pictured in *Training Day* (2001).
Pictorial Press Ltd / Alamy Stock Photo

Angeles Church of God in Christ (the largest Pentecostal denomination in the United States), has written and spoken of filmmaking as a way to use his "gifts" for God, whether he is playing heroes or villains.[63] The Bible and/or faith play a pivotal or symbolically important role – though sometimes only briefly – in almost all of his major films, but especially in *Malcolm X*, *The Preacher's Wife*, *The Book of Eli* (co-produced), and *Man on Fire*, among others. In *The Book of Eli*, the protagonist has committed the entire Bible to memory, in good Protestant *sola scriptura* fashion. Washington has addressed the Christian underpinnings of his films, such as the prominent role of scripture, and been forthright about his faith—reading the "Daily Word" and being "filled with the Holy Ghost"—in both mainstream publications like *GQ* and Christian news sources like CBN.[64] At the same time, he is far from being either an apologist or a purist. On the contrary, he has been quite critical of Pentecostalism, as depicted in his directorial debut, *Antwone Fisher* (2002). He has shown himself to be religiously open and sympathetic to devout practitioners of other religions, as evident in his portrayal of Malcolm X. While keeping Malcolm X's Islamic identity foremost, Washington's performance also resonates with Black Pentecostalism's (and the Nation of Islam's) emphasis on righteousness and justice.

Similarly, the Nigerian American actor David Oyelowo has spoken openly about his Protestant evangelical "born-again" experience and stated that God ordained him to play Dr. Martin Luther King Jr. in Ava DuVernay's *Selma* (2014), which was co-produced by Oprah Winfrey's Harpo Studios.[65] Building on previous civil rights documentaries, like *King: A Filmed Record . . . Montgomery to Memphis* (1969), *Eyes on the Prize* (1987), and *This Far by Faith: African American Spiritual Journeys* (2003), *Selma* is the first dramatic feature film to give prominence to Martin Luther King Jr.'s work and does not hide the fact that King was a Baptist minister. Oyelowo's Oscar-nominated portrayal, animated by his personal belief that "God used" King, convinces the audience that the on-screen figure's passion for racial equality and the political transformation of American life comes from his soul.

A key source of funding and a supporting actor in *Selma* was Oprah Winfrey. She has also discussed her Protestant faith to Hollywood and television. Raised in a Black Baptist Church, she now attends T. D. Jakes' Pentecostal Potter's House Church in Dallas. Winfrey actively talks about the power of her Christian faith, the church, and all spiritualities, for which she has a tremendous respect as resources for healing, hope, and empowerment. She has acted or helped produce numerous films throughout her career that highlight the importance and sometimes contradictory impulses of faith in *Malcolm X* (1992), *Beloved* (1998), *The Color Purple* (1985), *Selma* (2014), *A Wrinkle in Time* (2018), among others. Winfrey continues to bring her Christian faith to Hollywood movies and television through her TV series *Supersoul Sunday* (2011-) and the award winning documentary series *Belief* (2015-16).

Washington's, Oyelowo's, and Winfrey's public religiosity, like that of Perry and Jakes, has contributed to making racial-ethnic Christianity and Protestant evangelicalism a visible force in twenty-first-century cinema, no longer confined to church films. As this presence expands, it invites broader engagement with Protestantism's racial history as well as critique of its legacy. Seventeen-year-old African American Phillip Youmans's award-winning debut feature *Burning Cane* (2019), distributed by DuVernay's company ARRAY, meditates on the writer-director's Southern Baptist upbringing through the story of a church-going matron struggling to raise her grandson Jeremiah and heal the grown men in his life—including an alcoholic pastor—who use drink and domestic violence to flail against the emasculating effects of poverty in a backwater Louisiana town. In showing the duality of Youman's religious experience— a source of communal strength as well as an experience of patriarchal submission and entrapment in an insufferable past—*Burning Cane* indirectly rebuts perhaps overly optimistic evangelical films like the Kendrick brothers' domestic drama *War Room* (2015). Hopefully, it inspires other emerging filmmakers to continue a vigorous dialogue about what Protestantism in the United States has been, and what it can be.[66]

Protestant Influences on European films, New Hollywood, and Beyond

The Protestant influence on the European film industry has been especially noteworthy in Germany, Sweden, Denmark, and the United Kingdom. As the world observed the quincentenary of the Reformation, exhibits in Luther's birthplace, Wittenberg, highlighted the continuing popularity of Protestantism in Germany and Europe with discussions of the Lutheran presence in film.[67] Lutheran hymnody, the sacred music of Johann Sebastian Bach, and Stuart psalms and hymns have served in European film as acoustical symbols of Protestantism or the Reformation.[68] Calvinism, though less accented, has a presence in British cinema, especially in the genre of folk horror but also notably in *Cromwell* (see below) and the Oscar-winning sports drama *Chariots of Fire*, which shows the Scottish Congregationalist missionary Eric Liddell (Ian Charleson) triumphantly racing in the 1924 Olympics. Through historical dramas and religious biopics set in the sixteenth and seventeenth centuries, European filmmaking has mythologized the Reformation as well as critically reflected on its legacy in several ways: the political and religious consequences of the radical Reformation, and the drive to organize society around the new order of the Protestant ethic. In dramas about troubled pastors, European films have examined the trials of modern ministry that can cause vocational conviction to wane. Most especially, European art cinema has examined why religion persists in a secular age and amid evidence of God's absence. It has offered varied answers, such as chilling depictions in Michael Haneke's *The White Ribbon* (Germany, 2009) and affirming portrayals in Gabriel Axel's *Babette's Feast* (Denmark, 1987) and Hugh Hudson's *Chariots of Fire* (UK, 1981). In the last, Olympic champion Eric Liddell embodies the biblical Word as he races: "When I run, I feel His presence."

Biopics about Reformation leaders, most especially Luther himself, have been produced for decades on both sides of the Atlantic and continue to be shown, with subtitles, in churches as well as theaters. The most prolific producer of such films is Germany, where movies about Luther took the place of films about Jesus. In no other country does Protestantism have such an iconic and mythic national figure as a common touchpoint. Since his first appearance on German screens in 1911, the character of Luther has assumed many ideological complexions. Whether he is an embodiment of Weimar-era nationalism or the exemplar of the German Democratic Republic (East Germany), he is always a hero.[69] Apart from Luther films, the most widely distributed films about the Reformation have been British productions set in sixteenth- and seventeenth-century England. The success of *A Man for All Seasons* (UK, 1966), an Oscar-winning adaptation of Robert Bolt's play about Thomas More, Henry VIII, and the fraught establishment of the Anglican Church, inspired several period films, including Charles Jarrott's films *Anne of the Thousand Days* (UK, 1969), which also covers events that led Henry VIII to split the English church from Rome, and *Mary, Queen of Scots* (UK, 1971), which features the founder of the Presbyterian Church of Scotland, John Knox (Robert James); James Clavell's *The Last Valley* (UK, 1971), set during the Thirty Years' War (1618–1648), and Ken Hughes's ambitious *Cromwell* (UK, 1970) about the Puritan influences and social vision in Oliver Cromwell's English Civil War (1642–1651). In between, Michael Reeves's *Witchfinder General* (UK, 1968), an intelligent historical drama cross-bred with British folk horror and set during the English Civil War, had the mixed legacy of initiating a spate of period films featuring Puritan villagers, madmen, and torture. Though lucrative exports, most of them, such as *Mark of the Devil* (UK, 1970), *Cry of the Banshee* (UK, 1970), and *Twins of Evil* (UK, 1971), were exploitation fare. Reeves's own film transcends its imitators and anticipates Robin Hardy's *The Wicker Man* (UK, 1973), an equally potent representation of Protestantism as a parody of its religious Others.

Outside of religious biopics and historical dramas about the Reformation, explicit Protestantism in European movies has meant mostly narratives with a (male) priest or pastor at the center. John and Roy Boulting's wartime propaganda piece *Pastor Hall* (UK, 1940) is loosely based on the Lutheran pastor Martin Neimöller, who had been imprisoned at Dachau for organizing clerical opposition to Nazism in Germany's Protestant churches. Postwar dramas of Protestant clergy include Jean Delannoy's *La Symphonie Pastorale* (France, 1946), Ealing Studios' *Lease of Life* (UK, 1954), and Ingmar Bergman's *Winter Light* (Sweden, 1963). Prior to *Winter Light*, the most artistically accomplished film in this category was Delannoy's *La Symphonie Pastorale*, adapted from André Gide's classic novella about a Swiss Reformed pastor in the throes of an illicit passion for a blind girl in his spiritual charge; while controversial, the film was not hobbled by strictures like those in Hollywood's Production Code, which forbade negatively portraying ministers. Ministers are also often portrayed as flawed in Scandinavian movies, extending from Bergman's Lutheran-set dramas through *Babette's Feast* and films by Dogme 95 and post-Dogme directors like Lars von Trier (*Breaking the Waves* [1996], in which the church is Scottish Calvinist Presbyterian), Annette K. Olesen (*In Your Hands* [2004]), Anders Thomas Jensen (*Adam's Apples* [2005]), and Lone Scherfig (*Just Like Home* [2007]). In contrast with *Elmer Gantry* and other classic post-1950s American films, the ministers in these Scandinavian examples are not fraudulent, but fearful of flesh, harsh and bigoted, assailed by doubts, and taken by desperation or even loss of faith.

The ministers in most European films are male, which is also the case in most American movies. The rare U.S. exceptions feature characters that are Pentecostal faith healers like, or inspired by, Aimee Semple McPherson (see Part VI of the Introduction and Chapters 12 and 15). A number of Protestant denominations have ordained female ministers. The Salvation Army, which originated out of Holiness-Methodism, has had women "officers" who preach ever since the church's founding in 1865. Over the twentieth century and especially the past half-century, other Protestant denominations have made it possible for women to be clergy; in Europe, these have included the Swiss Reformed Church, the Church of Denmark, the Church of Sweden, the Church of Norway, the United Reformed Church in the UK, the Church of Scotland, the Evangelical Church in Germany, and the Pentecostal Church in Germany and Sweden. On-screen, Annette K. Olesen's *In Your Hands* almost uniquely reflects the increasing Protestant ordination of European women: in this case, a female seminary graduate assigned chaplaincy at a women's prison in Denmark. The one notable earlier exception is producer-director Gabriel Pascal's *Major Barbara* (UK, 1941), adapted by literary lion George Bernard Shaw from his 1905 satirical morality play. British thespian Wendy Hiller indelibly plays an idealistic Salvation Army officer, Barbara Undershaft, who is appalled when her organization accepts charitable donations from a munitions manufacturer (her own father). Though, as in the play, Major Barbara is forced to see the shortcomings of using Christianity alone to lift Britain's working class out of poverty, the film adaptation—quite daringly for a wartime production—still allows her plenty of speeches to attack those who profit from the "factory of death."

In European art cinema of the classic period (1940–1980), directors approached Protestantism through modernist narrative structures and styles that were designed to collide with viewers and make Christianity strange and new—startlingly, and at times disturbingly, out of step with modernity and even with Christendom itself.[70] For this purpose, they broke with the conventions of religious biopics, dramas of the pastorate, and Hollywood genre films. Employing a radical mise-en-scène, Carl Dreyer showed up the smallness of religious bigotry and theological fractiousness against the transcendence of God. Dreyer flayed both Protestant and Catholic institutions: the Calvinist inquisition in *Day of Wrath* (Denmark, 1943) and the warring Lutheran sects in *Ordet* (Denmark, 1955) as well as the French clerical court in *The Passion of Joan of Arc* (Denmark, 1928). Yet, as powerful as these indictments are, the most indelible moments of Dreyer's cinema remain those in which the filmmaking conjures a holy aura around characters who seem both blessed and absurd: the face of Renée Falconetti as Jeanne d'Arc, holding fast to God by personal faith; the image of Johannes, the Christian driven "mad" by his studies of Kierkegaard, challenging a roomful of mourners to believe again in the miracles performed by Jesus. In Dreyer's films, the failings of Christendom do not extinguish startling acts of faith limned by grace.

In the work of Ingmar Bergman, who admired Dreyer but did not choose to emulate him, characters and film author grapple with modernity and "its existential and oft-cited philosophical loss of faith—in religion, politics, and art."[71] Bergman, the son of a prominent Lutheran pastor, encouraged audiences to see his films as the unfolding of his own personal crisis of belief. Once asking, rhetorically, "how writers could assess his films if they had not even read Luther's shorter catechism," Bergman deploys his Lutheranism as a conceptual framework against which he rebels, accusing its God of hiding from humanity. Yet it is also a sensibility through which he differentiates himself from shallow rationalism and materialism.[72] Early Swedish masterworks, such as *The Seventh Seal* (1957) and *The Virgin Spring* (1960), as well as the much exegetized trilogy on "God's silence" and *Cries and Whispers* (1973), seemed, with help from Bergman's self-publicizing, to be chapters in an ongoing dialectic between artist and *Deus absconditus* that implicated Sweden's specific history of secularization as well as Western culture's alleged "death of God."[73]

Following in the path of Bergman and employing two of his stars, Max Von Sydow and Liv Ullman, director Jan Troell crafted the internationally acclaimed diptych, *The Emigrants* (Sweden, 1971) and *The New Land* (Sweden, 1972), adapted from the classic Swedish fiction series by Vilhelm Moberg. Combining modernist techniques (jagged editing, associative montage, narrative ellipses) with an epic-scale narrative, Troell roves beyond Bergman's chamber dramas to tell a story of Lutheran farmers and Åkian "heretics" leaving poverty and clerical

Figure 13 Scene from the 1981 British historical sports drama *Chariots of Fire* (1981). This scene depicts Eric Little's colleagues celebrating his Gold Medal in the 400 meters at the 1924 Olympics.
United Archives GmbH / Alamy Stock Photo

stigma in their native land to settle in Minnesota during the 1850s.[74] The New World dream that sustains them in their journey becomes weathered in America, as family members are peeled away by disease, gold fever, frontier violence, and wilderness. Kristina Nilsson (Liv Ullmann) finds her doubt in God growing wider, and her husband, Oskar (Max Von Sydow), suffers inscrutable loss in spite of his faith. *The Emigrants* and *The New Land* remain cinema's only tragic account of the transatlantic Protestant migration, a story that U.S. cinema had wrapped in a mythology of national origins: heroic Puritans seeking freedom.[75]

Through the foreign film market, European art cinema significantly impacted American tastes, especially those of the baby boomer generation.[76] The sixties "death of God" movement in American academic theology and the mainline/liberal cultivation of "a modernist high-cultural aesthetic" created a favorable intellectual climate for Bergman's reception on the art film circuit.[77] The New Hollywood, moreover, not only took the pulse of the counterculture and Vietnam-era America but also voraciously absorbed foreign cinema in its search for more mature subject matter and alternative ways of telling narratives.[78] Carl Dreyer and Ingmar Bergman, who won multiple Best Foreign Film Oscars (1960, 1961, 1983), signified auteurism. Together with the work of Catholic filmmakers like Roberto Rossellini, Vittorio De Sica, Robert Bresson (a Jansenist), and East

Asian writer-directors like Akira Kurosawa and Yasujiro Ozu (with Buddhist and Shinto influences), films like *The Seventh Seal* and *Ordet* had demonstrated to "movie brats" like Paul Schrader, Martin Scorsese, Terrence Malick, and William Friedkin cinema's potential for aesthetic experimentation as a means of more profoundly and jarringly exploring spiritual themes than had been possible in classic American film, which, while beloved, had been bound by the Production Code and the centrifugal cultural force of U.S. civil religion. Through European art movies, aspiring American auteurs found new interest in religious cinema, inflected by Protestant worldviews. Even when, as in Bergman, it had passed through a post-Christian critique, Protestantism remained enthrallingly concerned with ultimate questions of faith, doubt, and theodicy; the tension of spirit and flesh; the mystery of divinity; and the opacity of human words and symbols.

Beyond their contributions to the New Hollywood, European films remain a vital source of reflection on Protestantism and continue to mingle cultural legacies with American film. Figures like Michael Haneke, an atheist of Protestant upbringing, carry on the tradition of an anti-Hollywood European art cinema. In his *The White Ribbon* (2009), shot in stark black and white, a pre–World War I northern German village faces unsolved vicious crimes and acts of terror that implicate the Lutheran rector's children; the disciplinary structure of the German Protestant family seems to be an ingredient in forming the cultural psychology of post–World War I fascism.[79] Meanwhile, other European filmmakers have made popular Protestant film musicals, like Jonathan Lynn's *The Fighting Temptations* (US, 2003) and Hella Joof's *Oh Happy Day* (Denmark, 2004), and joined Americans Brian Dannelly (*Saved!* [2004]) and Stephen Cone (*The Wise Kids* [2011], *Henry Gamble's Birthday Party* [2015]) in expanding the genre of Protestant coming-of-age films: Terence Davies's *The Neon Bible* (UK, 1995), Wim Wenders's *Land of Plenty* (US, 2004), Garth Jennings's *Son of Rambow* (UK, 2007), and Mirjam von Arx's documentary *Virgin Tales* (Switzerland, 2012). Daniel Kokotajlo's *Apostasy* (UK, 2017), which probes family ties and patriarchy inside the Jehovah's Witnesses, a religious community rarely shown in movies, melds the coming-of-age genre with the story of a mother's mission to reinstate her disfellowshipped daughter.[80] The continuing influence of British Protestant folk horror pulses through the films of British auteur Ben Wheatley, whose uncanny *A Field in England* (2013) is set during the English Civil War, and American Robert Eggers's seventeenth-century-set *The Witch: A New-England Folktale* (2015).

Introduction Part V: Protestant Film Aesthetics

One of the more powerful rejoinders to the image of Protestants as anti-art or anti-aesthetic is the recent publication of Sarah Covington and Kathryn Reklis's

Protestant Aesthetics and the Arts (2020). In her introduction to the essay collection, Reklis defines "aesthetic" as a key idea of modernity: the "domain of feeling or spirit" through which the modern subject seeks wholeness, and the "domain where art can convey more than information and help the subject experience more than ordinary life allows."[81] The book demonstrates that, by criticizing the medieval church's "idolatrous" marriage of art and the sacred, Protestants laid the conceptual groundwork for the emergence of the modern idea of the aesthetic. But is there a *Protestant* aesthetic?

In her conclusion to the book, Covington argues that just as Protestantism has branched into many kinds of faith communities over the past five hundred

Figure 14 Carl Theodor Dryer (1889-1968) as depicted in 1965. He was a Danish film director and screen-writer.
Wikimedia Foundation #201009021007829

years, so it has also proliferated aesthetic expressions and theories. This variety has resulted from what Covington calls a productive unease with, and rethinking of, the status of art in relation to religion, and of both art and religion in relation to the immaterial (spiritual): "The rejection of idolatrous images raised new questions as to what, exactly, a post-iconoclastic . . . world was to be. How could one represent or express—or not—that which was used so falsely and idolatrously before? . . . [A] kind of unease if not anxiety resulted from these debates . . . one that endured through time, affecting future aesthetic forms."[82] In other words, Protestant art and theories of art reenact the Reformation's post-iconoclastic search for new forms to mediate the sacred through words, music, and images.

We recognize with *Protestant Aesthetics and the Arts* that Protestantism, motivated by productive unease, has given birth to numerous aesthetic expressions and theories. However, we stress that film, as a new medium, afforded Protestants many possibilities for experimentation. For all its comprehensiveness (theater, architecture, music, literature, painting), *Protestant Aesthetics and the Arts* does not address film art. We point to five defining Protestant aesthetic impulses expressed *in film* and variously featured in our case studies.

The first of these is *reform*, reflected in Protestantism's willingness to exploit new technologies and new media (like cinema and cinematic exhibition) and adapt aesthetic forms (like film genres) to create new artistic and religious expressions. Protestants see the world as intrinsically neutral—neither good nor bad. It can be utilized and transformed so long as the material representations and objects do not displace the Christian's relationship to God. In cinema, perhaps even more so than in other arts, Protestantism shows its "proclivity for hybridity, adaptation, and change."[83]

The second of these is, crucially, *embodiment of the biblical Word*. Some scholars have argued that Protestantism is far less cinematic a subject than Catholicism because it lacks the sensory appeal of pageantry, ritual, and materialized spirituality.[84] Rather than stress Protestantism sensory deficiencies vis-à-vis Catholicism, it is more helpful to recognize how Protestants differently practice their spirituality to respect the Reformation's emphasis on the written, spoken, and visually embodied word.[85] Films themselves do not embody this practice, but they represent embodiment through the actions of characters: (a) Biblicism (stress on a literal interpretation of the Bible and its teachings), (b) stress on righteousness and justice, (c) focus on moral societal and personal purity, (d) dress and comportment standards, and (e) an appeal to plain commonsense realism.[86] We would add that characters' striving to be true to these practices—whether it is the titular heroes of *Cromwell* and Luther biopics, Sonny and his congregation in *The Apostle*, Martin Luther King and his allies in *Selma*, Desmond Doss in *Hacksaw Ridge*, Will Munny in *Unforgiven*,

Figure 15 Ingmar Bergman (1918-2007) is here depicted editing one of his films in 1957.
Archive PL / Alamy Stock Photo

Jake Van Dorn in *Hardcore*, or the post-Rapture coalition of *Left Behind: The Movie* (2000)—makes for dramatic visual storytelling that gives special attention to the body of the protagonist or the bodies of groups united (a fellowship or social movement). These films show the converting body, the ecstatic body, the suffering body, and the righteously questing body.

The third aesthetic impulse, and closely related to embodiment, is *a reenchantment of the mundane*. Protestant-themed films tend to depict grace and holiness not in special sanctified objects and sacred places, like pilgrimage sites, but in the beauty, wonder, and mystery that limn earthly actions and naturalistic settings (*Tree of Life*, *Babette's Feast*, *Why Did I Get Married?*, *Higher Ground*). Even in Carl Dreyer's *Ordet*, which famously climaxes with a physical resurrection from the dead, the miracle is made more credible by the sustained level of sensuous realism that precedes it. Music (hymnody, Bach, gospel, and Christian pop), either diegetically (sung by characters) or non-diegetically (played on the soundtrack), acoustically evokes spiritual unity, hope, transcendence, or intercession in situations that seem quite ordinary or humble; for example, as Buck Williams in *Left Behind* (2000), sits on the floor of a public bathroom, the song "Believer" by Christian pop band Jake underscores that Buck is feeling convicted by the Holy Spirit and moved to salvation. Contrastingly, films can show grave respect for the ugliness of sin, reflected on-screen through grotesquerie, visual distortion, or audiovisual banality. Earthly depravity can be represented through terrifyingly hyperbolic violence (*Hacksaw Ridge*, *Witchfinder General*, *The Wicker Man*), through techniques like noir expressionism (*Hardcore*), or through a dulling lo-fi style deployed to signify a world filled with sin and emptied of faith (*Thief in the Night*). These artistic choices, withholding visual and/or aural balance and harmony, stress the privation of the holy and the corruption of the world's good.

The fourth aesthetic impulse, closely related to reform and embodiment, is *reduction*, a "decluttering" of art and distaste for aesthetic excess. This impulse takes more than one form in movies. The most common is a preference for straightforward literalism with regard to biblical history and miracle, reflected in the popularity among evangelicals of vintage Hollywood religious epics as well as recent epics designed for the faith-friendly market (*Son of God* [2014], *Ben-Hur* [2016], *The Young Messiah* [2016], *Risen* [2016], *Paul: Apostle of Christ* [2018]). Since they affirm the literal interpretation of biblical narrative, evangelicals enjoy miracles achieved on-screen through special effects as faithful representations rather than as virtuoso displays of technological illusion. *The Passion of the Christ* (2004), though deeply Catholic in its underlying theology, appealed to many evangelical Protestants because it focused in meticulous photorealistic detail on the physical suffering of Jesus as the sacrificial lamb. Films not set in biblical times, such as *Cromwell*, *The Apostle*, *Ordet*, or *The Scarlet Letter* (1973), can reflect the impulse toward reduction through direct quotation of scripture (or its written representation on banners, flags, and dress), naturalistic lighting, a plain camera style (frontal, eye-level, midrange), or a combination of these elements. Finally, films by Ingmar Bergman and those like Michael Haneke, whom he influenced, may reject literalism and biblical quotation as themselves clutter in favor of a cultivated audiovisual ambiguity approaching silence: an abstention as to the meaning of what the viewer is seeing or hearing, which deliberately creates doubt.

The fifth impulse, closely related to the reenchantment of the mundane, is the *interplay between literalism and symbolism*. This impulse arises from developments in modernity that conflicted with Protestants' desires to carefully control the mediating role of symbols in their art as well as their rituals and hermeneutics. For the reformers, a symbol—like a cross—was only a sign and not a real mystical presence like the body and blood of Christ in the Holy Communion (or the Lord's Supper) in Catholicism. Symbols in art or religion signified a meaning that had to be authorized with reference to the literal sense of the Bible, as illuminated and embodied by faith and practice in this world. Though the Bible was understood to contain figurative language, the supernatural events in the Bible were literal in the sense of being a factual recording of the past.[87] However, after the German Enlightenment's biblical criticism, miracles, visions, and theophanies could be interpreted as mythical symbols having cultural or psychological causes—and with the rise of Romanticism, symbols in art were seen as infusing representations of the secular everyday with impressions and intimations of transcendence.

Today, filmmakers can use the visual to signpost the presence of the immaterial, as with special effects, or they can use the visual to subtly imply the feeling of something beyond the material world gently breaking upon the materium or witnessing to a character internally. In the second case, how do we decide whether these representations are psychologically symbolic (reflecting a character's epiphany or yearning), iconographic (reflecting the filmmaker's ideology or deployment of cultural myths), or a symbol that is also part of the narrative's literal meaning (i.e., a small-scale revelation of the supernatural)?

In religious epics, with intentionally transgressive exceptions like *The Last Temptation of Christ* and *Noah* (2014), literalism has reigned with the crafted perception of verisimilitude (i.e., the appearance that something on-screen is real).[88] The Narnia series, which takes place in a meticulously visualized magical world, non-ambiguously blends the literal and the symbolic; Aslan is both the lion king of Narnia and, allegorically, "the lion of Judah" (Christ). However, when the setting is not biblical times or a magical place, the relationship between the symbolic and the literal can be open-ended and even slippery. Wim Wenders's *The Scarlet Letter* builds its entire visual strategy around the ease of this slippage, oscillating between iconographic images and a plain camera style that begs the viewer to take the image as a period depiction of the colonial Puritan past. *Tree of Life*, *The Apostle*, *Babette's Feast*, and *Higher Ground* include moments in which the viewer must decide for themself whether the representation on-screen manifests holy grace or symbolizes characters' subjective aspirations toward redemption or holiness. The heroine in *Higher Ground* spends much of the film's middle section looking for everyday signs that she is Spirit-filled, and the camera encourages identification with her psychological point of view and its attendant anxiety. The policemen in *The Apostle* represent civil authority, but they can also be interpreted, in keeping with the theistic sense of Sonny and his congregation, as symbolizing the Law minus the Gospel; the filmmaker seems in sympathy with this interpretation, but the film's naturalistic presentation does not make the symbol manifest, instead only suggesting it through the sermons, songs, and behaviors on-screen, which attest to characters' beliefs. At best, one might say that this interplay is fitting for a pluralistic age in which viewers of many beliefs,

Figure 16 *Son of God* (2014) poster. The movie was produced by Mark Burnett (1960 -) and Roma Downey (1960 -).

PictureLux / Hollywood Archive / Alamy Stock Photo

including nonbelief, are able to decide for themselves where (or whether) the real intersects with the transcendent.

It should be noted that a movie does not have to embrace all of these impulses in order to be considered Protestant. Indeed, few films do embrace all of them, and films may incorporate some tendencies while critiquing others. *Witchfinder General*, for example, often ironically counterpoises scriptural quotation with horrific violence to condemn Protestant notions of embodiment and the propagandistic use of Biblicism.

Introduction Part VI: Chapter Overview

The book begins with essays that examine how Protestants have influenced the rise of the film industry and discuss exemplarily the difficulties and explanatory potential of looking at movies from both Hollywood and Europe through the lens of Protestantism (Part I). It then provides a series of case studies that analyze Protestant themes, symbols, rhetoric, and worldviews in historical and contemporary films (Parts II–V).

Part I: History and Theory of Protestantism in Religion and Film Studies

William Romanowski's and Andrew Quicke's essays analyze how Protestants have embraced cinema as a new medium while trying to find a fitting and responsible public role for it. Romanowski tracks Protestant efforts to reform secular film industries in the United States and Great Britain during the Golden Age of movies. Quicke shows that the current wave of evangelical filmmaking (straight-to-video and theatrical features) has a long prehistory in the independent Protestant film industry, studded with attempts to find a proper means to balance economical and technical limitations with artistic ambitions and religious priorities. In the silent era, Protestants like Herbert Jump also pioneered efforts to define how the laity could use movies for evangelism and edification. Beginning in the late sixties, Christians influenced by neo-orthodox theologians H. Richard Niebuhr, from the Reformed tradition, and Paul Tillich, from the Lutheran tradition, moved beyond apologetics for cinema and developed what John Lyden (*Film as Religion*) has called a "dialogical or dualistic" approach that brings theology and film into dialogue in order to critically compare a Christian worldview with movie values and beliefs.[89] In his essay, Clive Marsh can be seen as continuing the dialogical approach. Focusing on a contemporary drama, *Crazy Heart*, Marsh asks why so many viewers see this not ostensibly religious film as a redemption story and thus credit it with power and insight. What project does it serve, what values does it reinforce, to find themes or motifs of salvation in a film like *Crazy Heart*?

Part II: The Protestant Reformation on Screen

Highlighting not only outstanding achievements of Protestantism's originary agents but also the dark side of revolution and new identities, the films in this section show that the Reformation has a decidedly mixed legacy. The essays by Esther Wipfler and Gastón Espinosa focus on biopics depicting clergy and lay leaders of the German and English Reformations: Martin Luther and Oliver Cromwell. The most famous Protestant leader in history, Martin Luther (1483–1546), has been represented in film since 1911. As Wipfler shows, his on-screen portrayal has been anything but uniform, and the cinematic representations of his story have purveyed contrasting myths that have served different ideological projects. Espinosa's essay on *Cromwell* addresses the difficulties that writer-director Ken Hughes faced bringing this highly controversial Puritan figure, Sir Oliver Cromwell (1599–1658), to British screens amid the Cold War and the countercultural ferment of the late sixties. In an original maneuver, Victor Sage's essay compares *Witchfinder General* to the British cult classic *The Wicker Man*. The two movies, one set in the seventeenth-century English Civil War and one in the 1970s, trade on scarlet memories of the Reformation and criticize Protestantism's ill-judged attempt, through propaganda and sacred violence, to police the boundaries between worship of the true biblical God and the "savage God" of paganism and the Catholic Eucharist.

Part III: Protestant Influences in European Art Films

These essays deal with art films made by European auteurs and cinematic modernists who reach into the Protestant tradition for new ways to make religious films outside the conventions of Bible epics, biopics, and melodramas. Maaret Koskinen examines Ingmar Bergman's trilogy on "God's silence"—*Through a Glass Darkly* (1960), *The Communicants* (U.S. title *Winter Light*, 1963), and *The Silence* (1963)—in the light of Bergman's Lutheran heritage and demonstrates that the three films reflect a Protestant notion of reduction: ridding movies of what she calls "sacred clutter." Mark Le Fanu's essay centers on the unconventionally long scene that concludes Carl Theodor Dreyer's classic film *Ordet* (1955) on a physical resurrection. Usually attributed to the Catholic faith, miracles like the resurrection in *Ordet* foreground for Le Fanu an often neglected strand in Protestantism—namely, the paradoxical Protestant *credo quia absurdum*, "I believe because it is absurd." Erik Redling's essay on Wim Wenders's *The Scarlet Letter* (1973), adapting Nathaniel Hawthorne's novel of the same title, demonstrates that Wenders shares with Luther and other reformers a Protestant skepticism toward allegory that shapes his visual strategies in the adaptation. Wenders departs from the dominant allegorical mode of the classic 1926 American silent film *Scarlet Letter*, but, as Protestants like John Bunyan discovered in the seventeenth century, he cannot forgo allegory entirely. Kjell Lejon's essay shows that *Babette's Feast* is gently yet pointedly criticizing Scandinavian Protestant Pietist Lutheranism; the movie, as Lejon argues, promotes the view that only reconciliatory grace (*sola gratia*), so central to Lutheran thought, can overcome long-standing Scandinavian religious and social conflicts. Apart from their commitment to cinematic experimentation, what unites the movies discussed in the four chapters is the prominence of Lutheranism in the category of "European art film." In American film, by contrast, we see many fewer films about Lutheran and Reformed churches (or heroes) and a greater focus on evangelicalism and contemporary society.

Part IV: Protestant Experience in American Movies

What happens when cherished certitudes of faith come up against the complexities of the contemporary United States? As in European films, we see faith and doubt colliding in conditions of suffering and spiritual confusion, but in American films this is often framed through quests for personal redemption or reconciliation, self-expression, or self-determination. Mark Scott's essay on Terrence Malick's acclaimed *Tree of Life* argues that the film uses the Bible, especially the text of Job, in a characteristically Protestant way to grapple with the problem of evil. Gastón Espinosa and Jason Stevens's essay on Robert Duvall's *The Apostle* argues that the film counters decades of screen misrepresentations of Holiness-Pentecostal churches in the American South. Though often playing (like most Hollywood films) to Black and Latino archetypes, such as the Black spiritual mentor and excitable Latino Pentecostal preacher, *The Apostle* approaches its subject with remarkable empathy, showing how Holiness and Pentecostal churches have fostered interracial friendships among poor and working-class whites and Blacks. Julius Bailey's essay on Ava DuVernay's *Selma* praises the film for not simplistically idealizing Martin Luther King Jr. but criticizes it for minimalizing the powerful place that Black Protestantism played in King's life and his leadership of the civil rights movement. Melanie Johnson's essay highlights African American writer-director-producer and star Tyler Perry, whose gritty dramas and comedies reflect a long Black Protestant tradition in which Jesus is consistently present, accessible, and one with oppressed Black men and women in their darkest times. In her essay on star and director Vera Farmiga's *Higher Ground*, from Carolyn Briggs's memoir, Paula Kane discusses a unique addition to American cinema. Though there is a wealth of scholarship on women in conservative evangelicalism and fundamentalism, this is an underrepresented subject on film, and the few examples—*The Miracle Woman* (1931), *Tobacco Road* (1941), *Elmer Gantry* (1960), and *Angel Baby* (1961)—tend to focus on faith healers like Aimee Semple McPherson. In Kane's nuanced and historically sensitive reading, *High Ground* is a tender and subtle but highly natural look at the role of faith across several decades in the heroine's life, which takes a path away from the religious patriarchy of her church community.

Finally, Alex Wainer's essay investigates the U.S. evangelical reception of the *Star Wars* franchise across four decades. Reading across a wealth of texts—books, magazines, online forums, and ad copy—Wainer's essay anatomizes how evangelicals have tried to reconcile the syncretic religious influences (Eastern, New Age, and occult as well as Christian) of the *Star Wars* universe with their own Gospel beliefs.[90]

Part V: Protestant Themes in Film Genres

Genres are "conventions of connection" that invoke, imitate, and complicate old forms.[91] Filmmakers working in a genre engage audiences in "a constant interplay of the latest instance [the film on view] and the history of a particular form."[92] The existence of audience expectations, rather than hampering creativity, can permit a genre film to play against its own tradition, its own past. The result can be ironic self-critique, a deepening of conventions that introduces new complexity to old themes, or a radical extension of conventions, combined with new elements, that thrusts new ideological perspectives into view.

The Western is a genre in which Protestantism is already embedded. From silent classics like William S. Hart's *Hell's Hinges* (1916) to early sound epics like Raoul Walsh's *The Big Trail* (1930) to the works of auteurs like John Ford, the Western broadly incorporates an American Puritan tradition. In her essay on Clint Eastwood's *Unforgiven*, Sara Vaux discovers an alternative Protestant ethic, what she calls "radical forgiveness," that avoids the genre's sanctified violence and portentous sense of destiny. Eastwood, whose *High Plains Drifter* (dir., 1973) echoes *Hell's Hinges* by having its hero burn an irredeemable town to the ground, has long been sensitive to the sermonic underpinnings of the genre, which often invokes the rhetoric of the jeremiad.[93] In Vaux's interpretation, Eastwood achieves his most mature vision of the Western, one that forgoes the genre's avenging angels and redeemers to live within forgiveness.

While Vaux finds the Western thoroughly indebted to American Puritanism for its ethos and narrative tropes, Timothy Beal's essay turns attention to a genre long disreputable to evangelicals and describes them boldly appropriating it.[94] Adding a significant chapter to Quicke's chronicle of the independent Protestant film industry, Beal highlights the importance of horror to the emergence, in the late 1960s and early 1970s, of filmmaking companies that sought to popularize evangelicalism among teenagers and twentysomethings. Donald Thompson's *Thief in the Night* (1972) launched the genre of evangelical horror and remains to this day one of the most widely seen independent films of all time. Extending his analysis through the Left Behind series to the present day, Beal tracks aesthetic shifts away from "horror" to "thriller" and back again, showing how these are symptomatic of the changing face of evangelical apocalyptic culture.

The essays by Matthew Rindge and Jason Stevens analyze how two filmmakers work within chosen genres—in one case the war movie, in the other film noir—to make personal statements about Protestantism. Mel Gibson's *Hacksaw Ridge*, about the World War II career of soldier Desmond Doss, a Seventh-day Adventist, pacifist, and improbable winner of a medal for valor—is the most overtly Christian war film produced in America since the Vietnam era. Rindge seeks to understand why Gibson, a Catholic, became attracted to this Protestant hero's story and to what extent *Hacksaw Ridge* remains a Protestant story in Gibson's telling. Haunted ex-Calvinist Paul Schrader, who is the subject of Stevens's essay, returns in *Hardcore* to his Dutch Reformed background through film noir, a genre that he helped to formulate. Schrader subjects *Hardcore*'s devoutly Reformed protagonist to a relentlessly probing and fragmenting gaze that holds the character to an accounting of his sins more rigorous than the character's perception of himself. *Hardcore* emerges as a Calvinistic anti-Calvinist noir.

C. S. Lewis scholar Devin Brown turns attention to one of the most successful fantasy film series of recent years. Lewis invented the genre of Christian fantasy fiction, imbuing the stuff of fantasy—childhood, enchantment, monsters, and dualistic violence—with meanings rooted in Anglican theology and Christian eschatology. The film trilogy, launched with *The Chronicles of Narnia: The Lion, the Witch and the Wardrobe* (2005), adapted Lewis's beloved books to the fantasy movie genre. Although the films were produced by Walden Media, a company owned by conservative Protestant Philip Anschutz, and were promoted to Christians using the niche marketing techniques that worked so successfully for *The Passion of the Christ* the year before, Brown finds that the film adaptation dilutes some of Lewis's key spiritual insights.[95] Brown is not making a simple objection of infidelity to the text but explaining how the filmmakers, perhaps under the constraints of the fantasy genre in a globalized film market, have transformed the Narnia stories into something more palliative to secular, therapeutic culture than Lewis intended.[96] Brown's essay returns us to themes that have always underlain Protestant engagements with popular culture, themes highlighted especially in the essays of Part I: in seeking to engage, transform, and create films within a larger culture and given different industries and markets, how much is Protestantism altered in the exchange?

In addition to the specific focus of each essay and section, we invite readers to track classic Protestant themes across films. These include, but are not limited to:

- Faith and doubt (Luther biopics, *Cromwell*, *Ordet*, *Tree of Life*, *The Apostle*, *Higher Ground*)
- Righteousness and justice (Luther biopics, *Cromwell*, *The Apostle*, *Unforgiven*, *Selma*, *Chronicles of Narnia*)
- Sin and depravity (Luther biopics, *The Silence*, *Ordet*, *Tree of Life*, *Star Wars*, *Thief in the Night*, *Left Behind*, *Witchfinder General*, *The Wicker Man*, *Unforgiven*, *Hardcore*, *Hacksaw Ridge*)
- Biblical literalism (Luther biopics, *Cromwell*, *Witchfinder General*, *Tree of Life*, *The Apostle*, *Higher Ground*, *Thief in the Night*, *Left Behind*, *Hacksaw Ridge*),
- Priesthood of all believers and its offshoots: democracy/individualism/manifest destiny (Luther biopics, *Cromwell*, *Babette's Feast*, *The Scarlet Letter*, *The Apostle*, *Unforgiven*, *Selma*, *Hacksaw Ridge*)
- Personal conversion and personal redemption (Luther films, *Crazy Heart*, *The Apostle*, *Higher Ground*, *Thief in the Night*, *Left Behind*, *Why Did I Get Married?*, *Unforgiven*)
- Holiness and sanctification (*Cromwell*, *Why Did I Get Married?*, *The Apostle*, *Higher Ground*, *Hacksaw Ridge*)
- Providence and secularism (*The Silence*, *Winter Light*, *Tree of Life*, *Higher Ground*, *Thief in the Night*, *Left Behind*, *Hardcore*)
- Apocalypticism/end of the world as the individuals know it (*Witchfinder General*, *The Wicker Man*, *Thief in the Night*, *Left Behind*, *Star Wars*, *Hacksaw Ridge*)
- Moralism/pietism (Luther films, *Cromwell*, *Babette's Feast*, *The Apostle*, *Higher Ground*, *Selma*, *Hacksaw Ridge*)

There is no such category as a Protestant film, but there are films bearing Protestant themes and shaped by identifiable Protestant sensibilities.

PART I

HISTORY AND THEORY OF PROTESTANTISM IN RELIGION AND FILM STUDIES

Figure 1.1 J. Arthur Rank (circa 1940s), Methodist and the head and founder of the Rank Organization, the United Kingdom's largest film company.
Glasshouse Images/Alamy Stock Photo

1

Protestant Responses to Hollywood, Censorship, and Art Cinema

William D. Romanowski

In 1922, Jewish studio owners in Hollywood selected Will H. Hays to head their new trade organization, the Motion Picture Producers and Distributors of America (MPPDA). It was no accident that Hays was a prominent Presbyterian layman with powerful Washington connections. His power depended on simultaneously improving the movies and protecting the industry's interests—mutual aims that were often at cross-purposes. His approach was encapsulated in a frequent assertion: Americans were fundamentally opposed to censorship and just as sure to demand it should the industry fail to control itself. Nothing scared the studio heads more than government intervention in their business practices.[1]

In 1915, the U.S. Supreme Court denied movies free speech protection, rendering them subject to censorship by a city, a state, or even a federal board—a ruling that was not reversed until 1952. Hays hoped the Protestant establishment, his natural constituency, would serve as a bulwark against legalized censorship. Drawing on their religious heritage, Protestants favored industry self-regulation and were averse to legalized censorship. They believed firmly, however, that freedom of expression was not unrestricted, and that a reasonable measure of self-restraint on the part of moviemakers was acceptable—even necessary—to protect the public welfare. Instead of exploiting the lurid tastes of a specific audience segment, Protestant leaders wanted the film industry to pursue long-term interests and develop the moral, artistic, and educational value of the cinema.

Meanwhile, despite Hays's repeated promise to maintain "the highest possible moral and artistic standards," profit-minded producers were putting out racy films like *One Hour with You*, which advertised: "She was his wife's best friend. He was her doctor and she wanted treatment three times a day."[2] Suffice it to say that by the late 1920s many Protestant reformers became convinced that the Hays organization was merely a public relations front to protect the studios' profits. This moment proved to be pivotal in both Protestant-Hollywood relations and the course of movie regulation.

The scholarly discourse on film regulation tends to focus on artistic freedom versus censorship (hegemonic control over public morals and movie content).

William D. Romanowski, *Protestant Responses to Hollywood, Censorship, and Art Cinema* In: *Protestants on Screen*. Edited by: Gastón Espinosa, Erik Redling and Jason Stevens, Oxford University Press.
DOI: 10.1093/oso/9780190058906.003.0002

The Protestant story, however, highlights another crucial dimension. Bluenose stereotypes aside, Protestant leaders hoped to secure a fitting role for the cinema, one that would protect individual freedom and expression under a shared ethos of self-restraint and public responsibility. The conflict between the film industry's relentless drive to maximize profits and the church's concern to protect civil liberties and the public welfare was at the crux of the struggle that Protestants waged over movie regulation.

It is helpful to understand Protestant strategies for reform in terms of what I call *pietist* and *structural* motifs. Briefly, the pietist tendency sees social problems as the result of personal shortcomings and failings, and not harmful social conditions. The structural motif finds the core problem in patterns of organization and emphasizes transforming institutions that influence and govern people's lives. It follows that pietists typically want movies to serve educational purposes by instilling right moral values, especially among youth. For that reason, there is more interest along the pietist spectrum in controlling movie content than among structuralists, who are more inclined to see the cinema as an arena for cultural discourse.

In this essay, I investigate the central ways that Protestants, and to some extent Catholics, engaged the cinema as an institution. Though I focus mainly on American Protestants, I draw comparisons with British initiatives. The juxtaposition of the "two countries separated by a common language" is illustrative.[3] Obscenity standards in both countries derived from the same English case, *Regina v. Hicklin* (1868). Movie reform progressed along a similar course, with Protestants employing much the same rhetoric, ideals, and values in their respective settings. Without judging the comparable merits, I hope to demonstrate something of the variety of Protestant approaches to the cinema.

For my purposes, this comparative approach highlights how much commercial imperatives set the parameters for American proposals, and to a lesser extent their effect on British initiatives. Market-based strategies were the linchpin of American proposals. British leaders, however, exhibited a less sanguine attitude toward commercialism. Actually, they loathed the prospect of American crass escapism washing over their national media and culture. Seeking to maintain high standards and protect their national interests, they preferred alternatives to either the market or direct government control in attempts to merge public and commercial values.

Broadcasting regulation in both countries provides a quick illustration here that will also serve later to highlight the persistent tension between public and commercial values in twenty-first-century media strategies. To protect broadcasters' free speech and the public welfare, public policy in both Britain and the United States was based on the principle of public ownership of the airwaves. In the States, funding came from advertising revenues; three major networks were licensed, in effect giving each company a monopoly contingent upon serving the "public interest, convenience, or necessity." In Britain,

John Reith, "an austere Scot of Calvinist upbringing," envisioned the British Broadcasting Company (BBC) as "a comprehensive public service" that provided education, information, and entertainment—dubbed the "Reithian Trinity." To maintain diversity and programming excellence, Reith believed that the public, not advertisers, should provide funding. The BBC was set up as a protected monopoly funded by a license fee—not advertising revenue or government taxes. As media historian Andrew Crisell explains, the aim was "to be institutionally and editorially *independent*—of commercial pressures on the one hand and, as far as possible, government influences on the other."[4]

Figure 1.2 Sir John Reith (circa 1930s), son of a Scottish Presbyterian minister and the first director general of the British Broadcasting Corporation.
Keystone Press/Alamy Stock Photo

Regulating the Movies

In the United States and Britain, film producers set up independent trade bodies that in effect censored movies to prevent legal censorship. A group of New York's elite, mostly Protestants, served on the National Board of Censorship (later Review) of Motion Pictures. This agency, created in 1909, existed independent of the film industry and was funded by fees that film companies paid to have their movies approved. That same year, Britain's Cinematograph Act empowered local authorities to grant theaters licenses. Like American filmmakers, British producers wanted protection from capricious local censoring and to create national standards to expand their market. They established the British Board of Film Censors (BBFC) in 1912, a nongovernmental agency that, like its U.S. counterpart, was funded by a fee structure. To maintain its independence, the board consisted of a panel of examiners without ties to the film industry.

To resolve the tension between freedom and public morality, the National Board treated movies as adult entertainment and therefore only minimized sensationalism when certifying films for general public viewing. Educating the public, not censorship, was the way to improve film quality. A constant complaint, however, was that the board passed adult-oriented movies that were not appropriate for impressionable young people. Protestant clergy disputed the board's logic that there was no principled reason to censor movies for adults; in the clergy's view, the purpose of regulation was only "to get pictures that are decent for young people."[5] Unable to maintain a broad enough consensus on standards, the National Board lost credibility; states began passing censorship measures—the very thing the board had been established to prevent.

Like the National Board, the British Board had no legal authority and was funded by distributor fees; statutory power remained with local authorities who could overrule the board's decisions. Whereas individual U.S. states were accustomed to taking legislative initiative, local councils in Britain did not share the same tradition and thus tended to be less restrictive than the BBFC. By occasionally permitting exhibition of a banned film, local councils provided a functional corrective to the board's rigidity and vulnerability to undue external influence. The British Board, however, differed from its U.S. counterpart in one important way: from its inception, the BBFC censored and also classified films for viewing by children (rating them U) or requiring adult accompaniment (rating them A). After a rocky start, the board's judgments eventually found widespread acceptance; BBFC film regulation, performed under the scrutiny of local authorities, was deemed adequate and even desirable.[6] As it was, the British Board managed to weather periodic crises, while its American complement lapsed into irrelevance by the end of the 1910s.

Hollywood Conquering the World

During World War I, with formerly vibrant cinemas in European countries devastated, Hollywood expanded its presence and control in the world market—a position it has never relinquished. By the late 1920s, the Hollywood studios had gained distinct advantages over British and European film companies. Hollywood's "Big Eight" studios had forged an oligopoly, their companies cooperating to eliminate competition. The major studios were now vertically integrated firms that not only produced and distributed films but also owned the key first-run theaters in major cities. This structure consolidated their control over the U.S. market—the world's largest—and ensured a regular outlet for their own releases while squeezing out independents and severely limiting screen time for foreign releases.

With Hollywood films making a profit from domestic earnings, the studios could sell them abroad for less, undercutting the competition in foreign countries while reaping additional revenues. With predictable and higher profits, average Hollywood production budgets increased, as did production quality, making it difficult for foreign producers to compete. Threatened by Hollywood's dominance, countries variously employed quotas, tax schemes, and financial support to keep indigenous production alive. Moreover, such was Hollywood's worldwide preeminence that to be commercially successful in the international market, U.K. and European filmmakers discovered they had to imitate Hollywood's highly commercialized style of filmmaking, which most of them detested.

One way to compete was to create a distinctive cinematic voice in contrast to Hollywood's use of cinema as mere spectacle and escapist entertainment. In the 1930s, John Grierson, a Scottish Presbyterian and pioneer of documentary film, argued for a different social function for the cinema—namely, that film should contribute to social and moral improvement. By setting a different standard for its national cinema, film scholar Andrew Higson explains, British documentary realism and Hollywood commercialism represented "two competing justifications for cinematic practice: the commercial film industry's ideology of showmanship, and the documentary movement's ideology of public service."[7] It also illustrates the importance of the relation between purpose, style, and content that preoccupied Protestant critics.

Protestant Principles and Film Reform

American Protestants saw their principles as being relevant to both personal and institutional life. To reform the cinema, then, they addressed the (im)morality of both movie content and the industry's trade practices. Protestant critics reserved their praise for movies that made an honest attempt to interpret life by presenting "artistically the deeper emotional struggles of the human spirit." They emphasized a movie's aesthetic worth and overall vision (theme, context, and treatment). Implied in this fusion of art and spiritual perspective was a critique of the Catholic Legion of Decency's approach, which Protestants discarded as mere nitpicking over immoral conduct on-screen. What bothered Protestants most, however, was the subtle and cumulative impact Hollywood's value system might be having on youth. Instead of instilling character and concern for the common good, too many Hollywood films glorified self-indulgence and material acquisition, stamping it with the approval of Hollywood glamour. In the Protestant judgment, Hollywood seemed to have "lost all sense of spiritual values."[8]

By and large, Protestant reformers became convinced that the only way to secure lasting reform, without resorting to official censorship, was to stop the major film studios from exploiting the system to gain advantage over competitors, whether independent companies in the United States or those from other countries. If the studios' stranglehold on the market could be broken, sensationalism would give way and lead to an increase in the supply of high-quality commercial films, in turn rendering prior censorship largely unnecessary. And so from the 1920s through the 1940s, Protestants supported federal legislation, not for government supervision of production but for breaking up the studios' monopoly by invoking antitrust laws. If their concern with the luridness used to boost box office receipts might seem to indicate a pietistic attitude, these reformers were actually advocating a structural approach to movie regulation that was at odds with the powers that be in Hollywood. This forceful initiative struck at the cornerstone of the studios' profitable monopoly. The Protestant strategy to restructure the film industry itself directly conflicted with Hollywood, the Presbyterian Will Hays, and soon enough, the Roman Catholic Church.

A Catholic Quid Pro Quo

His reputation crumbling, Hays launched a countermove to gain leverage over the producers. As is well known, in 1930 Hays persuaded the studios to adopt a new Production Code of standards that was composed with the input of Catholics. Then, in frustration over what they perceived as Hollywood's disregard for the code, the American bishops formed the Legion of Decency in 1934 and threatened a nationwide boycott of movies. In response, Hays put a Catholic layperson, Joseph Breen, in charge of a new Production Code Administration (PCA) that worked cooperatively with Legion of Decency officials to ensure that every studio release adhered to the code's provisions.

Figure 1.3 William H. Hays (circa 1930s), Presbyterian reformer who put Catholic layperson Joseph A. Breen in charge of the Production Code Administration.
History and Art Collection/Alamy Stock Photo

The Catholic method exemplifies the pietist motif. Basically, Catholic bishops entered into a quid pro quo with the studios: it was agreed that the church would monitor movie content in return for keeping quiet about the industry's monopolistic business practices. Studio enforcement of the Production Code was directly contingent upon their control over exhibition, which enabled them to prevent any film without Production Code—and now Catholic—approval from being shown in their theaters. Without access to the key metropolitan cinemas, no film could have a commercially successful run in the United States. Avoiding the Legion of Decency's dreaded C (condemned) rating also kept the Catholic market open.

Catholic leaders believed that the code represented their worldview and that its enforcement would make movies accord with universal moral principles. Their mode of criticism, which focused on the elimination of material deemed offensive based on the church's teaching on faith and morality, favored prior censorship since it protected viewers from false ideas and doctrine. In contrast to the

Protestant stress on the individual conscience, Catholics emphasized personal obedience to church authority to prevent the occasion of sin. Lay Catholics were compelled to obey the Legion of Decency's film classifications. Though greater in number, Protestants refused to restrict individual liberty by controlling the viewing habits of church members, which of course, prevented them from having anything near the consumer clout that Catholics enjoyed over cinema until the 1960s.

A Cinema for Christ in Britain

In comparison to the United States, the Catholic Church had much less influence in the British film industry.[9] J. Arthur Rank, a devout Methodist, was a dominant figure whose organization loomed large in British cinema from the 1930s into the 1960s. Rank, as a biographer put it, was "driven in business by an unshakeable religious faith." He believed that the only way to create a "Cinema for Christ" was to compete directly with Hollywood's vertical integration. Contra the American Protestant strategy, Rank aggressively put together corporations for financing, production, and distribution, and purchased theaters in the United Kingdom and other countries. His monopolistic pursuits were justified by an ambitious slate of religious and morally inspiring films—evidence of a pietist mindset. Personal motive and film content apparently outweighed consideration of the effect that a large-scale "Hollywood-on-the-Thames" might have on the production and marketing of movies that were an outright imitation of the American style of filmmaking.[10] Rank simply accepted Hollywood's terms and conditions, even submitting scripts to Breen's office prior to shooting.

The quest to profitably merge religious and commercial values in this way was fraught with conflict. That the British market was only a quarter the size made it necessary to either control costs or be successful in the North American market. It was possible to score at the U.S. box office and yet fail to return a profit against huge production and marketing costs. *Caesar and Cleopatra* (1945), for example, became a public relations disaster, with Rank criticized for releasing lavish and expensive productions that were "devoid of a sense of national identity."[11]

The disparity between British and American tastes proved troublesome for Rank. A morally ambivalent melodrama, *The Wicked Lady* (1946), topped the British box office in 1946, but overly revealing shots of star Margaret Lockwood's cleavage—something that Rank deemed typical of the seventeenth-century setting—had to be deleted for the American release. Although Rank interpreted such films as "moral fables" in which "patriarchal Christian good always prevailed," skeptics wondered why he would distribute such a film. *Variety* described the following year's release, *Black Narcissus* (1947), as "the story of two sex-starved women and a man. And since the women are nuns, there can be no happy ending except perhaps in the spiritual sense." U.S. Catholic protests of the film stunned Rank by asking whether he had lost his sense of Christian morality. Despite PCA approval, the Legion of Decency campaigned against *Black Narcissus* and initially slapped it with a C (condemned) rating. According to one scholar, Rank "did not relish finding himself under attack for allegedly straying from Christian rectitude."[12]

Rank's conglomerate charted a measure of success, but the critical U.S. market proved impossible for him to predict. Political, economic, and industrial changes, along with the rise of television, eventually forced a shift in priorities. The corporation diversified, investing in photocopying. By the 1950s, Rank had stepped down from leadership, film production waned, and the religious ideals that had been at its origin gave way to the goal of satisfying popular tastes.[13]

Ending the Production Code Era

Rank's empire began to sputter after World War II. Though there is no causal relation, the Hollywood studio system that inspired Rank's own film pursuits also came undone as part of a paradigm shift that occurred in the American cinema. In 1948, the Supreme Court dismantled the vertically integrated film studios, finally ending their monopoly—the eventuality for which Protestants had long labored. Then in 1952, the Court reversed almost forty years of precedent and defined movies as protected speech. Soon after, the *Hicklin* standards were rendered obsolete in both the United States and Britain. Film censorship was increasingly seen as a restriction on civil liberties. The combined effect of the Court's rulings was to undermine prior censorship and, with it, church oversight of film content. How would Protestant and Catholic leaders respond to these dramatic changes?

The National (previously Federal) Council of Churches represented the common front of the foremost Protestant denominations of the day. As I show in *Reforming Hollywood*, the council's long and complicated history with Hollywood constitutes the central thread in Protestant negotiations.[14] To engage the film and media industries, the National Council created the Broadcasting and Film Commission (BFC), with offices in New York and Hollywood. Two conflicting outlooks existed within the BFC. A group centered in the BFC's West Coast office perceived themselves as a counterpart to Catholic advisors. They wanted to consult with film producers to ensure that Protestants received the same flattering treatment in movies as priests and nuns, and then promote these Protestant-themed movies with church-goers. In this group's view, which was compatible with Catholic attitudes, producers with the right beliefs would make moral movies; otherwise, a filmmaker's freedom had to be restrained by the Production Code. They reasoned that a steady slate of uplifting films would prove box office gold for producers while also promoting the work of the church. This perspective epitomized the pietist approach. However, aside from the biblical spectacles, which were theologically contentious, uplifting films like these were usually mediocre: neither critically acclaimed nor huge commercial hits.

A second group, allied with the BFC's main office in New York, advanced a structural approach. Their aim was to engage media personnel in dialogue to ensure a pluralistic media with room for a Christian viewpoint. Movies were analyzed both as cultural texts and in terms of their social impact. The BFC's East Coast group pursued a two-pronged strategy: to use the annual Protestant Film Awards to encourage the production of outstanding movies that honestly explored the human condition, and to persuade the industry to replace the Production Code with an age classification system.

Parallel changes were taking place among American Catholics. In the wake of Vatican II, the Legion of Decency was renamed the National Catholic Office for Motion Pictures (NCOMP). The repurposed Catholic agency abandoned boycotts in favor of endorsing exceptional movies. As it was, two Protestant-Catholic alliances were formed: the BFC's West Coast office and Legion of Decency conservatives displayed a pietist tendency, while the two church film agencies embarked on cooperative ventures aimed at structural reform.

The courts had put an end to prior censorship, but the Hollywood studio heads remained adamantly opposed to a film classification system, which they were sure would only restrict attendance and diminish profit margins. However, when the U.S. Supreme Court issued rulings in 1968 opening the door to a proliferation of local, state, or national classification boards, the Motion Picture Association of America (MPAA) moved quickly to preempt any such occurrence. In cooperation with the Protestant and Catholic film agencies, the MPAA instituted an industry-wide age classification system, becoming the last developed country to do so. The purpose of movie ratings was twofold: first, to safeguard artistic freedom for filmmakers and an adult's right to decide which movies to see, and second, to inform parents about the suitability of a film for children and adolescents. It was a classic articulation of the Protestant structural motif.

The attitudes of the British Board of Film Censors also became more liberal, especially during the 1960s, and even more relaxed with the introduction of an R18 rating for pornography in 1999. When Parliament extended the BBFC's scope in 1984 to assess films on videocassette for "suitability for viewing in the home," the board underwent a name change to better "reflect the fact that classification plays a far larger part in the BBFC's work than censorship."[15] Having survived sporadic controversies, the board, renamed the British Board of Film

Classification in 1984, continues to rate films as a not-for-profit organization that is accountable to both the public and Parliament.

Media Consolidation

Since the 1980s, the media landscape has undergone a huge transformation. The studio system that Protestants had worked to abolish was reassembled through corporate mergers and acquisitions. Today the major film studios are subdivisions of global media oligopolies. In the early 1980s around fifty companies controlled a majority of the U.S. media; today six firms provide news, information, and entertainment for the vast majority of Americans.[16]

Media consolidation was made possible by deregulation policies that brought about a fundamental shift. A direct result of the neoliberalism espoused by the Reagan administration, media companies operate chiefly as profit-oriented businesses under minimal government oversight, rather than as trustees serving the "public interest, convenience, or necessity." It follows that the public interest is defined now by what people supposedly choose through the marketplace—not by diversity, quality, competition, or social value. In response, the National Council of Churches released an extensive study in the mid-1980s with proposals to make "some adjustment to the conflict between artistic freedom and commercial exploitation."[17] The call for industry reform went unheeded and marks the end of any structural initiatives by the old Protestant establishment.

With the decline of mainline Protestantism, the structural motif lost import; the pietist approach moved to the forefront, with American life increasingly characterized by the "privatization" of religion and the diminishing scope of religious authority.[18] By the end of the twentieth century, concerns about artistic quality and social responsibility had receded further into the background. One evangelical argued for release of altered PG-13 and R-rated films based purely on a supply and demand hypothesis. The persistent promise was that an "untapped market of consumers" would boost revenues for "family-oriented" films, producers would reap a financial bonanza, and everyone would live happily ever after—as if simply removing "all that crude stuff" was enough to redeem Hollywood's hyperindividualism that in crucial ways runs against the grain of biblical sensibilities.[19]

The belief that profits and morality are compatible is a recurrent theme, even as box office statistics lend themselves to contrary readings of public tastes. Film producers still insist that they are only meeting market demands with shocking or salacious movies; religious groups counter that most people desire clean entertainment. This supply-and-demand model, however, rests on an optimistic assumption about the high moral tastes of the majority that an unrestrained market will supply. If everyone adheres to the notion that "good" movies equate with profitable ones, then on what basis can screen exploitation be limited other than profitability? Today's market does not necessarily produce quality—whether aesthetic or moral—but rather generates mostly entertaining spectacle, which has become key to success in today's global market.

The values discourse has been limited to specific programming content and not the corporate systems that provide it. The recent debate in the United States over net neutrality, the equal treatment of all traffic to ensure open access to the internet, revived the structuralist theme. Corporate ownership of the internet was judged by some politicians and consumer advocacy groups to be harmful to consumers, innovation, and democratic values. As it became entwined in these issues, Comcast—the largest U.S. cable provider—had to withdraw its proposed $45 billion merger with Time Warner Cable in 2015. Opponents of the deal argued that this concentration of power would stifle competition, restrain programming, and diminish the presence of independent and diverse voices in the media—persistent dynamics in movie regulation since the dawn of the cinema.

A healthy media environment is obviously critical to the functioning of a pluralistic democracy. For that reason, the religious community, including traditional Protestantism, has a stake in seeing that the media provide access to a broad dissemination of news, information, and entertainment from divergent sources. Perhaps recovering communal values—service and love of neighbor, sustaining community, and concern for the public welfare—will better prepare us to confront the challenges presented by the digital age.

Figure 2.1 The Son of God (Brian Deacon) sups and teaches among outcasts in *The Jesus Film* (1979), based on the Gospel of Luke and financed by the Campus Crusade for Crusade.
Allstar Picture Library Ltd./Alamy Stock Photo

2

Independent Protestant Film, from the Silent Era to Its Resurgence

Andrew Quicke

The American film industry has always covered wider ground than its dominant Hollywood narrative film output. American films come in many forms, with underground films, political films, experimental films, educational films, and documentary films all representing alternative ways of looking at life and proposing ideological or pedagogical perspectives differing from those of the dominant media corporations.

What we term the Protestant Christian film industry has been a marginalized area of independent nontheatrical films that during the period 1898 to 2019 were not usually made for general theatrical release. However, currently a radical shift is beginning to occur within the ranks of Christian filmmakers, especially those with African American origins. The twenty-first century has seen Protestant films made for a general audience, and Protestant films like *The Lion, the Witch and the Wardrobe* (2005) have earned millions at the box office.[1]

Terry Lindvall has become the leading scholar in this specialist historical area. He defines Christian films in America as "films of, by, and for the people of the church, neither aspiring to high aesthetic values nor aiming for economic profit, but seeking to renew, uplift and propagate."[2] Christian films are sectarian, ideologically theological, and primarily didactic. You could describe them as tribal films: the biblical narratives told and retold as Christians seek to address their own communities, preserving and proclaiming their traditions and values. Until the twenty-first century, Protestant films had been crafted primarily to preach rather than to entertain, to emphasize moral and religious concerns rather than aesthetic delights.

The American Protestant Film Industry, 1898–2019

When we examine the history of Protestant filmmaking over the past 120 years in the United States, we find it can be divided into three distinct periods. The first covers the period of silent film, approximately 1898 to 1927, when films

Andrew Quicke, *Independent Protestant Film, from the Silent Era to Its Resurgence* In: *Protestants on Screen*.
Edited by: Gastón Espinosa, Erik Redling and Jason Stevens, Oxford University Press. © Oxford University Press 2023.
DOI: 10.1093/oso/9780190058906.003.0003

were often projected in churches and church buildings. In the very early days of cinema before movie theaters were built, the church was the midwife to this infant industry. Silent-film projectors, which utilized 35 mm film, were cheap to buy and required no special architectural changes to the churches. This all changed when Warner Bros. promoted commercially viable movies utilizing the new sound technology by releasing *The Jazz Singer* in 1927. However, the high costs of this technical advance temporarily stopped churches from making films.

The second period of Protestant filmmaking began in the 1930s with the growth of 16 mm film and the invention of the 16 mm optical sound projector. After World War II, this new, smaller sound-on-film gauge was a boon to churches but had the unfortunate effect of creating a 16 mm Christian ghetto for filmmakers, since none of their 16 mm productions could be shown in any neighborhood theater. The only filmmakers who worked in 16 mm were documentarians, educators, and specialist Christian directors and producers. As a result, ordinary movie theater patrons did not see movies made for churches; church movies evolved into a separate production and distribution system. The period of 16 mm church movies ended around the mid-1980s, when the advent of videocassettes destroyed the economics of faith-based church 16 mm movie distribution and led to the closing of most church-based production companies.

The third period of faith-based movie production in the United States began when churches returned to the professional 35 mm gauge filmstock for their narrative films, which could therefore be shown in neighborhood theaters again. This change began in the late 1990s but really got under way after the year 2004.

Let us go back to the dawn of the motion picture industry in America. In 1885, the Reverend Hannibal Goodwin, an Episcopalian rector in Newark, New Jersey, invented and patented the flexible, transparent filmstock that allowed successive photographic images to be coiled on one long celluloid strip. His invention was either copied or stolen by George Eastman, of Kodak fame; a long legal battle followed, with Goodwin finally being awarded compensation for the theft of his very profitable invention.[3]

The greatest Christian prophet of the moving picture was the Reverend Herbert A. Jump, who believed (as theologian Paul Tillich did at a later stage) that any cultural form, however secular in origin and intent, could potentially be made religious. Jump's pamphlet "The Religious Possibilities of the Motion Picture," which he privately printed in 1910, set out five ways in which the motion picture could function as a religious tool. First, Jump argued that movies attract people as an entertaining storytelling device. Second, films help in giving religious instruction in Sunday school. Third, the motion picture does "more for foreign and home missions than any agency yet utilized by our missionary secretaries. Fourth, it provides an agency for the religious and social education of the needy within the community, and finally, it helps the preacher by dramatizing his proclamation of moral truth."[4]

The silent period of Christian filmmaking concluded shortly after 1927; sound films killed the demand for them. To replace silent movies with sound films was technologically difficult and financially risky; no church wanted to invest in 35 mm sound films.

Celluloid Sermons

Three principal factors explain why the church remained slow to start making movies with sound technology: (1) the high cost of production, (2) the costly necessity of equipping all the churches and church halls with film sound systems, and (3) the advent of radio, which provided a rival, low-cost method of evangelism. Christian suspicion of Hollywood deepened in the 1930s. Films were seen by some Christians as the source of all vice, and both Protestant groups and Roman Catholics became justifiably concerned for their parishioners. At first Protestants partly agreed with the Catholic pressure group the League of Decency, attempting to get Hollywood filmmakers to pull back from their most objectionable content, but within five years Protestant support for the overly judgmental League of Decency evaporated. Spearheaded by the Protestant magazine *The Christian Herald*, Hollywood films with moral values, such as *Sergeant York* (1941) and *Mrs. Miniver* (1942), were often favorably reviewed.

Postwar Developments

At the end of World War II, the US military sold off its surplus film equipment, including many 16 mm sound projectors, which had been used for military training. Three evangelical film auteurs sprang into production in the 1940s and 1950s: James Friedrich, Carlos Baptista, and Irwin Moon. They decided to give churches projectors so that those institutions could show their Christian training films.[5]

The father of the 16 mm church film industry was the Reverend James Friedrich, an Episcopalian priest who believed that "we can reach the largest number of people through motion pictures: it is the easiest and most influential medium today."[6] After the war, Friedrich established Cathedral Films, which would make short, high-quality 16 mm sound films for churches to use in their Sunday schools. Friedrich shot short incidents in the life of Christ, filmed in fifteen-minute black and white reels. His first release was *The Good Samaritan* (1940). Two more twenty-minute films followed: *A Certain Nobleman* (1940) and *The Child of Bethlehem* (1940), both directed by Edwin Maxwell and John Coyle for about $12,000 each. Friedrich's main aim was to educate, not merely to entertain.[7]

Cathedral Film's crowning glory was the twelve-part series *Life of St. Paul* (1949–1952), followed by a color series, *The Living Christ* (1951–1957). In the *Life of St. Paul* films, Friedrich had four clear teaching aims: first, to introduce the dynamic character of Saul of Tarsus; second, to show the power of the forgiveness of sins; third, to dramatize the hardships of early Christian followers; and fourth, to show how an enemy of God could be transformed into a "chosen vessel." As a Protestant filmmaker, Friedrich articulated four general goals: (1) to edify and educate the church, (2) to enhance interest in civic affairs, (3) to promote mission work around the world, and (4) to evangelize.[8]

The two most lasting legacies of Friedrich's work were the development of a church market and the supplying of the necessary projectors, which could show all sorts of 16 mm sound films—not only his own, but those of other traditions as well. Above all, Friedrich stressed quality Christian filmmaking, using professional writers, directors, and camera crews. Detailed notes and sample questions to ask the Sunday school viewers also backed up every teaching film he made.

A second auteur Christian filmmaker, Carlos Baptista, followed Friedrich. In his life and practice, he was very different from the highly organized Friedrich. Unfortunately for the quality of Christian films at that time, Baptista was far more concerned that his amateur camera crew were born-again Christians than that they had any camera experience. As a result, his films are virtually illustrated sermons, poorly lit and badly directed.[9]

The third historically important Christian film auteur was Dr. Irwin Moon, a modest but creative scientist who experimented with illustrated sermons at his church in Los Angeles in the years 1931 to 1937. His sermons incorporated electronic, photographic, stroboscopic, and sonic devices to demonstrate the kinship of the Christian faith and true science. Moon set out to communicate the creative truths of God by illustrating them on film through science and nature. In 1945, Moon formed the Moody Institute of Science, which produced live demonstrations (e.g., Moon conducting a million volts of electricity through his body) and film presentations of his series *Sermons from Science.*[10]

The celluloid sermons materializing from these three pioneers, Friedrich, Baptista, and Moon, illuminated the path for other individual Christian filmmakers and denominations to follow. While their forays into filmmaking reveal contrasting strategies of communication with their intended audiences, they approached their audiences through the recreation of biblical stories, the construction of direct propaganda, and the creation of indirect appeals through the marvels of the natural world. Each guided spectators to the same theme of God's presence in the world. Their primary success was to awaken churches and denominations to the efficacy of using film for various church purposes. Friedrich, Baptista, and Moon shared a sense of ecumenical, albeit evangelical, focus, making films that could be used in any church community and which might also unite diverse churches in a shared visual tradition.

Protestant film studios like Gospel Films, World Wide Pictures (with the Billy Graham Evangelistic Association), Gateway Films, and other large production companies dominated the Protestant film industry in the 1960s and 1970s. World Wide Pictures, started in 1951, was an important pioneer, producing higher-budget films that effectively utilized the star power of Billy Graham, who appeared in the films as himself, and presented technically proficient and eventful feature-length narratives in contemporary settings. The studio produced, for example, a gospel-themed modern Western, *Mr. Texas* (1951), which premiered at the Hollywood Bowl, and a gangster biopic, *The Wiretapper* (1955), based on the life of Jim Vaus, a Billy Graham convert who had previously spied for racketeer Mickey Cohen. The company could also be said to have launched the genre of the evangelical youth film with the theatrical release of *The Restless Ones* (1965), which combined scenes of juvenile rebellion and delinquency with a bopping beach party musical number. The films of World Wide and the other large Protestant studios were circulated through a network of more than eighty Christian film libraries, which provided a range of evangelistic and teaching films that rented for $30 to $100. Most churches included a special budget line to pay for film rentals.

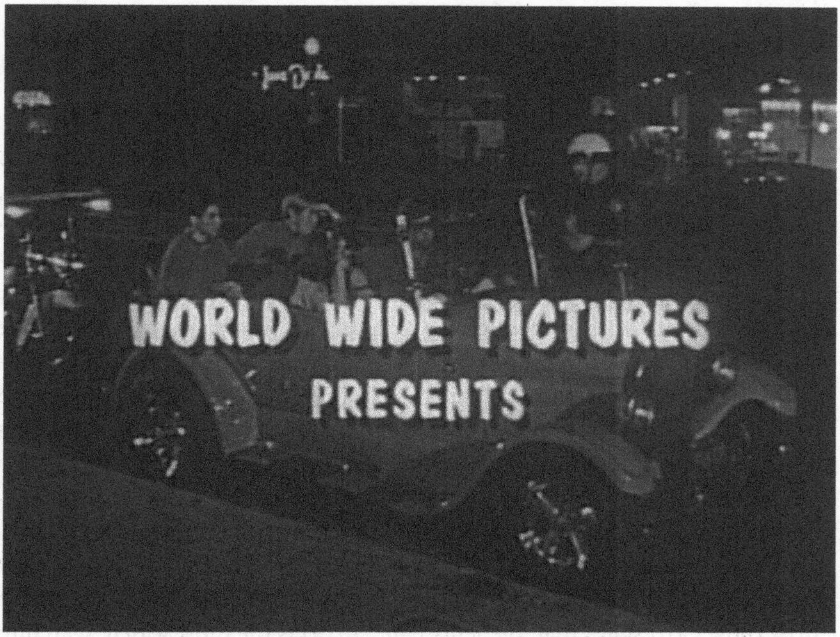

Figure 2.2 The Billy Graham Evangelistic Association's World Wide Pictures told stories in contemporary settings.
DVD screen capture, fair use

Figure 2.3 World World Pictures utilized the star power of Billy Graham. He appears as himself in *The Restless Ones* (1965).
DVD screen capture, fair use

While the audience for Protestant films patronized those movies mainly in the United States, missionary organizations believed that film could help with the task of fulfilling the Great Commission. One film has historically met the criteria for spreading the story of the biblical Gospel for many missionary organizations: *The Jesus Film* (1979), which was produced by well-known filmmaker John Heyman of Genesis Productions in England. Almost every word in the movie was derived from the *Good News for Modern Man* translation of the biblical Gospel of Luke. Key passages like the Lord's Prayer and the Beatitudes were taken from the King James Authorized Version. A panel of biblical scholars was invited to participate in every stage of the production. Released theatrically by Warner Bros. in 1979, it only earned some $4 million at the box office, and lukewarm reviews. However, taken by Campus Crusade for Christ missionaries to nearly every country in Europe, Africa, Asia, and the Americas, it was warmly received in over a thousand different language versions.[11] Campus Crusade for Christ (now Cru) states that *The Jesus Film* (1979) is the most widely seen film ever made; they claim that it has been viewed five billion times by more than three billion people and is responsible for saving some 225,873,100 souls.[12]

Few foresaw that technological change would effectively wipe out the 16 mm Protestant film industry. But with the growth of videocassette sales and drastically lower rental prices in the 1980s, the market for dramatic 16 mm Protestant Christian films died abruptly. Although various series on bringing up children, like Dr. James Dobson's movies from *Focus on the Family*, still sold to the few remaining film libraries, the specifically Christian audience evaporated as new inventions changed the way people consumed media.[13] Videocassettes and DVDs, the internet, and the ubiquitous cellphone would change the way people spent their leisure time.

The next generation of Protestant filmmakers in the transitional 1970s and 1980s were forced to move into the mainstream of theatrical productions with movies good enough to be shown in commercial theaters, creating a Christian film industry where box office profits decided which faith-based stories could be financed.

Christian Box Office

The collapse of the 16 mm Protestant film industry in the 1980s caught producers and distributors by surprise. The first victims were the eighty-four Christian film libraries spread throughout the nation. Slowly they found they could no longer command $30 to $100 per rental for their Christian dramatic films. Churches decided not to rent movies that their young people considered old-fashioned and out of date. If the 16 mm church market business model was no longer viable, then Protestant filmmakers would need to make films for the much larger and more difficult theatrical market, where standards of filmmaking were much higher and budgets much bigger. This was a completely new business model, and few investors wanted to risk their capital on an untested market. Investors cautiously asked whether it was even possible to make faith-based films for a general market.[14]

The first Protestant filmmaker that dared to enter the expensive world of theatrical production and distribution was Cloud Ten Productions. Lacking sufficient funding, the company tried to make cheap films with second-tier actors. The results were, predictably, disappointing. Cloud Ten Productions made four low-budget apocalyptic films, increasing the budget—but not the audience—for each subsequent film. *Apocalypse* (1998) cost $1 million; *Revelation* (1999) cost $5 million; *Tribulation* (2000) cost $9 million, and *Judgment* (2001) cost $11 million. Most secular reviews were negative, to say the least. These films deservedly failed at the box office, though they sold 300,000 copies of their DVDs. The sad fact is that the screenplays were weak, the production values substandard, and the acting second-rate.

A pair of Christian authors, Tim LaHaye and Jerry Jenkins, believed they could provide the stories that a general public would want to see. The pair had already written a hugely successful series of end-times novels that earned millions in bookshops across America.[15] Unwisely, their own film company, Namesake Entertainment, joined with the low-budget experts Cloud Ten Productions to release *Left Behind* (2001). The shooting cost amounted to $17.5 million against box office earnings of only $4.2 million. Condensing LaHaye and Jenkins's four-hundred-page book into a ninety-minute movie proved a challenging task. The book version of *Left Behind* ends abruptly in the hope that readers would be motivated to read the next installment. But that same abrupt ending translated into film deprived viewers of *Left Behind: The Movie* of a real conclusion, and audiences stayed away. The first sequel, *Left Behind II: Tribulation Force* (2002), cost $3.8 million, and *Left Behind III: World at War* (2005) cost $4.6 million; if the DVD sales by Cloud Ten Pictures are accurate, then the company has likely made a return of investment on the sequels.[16]

Other Christian ministries also planned to make movies. One Protestant Christian broadcaster in California, the Trinity Broadcasting Network, formed a movie company with the curious name Gener8Xion Entertainment. Their first film, *The Omega Code* (2000), was one of the most successful independent films of the year, earning $12.6 million at the box office from only 304 theaters.[17]

A major breakthrough in successful Protestant filmmaking came from an unlikely source. Two educational idealists, Cary Granat and Micheal Flaherty, created a movie company that focused on adapting children's books to the screen, which in turn could be leveraged to create educational programs. Their company, Walden Media, backed by millionaire oilman Philip Anschutz, began in 2001.[18] Walden Media avoided labeling themselves a "Christian company," but when they bought the rights to the C. S. Lewis Narnia series of children's books, they became the most successful Protestant filmmakers of all time. Lewis called his stories and his iconic characters a "supposal," but they are also allegories that clearly incorporate the biblical gospels and thus broadly appeal to Christian audiences. Thanks partly to the detailed supervision of Douglas Gresham, C. S. Lewis's stepson, the first of the Chronicles of Narnia series, *The Lion, The Witch, and the Wardrobe* (2005), mixed wonder, mythical creatures, and Christian themes, and earned $760 million worldwide.[19]

Much of the credit for the success of the Narnia series should go to Disney and their distributor Buena Vista, who also worked on the next film, *Prince Caspian*, released in 2008. *Prince Caspian* earned $375 million worldwide against a production budget of $225 million, a 43 percent drop in profits at the box office compared to the earlier film.[20] Walden Media moved their production and distribution partnership to Fox to make *The Voyage of the Dawn Trader* (2010), which cost only $155 million against worldwide earnings of $418 million, a much healthier result.[21] But no more films in the Narnia series have been forthcoming since the contract between Walden Media and the C. S. Lewis estate expired in 2011.

The strategy behind the Narnia series, to adapt well-known Christian family classics, was swept aside, at least temporarily, by new players in what would come to be called the faith-based film market. Major movie companies took note of *The Passion of the Christ* (2004), which earned astonishing box office receipts totaling $612 million worldwide.[22] Due to skillful pre-marketing by its director, Mel Gibson, many evangelical Protestant churches also supported the film despite its deep connections to Roman Catholic theology and traditions. *Passion*'s financial success prompted the Rupert Murdoch company 21st Century Fox, to invent a new subsidiary company named Fox Faith, which planned to release as many as twelve faith-based movies every year. Fox Faith aimed to target evangelical Christians, who often have shunned popular entertainment as offensive.[23]

Fox Faith spent four years building a network of ninety thousand church congregations and a database of more than fourteen million mainly evangelical Protestant households.[24] Fox Faith found its stories from Christian bestselling books but provided only $5 million budgets for each production, plus $5 million marketing expenses for each film. It was a recipe for disaster. In the six years before Fox Faith shuttered its doors in 2012, it only had one success: *The Ultimate Gift* (2007). Adapted from a successful novel by the same name, *The Ultimate Gift* made $3.4 million; the producer said bitterly, "We got pigeon-holed into this little Christian niche."[25] Fox Faith might have had a better chance at success with a film shot in India about Queen Esther with the racy-sounding title *One Night with the King* (2006). Costs were $20 million, but the domestic gross earnings were only $13 million.[26] Every other Fox Faith release failed even more significantly, so Fox Faith attempted no more theatrical releases.

The next candidate to try Protestant moviemaking arose from a totally unexpected source. Sherwood Baptist Church in Georgia had zero experience in movie making, but in 1999 the church invited youth leader Alex Kendrick to join their staff as minister of media. Sherwood approached moviemaking as a ministry: "We don't compromise the message, and we don't put style ahead of substance."[27] In a cursory analysis of Sherwood's first four films, *Flywheel* (2003), *Facing the Giants* (2006), *Fireproof* (2008), and *Courageous* (2011), "substance" appears to mean wholesome, uplifting stories with strong elements of Christian redemption, delivered with overtly evangelistic dialogue. In the Sherwood producing model for their first three films, no one got paid apart from TV actor Kirk Cameron (*Fireproof*). This policy changed with *Courageous*, a much better-made film, which cost Sherwood $2 million to make and earned $34 million in the United States alone. Sherwood claims that the "secret" to its success is an application of fervent prayer and faithful commitment to honor God and to do

His will. These factors alone may have been important, but Sherwood shrewdly marketed their films through grassroots organizations (read: churches), pre-sales, and social media campaigns, ensuring success at the box office.[28]

African American Protestant films look completely different from any other Protestant films because they deal with sin, crime, sexual lifestyles, and shame in real R-rated terms. For example, megachurch pastor and writer-producer Bishop T. D. Jakes's first film was adapted from his novel *Woman Thou Art Loosed* (2004), about a Black woman on death row. Critics welcomed the gritty nature of this R-rated movie, suggesting that subjects like rape, violence, and drug addiction are the stories that Christian filmmakers ought to be addressing.[29] Unlike Sherwood Baptist Church, Bishop Jakes determined to employ only experienced Hollywood actors, directors, and producers. The quality of his many profitable films is a tribute to his expensive casting and production decisions. Bishop Jakes's movies at first averaged about $8 million in production costs. His 2014 epic *Heaven Is for Real* cost $12 million to make and had earned $90 million by 2018.[30] Bishop Jakes has become one of the most successful independent filmmakers in the United States, at least by the numbers.

Black Protestant filmmaker Tyler Perry began writing comedies and comedy-dramas for African American theaters in 2001. Following the process of the Marx Brothers, he perfected the story and delivery on the stage before producing the material for film. His first movie, the raucous yet inspirational *Diary of a Mad Black Woman*, introduced his famous black grandmother character, Madea, to screens. It also contained explicit Protestant messaging in the voice of the main character's mother, who encourages her daughter to seek personal guidance from God. Costing a mere $5.5 million, *Diary of a Mad Black Woman* earned $50 million at the box office.[31] Fifteen movies later, Tyler Perry has earned over $500 million from his films and now owns his own studio complex in Atlanta, Georgia.

That a filmmaker like Tyler Perry with a strong Protestant faith commitment should become the most successful independent director of the twenty-first century is remarkable. Overtly Christian movies with self-professing Christian stars of real ability have become a new norm in comedy filmmaking. This trend toward comedies has inspired young Protestant filmmakers to try their hand at more serious fare. For example, a small company called Pure Flix made a drama about a Christian college student who challenges his agnostic professor in class and convinces his classmates of the truth in Jesus. Though as crudely direct in its evangelizing as the 16 mm church movies of the 1970s, the 2014 release *God's Not Dead* still struck a chord, making $60 million and spawning two less successful sequels.[32]

Conclusion

Protestant filmmakers have become a new force in Hollywood; their faith-based movies have expanded from a niche market to a new genre of Christian movies accurately reported weekly by the trade organization Box Office Mojo. For both Black and white audiences, these movies have proven themselves able to articulate the sufferings and the joys of the poor and encourage them to become upwardly mobile. In the first decades of the twenty-first century, Protestant moviemakers have touched the religious and moral perceptions of an audience largely ignored by Hollywood producers. Increasingly, Protestant storytellers have climbed out of their niche market and have become well-known producers with a distinctive faith-based movie output.

Figure 3.1 Jeff Bridges as Bad Blake, the down-and-out country-western singer in *Crazy Heart* (2009).

AF archive/Alamy Stock Photo

3

Protestant Themes Within Secular Models of Salvation—"Redeemed" or Just "a Bit Happier"? The Example of *Crazy Heart*

Clive Marsh

In his study of the theme of redemption, David H. Kelsey notes how frequently the term is mentioned in film, theater, and book reviews, even if the meaning of the term is often left unclear.[1] This being so, it is right to ask how contemporary Christian construals of redemption, with all its cognate terms, may be affected by contemporary Western artistic and cultural products as these carry or interact with specific theological ideas.[2] For the purposes of this collection, I am interested in Protestant notions of redemption in particular.

In exploring the theme and in affirming the accuracy of Kelsey's insight, the chapter does three things. First, it recognizes that many Western cultural products do indeed locate themselves within narratives of redemption and hope.[3] Second, it acknowledges that theological terms remain prevalent within Western culture, whether or not their theological resonance is recognized or intended. Third, by adopting a dialogical approach—moving back and forth between theological tradition and cultural expression—the chapter slots into a historical strand of modern theological engagement with the arts, as mapped out in particular by Paul Tillich. By engaging with a work of popular culture, the chapter moves beyond Tillich while remaining indebted to the contours of his cultural theological approach.[4]

A wide range of films are held to be "about" redemption. Even if not explicitly or self-consciously theological in origin, works of art and culture (such as film) that present and explore what "looks like" a redemption story are drawing on residual memories or embedded cultural codes when telling their tales. Critics and viewers then hold that films are "about" redemption whether or not their directors, their screenplay writers, or the authors of original works (in the case of adaptations) suggest that redemption is a theme, or the key theme, of what they have produced. Film fans contribute to websites in which the "best movies about redemption" are listed (e.g., www.ranker.com). A long list of contenders can be easily compiled: *The Shawshank Redemption* sits atop the list—number one not

Clive Marsh, *Protestant Themes Within Secular Models of Salvation—"Redeemed" or Just "a Bit Happier"? The Example of* Crazy Heart In: *Protestants on Screen.* Edited by: Gastón Espinosa, Erik Redling and Jason Stevens, Oxford University Press. © Oxford University Press 2023. DOI: 10.1093/oso/9780190058906.003.0004 only in the ranker.com redemption list but also in the IMDb top 250 films of all time, based on votes by 2,055,632 users.[5] But plenty more, many less explicit in their engagement with theology than *The Shawshank Redemption*, quickly take their place as a result of the multiple lists and verdicts available: *The Green Mile*, *21 Grams*, *Rain Man*, *Good Will Hunting*, *Cinderella Man*, *Seven Pounds*, *Gran Torino*, *Invictus*, *Leon: The Professional*, *The Wrestler*, *Crash*, and *The Dark Knight*, to name but twelve. Some of these (e.g., *21 Grams*) contain characters who explicitly engage with religious resources; others (e.g., *The Dark Knight*) tap into the often clichéd world of "Christ figures."

My purpose is neither to discuss whether such films are "about" redemption or are to be adjudged "redemptive" in some way, nor to identify those that clearly are salvific. Nor will I ask why it is that critics (not necessarily religious ones at that) throw the term "redemption" into their reviews with such ease. I wish simply to explore what is actually being claimed when references to "redemption" are being made in relation to a film.[6] What Protestant archetypes and motifs are present? What does it mean to be "redeemed"? What cultural influences in the setting, making, and watching of films make such claims possible? And what, if anything, do such claims, and the use of such terminology, have to do with Protestant Christianity? More particularly still, is there anything specific about Protestant approaches to redemption that may be at work here, whether or not judgments can ultimately be made about whether films "really" reflect Protestant doctrine? And what does all of this reveal about Protestant-themed films?

Redemption in Protestant Perspective

I begin by defining and characterizing a Protestant understanding of redemption.[7] First, in Protestant understanding, all human beings stand in need of redemption, for all human beings fall short of the glory of God (Romans 3:23). All people have willfully refused to follow God's will for the world and thus need to be saved from the consequences of this sinfulness (eternal separation from God). In films that critics and viewers may consider to be "about" redemption, it could thus be said that all characters are sinful, and thus all need salvation. Yet in order to accentuate redemption's meaning, not all characters in the narrative of a redemption film appear sinful. Viewers need to be able to identify, and potentially relate to, characters who are either more sinful or more tormented than most and who seem especially in need of rescue.

Second, God has provided the means of redemption since it is not God's will that any should perish. Hell has pervaded the history of Christian theology as the destination of those who do not turn to God for salvation.[8] Whilst less emphasized now in much Protestant theology, it serves as a reminder of the awfulness of separation from God. The visual portrayals of the torment that punctuate the history of Western art (the works of Hans Memling, Hieronymous Bosch, and the Brueghels, for example) present this graphically.[9] However these works are to be received now, they make a telling psychological point: hell is not to be desired. Even so, the possibility of redemption is always there. It is not God's will that people be tormented eternally. In films, how does a character in a film being redeemed become aware of their situation, or perceive that there is a "way out" of whatever life-threatening context or condition confronts them? Who makes the character aware of this alternative and how? These are the motifs that one would expect to find in a film "about" redemption. *The Fisher King*, *Good Will Hunting*, and *Groundhog Day* are examples of films where such motifs appear. It becomes clear what kind of "hell" is being escaped from (in this life at least).

Third, Protestants believe that God has provided the means of redemption through the life, death, and resurrection of Jesus Christ for all who turn to God. No form of Christianity, Protestantism included, has identified a definitive theory of atonement to account for *how* God affects this redemption in Christ.[10] Nor is it always clear that personal repentance is a *condition* of receipt of the forgiveness of God, God's mercy being so great, though like most versions of Christianity, Protestantism has emphasized the wisdom, value, and effectiveness of such repentance. Highlighting the role of Jesus Christ emphasizes that human beings do not save themselves. Redemption is brokered in some way. Where Christ is not named in a screenplay, brokers are present, even if they may not be Christ figures in any overt way. For example, a redemptive context might be a situation of rescue in which the broker is a community that embraces a seriously flawed character. In the same way that the church—as a corporate phenomenon—constitutes Christ's living body, so also a community may prove redemptive, and hence redemption happens in Christ, in community. But however understood and articulated, it is vital to perceive such redemptive activity as being "in" or "through" Christ in some way for it to be seen as a traditional Protestant construal. All redemption, all forgiveness, all reconciliation is ultimately participation in the activity of a merciful God, the Father of Jesus Christ.

Fourth, people can change. They can seek to amend their lives and receive help as their lives are turned around. While remaining sinful, people can nevertheless be made right with God. They can live in the light of God's grace having encountered it in Christ, in anticipation of ultimate release from the consequences of their evil actions, past, present, and future. There is a new freedom in which, with the help of the Holy Spirit, they can live as a new person. A person living a new life, as redeemed, is being made holy (sanctified), with the consequence that forgiveness of others and reconciliation with those with whom relations are difficult, while still hard to bring about, become more of a way of life than before. Films portray redemption as evidence that people can change in this way. Perhaps there is a happy ending, or at least the promise that life begins to be lived more positively for a character who experiences redemption. Often, though, viewers do not see much, in practice, of the sanctified life on-screen, simply because bad characters make for more compelling viewing. The more fulfilled life may end up being more implied than stated—that is, what continues after what is contained within the film's diegesis.

Fifth, and I say this with some caution as it is emphasized less equally across Protestant notions of redemption than the four points already highlighted, the redeemed person steps onto the road to perfection. This is not a moral journey in the sense that perfection results from human effort, since Protestants stress that people are saved by God's unmerited grace. However, as with all forms of Christianity, the recognition of human frailty is easily allied with demanding expectations and hopes for what it is possible for human beings to become. In films, "happy endings" in redemption stories could be criticized for underplaying the struggles of actual living, tapping into perfection traditions too easily, and implying that release from past burdens makes life easier to live. Yet, while redemption films may end happily, the lack of attention to the redeemed life as such should leave a viewer with a sense that much needed to be overcome, and that the journey to redemption was tough.

These five hallmarks are key points in a Protestant understanding of redemption. The next step is to see whether these points are reflected in films that are deemed to be about redemption. Afterward, I will explore whether the reflection of these hallmark points in "redemption" films matters, either for the use of the term in cultural discussions or for theology as carried by Christian churches.

Redemption in Practice: *Crazy Heart* as a Case Study

To explore the continuing prevalence and potentially lingering usefulness of such themes in contemporary culture, I use the film *Crazy Heart* (2009) as a case study. The film is based on a 1987 novel by Thomas Cobb, is directed by Scott Cooper, and secured Oscar-winning performances from its lead actor, Jeff Bridges, and from Ryan Bingham and T Bone Burnett for their song "The Weary Kind." Neither the book nor the film will be regarded as a classic. Each is enjoyable in its own way; the musical soundtrack to the film functions as a celebration of American country music, and the film as a whole as a "powerful story of a country music star's rocky road to redemption."[11] Our task is to explore what this claim means, whether it is justified, and, if so, in what sense.

Crazy Heart is a study of the later years of Otis Arthur Blake, more commonly known as Bad Blake, a country singer who has fallen into hard times because of alcoholism. Four times married and four times divorced, the film follows his attempt to recover his career and recreate the experience of his earlier life through returning to a life of touring. In the process, he meets Jean Craddock (Maggie Gyllenhaal), a journalist who interviews him for an article she is writing and who falls in love with him. Though their relationship helps Bad to reassess his life and enables him to resolve to become sober, they do not end up together, parting on good terms. Here the contrast with the novel is telling, since Cobb ends Blake's story with him returning to drink. He is not released from, nor does he appear to be able to live with, his alcoholism. The film, by contrast, is more positive. There is no suggestion that Blake remains mired in his alcohol addiction.

Why, then, is the film said to be about redemption? Is it simply because of the relatively happy ending? It certainly cannot be said in any unqualified sense that the book is about redemption, although, as we shall see in due course, the book contains more resources than the film that invite a theological interpretation of what the story presents. At its simplest, of course, the film is said to be about redemption because it presents a story of a life turned round, from destructive tendencies to a more hopeful and healthy way of living. Typically, the narrative shape or arc of a story that is said to be about redemption plots the movement from a negative situation to a more positive state, with ups and downs and external intervention on the way. It also portrays some kind of inner change in the life of the main character, in this case Blake's resolution. However, the film scarcely articulates the five theological features of redemption outlined earlier in any explicit sense.

Crazy Heart's reception illustrates that although the theologically loaded term "redemption" remains in use in Western culture, film criticism and interpretation often apply it in a weakened sense. Perhaps it is only the theologically sensitive or religiously committed who see the term as theological in the first place. Linguistically, the word "redemption" simply means "being bought back"; it is a commercial term, even if it has come to have religious or theological resonance. Yet even if one applies the commercial analogy to *Crazy Heart*'s narrative themes, who in the film's story is doing the buying and what costs are involved? What, in short, is at stake when this story is called redemptive?

In the case of the first theme—the universality of sin—Bad Blake certainly embodies an inconsiderate character who, while perhaps earning viewers' sympathy, is destructive of self and others. It is easy to say that Bad Blake is a character in need of redemption.

Figure 3.2 Bad Blake, mired in alcoholism, is destructive of self and others. He seems in need of redemption.
DVD screen capture, fair use

Second, redemption is available in the sense that there are characters around who are willing to help and support him, ask him awkward questions about his lifestyle, and challenge his basic assumptions. The means of rescue are laid out before him, even if not in formal ways. These are human agents offering help. Even if a theological interpretation might suggest that it is precisely through human agency that an incarnate God works, there is no sense whatever in the film that the means of rescue is an expression of divine action.

As a result, the third theme of redemption in Protestant understanding—the fact that God works in Christ to effect redemption—has no chance to surface. There is no explicit reference to grace (theologically understood). Nor is there any clear reference to a system of values and beliefs that relates to the action of God in Christ. Whatever self-giving or self-sacrifice may be evident in any character's actions in the film, there is no hint that it is a reflection of God's self-giving in Christ.

There are, however, signs of the fourth redemptive theme: amendment of life. The film dramatizes the theme in a number of ways. Blake begins to seek to repair damaged relationships—with Tommy Sweet, a performer with whom Blake had fallen out over the years, and with his long-lost son Steven, with whom he makes contact after twenty years of silence. Though neither of these subplots ends on a wholly happy note, Blake and Sweet do start to work successfully together again. There is thus more hope for this relationship than for that between Blake and Steven because the son seems to want no further contact with his father. In addition to his attempts to repair relationships, Blake resolves to be sober and stay sober. If the recovery process, even with the aid of an Alcoholics Anonymous group, seems a tad too easy, at least Blake shows conviction. Moreover, the amendment of life takes shape in the fact that Blake looks after himself more, and looks better physically as a result of his getting on top of his alcoholism.

Still, the amendment-of-life theme is far from any sense of being a road to perfection. It is a road to improvement, recognizing the support of others, but very much based on an inner resolve, a human act. External agency is contained within the context of interpersonal support provided by friends old and new. Blake is much happier at the end of the film, potentially a little bit happier at the end of the book (though this is unclear), but quite why and how he is "redeemed" might be open to challenge.

Crazy Heart as Film and Book: Some Further Reflections

To take us a stage further in our exploration of why a film such as *Crazy Heart* is deemed by critics and viewers alike to be about redemption, and what this might mean in practice, it is important to dig deeper into the differences between the book and the film and note what has happened in the transition. To anticipate my conclusion: though the book may in no easy sense be considered a theological novel or a literary classic, in the passage from book to film we see the clear *reduction* of explicit theological content. Blake's Protestant background, the motif of his wrestling with religious imagery from different directions, and his decision whether or not to support an evangelical politician are all excised from the plot. The film adaptation can be taken as an example of what I shall call the secularization of penance, which is a result of the secularizing tendencies prevalent in Western culture. Through the secularization of penance, life's amendment through Christ is so emptied of theological reference that the residual motifs align entirely with human works. In this way, Protestantism ends up producing, in a secular context, forms of the works righteousness that the Protestant tradition's very existence is meant to oppose.[12] I shall work towards this conclusion in four steps.

In the transfer from book to film, there appears to be only one clear residual reference to the religious motifs in country music within the film's dialogue. This is the retention of an observation made by Jean Craddock that Bad Blake surprisingly keeps gospel music as part of his playlist. What is removed in the film is an entire level of explanatory background as to how and why Bad Blake became a singer and how he relates to the kinds of music he performs. In the book Blake declares: "I learned to sing in church. Everybody sang. We were Southern Baptists."[13] That appears in a section where he reflects on his upbringing and what music was deemed acceptable and what was not. The quotation is not in the film.

Figure 3.3 Bad Blake surprisingly keeps gospel music as part of his playlist, but the film offers no explanation why.
DVD screen capture, fair use

Second, the extent to which Blake remains rooted in—we might even say is haunted by—his evangelical past is presented in the book, though not in the film. The opportunity for him to make a choice for God and against the possibility of falling "naked into the everlasting flames that burn and blacken but never consume" remains with him and is folded into his contemporary experience of wrestling with drink.[14] It is not clear whether he realizes that he needs saving in some way from his alcoholism, even if not within the religious system he knew in his youth, or whether his alcoholism implies the inadequacy of the evangelicalism against which he rebelled. Readers are simply left to reflect on the relationship between his religious upbringing and his self-destructiveness; we might even be led to conclude that *any* kind of religiosity promotes a destructive lifestyle. All of this material, which raises theologically provocative questions, is excised from the film.

Third, the film contains no representation of a scene in the book where Blake wanders into a cathedral that appears to be Roman Catholic. Inside, Blake is struck by "a crucifix with a twisted, tortured Christ . . . His Baptist upbringing has never prepared him for this graphic representation of Christ in agony."[15] Despite the emphatic redemptive significance of the figure on the cross in Protestantism, Blake's evangelical background has not enabled him to be faced with the full import of the crucified figure or, up to this point, to appreciate how and why the message of redemption works for Christians, whose experience of pain the incarnate, crucified God shares. Since this material is excised, the film hides the religious backdrop against which Blake's story is being played out.

Fourth, and finally, a Republican politician's invitation to Blake to sing for campaign events provides a subplot in the book for pointing out the common alliance between a particular kind of conservative evangelicalism and right-wing politics. Though it scarcely leads to Blake's political awakening, he does start to ask questions that he may not have asked before about the significance his music might assume in an American election. Even if there is so much more to be said about the relationship between music and politics, and between evangelicalism and U.S. politics, than this simple, rather clichéd reference suggests, it is nevertheless a further element from the book excised from the film.

These four observations are not intended as a simple complaint that "the film is not as good as the book." When books become screenplays, tough and selective choices have to be made in order to capture a story's essence and turn it into a compelling visual and aural experience. My basic point is that the country music of the southern United States—so prominent in the film—is being decontextualized. The sound of the music is celebrated and made full use of in the film, but key religious associations that the music carries are overlooked. The simplification process has removed important dimensions of the music itself. As a result, the film is sold short precisely because of what is removed, perhaps simply for commercial reasons. A film said to be "about" redemption removes from one of its key elements—the music—a main feature that would make such a claim tenable. The underlying assumption seems to be that to make a country music film too much about religion will alienate audiences or incur the disapproval of secular Hollywood. Yet if one advertises this film as about redemption and links it with country music, as the DVD cover itself does, then arguably there is no choice but to include its religious dimension and cultural context in order to capture the authenticity of southern culture, music, and way of life. This lack of cultural integrity and authenticity may explain its modest showing at the box office, despite relatively positive reviews by some critics.

There is, in short, no escaping the Protestantism out of which Blake came and to which he continues to relate. What is more, not to attend to that Protestantism results in a film that glosses over important and profound themes embedded in southern culture, undercutting the originality and integrity of the film and ultimately the people it purports to represent.

Conclusion

One further, film-historical point is worth making as a preamble to my conclusion. The casting of Robert Duvall as Wayne Kramer, owner of a bar that Blake frequents, invites consideration of Duvall's Oscar-winning performance nearly three decades earlier as Mac Sledge in *Tender Mercies* (dir. Bruce Beresford, 1983). In that film Duvall also played a recovering alcoholic and country music artist, but the religious background of his recovery is much more prominent through the activity of an evangelical widow, Rosa Lee (Tess Harper), who supports his recovery, leads him to her church, and attends his baptism. Between *Tender Mercies* and *Crazy Heart*, Duvall also undertook a personal project of his own, *The Apostle* (1997), a film that he funded, directed, and starred in. Duvall also functioned as a mentor for the director of *Crazy Heart*, Scott Cooper. Yet while the two earlier films accentuate forms of Protestantism in the American South, in *Crazy Heart* the religious element has been airbrushed out. The American South thus plays a key role in locating geographically the *music* that lies at the heart of the film, but the music is in effect deracinated and the loss of its broader context makes reception of the film problematic.

If I am right and the explicitly Christian—here, specifically Protestant—motifs that have created a character are removed from view, then a film about spiritual redemption becomes a film about self-help mixed with a story of the support of good friends. That is fine as far as it goes, but the term "redemption" is not being explored or fully mined even at the interpersonal level, let alone the theological. "Redemption," a commercial term that has developed deep theological resonances and which remains widely used, demands a broader linguistic and cultural attention than it receives in this movie adaptation.

If the film becomes only a therapeutic plot, as in *Crazy Heart*, then even if the lead character is remorseful and seeks amendment of life, in Protestant terms the redemptive plot narrative has slid into an exercise in works righteousness. It is the human effort alone that brings about the dramatic change. Theologically—in both Protestant and Roman Catholic readings of Christianity, it should be noted—this strains the extent of human possibility too much.[16] The shift of redemptive power to human agency especially undermines the Protestant emphasis on being saved by God's unmerited grace. In Protestant understanding God brings about more than human beings can achieve. Such activity, embodied and effected in and through the work of Jesus Christ, continues to work by the Holy Spirit on the life of an individual and can function at a depth in the inner person that is truly life-changing. There is, in other words, psychological and therapeutic power in the Protestant perception of human limitation and sheer incapacity, though secular Western individualism is more prone to pay attention to the motif of self-help.

In theological perspective, such elements need to be part of any story considered to be "about redemption." Without such observations being drawn out, penance is secularized to a striking degree and stripped of its potential power and impact upon viewers. Blake appears to be penitent in this film (though the book makes us wonder whether he will stay the course). Even if he is getting help and feels a bit happier, however, the efforts are largely his own. So if this is a story of redemption, then I suggest that it is deficient in the necessary background that the book at least in part provides. Without this background being filled out, Protestantism as it is known across the American South is prevented from contributing in a creative way to critical, public discussion about the manner in which its key insights are carried not only within Protestantism but in cultural life more generally.

Whether or not a Christian (and a specifically Protestant) understanding of redemption can be held to be "true" in all respects, there remains a profound insight in theological discussion about redemption that has value beyond religious circles. The basic claim that human beings cannot redeem themselves has far-reaching psychological, social, and political implications. For this to be lost in hazy allusions to redemption in popular cultural discourse may have damaging consequences. While, on the one hand, it can be considered positive for humans to seek amendment of life, or a release from destructive practices such as addictive patterns of behavior, the too-easy labeling of such initiatives as "redemption" can overlook what traditions of theological discourse contribute to the understanding of human behavior and well-being. To start from the assumption that one cannot redeem oneself is a positive insight in a manner different from self-help culture. It recognizes that the assistance of others is always needed for lives to be turned around. Whether or not the redirection of the amended, transformed life is then also viewed within a transcendental or theistic framework, concepts and practices that constitute key elements in the redemptive process—repentance, atonement, resolve, reconciliation—are exposed, and scrutiny of these is invited, when a theological interpretation of human experience is offered. In this way, theology enriches life whatever the religious commitments of those who watch the film. The film's reception invites viewers to carefully examine, and examine deeply, what it means to call *Crazy Heart* a film "about" redemption.

PART II

THE PROTESTANT REFORMATION ON SCREEN

Figure 4.1 Stacy Keach as the psychologically tormented title character in *Luther* (1973).
Allstar Picture Library Ltd./Alamy Stock Photo

4

"Here I Stand I Can Do No Other": Martin Luther in German and American Biopics

Esther P. Wipfler

The famous Protestant leader in history, Martin Luther (1483–1546), has been represented in film since 1911. Although more than two dozen feature films about the reformer have been created, the phenomenon has more or less been ignored by scholars.[1] Luther films have always been—apart from some exceptions at the very beginning of the history of the genre—ambitious undertakings. As far as we know, all the initiators of these films sympathized with the protagonist and his issues, and so for them the status of the historical figure as a national myth in Germany or a church founder in America required an adequate form.[2] Unlike in other media—especially print—there were never any films dedicated to the polemic against the reformer.[3] When the Lutheran Church was involved in the production, leading scholars of theology and church history were invited to advise the scriptwriters, since the film's content also referred to theological issues and mirrored the self-image of the Lutheran Church.

The filmic representation of the reformer stands at the end of an iconographical tradition that goes back to Luther's lifetime. Reference to topoi formulated in the sixteenth century continued even into film—they were often cited to lend the protagonist or the setting the aura of authenticity. Even in the Reformation period (beginning in 1517), the image of Luther was multifaceted. The spectrum included polemic names: "Luder" ("rascal," "scoundrel"—a pun on the name Luther), "Septiceps" (the seven-headed dragon of the Apocalypse), "mad dog," "grim bear," and "Devil's apprentice." On the other hand, Luther's followers characterized him as a "man of God," a "herald of peace," a "great prophet," "the third Elijah," and "another Plato," as well as "a true Cicero," the "father of the Church," the "bringer of Enlightenment," a "German hero," and the "father of his house."[4] Moreover, the filmic image of Luther is also part of a specific Lutheran approach to the visual arts: the image is accepted as an adiaphoron, something not essential but acceptable for the purpose of evangelization.[5] By contrast, the Swiss Reformed Church tradition has failed to produce any feature films on John Calvin, apart from documentaries.[6] The first feature film about the Swiss

Esther P. Wipfler, *"Here I Stand I Can Do No Other": Martin Luther in German and American Biopics* In: *Protestants on Screen*. Edited by: Gastón Espinosa, Erik Redling and Jason Stevens, Oxford University Press.
 DOI: 10.1093/oso/9780190058906.003.0005

reformer Huldrych Zwingli (1484–1531) was shown in 1983, and a second one *Zwingli* appeared in 2019.[7]

In Germany, the Luther film represents a specifically Lutheran response to and substitute for the Jesus films (e.g., *La passion du Christ* [Albert Kirchner, Georges-Michel Coissac et Frère Basile Kirchner, France, 1897], *The Life and Passion of Jesus Christ* [Pathé, 1902–1905], *The King of Kings* [Cecil B. DeMille, 1927], etc.), which followed traditional Christian iconography and were promoted by the Roman Catholic Church, which had been producing its own films since 1917. In Germany, however, the First Protestant Film Congress (Erster Evangelischer Filmkongress) did not convene until 1931. Moreover, in the early twentieth century the proper representation of Jesus was still an issue for German Protestants. In 1908, for instance, the Oberkonsistorium (High Consistory) of the Bavarian Lutheran Church categorically rejected a petition from the Bavarian State Ministry of the Interior for Ecclesiastical and Educational Affairs to permit the life of Christ to be represented in film (although they had approved a film about the Passion).[8] In the United States, by contrast, while Protestants had reservations about the filmic image of Christ, especially in secular productions, many churches exhibited photoplay versions of Passion plays and, with persuasion, embraced even Hollywood's Jesus films. So George Reid Andrews, a Congregationalist reverend and representative of the Federal Council of Churches, acted as one of the clerical advisors on *The King of Kings*.[9] *The Jesus Film*, initiated by evangelical Christians in the United States, was released in Germany in 1979.

The representation of Luther in feature films has been—apart from the protagonist's physical similarity with the portraits by Lucas Cranach the Elder—anything but uniform, not even when only the positive sides of the reformer's character have played a role.[10] Luther was supposed to remain a likable and admirable character, providing a model for Christian life, the respective concept depended on the screenplay writer, the theological advisors, or the spirit of the times. For these reasons, Luther has variously appeared in movies and television as a romantic lover, a titan of German nationalism, a talent in the arts, a delight to children, a man racked by doubt, a groundbreaking theologian, or the passionate antagonist to several religious opponents (the emperor, the Catholic Church, radical Protestant theologians such as Andreas Bodenstein [alias Andreas Karlstadt, c. 1486–1541] and Thomas Müntzer [c. 1489–1525], the Anabaptist movement, and the revolting peasantry).

The character of Luther has also been shaped by those who played him. Directors chose actors who were famous, who often had years of stage experience, and who in some cases had even attained "star" status. Today many of the names (Hermann Litt, Rudolf Essek, Karl Wüstenhagen, Eugen Klöpfer, Niall McGinnis, Hans Dieter Zeidler, Christian Rode, Bernard Lincot, Lambert

Hamel, and Ulrich Thein) have been forgotten, but others, such as Stacy Keach and Joseph Fiennes, are still well known. Through these portrayals, the filmic Luther speaks not only German but also French and English, which has considerably expanded an awareness of the historical person.

The Luther film is also recognizably associated with the context of the German middle-class Protestant culture of commemoration.[11] Luther anniversaries—the officially commemorated "Luther Years," 1983 (the 500th anniversary of his birth) and 1996 (the 450th anniversary of his death), as well as other anniversaries of his birth, such as 1913, 1923, 1953, 1973, and 2003—provided the impetus for new treatments of the reformer, which influenced cinematic history. This orientation toward the year of Luther's birth rather than the pivotal dates of Reformation history, such as the publication of the Ninety-five Theses in Wittenberg in 1517 or the presentation of the Augsburg Confession in 1530, reveals how strongly the commemorative culture of the Lutheran Church is centered on the reformer's life.

Even as early as the sixteenth century this cult was stylized, most notably in pictures: a famous example is the woodcut designed by Hans Baldung (known as Baldung Grien) published in 1521, in which Luther is hagiographically depicted as a monk with a nimbus and the dove of the Holy Spirit.[12] Luther himself, as is well known, contributed to the stylization of his own person; for example, although he enrolled in 1501 at Erfurt University under the name Martinus Ludher ex Mansfeldt, in signing the October 31, 1517, letter to the archbishop of Mainz that accompanied his Ninety-five Theses, he styled himself as Luther for the first time. That was because he saw himself as Eleutherius, meaning "the one who has been made free [by God]."[13] In the films, he is consistently addressed as Luther.

Viewed against this background and the regularity with which it continued to be revived, the Luther film seems to refute the much-cited thesis that historical biography is a crisis phenomenon.[14] The idea that the biopic served as a medium of self-assurance in times of political and ideological uncertainty only seems to apply to the production *Luther: Ein Film der deutschen Reformation* (1927), directed by Hans Kyser. The extremely nationalistic view of the protagonist in this film reflected the situation of Lutheranism as a former state church that was forced into a defensive position during the Weimar Republic. Although the churches had received a privileged status in the Weimar Constitution of 1919, the fear of anarchy that arose during the short revolutionary period after World War I remained and was projected mainly onto the left-wing parties (KPD, SPD, USPD). Moreover, the ideological neutrality of the Weimar state was interpreted as a weakening of the Christian faith. Lutheranism at that juncture wanted to express its claim to spiritual leadership in political terms, and it used the nationalist lexicon to do so. With the 1927 film, it becomes clear how the medium of cinema contributed to ensuring the continuity of the Kulturkampf (cultural struggle) of the nineteenth century. This struggle was enacted by the prime minister of Prussia and later Reich chancellor Otto von Bismarck (1815–1898) in order to reduce the influence of the Roman Catholic Church on education, social life, and politics, first in Prussia and then in the Kaiserreich.

Even though the anniversary of Luther's birth provided an occasion for representing his life story, most Luther films begin not with his birth but rather at a biographical turning point, such as his entering the monastery or taking monastic vows—that is, with the official beginning of his religious life. This treatment corresponds to the traditional structure of filmic biography, or biopic, which often starts at the moment that the idea embodied by the protagonist takes hold.[15] Apart from Leopold Ahlsen's 1964 television film *Der arme Mann Luther* (Poor Man Luther), the character Luther always remains the driving force of the diachronically structured narrative, a typical feature of the traditional closed biographical narrative system, which is indebted to both a belief in progress and the cult of genius.[16]

All Luther films also share the canonical key scenes originally drawn from the repertory of motifs first formulated in illustrated Luther biographies, in history paintings, and in the theater. These motifs include Luther entering the Erfurt friary, nailing the Ninety-five Theses to the cathedral door, burning the papal bull at the Elster Gate in Wittenberg, standing fast at the Diet of Worms, staying incognito as Junker Jörg at the Wartburg, and dramatically crying out in a thunderstorm near Stotternheim in 1505: "Help! St. Anna, I want to become a monk!" This last turning point has more than once occupied a pivotal position in filmic representations (*Luther: Ein Film der deutschen Reformation* 1927, *Martin Luther*, 1983, *Luther* 2003).

The Luther film genre, which originated in 1911 as an expression of an ongoing Luther renaissance, reveals a paradigm shift in the way that Luther was perceived within the span of only two decades—from romantic aesthete in the 1913 *Wittenberger Nachtigall* (Wittenberg Nightingale) to hero of the German Reformation in 1927. The paradigm shift was not triggered by the discovery of Luther as a national hero; that had happened much earlier.[17] Instead, it can be traced to the intentions of each set of producers, which were at first probably commercially oriented. That may also have been the reason sentimentality was first given priority, echoing dramatic models such as Friedrich Ludwig Zacharias Werner's romantic tragedy *Martin Luther, oder Die Weihe der Kraft* (Martin Luther, or The Sanctification of Power), published in 1807, or August Strindberg's play *Näktergalen i Wittenberg*, which premiered in Stockholm in 1903 (the German version, *Luther, die Nachtigall von Wittenberg*, was staged for the first time in 1914 in Berlin).

Afterward the thrust became increasingly clerical. Serious involvement on the part of the Lutheran Church cannot be verified until the 1923 Luther film.[18] In this case, the top-ranking church authorities promoted the project only through advising on the screenplay and having the film distributed by the Evangelische Bildkammer, the media center of the Innere Mission (Inner Mission) of the Lutheran Church. Yet opinions were divided on the film because of weak acting by the principals and because of fundamental doubts about the capacity of the film medium to do justice to religious subject matter. The production of *Luther: Ein Film der deutschen Reformation* from 1926 to 1927 was far more professional and sophisticated. Remaining in circulation until 1939, it served the propaganda supported by the Evangelischer Bund (German Protestant League), founded in 1886–1887 in order to pursue "German-Protestant intentions." This league established the corporation responsible for the film's production, and its head, the Berlin cathedral pastor and university instructor Bruno Döhring (1879–1961), had a paramount influence on the screenplay. Döhring, who would found the Deutsche Reformationspartei (German Reformation Party) in 1928, a late answer to the Deutsche Zentrumspartei (German Center Party), a lay Catholic political party founded in 1870, definitely wanted to win over a wider public to this political cause. This is evident in several explicitly anti-Catholic scenes and motifs: the luxurious life of the papal court, monks with alcohol and prostitutes, the quasi-delirious veneration of a statue of the Virgin Mary (intended to illustrate idolatry), and the casting of a then well-known comedian as the Dominican preacher Johannes Tetzel. These led to such severe conflicts between Lutherans and Roman Catholics that the tradition of the Luther film in Germany ended for the time being.

It was not until after World War II that the next big Luther film project would be produced in West Germany by Louis de Rochemont and RD-DR Corporation in cooperation with Lutheran Church Productions and Luther-Film-Gesellschaft M.B.H. The film *Martin Luther* premiered in Minneapolis in 1953 and was released to West German cinemas in the following year (first in Hanover and then in Nuremberg). It was the first talking motion picture about Martin Luther. Entirely different intentions informed it; the group that commissioned it was of course not interested in stylizing the reformer into a German national hero. Rather, it moved toward demythologizing the figure of Luther by portraying the reformer as an introverted intellectual rather than as a superhuman being. To do so, the canon of scenes prescribed for a Luther biography did not have to be changed. However, critical aspects were omitted, such as Luther's late hostility against Jews, his adversarial attitude toward the peasants' cause, and his tolerance for the bigamy of Landgrave Philipp I of Hesse. So it was possible to present Luther as an immaculate champion of freedom of thought. In 1953 this ideological model could also serve to support the denazification of postwar Germans and to vaccinate them against communism. In the United States it was intended to do the latter, as the propaganda material shows.

Figure 4.2 Niall MacGinnis plays Martin Luther in the 1953 American-West German film biography, where he is here depicted as a champion of free thought and conscience in his debate with John Eck at the Leipzig debate on grace and free will.

This changed with the American Film Theatre's ambitious 1974 production of John Osborne's play *Luther* (1961). Producer Ely Landau was able to attract Broadway and Hollywood stars, such as Stacy Keach, who played the lead, and Judi Dench, cast as Katharina von Bora. The employment of Stacy Keach, an actor whose face is marked by a scar from the repair of a cleft lip, meant a break with the "handsome Luther" tradition. In a film that otherwise followed Osborne's play, the radical new idea was the staging of Luther's life and work from 1506 to 1530 in the setting of a Gothic church.[19] This location served, albeit maybe unintentionally, as a metaphor for medieval society. Director Guy Green deleted from Osborne's play the scene showing Luther nailing his theses to the portal of Castle Church, perhaps because the scene is not part of the collective memory of English or American audiences. However, Green did stage the burning of the papal bull at the Elster Gate as an expression of disobedience and protest against the authorities. In contrast to the 1953 film, the 1974 production didn't get much feedback; there are only a few uninspired reviews.

It was not until 2003 that cinema once again linked up with the sentimental beginnings of the Luther film. Initiated by the German film producer Alexander Thies (Neue Film Produktion GmbH, Berlin) and mainly sponsored by Thrivent, an American Lutheran fraternal benefit society, *Luther* (2003) was made for a worldwide cinema audience. In the cinema the film had 3.5 million viewers in Germany, Austria, and Switzerland; on TV, the screening reached 5.87 million people; moreover, 510,000 DVDs were sold.[20] In an interview recorded on the DVD, director Eric Till emphasized that previous characterizations of Luther had lacked sensitivity and passion, the very values that should be imparted to audiences today. Joseph Fiennes, who played the lead, had received the accolade "the handsome Luther" even before the official German premiere of the film on Reformation Day (October 30) in 2003. He is depicted as a figure of suffering who is accompanied by Johannes Staupitz, played by Bruno Ganz as a caring father figure. This Luther quarrels with his opponents, specifically with the papal legate Girolamo Aleandro, played by Jonathan Firth as a power-mad intriguer, and Cardinal Cajetan, intelligently accounted for by Mathieu Carrière. The rebel friar is under the protection of Frederick the Wise (Frederick III, elector of Saxony), played in a quirky rendition by screen legend Peter Ustinov, whose Frederick seems senile on the surface but is secretly sly and resourceful. As Ustinov explained in an interview, the elector of Saxony had learned from Luther to have the courage of his convictions. Accordingly, what could be learned from Luther above all was belief in oneself. Further, Ustinov stated in an interview given in 2003: "Luther was too good a Catholic to remain a Catholic. . . . [H]e was so critical of some of the habits of the clergy. . . [H]e was . . . scandalized by this commercialization. . . . [H]e took action against it and started the Reformation. . . . It [the film] does speak of the independence of the human being to think and to think deeply."[21] That Ustinov has been engaged here to provide a Luther exegesis tallies with the concept of the film. Rather than being intellectual, the movie was primarily intended to affect the emotions. This slant was conveyed chiefly via the star of the film, Joseph Fiennes, who was the prime vehicle for eliciting viewer sympathies. He explains the film's interpretation of Luther and his era in the bonus material marketed with the DVD: "I think it is very much about the minority and the suppressed. . . . [I]t's about the control the Catholic Church had on the masses during that time through language and interpretation. . . . [Y]ou can't keep man down and you can't control [him . . .] sooner or later he will gain knowledge and through knowledge, power to be liberated in freedom of . . . conscience . . . As he starts out he is an innocent man who gets driven by a clause . . . an argument in the Testament which, in the interpretation of the Catholic Church, amounts more or less to a debit and credit account. . . . Martin Luther very much saw . . . it is a gift . . . that one doesn't need to buy . . . one's way into heaven."

In this film, the reformer usually acts alone, and the leitmotif is a close-up of his face. Melanchthon and other contemporaries of Luther play only a marginal role in the events of the Reformation, as, for example, in the cursory treatment of Luther's quarrel with Karlstadt about the iconoclasm unleashed by the Peasants' Revolt. The historical background is scarcely intelligible to the average viewer.

Figure 4.3 In *Luther* (2003), the reformer usually acts alone, and the leitmotif is a close-up of his face.
DVD screen capture, fair use

Conclusion

In no other medium besides film can one so clearly read the change in the Lutheran mindset during the past century. This mass medium popularized scholarship on a grand scale, whether in respect to psychology or the interpretation of the Reformation as a media reformation. Biopics, like other film narratives, have mythological functions, and Luther films fairly consistently adhere to the positive image of the hero. Other important historical figures from the Reformation who also influenced Luther, such as Philipp Melanchthon, are thrust into the background so that the impression remains that "great men" always "make history" on their own.[22] Whereas the view of Luther in German films increasingly emphasized the nationalist element until 1927, the Anglo-American tradition has placed the emphasis on the theme of emancipation from conventional thinking, liberation from the authorities of the Middle Ages, and new beginnings.[23] The films in this tradition extol the rejection of an exploitative system informed by the doctrine of justice as interpreted by the Catholic Church: salvation for righteousness accompanied by good deeds. In the film narratives, these teaching are overcome through Luther's doctrine of imputed righteousness (salvation "by grace alone, by faith alone," without personal merit).

The Anglo-American image of Luther replaced the German one and became the basis for later filmic representation in cinema, but not on TV. Nevertheless, it is legitimate to speak of an Americanization of Luther in film. This should not be underestimated, because film has been the main medium of Americanization in western Europe since the late 1920s.[24] The success of the 1953 Luther film disproves Heide Fehrensbach's thesis that "throughout the 1950s, West German films and German rereleases from the Weimar and Nazi periods surpassed imports in popularity."[25] Certain main aspects of Luther's image can be seen in both the European and the American traditions, such as the omission of Luther's mistakes and inconsequences. Problematic stances, such as his invectives against the Jews, appear only in other filmic formats such as documentaries.[26]

Life with his family is given increasingly greater scope in the presentation beginning with the film adaption of John Osborne's play in 1974, but Luther's illnesses of his later years, his six children, and the death of his daughter Magdalene are not mentioned until the German TV productions of 1983. However, one can discern a paradigmatic shift in the image of Luther from Europe to America. His image mutates from that of a German national hero into a champion of freedom of thought and a rebel against traditional authorities. His rebellion remains limited to the church because Luther never wanted political change. Even Martin Luther King Jr. himself did not refer often to his namesake.[27] Some historians have interpreted the political, social, and economic consequences of the Reformation as a "Protestant revolution" and see an analogy between the sixteenth-century Reformation and the civil rights movement of the twentieth century.[28] However, this trend of historical argument did not inform the propaganda for any of the biopics; for these, the producers had other intentions.

Luther, rather, corresponds to the American role model of the intellectual pioneer opening new frontiers of thought and experience. Heading a populist movement, he breaks down institutional barriers and promotes spiritual freedom. Thus, Martin Luther has become a character who is fighting for certain values much more than he is fighting against an institution and/or a different nation. Nevertheless, Luther remains a member of the bourgeoisie and thus gives mainly middle-class audiences a chance to identify with the reformer as a role model. Luther also personifies the Protestant church and its values. Since the representation of his individual faith does not eliminate the idea of the Christian community, the cinematic Luther is absolutely not an "anti-ecclesiastic character," as is described by Werner Schneider-Quindeau.[29]

Moreover, viewer response to the Luther film has proven to be an indicator of the degree of secularization in a society. It also shows whether links to a particular religious affiliation are perceived at a given time, and if so, how strongly. Between 1953 and 2003, one observes a change from emotionally charged reaction expressed in extreme polemics by those who were for or against particular films to moderate, objective commentary.[30] The extra material on the DVD of the German 2003 film shows a significant role allocation: Luther's life is interpreted by the actor Joseph Fiennes, but the theologian Dr. Hans Christian Knuth, at that time bishop of the Nordelbische Evangelisch-Lutherische Kirche, is limited to reading out Luther's Small Catechism without any comment. The special features on the DVD for the English-speaking market offer interviews with the cast, the crew, the director, and the producers, but no theologian is included. This reveals a phenomenon described in 1962 by Hermann Gerber: "that a good bit of conveying the message has shifted from theologians to laymen."[31] What has been called secularization has evidently not eliminated religion but instead has changed the way it is handled.[32]

New icons emerge over time, as reflected in film. The film *Katharina Luther*, broadcast by the German TV channel ARD in 2017, focused on the character of the reformer's wife; it attracted 7.28 million viewers.[33] In this film, directed by Julia von Heinz, the change of perspective permitted the filmmaker to portray some of the negative aspects of Luther's character, such as his later hostility against the Jews and his unbalanced temper. However, this won't be the last representation of the German reformer in film.

Figure [illegible]

Figure 5.1 Richard Harris, as the titular hero of *Cromwell* (1970), riding with Puritan Parliamentary battle standards during the English Civil War.

Photo 12/Alamy Stock Photo

5

The Vexed Man: Oliver Cromwell and the English Reformation and Civil War on Screen

Gastón Espinosa

Ken Hughes's 1970 historical drama *Cromwell* traces the story of one of England's most celebrated political leaders—Sir Oliver Cromwell (1599–1658). An adult convert to the Protestant Puritan faith, he led the English Parliamentary forces against King Charles I during the English Civil War from 1642 to 1651. The film's main theme is overcoming corruption, and the plot is driven by Cromwell's desire for religious freedom and attempt to promote a constitutional monarchy led by Parliament rather than King Charles I's claim to universal power via the divine right of kings.

With a distinguished star cast, Richard Harris fills out Cromwell's earnest and hot-tempered Puritan spirit, while Alec Guinness creates a highly sympathetic King Charles I, with Robert Morley and sprightly Timothy Dalton as the ever-calculating Earl of Manchester and giddy Prince Rupert of the Rhineland. Hughes wrote and directed the film, and despite its modest $8 million budget, it was nominated for two Oscars, a Golden Globe, and a BAFTA award. At the Moscow Film Festival, Harris won for Best Actor and the film was nominated for Best Picture, perhaps because of the film's seemingly anti-bourgeoisie spirit.

Plot

The inciting incident occurs when Cromwell's steward is punished by having his ear cut off for protesting the confiscation of common grazing lands by the king and after his Puritan church is forced by the Crown-controlled Church of England to adopt Catholic-sounding liturgy and ornate religious paraphernalia in their Sunday worship services. Cromwell reacts strongly against this cruel violence and Crown's imposition on his Puritan church, and this sets him on his journey for political justice, religious freedom, and ultimately a constitutional monarchy led by Parliament. However, Cromwell must first overcome a series of conflicts and

Gastón Espinosa, *The Vexed Man: Oliver Cromwell and the English Reformation and Civil War on Screen* In: *Protestants on Screen*. Edited by: Gastón Espinosa, Erik Redling and Jason Stevens, Oxford University Press.
 DOI: 10.1093/oso/9780190058906.003.0006

obstacles that increasingly put him in jeopardy, such as accusations of treason, house arrest, betrayal, mutiny, civil war, the death of his son, fears of Irish Catholic and Scottish invasions of England, and regicide. The crisis and reversal occur after Cromwell learns that King Charles I has used his protracted peace negotiations with Parliament to buy time to bribe the Kingdoms of Ireland and Scotland to invade England and crush the Parliamentary forces. The climax is the tortured decision about whether Parliament will vote to execute the king or turn against Cromwell. The resolution takes place after the king's execution and Cromwell is named lord protector of England, but he finds the new Parliament is not much better than the previous one ruled by Charles I. This leads him to disband it and serve as a symbolic de facto "king"—a title he hitherto rejected and scoffed at—in all but name.

In what follows, I will sketch the historical backdrop to the movie by outlining Puritanism, the English Reformation, Cromwell, and the English Civil War and then I'll analyze historical interpretations of Cromwell, inaccuracies in Hughes's film, critical reception of the film, and then its political, religious, and social commentary.

Protestant Origins of the English Reformation and Puritan Tradition

The Puritan tradition traces its roots to the Protestant Reformation in Europe (1517–1648) led by Martin Luther (1483–1546) in Germany, John Calvin (1509–1564) in Switzerland, and John Knox (1514–1572) in Scotland. While Luther's Reformation spread primarily north into Scandinavia, Calvin's Reformation spread west into France, Holland, England, Scotland (Knox), and eventually to the English colonies in America. Although once hailed the "defender of Catholicism," for numerous reasons Henry VIII embraced Protestantism and established the Church of England (aka Anglican/Episcopalian Church), which was Protestant in theology but Catholic in rituals, iconographic style, and liturgy. Rather than answer to the Pope in Rome, King Henry VIII invoked the divine right of kings to claim that he was the head of the Church of England (Anglican Church) and answerable only to God.

By the 1550s, a number of English Protestant reformers, driven by a desire to practice only what Christ taught in the Bible, called on the Church of England to purify itself of unbiblical Catholic-style beliefs, rituals and practices. After King Henry's successor Edward VI died, his Catholic half-sister Queen Mary I ascended the throne and attempted to reestablish Catholicism in England and crush Protestantism. She unleashed a bloody reign of terror on Protestants and had the Anglican archbishop Thomas Cramner and many others tortured and burned at the stake, which helps to explain Cromwell and the Puritans' hatred for

Figure 5.2 Historical Portrait of Oliver Cromwell (1599-1658). He was the Lord Protector of England, Scotland, and Ireland and an English general and politician who led the Parliamentary armies against King Charles I during the English Civil War.
Library of Congress

Catholicism. The anti-Protestant persecution ended in 1558 after Queen Mary died and her half-sister Elizabeth (a Protestant) became Queen of England. She reestablished Protestantism as the official religion of England via the Elizabethan Religious Settlement, which also allowed Catholics to practice their faith.

Fearful of Catholic resurgence, Puritans in the Church of England pushed harder for spiritual reform. They called for an end to the Catholic Mass, kneeling for the Eucharist in front of a priest, wearing ornate priestly vestments, the use of graven images of saints and ornate decorations in churches, and the widespread abuse of the Sabbath. Disgruntled Anglicans pushed the Puritans out of church leadership and persecuted them, which led to thousands fleeing to Europe and then to the English colonies in America, thus giving rise to Puritanism in America.[1]

For our purposes, it's important to note that the Catholic-driven anti-Protestant persecution, religious intolerance, divine right of kings, and the push for spiritual reform were all factors that shaped Cromwell's life, outlook, and work.

Cromwell's Origins and the English Civil War

Cromwell was born on April 25, 1599. Scholars know surprisingly little about his early years. At age twenty-nine, he became a member of Parliament representing Cambridgeshire. He came from an upper-middle-class family and attended Cambridge University, the intellectual center of the Puritan movement. He converted to Puritanism in the 1630s. By all accounts, he was an intensely spiritual man who tried to live his life according to the Bible. He believed God watched over him and guided his life and actions.[2] He and his family planned to join the twenty thousand other Puritans in the great Puritan migrations to New England (1620–1640s), but changed his mind after he was swept into the English Civil War.

Cromwell rose up in opposition to King Charles I after the king tried to suppress the religious liberty of Puritans and other Nonconformist Separatists by forcing them to embrace high church Anglican practices (which smacked of Catholicism to him) and attempting to confiscate public lands from the poor for his rich aristocratic supporters. Cromwell connected King Charles's religious oppression to his universal authority, which was allegedly based on the divine right of kings. According to this view, God had made Charles king, and therefore Charles did not have to answer to any legislative body, even Parliament. Cromwell wanted to change Parliament from a rubber-stamping band of wealthy aristocrats to a powerful legislative body that truly represented the people and checked the abusive power of the king. Cromwell promoted freedom of conscience, religious liberty, and a constitutional monarchy run by Parliament rather than solely the king.[3]

The English Civil War erupted after Charles I called Parliament into session in 1642 for the first time in eleven years to raise funds to invade Ireland and Scotland. This outrage led to the first English Civil War, with King Charles I on one side and Cromwell and Parliament on the other. When Cromwell crushed the king's forces at Marston Moor in 1644 and Naseby in 1645, Charles I came to the bargaining table.[4]

After a series of protracted negotiations during which time the king conspired with Irish Catholic and Scottish Calvinist armies to destroy Cromwell and the Parliamentary forces, Charles invoked the divine right of kings to override Parliament and tore up their peace proposal, which led to the second English Civil War, from 1648 to 1651. In 1648, the Irish and English royalist forces in Ireland rebelled against Parliament. They killed twelve thousand English Parliamentarian supporters, almost all Protestants. Cromwell and his New Model Army of redcoats smashed the royalist forces throughout England and then sailed to Ireland in 1649 to crush rebellions at Drogheda and Wexford, killing close to sixty-five hundred English royalist soldiers, sympathizers, Irish rebels, and a few Catholic priests, before sailing to Scotland to defeat the Scotts at the Battle of Dunbar in 1650. For Cromwell's conquests in Ireland, Catholics called him "Cromwell the Destroyer." By 1651, his conquests of royalist sympathasizers in England, Ireland, and Scotland were complete and led to the birth of the English Commonwealth (England, Scotland, Wales, Ireland). King Charles I was arrested, tried, and found guilty of treason for plotting the Irish and Scottish invasions and summarily executed—off with his head.[5]

On the religious front, Cromwell sought to re-Protestantize the new commonwealth by bringing Calvinist theologians together to create the Westminster Confession of Faith and the Shorter Catechism (1647), which he made the official confession and catechism of England and Scotland. In all of his efforts, Cromwell sought to complete the Reformation in England that Luther and Calvin had started in Europe.[6]

After Cromwell's death, his less charismatic and zealous son Richard governed for about twenty months, but because Richard did not have the confidence of the army, King Charles II returned from exile in France in 1660 and reestablished the Tudor Stuart monarchy. He had Cromwell's body dug up and publicly beheaded, and had the skeletal remains dangled from the Tower of London for years. Cromwell's New Model Army and conquests contributed to the birth of the British Empire, and his notions of religious freedom, a social contract, and individual rights were later developed by John Locke and the English Enlightenment and brought by the Puritans to America, where they laid the foundation for the Declaration of Independence, Constitution, and Bill of Rights.

Cromwell: Man, Myth, and Legend—Previous Interpretations

Cromwell is highly controversial to this day. His admirers and detractors have interpreted him as everything from an ideological champion of liberty and democracy to a pragmatic, ruthless, and regicidal dictator. Puritan poet John Milton called Cromwell "our chief among men" and praised the new republic because of its promotion of civil and religious liberties. Puritan leaders likened him to a new Moses and lawgiver for the English people. Religious radicals like John Lilburne and the Levellers (a populist movement committed to religious liberty, natural rights, and representative government) depicted him as a treacherous, Machiavellian figure who betrayed the English revolutionary cause by not going far enough to destroy the monarchy and aristocracy. And royalist Edward Hyde described Cromwell as that "brave bad man." By contrast, Victorian-era historians such as Thomas Carlyle described Cromwell as a national hero who anticipated the modern liberal state on church-state relations, freedom of conscience, parliamentary government, and religious tolerance. W. C. Abbott disagreed, interpreting him as a proto-fascist, and Winston Churchill viewed him as an "earnest military dictator." Marxists like Friedrich Engels saw Cromwell as Robespierre and Napoleon wrapped up in a single person, and Leon Trotsky viewed him as a working-class revolutionary fighting for the proletariat, which may help explain why *Cromwell* did so well at the Moscow Film Festival. In sharp contrast, Irish Catholic writers cursed him as "Cromwell the Destroyer" for his devastating invasion of Ireland, while Blair Worden described Cromwell as an ideological schizophrenic, torn between the contradictory impulses of social conservatism and religious extremism. Austin Woolrych's more textured analysis interpreted Cromwell as a very modern and contradictory man who simultaneously espoused religious radicalism and constitutional conservatism.[7]

Thesis and Purpose

With so many competing visions of Cromwell at stake, what does filmmaker Ken Hughes make of him? For Hughes, Cromwell is neither a conniving hypocrite, a dictatorial tyrant, a religious zealot, or a proto-Marxist class-based revolutionary, but rather a psychologically contradictory modern man—a vexed man—with religiously garbed secular goals who sought to replace a bygone era of the divine right of kings with a modern parliamentary-led constitutional monarchy.[8] Hughes creates the image of a reluctant hero who, although having psychologically vexed moments about how to proceed during the English civil war, is nonetheless able to rein in his prophetic stridency via middle path approach to saving England from an increasingly out-of-touch monarch and antimonarchial Levellers on the other. He portrays him as a relatively progressive, modern, and forward-looking political reformer and champion of Western-style democratic values. In telling Cromwell's story, he also provides (perhaps unwittingly) a kind of social commentary and road map on how to navigate and move forward on the social divisions vexing British society in the 1960s and 1970s like the Troubles in Northern Ireland, the British Empire and colonialism, countercultural movements, growing racial-ethnic divisions (via representations of the Irish and French), and secularism.

The film focuses largely on Cromwell's service in Parliament during the English Civil War until his death in 1658. Hughes portray's Cromwell at the eleventh hour of his life with a fully formed man. He does not take the traditional cradle-to-grave Moses-style biopic story arc popularized by Joseph Campbell's and Christopher Vogler's hero's journey, though many of these markers are still discernable. In fact, despite fanciful stories and prophecies about Cromwell's

Figure 5.3 Cronwell throws the gavel down in a meeting of Parliament after they proposed to name him King, something he roundly rejected because he wanted to see England transform into a liberal democracy
Moviestore Collection Ltd / Alamy Stock Photo

birth, the movie skips over Cromwell's childhood, youth, conversion, marriage, eight children, and family life (for the most part), and the reasons why he went into public service. The film does not portray or explore his formation and development. His story arc takes him from being a reformer to a regicidal revolutionary to a promoter of constitutional monarchy, wherein religious liberty and secular democracy were mutually reinforcing and accommodating forces that nurtured a virtuous citizenry. For these reasons, it would be inaccurate to classify Cromwell with Bible-and-sandals movies from the same period. In fact, Hughes offers a distinctly modern and quasi-secular psychological interpretation of Cromwell rooted in Cold War values and religious sensibilities that blended God, country, and constitutional democracy.

Historical Inaccuracies

Despite Hughes's decade of research on Cromwell and Roger Ebert's and Glenn Erickson's claims that the film "is faithful to the facts," scholars have noted more than two dozen historical errors, oversights, and examples of "creative license."[9] Most of these changes tend to exaggerate Cromwell's role and leadership in the English Civil War, though some also distort his family life. Hughes paints

Cromwell as a Moses-like lawgiver for the English people by having him tell Charles I that England should be a God-honoring nation that brings light to the masses suffering in darkness, an event that is debated among scholars. In his final farewell speech, Cromwell states: "I will liberate man's souls from the darkness of ignorance. I will build schools and universities for all. . . . This nation will prosper because it is a godly nation."

Hughes's decision to leave out major events in Cromwell's life, such as the Battle of Marston Moor in July 1644, is also puzzling because it was not only the biggest battle of the first English Civil War, but also one where Cromwell played a critical role in achieving victory. More problematic is his depiction of the Battle of Naseby in June 1645, wherein Cromwell's New Model Army is portrayed as vastly outnumbered by Charles I's royalist army, when just the opposite was true. However, by recasting the royalist army as larger and more menacing, he placed his protagonist in greater jeopardy—which heightens suspense and sympathy for Cromwell. In an effort to humanize Cromwell, Hughes has his oldest son, Oliver, killed at the Battle of Naseby in 1645, when in fact he died from smallpox in the spring of 1644. To reveal his transformational story arc and growing courage, Hughes has Cromwell's gallantry and bravery rewarded by the Parliamentary forces, who name him commander-in-chief of their army, when in fact Sir Thomas Fairfax first held that post. In real life, Cromwell served as lieutenant general and second-in-command until he was given the title of commander-in-chief of the army for the invasion of Ireland. Hughes gives viewers the impression that after rejecting the offer of the crown from Parliament, Cromwell went back to his farm in Cambridgeshire to live a simple life, when in fact he led a devastating invasion of Ireland.

These historical inaccuracies and oversights have led some to criticize the film for its incomplete and somewhat varnished picture of Cromwell. But this overstates the case. Hughes portrays Cromwell not as a classic hero, but rather as a dynamic, imperfect, and contradictory man who helped lay the foundations for the British Empire and for the modern secular state, where religious freedom is guaranteed but also kept in place, with neither state nor religion controlling or corrupting the other.[10]

Interpreting Gender and Race

Women do not play a central role in the film. Patriarchal values are reinforced, except in the case of Queen Henrietta, though her stubborn defiance is arguably driven as much by her zealous Catholicism as by her gender. However, she is given considerable voice and agency within her world, and, like first- and second-wave feminists of Hughes's day, she is outspoken and won't have her voice muffled even by strong men like Charles I or Cromwell. Despite her strong will and defiant spirit—and perhaps because of it—she is depicted in an earnest but negative light and as someone who indirectly cajoles her husband to make terrible decisions that ultimately lead to his downfall, such as inviting the Catholic Irish to invade Protestant England. This decision leads to charges of treason and ultimately King Charles I's execution. Cromwell's own wife, by contrast, is portrayed as someone who reinforced traditional feminine values as guardian and mistress of hearth and home.

Like gender, race-ethnicity does not play an overt role in *Cromwell*. However, one could argue that the Irish served as a racialized group throughout much of English history. The Irish are uniformly and collectively presented in a negative light as rowdy Catholic papists who can be bribed by Charles I to destroy democracy. Similarly, French nationals are cast as Catholic, manipulative, smug, and naive, with few redeeming values. Religion and ethnicity are thus combined to create a kind of religio-racialized other. The Scots are treated neutrally since they are kindred Protestant Calvinists from lands north of England.

Critical and Popular Reviews

Although *Cromwell* was nominated for two Academy Awards (Best Costume Design and Best Musical Score), many professional critics have not found the story compelling—and some have been outright scornful. Roger Ebert lays out a litany of criticisms about the overly strict historical retelling, the lack of personal character development, and the acting of Richard Harris, who "does not inhabit the role or seem to care much about it."[11] Glenn Erickson contends that Cromwell comes off as a "pretty insufferable guy, a Puritan who wants to drive every Catholic into the sea, especially in Ireland," and that the script doesn't provide any real insight into the internal working of the man—whether he's "a saint or opportunist."[12]

In contrast, Tony Mastroianni argues *Cromwell* is a "moving portrayal" of "a reluctant leader" whose "virtues" seem to come "out ahead" of "his faults."[13] Andy Webb notes that this film was part of a series of English historical epics like *Becket* (1964), *A Man for All Seasons* (1966), and *Alfred the Great* (1969) and that Hughes uses Cromwell to capture the "radicalism" of the late 1960s and "reflects it through the prism of the Lord Protector's righteous pulverizing zeal in another time of upheaval and furiously questioned social precepts." The film suffers from "attempting to present a shaded portrait" of Cromwell as a "conscientious traditionalist pushed first into radicalism and then into repeating the mistakes of his enemies" and finally by "transcending hypocrisy through the ardor of his idealism."[14]

Figure 5.4 Cromwell, dressed in his Puritan garb, embracing his wife with a worried look because he is concerned about the fate of his family and the English people.
Moviestar Collection Ltd / Alamy Stock Photo

The general public in recent years has viewed *Cromwell* favorably, giving it a 69 percent positive rating on RottenTomatoes.com and 6.9/10 stars on IMDb.com and praising its epic-style, lavish costuming, faith dimension, and window (however incomplete) into Cromwell, the Puritans, and the English civil wars.

Political, Religious, and Social Commentary

Films are like time capsules that provide a window into the historical period they depict and the decade in which they were made. They are not value neutral, but instead reflect the attitudes of the writer, director, and producer—and the larger society that consumes the film. For many, the goal is not simply fame and fortune, but also influence and social change. In order to do this, they use their films to create narratives that provide social, political, religious, racial-ethnic, gender, and other forms of commentary about a person, group, community, event, or time period with the goal of changing how audiences perceive and/or respond to it. While some directors claim that they aren't seeking to provide commentary (perhaps to avoid lawsuits and negative publicity), their stories and dialogue often belie the claim and even if they weren't, most can't escape attitudes, values, and social and political views of their day and their films reflect them.

If we stand back from the film, how might we view Hughes's interpretation of Cromwell? What trends, events, and developments shaped his interpretation and narrative construction? His interpretation of Cromwell's story reflects and provides social commentary on different issues vexing Great Britain in the late 1960s: Ireland and the Troubles, the magnanimity of the British Empire and colonialism, the Cold War, the countercultural movement, growing racial-ethnic divisions, and secularization.

Ireland and the Troubles

Instead of Cromwell the Destroyer, Hughes portrays him as a relatively progressive, modern, and forward-looking political reformer, social justice advocate, and champion of Western-style democratic values. Hughes uses Cromwell to provide commentary on the religious and racial-ethnic sectarian origins of the conflict in Northern Ireland during the Troubles of the 1960s and 1970s, when Irish Catholic nationalists called for the British to pull out of Northern Ireland—a Protestant colony of the British Empire in Catholic Ireland. After Cromwell's conquests, the British Empire brought the conquered Scottish Calvinist Presbyterians to settle Northern Ireland, which set the stage for centuries of Protestant-Catholic and interethnic tensions.

In many ways Hughes's depiction of the English Civil War mirrored the relatively hard-line approach the British took to Northern Ireland in the late 1960s. Thus while many scholars have interpreted the Troubles as being driven by scarce resources, civil rights violations, and historic ethnic divisions, Hughes stresses the sectarian religious nature of the conflict throughout the film by portraying Charles I's French Catholic queen Henrietta Maria as prodding Charles to invite an army from Catholic Ireland to invade Protestant England to help save the throne. He also has the Catholic archbishop state that for the right concessions the Pope could authorize a Catholic army from Europe to invade England. In reaction to these moves, Hughes has Cromwell meet Charles I and boldly make a speech that could easily echo Protestant Presbyterian minister Iain Paisley's views on the conflict in Northern Ireland from the 1960s to the 1990s. Cromwell declared: "Catholicism is more than a religion, it is a political power. Therefore, I am led to believe there will be no peace in Ireland . . . until the Catholic Church is crushed."

Figure 5.5 King Charles being persuaded by his French Catholic Queen Henrietta to stop Parliament by supporting a Catholic Irish invasion of England, which results in his being tried for treason and executed.
Album / Alamy Stock Photo

How do we know that Hughes is offering a religious interpretation of Cromwell's views? There is no historical evidence that Queen Henrietta ever called for a Catholic invasion. Furthermore, we know that this alleged meeting between Cromwell and Charles I never took place at the king's palace and that Cromwell probably never uttered these words. It is also highly unlikely that Cromwell's declaration that Catholicism was a political power and that there would be no peace in Ireland until the Catholic Church as a political power was crushed would have been read by the Irish and IRA as anything other than a religiously laced solution to the Troubles. Having Richard Harris—an Irish Catholic—play Cromwell and offer a colonial-minded military solution served as a supreme irony, something for which Harris was roundly criticized. While some might be quick to note that the film does not depict Cromwell's bloody invasion and suppression of the Irish revolt, this is because it would have shifted the moral blame for the English civil war away from the Irish and Catholic antagonists and placed it squarely on the backs of Cromwell and the English Parliament, something that Irish propagandists in the 1970s might have exploited in their struggle against British colonialism in Northern Ireland.

Decline of the British Empire and Defense of Colonialism

In this respect, the film may also reflect Hughes's political commentary on the decline of the British Empire and defense of colonialism. Why else would he make the case that the suppression of Ireland (and by inference all rebellious overseas colonies) is a reaction to external provocations by outside forces (French, Irish, Catholics with loyalties to Rome) for which military solutions are sometimes an acceptable if lamentable option? He also uses the freedom-loving Cromwell to push a vision of a benevolent British Empire that—if it continues to hold true to its foundational principles—will prosper. In the final scene, the narrator states in a rather unqualified way and tone that Cromwell "raised England to be a great power . . . feared and respected throughout the world." In short, Cromwell both defends British colonialism and provides a road map for how Great Britain can regain its greatness during the Cold War.

Completely left out of Hughes's interpretation are Cromwell's invasions and suppression of Ireland in 1649-53 and Scotland in 1650-52, because they would undermine his notion of a benevolent empire and inflame the strife in Northern Ireland. In short, the English are victims of external provocations, and the actions they took were responses to them, not the product of any policies initiated by Cromwell, the Parliament, and the modern political establishment.

Cold War Film

In many ways, *Cromwell* also can be interpreted as a Cold War film. This is underscored not by a message of peace but rather by the view that one must confront totalitarian regimes with military might. This is evident in Cromwell's affirming military solutions to tyrannical and totalitarian governments, emphasizing political democracy and religious liberty, and stressing Christian civilization over absolutist and dictatorial (i.e., Marxist) governments. Hughes also portrays the Levellers as social radicals and completely strips them of their original religious motivations in order to make them less sympathetic. He avoids Marxist interpretations of Cromwell by affirming his Puritan faith, which the script connects to his middle path blending of democracy and constitutional monarchy, as well as his rejection of the Levellers' demands for the abolition of the monarchy. Although not a Marxist, Hughes portrays the king as embodying many of the attitudes of Marxist totalitarian regimes that must give way to Western-style liberal democracies.

Countercultural Movement

Although Hughes somewhat reflects Churchill's idea of Cromwell as an earnest law-and-order military dictator, Hughes also interprets him as a person in tune with the times and part of a new generation of leaders who take a countercultural stance against the reigning establishment and thousand-year-old tradition of the divine rights of kings. In good moderate English fashion, this countercultural spirit is not anti-religious like some contemporary versions because in the 1970s Soviet Marxism was still a global threat to religion, freedom of conscience, and liberal democracy. We see Cromwell's countercultural spirit in his speeches about liberty, freedom, and democracy and in the decision—at least at first—to align himself with the revolutionary Levellers. Additionally, he supports the execution of the king, a radical act. Yet, rather than paint Cromwell as a revolutionary radical who might be used for Marxist causes, Hughes ultimately portrays him as taking a middle path between monarchal absolutism and the Levellers' call for the complete abolition of the monarchy. In this sense, he seems to be speaking to the countercultural movement of the day by emphasizing a need for religious, social, and political tolerance, but at the same time rejecting its scathing dismissal of the established political, religious, and social order. In the end, Hughes seems to have Cromwell ironically saying that both unrestrained democratic and revolutionary impulses must be reined in and that some measure of conformity via a constitutional monarchy for the common good must prevail.

It should be noted that one could also interpret Hughes as using Cromwell to critique the countercultural movement via his treatment of the Levellers and antipathy to external foreign influences (Irish, French, Scottish) on England, which are portrayed as largely threatening much like Soviet Marxism was viewed in the day. However, his decision to support the execution of the king and promote freedom of thought, freedom of religion, and a constitutional Parliament-driven monarchy seems to undermine this interpretation, since he is clearly challenging the established quo while also in some ways reinforcing it.

Secularized Vision of Cromwell

Hughes's religious commentary is interesting because he underscores the value of religious liberty but at the same time does not make it an explicit theological or ideological driving force in Cromwell's thinking, despite the fact that most scholars agree that it played this role in his political thought. Cromwell's middle path but still robust Puritan religious vision is underscored by Cromwell's rejection of the unrestrained religious radicalism of the Levellers. Although we see few explicit theological references, we do see the Puritan temperament and a Protestant aesthetic of the embodied Word in Cromwell's actions, in his brooding self-righteousness, and in biblical allusions and army banners with Bible passages embroidered on them in the battle scenes. Puritan themes that appear in the film are the movement's dissenting spirit; the focus on personal conversion and piety; the sense of divine election not only for Cromwell but also for the English people; the representation of simple and unadorned sacramental services; a low-church congregational government where the pastor is elected by the people; and a view of government as a correcting and restraining force in society with a responsibility to inculcate Christian morals and virtues. All of these appear not as explicit doctrines and teachings but rather as embodied aesthetic practices reflected in Cromwell's life and actions throughout the film, albeit with a secular framing for the common good.

Puritanism is also refashioned not as a primary value in itself but rather as a respected middle path conduit and vehicle for promoting political freedom and parliamentary democracy. Hughes seems to be affirming a slightly more secularized version of Cromwell, Puritanism, and English society than the historical record indicates. We see this secular impulse in his film's implicit criticisms of the Catholic influence in Ireland and France, the Church of England's rule by the king, and Charles I's invocation of the divine right of kings to justify his absolute power. In all cases, the film has Cromwell arguing for a kind of separation

Figure 5.6 "Dictator! Dictator!" cries Parliament after Cromwell dissolves it. Hughes rescues him from the appearance of totalitarian hubris by depicting him as a Moses-lawgiver type.
Moviestore Collection Ltd / Alamy Stock Photo

of church and state. However, this is contrary to the facts. Although Cromwell disestablished the Church of England in 1646, he replaced it with the Scottish Calvinist Presbyterian Church, which served as the state church until the restoration of the monarchy by Charles II in 1660—none of which is mentioned or alluded to in the movie. More surprisingly, Hughes completely skips over Cromwell's adult conversion to the Puritan faith—a topic normally rife with emotion that would be included in most films about religious leaders. However, representing Cromwell's Puritan conversion on-screen would have run the risk of casting him in the light of a religious radical and revolutionary rather than a countercultural democratic reformer. In addition, Hughes does not develop Cromwell's Puritan faith, which seems at first glance to change very little if at all throughout the film except in terms of his political stances. Although he goes from supporting the monarchy to opposing it to reaffirming the call for a constitutional monarchy, Cromwell's original religious concerns seem to fall by the wayside as the film progresses. He tends to stress the cultural and political rather than the spiritual value of religion. He also seems to be more motivated by a love for democracy than by religion, when most scholars agree that his Puritan faith and biblicism profoundly affected and helped drive his political philosophy and social vision. Perhaps Hughes was attempting to make the character more appealing to an increasingly secular British society.

Cromwell the Psychologically Contradictory and Vexed Man

Despite Hughes's relatively positive portrayal, he studiously avoids the Victorian and Whig interpretations of Cromwell by stressing his psychologically contradictory tendencies. These tendencies are manifested throughout the film in his outbursts of righteous anger and indignation, his rage against betrayal, deception, and Irish Catholics, and his generally brooding temperament. However, his contradictory tendencies do not appear to be as driven by his religious devotion as they might have been portrayed in so many Hollywood movies today, but rather by an unquenchable thirst for righteousness and justice—though more in a civil religious tone than in a strictly Puritan one. Although his personal style was forceful, he still continues to portray Cromwell as steering England on a middle path between an absolute monarchy and the Levellers. This results in Huges making Cromwell a complex modern man, without interpreting him as the genocidal and regicidal dictator parleyed by his detractors.

The one notable exception is—perhaps—the film's finale, when Cromwell dissolves the hopelessly corrupt Parliament, which cries, "Dictator! Dictatorship!" Even here, Hughes softens the harder edges of this scene by having Cromwell justify his actions, accusing the new Parliament that replaced King

Charles I of being more Machiavellian than the king and made up of "tricksters, villains, whoremasters, and godless scum no more capable of conducting the nation's affairs than running a brothel." Hughes then has Cromwell wax glorious about how he will liberate man's soul from the darkness of ignorance, provide bread for all, and bring law and order within reach of every common man even if—irony notwithstanding—he has to do it himself! While this might have been a last-minute reversal that left viewers with a bittersweet taste of hypocrisy, the narrator then steps in and pushes through the irony by declaring that Cromwell made England a great power, despite his hubris, and laid the foundations for a truly democratic nation, thus snatching victory from the jaws of defeat.

Conclusion

In the end, Hughes interprets Cromwell as a paradoxically modern but contradictory vexed man whose push for a Parliament-driven constitutional monarchy paved the way for the British Empire and for Britain to enter into the modern world chief among nations. He portrays Cromwell as oscillating between a countercultural liberal force in his promotion of a constitutional monarchy and religious freedom and yet also a conservative force in his promotion of political stability, military solutions, family, righteous idealsm and suppression of radicals like the Levellers. His Protestant Puritan religious orientation—which is aesthetically embodied chiefly in his actions—is the quiet engine that seems to drive his populist political reforms. Hughes's Cromwell is ultimately an honest man whose commitment to God, righteousness and justice, and the people makes him a virtuous reformer—one who was incredibly successful in his own life, but also one whose promotion of a democracy could not withstand the backlash of the monarchy after his untimely death. Despite Charles II's restoration, Hughes shows how Cromwell's revolutionary ideals set the stage for religious freedom, secularism, and full-scale liberal democracy.

Figure 6.1 Vincent Price as English witch-hunter Matthew Hopkins (1620–1647) in *Witchfinder General.*
AF archive/Alamy Stock Photo

6

Propaganda, Blasphemy, and the Savage God in *Witchfinder General* and *The Wicker Man*

Victor Sage

The famous pre-credits sequence of director Michael Reeves's *Witchfinder General* (1968) begins with some shots of an estate park in which sheep are grazing. The sun gleams through the branches of ancient English oak trees in such a way that its suddenly blinding rays polarize on the camera's lens into the form of a cross made of light. These shots are accompanied by the ringing blows of a hammer on the ridge of a hill where a sturdily built carpenter is putting the finishing touches to a gibbet.

Screaming interrupts the scene, and a voice begins to recite. The camera cuts to a long path by the side of a house, along which, at the end, we see that some people are dragging out a woman while a man dressed in a plain cassock is intoning a text. David Pirie in his book *A Heritage of Horror: The English Gothic Cinema 1946–1972* takes up the description of the rest of the scene:

> Then Reeves cuts to show us the pathetic witch being dragged along. . . . The witch is pushed on to the scaffold and the rabble subsides until, as she hangs, there is only the creaking of the wooden cross-bar and the sound of the wind; after a pause in which the nightmarish figure of the old woman swings stiffly to and fro, Reeves suddenly zooms in close on a dark figure on horseback observing the execution from a distance, revealing an imposing face with gaunt supercilious features, and instantaneously the music comes in for the first time[] as the credits roll.[1]

Pirie's auteurist focus, quite consistently, is on the director's priorities and on the degree of alienation infused into the horror and incipient violence of this disturbing scene. This is effectively a lynching party, he implies. As far as it goes, Pirie's commentary is arresting and often just, but my argument here seeks to take into account other priorities: if we begin instead from the historical crisis

Victor Sage, *Propaganda, Blasphemy, and the Savage God in* Witchfinder General *and* The Wicker Man In: *Protestants on Screen*. Edited by: Gastón Espinosa, Erik Redling and Jason Stevens, Oxford University Press.
 DOI: 10.1093/oso/9780190058906.003.0007

of Protestantism that forms the context of this scene, then we can see that the horror is associated at every step with a propaganda war, in which the boundaries between the "true" God of scripture and the deformities of Catholic or pagan or even Puritan heresies must at all costs be policed. British horror, whether verbal or visual, is rich in religious themes rooted in bloody memories of the Reformation.[2] As a classic of British horror, *Witchfinder General*, I shall argue, locates its horror in the violence that results from policing the boundaries between the godly and the ungodly. I shall then conclude my discussion by considering another example of a classic British horror film, *The Wicker Man* (1973), which represents a quite different attempt to police the boundaries between Protestant Christianity and pagan heresy on an island off the coast of Scotland, and which questions the authority of the Protestant religion to police that boundary.

"Listening" to the Text

This scene functions as a generic introduction to the film's Protestant context, supposing that we "listen" more closely to the text, Revelation 19:1–6 and 11–21, that the priest is actually reading.[3] Initially we hear interrupted fragments. The opening of the chapter concerns God's righteous judgment of the Great Whore and her corruption of the servants of the Lord. We cannot quite hear these passages, as we first struggle to attune ourselves to the voice that is, at a distance, competing with the screams of the woman:

> And after those things I heard a great voice of much people in heaven, saying: Alleluia; Salvation and glory and honour, and power, unto the Lord our God. (Revelation 19:1)

This verse marks the point at which they drag the alleged witch howling along the side of the house toward the camera. We next hear fragments of the following:

> For true and righteous are his judgments; for he hath judged the great whore, which did corrupt the earth with her fornication, and hath avenged the blood of his servants at her hand. (Revelation 19:4)

As the camera approaches the struggling group and focuses on the woman, we hear the word "fornication" from this sentence. We could be forgiven for momentarily trying to match the image to the word, but the text gives us a glimpse of the context of this term, inviting us to think of this verse allegorically—that is, as a description of the propaganda put out by the Great Whore of Babylon, the

Church of Rome, and not simply of those elderly witches in 1645 and the following years who "confessed" to fornicating with the devil.

The camera cuts, shooting now from the rear of the procession, and the soundtrack skips the rest of the intervening verses. Now we can hear quite clearly as the priest, stalking in front of the procession huddled round the alternately whimpering and screaming prisoner, intones the following, while the villagers drag the woman up the hill, revive her brutally when she faints, tie the rope, and poise her on the stool:

> And I saw the beast, and the kings of the earth, and their armies gathered together to make war against him that sat on the horse, and against his army. And the beast was taken, and with him the false prophet that wrought miracles before him, with which he deceived them that had received the mark of the beast, and them that worshipped his image. These both were cast alive into a lake of fire burning with brimstone. And the remnant were slain with the sword of him that sat upon the horse, which sword proceeded out of his mouth; and all the fowls were filled with their flesh. (Revelation 19:19–21)

At this point, the priest ceases reading—Chapter 19 has come to an end—and nods firmly to the executioner; the stool is kicked away and the woman lurches into space with a resounding crack, swinging inert. The following shot cuts and zooms to a man sitting on a white horse, an image of Matthew Hopkins (Vincent Price), which freezes into an emblem in the credit sequence of the film and then threads its way through the rest of the film.[4] Hopkins is "him that sat upon the horse" and his word is "the sword of truth."

Idolatry and Witchcraft: The Search for "Evidence"

Witchcraft in England divides into two aspects: the pact with the Devil, the sign of which is the invocation of demons; and the *maleficia* (Lat., "evil actions"), the deeds that are done against people and property. Originally the first aspect was tried by ecclesiastical courts and the second by secular law. By 1600, Protestant clerics had begun to raise the status of witchcraft from a series of petty rural squabbles and feuds to the ultimate spiritual crime. In the tract *Daemonologie* (1598), King James further accentuated the stress on diabolic possession; insisting on the primacy of a pact with the Devil in cases of witchcraft, James provided the basis of the Witchcraft Statute of 1604. The statute in turn had the paradoxical effect of promoting the search for evidence of a pact in the *signs* of possession by the Devil, which could be credibly presented to a secular court of law. The arguments of *Daemonologie*, which directed the reader toward the typical forms of the "mark of the Beast" (the so-called witches' teats, the signs that the Devil sucked their blood, in reality anything from skin blemishes to genital warts) read in places like the manual for a witchfinder that the historical Matthew Hopkins (1620–1647) later took it to be.[5] When James came to the throne, however, the new king performed a volte-face, appointing a "liberal" (i.e., anti-Puritan) archbishop of Canterbury, Richard Bancroft, and himself becoming skeptical about the large amount of fraud involved in cases of witchcraft. He even rebuked some magistrates for hanging a group of people in Leicester.

Under Charles I, during whose reign the action of the film takes place, the number of successfully brought cases of witchcraft declined because Archbishop Laud, who was actually not interested in witchcraft at all, revived the ecclesiastical courts and gave back power to them. The magistrates of the civil courts were listening. As a result, as one commentator puts it:

> By the time Charles became king in 1625, witch-trials were highly likely to fail, for one or more of three reasons: exposure of the accuser as a fraud; insufficient evidence; or a natural medical explanation that chased witchcraft from the courtroom. The witch-hunt that flared up in 1645 was therefore partly a reaction against the decline of prosecutions under Charles I, and partly a sign that witchcraft and the persecution of Catholics were linked in people's minds.[6]

The Elizabethan reformed settlement after the reign of Mary Tudor was not an entirely fresh start, and the Book of Common Prayer preserved many of the old Catholic forms. Idolatry was still a live issue for many Puritans in the seventeenth century, as it was for Catholics, both of whom claimed to be able to exorcise demonic possession. The episcopal Protestant establishment under James had to steer a middle way between them by both punishing witches and discouraging private exorcism: Puritans, in particular, were forbidden to fast and pray, which was their directed method of exorcising witches. The landscape of East Anglia and, in particular, the area where Michael Reeves's film is set (on the border of Suffolk and Essex around the Stour Estuary, in an area called the Tendring Hundreds) was a palimpsest of old Catholic villages, some of them founded on ancient priories, like St. Osyth's, whose churches still preserved the icons of the old faith. The Earl of Manchester, a moderate Puritan, had commissioned in the name of Parliament one William Dowsing (a curiously appropriate name) to go around to these village churches, remove the idolatrous icons of the old faith from these places, and destroy the icons. His post was called iconoclast general, to signify the sanction of Parliament. This was the prototype of Matthew Hopkins's self-appointed post of witchfinder general under the old formula "witchery-popery, popery-witchery" (i.e., "where Catholics exist, witches will be found; and where witches, Catholics"). Dowsing provided Hopkins with an iconoclastic "track" in which he could find witches.[7]

The Case of John Lowes

The movie condenses the loosely picaresque wanderings described in the Ronald Bassett novel on which the script is based and goes straight to the village of Brandeston, where we see the overlaps between witchcraft and idolatry to which the opening text of Revelation refers. The parson John Lowes, who opens the door of his rectory to Cornet Richard Marshall, is wearing his surplice, a ruff, and a small embroidered blue skullcap. His dress is an aggressive signal of high Anglican, probably Laudian, sympathies that Puritans would have judged idolatrous. Lowes is a real historical person, unlike Marshall himself and Sara, whom Marshall has come to see. Bassett's novel, notes a Laudian connection and also has the following separate note:

> One account suggests that he was a "reading parson," which was the Puritans' description of a cleric who read matins and evensong but did not exalt the sermon to a Sacrament. However, the fact that he had been summoned by the Bishop's court on a charge of failing to conform to the rules of the established church suggests that he retained Catholic loyalties, and his advanced age supports this probability.
>
> A parishioner and a neighbouring divine gave as their opinion that Mr Lowes, being a litigious man, made his parishioners (too tenacious of their customs) very uneasy, so that they were glad to take the opportunity of those wicked times to get him hanged, rather than not get rid of him.[8]

John Lowes was in reality over eighty when Matthew Hopkins and John Stearne visited him, as they do in the movie at the instigation of some of his parishioners. He had already been arraigned for witchcraft and acquitted, but the actor Rupert Davies plays him with expansive benevolence, welcoming Richard Marshall with open arms. Marshall is a local farmer's son who has just killed his first royalist and been promoted to cornet by Cromwell himself. Lowes is encouraging his relationship with Sara Lowes, his surrogate daughter, in reality a foundling whom he has taken in. He refers vaguely to "troubles" in the parish and is nervous about making sure Sara secures the door. The supper Lowes invites Richard to is shot in an original composition: the camera makes a lateral exposure of a long ecclesiastical-looking old oak dining table at which the three of them sit with candles before the fire. The wide shot suggests a warm and comfortable but also ceremonial atmosphere. These tables had sometimes been altar tables that were banished to the vestries of churches, and Charles I's Archbishop Laud mounted a campaign to get them reinstated, among all other church ornaments, much to the fury of the Puritans. Now that he has given their marriage his blessing, John Lowes retires jovially to bed, turning a blind eye to their lovemaking, while the camera follows them devotedly into the bedroom.

The film's main theme, however, is not the erotic mutual confirmation of the young lovers, lyrical as it is, but the deformity of violence in the culture that will destroy them both. In the morning, Richard departs back to his unit, and that night Hopkins and Stearne arrive and reduce the bluff but dignified parson to a wreckage of his former self by "pricking" and then "running" him. Pricking is done with maximum brutality: Stearne pushes a spike repeatedly into his back in a dozen places, which could easily have damaged some internal organs. In reality the historical Hopkins and Stearne had to be careful not to leave marks that could become evident to magistrates, or to a jury. Here is an account, from one Mr. Rivett, a sympathetic (royalist) parishioner, of the two "running" the real Mr. Lowes:

> I have heard it from them that watched with him, that they kept him awake several Nights together, and run him backwards and forwards about the Room, until he was weary of his Life, and was scarce sensible of what he said or did. They swam him at Framlingham, but that was no true Rule to judge him by; for they put in honest people at the same time and they swam as well as he.[9]

Figure 6.2 Violence in *Witchfinder General* is vividly shown deforming the characters, and sacred violence against heretics escalates in brutality and grotesquerie.
DVD screen capture, fair use

The swimming scene, in which suspected witches are dropped, their hands and feet bound together, into a river to see whether they float (if so, then they are witches), is also depicted in the film. Later, when Hopkins and Stearne get to Lavenham, they retire to a gothic castle keep on a hill outside the village so that they can torture prisoners as violently as they wish. Violence is vividly shown in this film as deforming the characters, and *sacred* violence (i.e., violence employed against pagan and Catholic heretics, and "justified" by propaganda) escalates, as the film goes on, in brutality and grotesquerie: even Richard Marshall is sucked into sacrifice to the savage god.

The Savage God

In the film, Sara sacrifices herself sexually to Hopkins in return for John Lowes's freedom, and later she is betrayed by him and raped by Stearne. When Richard Marshall returns again from the battlefield, he is confronted with chaos; the church has been completely desecrated and Sara is nowhere to be seen. After he has found her and heard Sara's story, he does not forgive her overtly, but, taking her hand in his, they enact a "wedding scene" in the ruins of the church in which they kneel together at the desecrated altar and ask for God's blessing. Marshall then pointedly sets Sara's hand aside and adds a coda for himself: he invokes the jealous God as their witness, dedicating the murder of Hopkins and Stearne to Him. Marshall thus becomes the avenging knight. Sara looks disturbed by this savage ritual, in which she has no place, and which has, in fact, usurped the formal ceremony of their union.

This ritual dedication to revenge determines the horrific climax of the film, in which, after Sara is tortured in front of him, still in the sumptuous blue dress worn for his return, Richard Marshall frees himself, puts out Stearne's eyes, and hacks Hopkins to death with an axe. When his two trooper comrades emerge into the basement cellar, one of them is so horrified that, after putting the half-butchered Hopkins out of his misery with a pistol, he momentarily forgets which side of the war he's on and makes the sign of the cross.[10] A transformed Richard Marshall approaches him, his face increasingly contorted as he repeats accusingly three times: "You took him *away* from me!" For different reasons, both of them have abnegated their former identities.

Here in this climactic scene we see the two structures face-to-face. Reeves has included the propaganda war in this gesture of Marshall's trooper comrade that shows him to be an ex-Catholic or Anglican Protestant, now fighting for Cromwell. At the same time, the sanity of Marshall has become irrevocably corrupted by the savage ritual of blood revenge, to which he has given up all traces of his former self.

Policing the Eucharist

The film of *The Wicker Man*, directed by Robin Hardy and scripted by Anthony Shaffer, tells the story of a piously Christian rural police sergeant, Neil Howie, on the west coast of Scotland who is lured to an island off the coast on the pretext of the disappearance of a young girl, Rowan Morrison. The sergeant's investigation is constantly frustrated, and he himself is progressively mocked and humiliated by the islanders and his authority undermined. For example, the schoolmistress, Miss Rose, teaches a form of pagan religion and mocks his authority in front of her children, yet he discovers clues that the missing Rowan Morrison was one of her pupils. The atmosphere becomes notably paranoid as the story goes on: Miss Rose (Diane Cilento) turns out to be the companion of the sinister laird (played by Christopher Lee), the absolute ruler of the island—until it dawns on the viewer, but not yet on Howie himself, that the sergeant has been cast as a human sacrifice in a fertility rite to redeem the island's crops. This film begins with another unnamed but familiar biblical text. We open with the church in Portlochrie where Howie, an Episcopalian Christian, reads the lesson. Mary Bannock, his fiancée, is together with him in the congregation. The lesson is from St. Paul:

> For I have received of the Lord that which I also delivered unto you, That the Lord Jesus just the same night in which he was betrayed, took bread: And when he had given thanks, he brake it, and said, Take, eat, this is my body, which is broken for you; this do in remembrance of me. After the same manner also he took the cup, saying the cup is the New Testament in my blood: this do ye, as oft as ye drink it, in remembrance of me. For as oft as ye eat this bread, and drink this cup of the Lord, ye do shew the Lord's death, till he come. (1 Corinthians 11:23–26)[11]

I quote here from the King James Bible, but the text Howie reads is probably the Scottish Episcopalian Bible, because Howie adds—on a rising preacher's intonation, which is significant—the word "again" to the final phrase "till he come," making sure that the text's focus on the Resurrection as a second coming is absolutely clear. In the passage, St. Paul is preaching to the pagans at Corinth, whom he converts. The camera then peeps over Howie's shoulder as he takes the bread of Christ's broken body into his mouth.

The gothic horror tradition is littered with anti-Catholic propaganda, and one of the insistent traditional jibes by Protestant writers against Catholic forms of belief centered around the cannibalism implicit in the Catholic Eucharist.[12] In Hardy and Shaffer's 1978 novelization of *The Wicker Man* there is a scene that is not in the movie, in which Howie sees Miss Rose cycling toward him and determines to ask her where Rowan Morrison is, but begins by producing tactical flattery, getting her to describe what the May Day dance means to her as "a teacher of comparative religion." She expounds the carnival structure of the dance procession at length:

> "And fourthly, there is the sacrifice, whose death and resurrection, of course, is the climax of the dance . . ."
>
> Sergeant Howie had taken out his notebook and a pencil.
>
> "Would you care to make a statement on where the victim is being kept?"
>
> "The victim is as symbolic or not as the Christian's bread and wine, my dear Sergeant. What does that represent?" asked the schoolteacher.
>
> "The body and blood of our Lord Jesus Christ," said Howie.
>
> "You eat it at Communion, do you not? And the Roman Catholic Christians believe it is turned miraculously to the real thing in their mouths. Others believe it is symbolic. A matter of taste, I suppose, if you'll forgive the pun."[13]

Miss Rose hints knowingly to the reader that Howie (as an Episcopalian, but perhaps in her mind merely as a Christian) is close to Catholicism. She dodges him while spearing him, like a matador. Confessing that they have not even told "the sacrifice" of its "honourable, indeed, sacred fate," she then adds pointedly, "It is doubtful that the sacrifice would understand if the truth were suddenly made plain."[14]

The "sacrifice" suddenly refers here not to Rowan Morrison, who is an invented victim, but to Howie himself. The game of blindman's buff is evident here, with Howie as both fool figure and sacrifice. There is another play on sacrifice in a later encounter that is exclusive to the novel. When Howie is searching the houses he meets three cackling old ladies and tries, equally vainly, to quiz them about the same topic:

> "I have reason to believe she is going to be a sacrifice today."
>
> "Lucky girl. How well I remember when I first sacrificed myself. It was with the young lord's grandfather. What a magnificent figure of a man he was," said Swallow most nostalgically.[15]

Apparently the old lord organized a "priapic ball" at which they were all "sacrificed." The sexual register here is a carnivalistic counterpoint, in which Howie, who is to become the carnival fool, is made a fool in the colloquial sense by the population, since he does not understand his ritual role in these verbal exchanges.[16]

Policing the Resurrection

An associated nodal point of transfer between Christ and the carnival fool in the carnivalistic structure of the movie is the nature of the Resurrection and how literal we may suppose it to be. This also often forms a point of horror, because a profane resurrection will involve promiscuous revenancy. Paul controls this point in 1 and 2 Corinthians in some famous passages, but in horror fiction the image of blood sacrifice cannot be cleansed of its residual pagan roots.[17] For example, Goethe's famous gothic ballad "The Bride of Corinth" shows the Eucharist reversing into its disavowed pagan source. The young daughter in the ballad has been left lingering among the old pagan gods by her mother's newly converted zeal for the single God in human form, preventing the daughter's union to her childhood betrothed, and the girl turns into an unholy, blood-feeding vampire out of spite.[18]

The opening sequence of the film thus introduces us to the ironic and blasphemous juxtaposition of the blood sacrifice in the Eucharistic ceremony of Howie's zealous Episcopalian Protestantism and the developing countertheme of the savage god's need for blood sacrifice in pagan ritual. That tension between things that are supposed to be opposites carries on, culminating in the fool figure Howie's final childhood prayer, in the midst of his own blood sacrifice, as the flames inside the Wicker Man lick around his feet. I quote from the novelization:

> "O God," whispered Sergeant Neil Howie in his last moment, for only by whispering could he keep his lungs clear of smoke, "Whose nature is ever to show mercy and forbearance, I humbly entreat, Thee, for the soul of this Thy servant, Neil Howie, who will this day depart from this world. Do not deliver me into the enemy's hands or put me out of mind forever, but bid Thy holy angels welcome me and lead me home to Paradise. Let me not undergo the real pains of hell, because I die unshriven, but establish me in that bliss which knows no ending . . ."
>
> The floor collapsed before he had time to say "through Christ Our Lord. Amen." But he thought it as he fell into the thirty foot bonfire between the Wicker Man's legs.[19]

The mention of dying unshriven (i.e., unconfessed) shows us just how close Howie's Episcopalian childhood has been to the confessional of Catholic tradition. This whole prayer is reduced in the film to the Psalmic phrase "Do not deliver me into the enemy's hands, or put me out of mind forever," which strikes the viewer either as a moment of great pathos or as a pathetically understated description of what might indeed be happening, because oblivion awaits, and if anyone were ever in the enemy's hands, it is surely Neil Howie.[20] The ambiguity of

Figure 6.3 Neil Howie shrieks in a blasphemous double entendre on first seeing the Wicker Man, "God!" "Christ!"
DVD screen capture, fair use

this cry to God echoes the way he shrieks in a blasphemous double entendre on first seeing the Wicker Man: "God!" and "Christ!" The viewer cannot help feeling the ambiguity of these shrieks: are they unconscious curses, or are they a solemn reaching for Howie's own God in defense, or are they a vernacular acknowledgment of sublimity in the giant pagan effigy?

It is not completely unknown for viewers to laugh in these final scenes. There's an almost perfect fusion of horror and humor here, caused by this carnivalized "traffic" in the novel's text between the opposites of Christian and pagan sacrifice, which is more overtly expressed in the novelization but still present in the film's images.

Conclusion

The two films I have been discussing are in some ways quite different works. *Witchfinder General* is set back in the seventeenth century, during a period of mass terror in the English Civil War. *The Wicker Man* is set in a modern time, near contemporary with the film's own appearance in 1973—Sergeant Howie flies a seaplane and has a two-way radio. It is sometimes seen as a parody of modern "alternative" religious cults, which became a feature of the 1960s. But both films create horror in the viewer, I have been arguing, not simply because of their aesthetic tactics but because of their underlying structure: they examine and expose to a withering or mocking gaze the doomed attempts of Protestantism to police the theological border (in the textual representations of the Christian ceremonies of the Eucharist and the Resurrection) between the "true" (or "rational") faith of the godly or the civilized and what no longer, in each of these films' narratives, lies clearly beyond that border—namely, the grotesquely "irrational" aspects of the savage god's demands for blood sacrifice.

PART III

PROTESTANT INFLUENCES IN EUROPEAN ART FILMS

Figure 7.1 An emotionally charged dialogue between two women (Ingrid Thulin, Liv Ullmann) falls silent in *Cries and Whispers* (1972).
Entertainment Pictures/Alamy Stock Photo

7

Words Versus "the Word": Language and Scripture in Ingmar Bergman's Films and Writings

Maaret Koskinen

Ever since a number of Ingmar Bergman's films have become iconic, his work has been analyzed in religious terms, and from virtually every perspective—high and low, horizontally and vertically, and not least in regard to the relations between human and divine powers.[1] Perhaps the best-known among these films are *The Seventh Seal* (1957), in which a medieval knight wages his battle with faith, and the three films that Bergman called a trilogy on "God's silence": *Through a Glass Darkly* (1960), *The Communicants* (U.S. title *Winter Light*, 1963), and *The Silence* (1963).[2]

It follows that it would not be difficult to name and delve into at least thirty books and dissertations on the subject of Bergman and religion, ranging from religious experience, quests of reconciliation, relational ethics, and existentialism to the fact that Bergman himself often, both in writings and in interviews, returned to his childhood at a parsonage presided over by his father, a stern Lutheran minister of the Swedish church. But rather than repeat history, I will take hold of a strand in which Bergman's art and religion meet—namely, the question of faith and doubt, which in various ways turns out to deal with religion, aesthetics, and Protestantism on-screen.

In interviews as well as in published articles, Ingmar Bergman often spoke about art in terms of cult and worship. As early as 1954, when contemplating the cathedral of Chartres, he wrote about his longing to be an anonymous craftsman among others:

> I want to be one of the artists in the cathedral on the great plain. I want to carve a dragon's head, an angel, a devil or perhaps a saint out of stone. It does not matter which. Regardless of whether I believe or not, whether I am a Christian or not, I would play my part in the collective building of the cathedral, as I am an artist and a craftsman.[3]

Maaret Koskinen, *Words Versus "the Word": Language and Scripture in Ingmar Bergman's Films and Writings*
In: *Protestants on Screen*. Edited by: Gastón Espinosa, Erik Redling and Jason Stevens, Oxford University Press.
 DOI: 10.1093/oso/9780190058906.003.0008

Bergman sets up a clear analogy between (Christian) religion and art. Or as he put it in 1961, "The creative artist performs an act of cult, similar to the priest, and the stage or the podium is the place of the cult."[4] Some years later, in 1968, the wording was even stronger: "The practice of art as sorcery, as ritual action, as prayer, as reciprocal gratification of needs—this I have always felt very strongly."[5]

However, the relationship of art and religion was for Bergman not unproblematic. On the contrary, the act of cult, be it religious or artistic, was seldom an expression of faith, clear and pure. More often than not it was shot through with doubt and uncertainty or, more specifically, characterized by a constant oscillation between trust and denial, faith and doubt. It is this constant dynamic movement between opposites that makes Bergman of philosophical interest today—aside from his undeniable mastery in the art of filmmaking.

The oscillation between faith and doubt is clearly seen in the abovementioned trilogy about "God's silence." The titles reverberate with religious references—*Through a Glass Darkly* is a biblical citation (from 1 Corinthians 13:12), while *The Communicants* is named after one of the remaining and arguably most important sacraments in the Lutheran Church, Holy Communion, and *The Silence* summarizes the overarching intent of the whole project, which is to explore God's silence. The trilogy as a whole describes a trajectory that can be best summarized in one specific word: "reduction." Bergman himself used it in the epigraph of the published scripts, where he notes that "the theme of these three stories is a 'reduction'—in the metaphysical sense of the word," describing a movement from "certainty achieved" in the first film to "certainty unmasked" in the second and finally to "God's silence—the negative impression."[6] In the interview book *Bergman on Bergman* (1970) he put it even more succinctly when he stated that "I swept my house clean" with this trilogy and got rid of "my top-heavy religious superstructure."[7]

If there is one scene in this trilogy that summarizes this cleaning out of religious faith, it is the one in *The Communicants* (U.S. title: *Winter Light*) in which we find the parson Tomas alone in his empty church, some hours before the Sunday service is supposed to commence. For a long time he has been beset by doubts regarding existence of the God to whom he prays every day and yet in whose service he remains. On this bleak, cold Sunday in November he is also suffering from a bad cold, and he is contemplating canceling the service when suddenly he is seized with deep despair. "God, my God, why has thou forsaken me?" he stammers—and falls on his knees on the stone floor, racked by hollow coughing.

Particularly noteworthy in this scene is the washed-out quality of the black-and-white cinematography. It was a quality that Bergman and his cinematographer, Sven Nykvist (later also known for his work with Woody Allen), worked hard at achieving—something they called a "leaden grey" effect, without harsh contrasts.[8] This was a lighting technique that, one can assume, would correspond to Tomas's despair over his lost faith, while at the same time remaining a perfectly realistic rendering of Nordic November light.

In other words, the reduction that Bergman noted in the epigraph to the published scripts seems to refer not only to religious faith but also to a conscious reduction or paring down of cinematic aesthetics. In hindsight, it is a reduction that could be called a counterpart to Lars von Trier's and the other Dogme brethren's ascetic deconstruction of cinematic aesthetics in the mid-1990s, which proved so successful for Danish cinema. Bergman's equally conscious attempt at dismantling the undeniable skill and international outreach that he had reached by this time as a filmmaker (confirmed by his winning of two Oscars, for *Virgin Spring* in 1960 and for *Through a Glass Darkly* in 1962) was achieved by, so to speak, voluntarily abstaining from his own virtuosity.

Indeed, given the twofold nature of this abstinence—thematic and aesthetic—it could even be called a kind of cinematic counterpart to Luther's elimination of Catholic rituals, in this case the rituals of narrative conventions and traditions tainted with Hollywood orthodoxy. Away with aesthetically sacred clutter! Get rid of the sacraments! Keep only what is necessary! Interestingly, several years later, in his memoir *Images* (1990), Bergman wrote: "I have always been embarrassed by my need to please. My love for the audience has been rather complicated. . . . The only thing is, sometimes one feels to shoot [at point-blank range], to leave all the ingratiating stuff behind." So, he continued, with *The Communicants* he risked a "death-defying" leap, because "I was not so stupid as to believe that *Winter Light* [the American title for *The Communicants*] would be a public favorite."[9]

Silent Signs, Incontestable Words

With his trilogy, then, Bergman's intention was to throw out the sacred clutter on two fronts, in both religious and aesthetic terms. However, although religion as a subject or theme vanished from Bergman's films, it never vanished as a pattern of thought or, in a generalized sense, cinematic aesthetics and style, for Bergman's post-religious films still disclose a deep affinity with a Protestant conceptual world.

There is a scene in *The Communicants* that introduces a thought pattern that will govern other post-religious Bergman movies. Again, this scene involves the deployment of light and the fact that its compact, leaden quality is broken only once or twice in the film. One of those occasions is in the scene discussed above when Tomas, in his suffering, walks toward the window and there is suddenly a streak of sunlight that breaks through the clouds and washes over him in the

Figure 7.2 Tomas, in *Winter Light*, walks toward the chapel window, and a streak of sunlight washes over him in the moment of his deepest doubt.
DVD screen capture, fair use

moment of his deepest doubt. A streak of grace, perhaps—redemption or justification by grace alone?

Regardless, the fact remains that such a light—or, rather, sudden illuminations—tends to return in Bergman's later films as well, and now almost with a vengeance. One example can be found in *Passion of Anna* (1969), in which an elderly loner is found in his small cottage savagely beaten to death, and his dead body is suddenly awash in an illuminating and yet inexplicable light. Another example can be seen in *Cries and Whispers* (1972), where Agnes, a woman dying of cancer, is woken by the sunshine falling through her bedroom window. Here too, just as in *The Communicants*, it is a realistic early morning light from the outside, but the way it breaks forth so suddenly turns it into something otherworldly. In any case, this phenomenon in Bergman's post-religious films, with light flooding over someone who suffers or is downtrodden, could be described as a kind of lingering religious "hangover" or remains from a fallen world.[10]

There is yet another dimension to this light, particularly in the case of Tomas in *The Communicants*, where there seems to be a battle or a crisis between various means of communication. If this light in its glaring clarity is a sign, a kind of a prophetic "as if," Tomas seems to be oblivious to its presence. Indeed, he literally turns away from it while citing the Bible (somewhat self-pityingly, one might add). And certainly Tomas is one of those many rationalist characters in Bergman's films who tend to rely on words and who talk and talk obsessively—a bit like the medieval knight in *The Seventh Seal*, who is not content with believing but desperately wants to *know*.[11] So, too, Tomas seems to be demanding to hear the Word of God, concretely and definitively, in order to believe, and does so to the extent that he fails to notice what happens around him in the physical, empirical world, which is arguably God's creation, too.

In short, we have silent, mysterious signs, hardly visible (because embedded in the natural world), let alone easy to interpret, which are pitted against abstract, rationalist words and language. All of which, I would say, conflates in an interesting way with the film medium itself and its specific means of communication: audiovisuality. If in this church scene there is a battle between various means of communication, it is one that concerns not only Tomas but his cinematic creator as well—Ingmar Bergman and his faith in the means of communication at hand.

Fear of Words

When Bergman wrote the scripts for the trilogy, his ambition was to reduce not only the clutter of the film *image* but also very much the clutter of *language*—in this case the spoken word in the form of dialogue. In particular, the final film of the trilogy, *The Silence*, is an explicit attempt to liberate film from words and spoken language and, instead, replace them with other phenomena, such as sound—noise, music, and, of course, silence. Aesthetically speaking, then, the film's title is not accidental.

In this context it is illuminating to cite from Bergman's notebooks, which he wrote while conceiving the film trilogy. Apparently the process of paring down the dialogue was complicated for Bergman. In his notebook, he writes the following thoughts on the emotional process of scripting the first film of the trilogy, *Through a Glass Darkly*:

> This anxiety before starting to write. The inability to translate the images, which are clear and direct, into understandable words. [My] dialogue disease. Words that I hate: since, because, and, to, suddenly, silence, violently. Unreliable words that take the opportunity to hide when you need them the most. . . . My inhibition over the act of writing itself. My reluctance to lift the burden and carry it. To be an amateur.[12]

Two years later, in the notebook for *The Silence*, the complaint was the same: "How hard it is with all these transformations that every image has to go through, before I can work with them. How often the result is unsure and half-baked."[13]

Two key phrases stand out in the quotations: "transformation" and "dialogue disease." In the first case, what is clearly meant is a kind of double transformation: first a transformation from the author's internal images to their material manifestation (written words), which in turn have to be transformed into

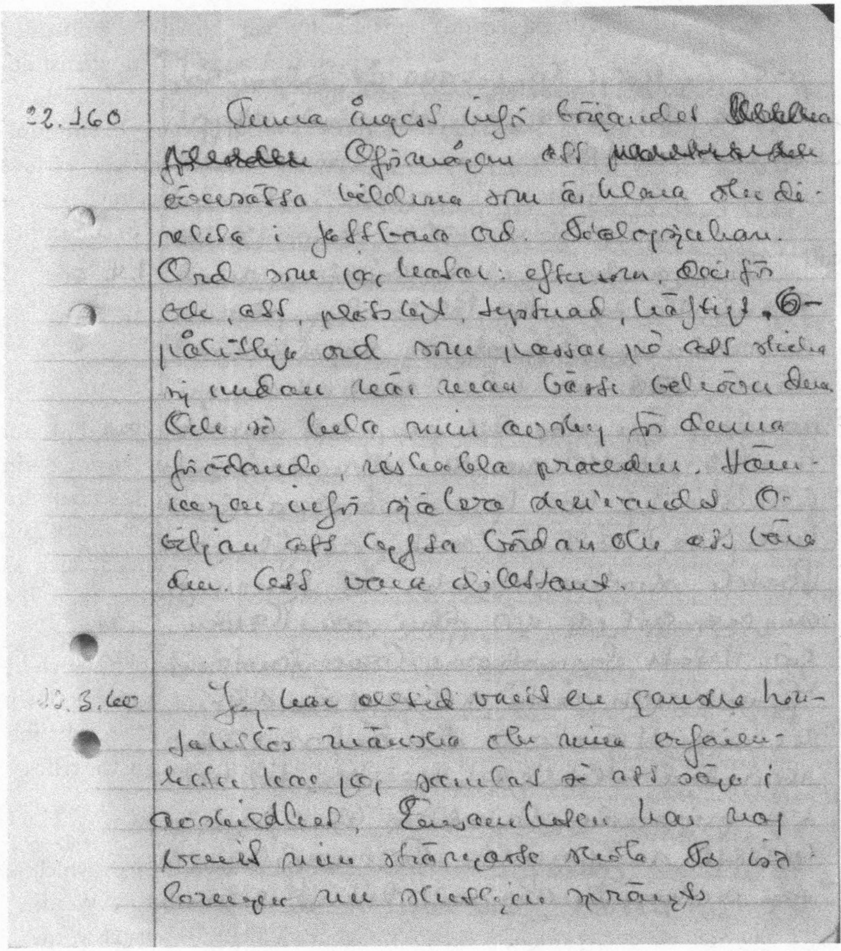

Figure 7.3 In his notebook, Bergman writes of feeling "the inability to translate the images, which are clear and direct, into understandable words."
Photo by Maaret Koskinen.

another material manifestation (sounds and moving images). One would think that for an auteur, who writes their own scripts, this transformation from written screenplay to finished film is a natural part of the package. In Bergman's case it was precisely the fact that the writer was the same person as the director that seemed to have been particularly troublesome.

Then there is the other term: "dialogue disease." "I really," Bergman wrote, "once and for all, have to get away from dialogues. I'm damned tired of all these meaningless words and discussions."[14] "Besides," he continued, "it's very hard finding oneself mute. Given that all my life I've practiced [writing] dialogue, it certainly gives you a sense of loss and anxiety not to be allowed to use it anymore."[15] At times he even envisioned that *The Silence* would be entirely without dialogue. "In this film the dialogue will be entirely subservient and only an accompaniment on the soundtrack," or "only a rattle on the soundtrack without any meaning. Ignoring all that talk will be delightful . . . [and] cinematographic."[16] The truly cinematic, then, seems at this point in time for Bergman to hark back to silent cinema, which was capable of transmitting something that cannot be described. Aesthetically speaking, this is a positively austere discipline for a filmmaker to impose on his art.

In any case, there is clearly a rift here between the order of the word and the order of the image—between the author, still mainly a wielder of words, and the future film director.[17] Indeed, should one believe Bergman, he suffered from a virtual fear of writing—a fear of the word as an artistic medium. He jotted down in a shooting script as early as 1959: "To realize one's inadequacy on both the human and the artistic level. And particularly the writing, that constant thorn, fear, bitterness, the embitterment, sorrow, humiliation . . . my tender spot, my terror."[18]

How, then, could he compensate for his self-imposed censorship and rules about not using words and film dialogue? Besides using silences and other sounds, Bergman drew on classical music, most especially secular compositions by Johann Sebastian Bach, a Lutheran. *Cries and Whispers*, for instance, contains an often cited scene in which an emotionally charged dialogue between two women suddenly falls silent, yielding to music, as they continue talking, now inaudibly moving their lips. The composition, Bach's Suite No. 5 for solo cello in C minor, fourth movement ("Sarabande"), becomes a kind of *Ersatz* for words, in a way confirming the inadequacy and frailty of words as a communicative medium.

The Silence features a comparable scene in which the music of Bach is similarly used. During a sudden truce between the two female protagonists, they find themselves listening to the music of Bach's "Goldberg Variations" (No. 25, from 1742) on the radio at their hotel. This unexpected lacuna of harmony, interrupting the otherwise constant tension, is also emphasized visually. While

Figure 7.4 With Bach playing on a record, the normally tense sisters in *Silence* enjoy an unexpected moment of harmony.
DVD screen capture, fair use

their differences are normally accentuated by spatial separation, in this scene they are seen in the same shot, one woman in the foreground, her sister in the background with her son on her lap, pietà style.

Interestingly, while Bergman was writing the screenplay for the film, notes on music became more frequent in his notebooks. It was possible, he wrote, "to be able finally to break out of all conventions and take the step from narration to music. No longer using the giant's small finger but at least the whole hand."[19] Continuing, he explained: "Words are almost always double and prostitutional and inflationary. If one only could make a musical score directly, without any touch-downs in words."[20] Not surprisingly he returned to the subject in interviews. He claimed that *Through a Glass Darkly* was "composed" as "a string quartet in three movements," while he regarded *The Silence* as a sonata for two voices, and *Persona* (1966) as a composition "for different voices in the same soul's concerto grosso."[21]

In this context, it is of special interest to cite a passage from Bergman's notebooks on Johann Sebastian Bach, for it displays how he was tired of religious discourse:

> People can no longer stand all those words that belong to the rituals of religion. . . . In the music of Sebastian Bach our homeless longing for God finds a security which isn't confused by the equivocality of words or the contaminations of speculation. We let our wounded thought become silenced and feel no need to revolt against a trust so boundless that it encompasses all our divided anxiety. Bach's music lifts us beyond the raw concretion of ritual and dogma, and takes us to a communion with a holiness that remains nameless.[22]

Once again he voices his distrust of words—"all those *words* that belong to the *rituals of religion*." Put differently, there is in Bergman's work a fascinating conflation of skepticism toward the word in human affairs, as writing or speech, and skepticism of the Word, as externalized in the forms of religion.

Words: Promise and Contingency

At first glance, the observations made above may seem contradictory, especially if Ingmar Bergman is perceived in the light of Protestantism. After all, Martin Luther was a man of words *and* the Word, as Protestantism advocated precisely the centrality of writing and the Scripture, protesting the various rituals of Catholicism and, not least, advocating vernacular dissemination through the printing press.

Yet, as we all know, Luther did allow quite a few sacraments. Moreover, as we have already noted, Bergman seems not entirely to have escaped certain rituals, be they religious or cinematic. What could be better proof than the fact that he ended his career as a writer, pure and simple? Consider his worldwide-bestselling autobiography, *Laterna Magica* (1987), and also his film scripts for other directors—highly literary scripts at that. Not surprisingly, most of them have been published.[23] These texts document the disappearance of not only his fear of the word but also his loathing of the word as an artistic means.

Of particular interest in this regard, one of Bergman's last scripts (directed by Liv Ullmann in 1996) is called *Private Confessions*, probably in reference to Martin Luther's spiritual practice. Luther is explicitly discussed in the first chapter of the script, in which one of the male protagonists states: "Most people think Luther abolished confession. But he didn't. He prescribed what he called 'private conversation.'"[24] The person who points out Luther's true idea is, furthermore, a parish priest called Jacob. He is a stubborn but intensely likable character who is engaged in intense conversations with Anna, a married woman unfaithful to her husband, and who encourages her to open up to him.

In comparison to the sternly puritan Tomas in *The Communicants*, Jacob seems to have arrived at some sort of sustainable human compromise with regard to earthly and divine matters. (In fact, there is good reason to believe that Jacob serves as a spokesperson for Bergman's own views, as will be discussed below.) As Jacob continues to discuss the idea of the private conversation, he says, with a soft jab in Martin Luther's direction: "But he didn't know much about human beings, that splendid reformer. Face-to-face in broad daylight is difficult. So it's better done in the semidarkness of the confessional, the mumbling voices, the smell of incense."[25] Again, this is part of Jacob's gentle attempt to make Anna talk, but in the context of Bergman's previous rendering of Lutheranism, Jacob's remark is highly surprising. Luther could have remained a bit more Catholic: instead of advocating greater clarity, stern face-to-face confrontations, and truths, he could have favored murmurs and incense. Perhaps this turn in Bergman's thought is, metaphorically speaking, the return of the repressed, both religious rites—the Word—and the ritual of words as human discourse? In any case, it seems that language, with all its shortcomings and potential for misunderstandings and "mumblings," is at the end of the day all we have at our disposal.

In light of Jacob's irresolution, it is worthwhile to refer to yet another parson, the one in *Cries and Whispers* who is called to the bedside of the newly deceased Agnes. He prays for her, and in his prayer one small word stands out:

> If it is so that you have gathered our suffering in your poor body,
> if it is so that you have borne it with you through death,
> if it is so that you meet God over there in the other land,
> if it is so that He turns His face toward you,
> if it so that you can then speak the language that this God understands,
> if it is so that you can then speak to this God. If it is so, pray for us. . . .
> Ask Him to free us at last from our anxiety, our weariness, and our deep doubt.[26]

The word "if" indicates that grace and redemption are highly conditional, provisional, and contingent. And yet the parson still performs the ritual, a religious act, even though he is racked with doubt. Tomas does the same in the closing scene of *The Communicants*. He holds his service, and the film ends with him chanting the words "Holy, holy, holy Lord of Hosts, heaven and earth are full of Thy glory." Something similar occurs in *Private Confessions* (1996), because in the film an important theme of the drama and the conversations between Jacob and the female protagonist revolves around the question of whether she should participate in the Holy Communion or not, as she feels it would be hypocritical.

Still, Jacob insists that she should go, because, as he puts it, "there is grace in the action itself."[27]

So if there is grace, it seems to reside in performing the act, regardless of whether you believe in God or not. The act itself matters, even when (or precisely in the moment that) it seems meaningless.

Conclusion

It is in dynamic oscillations between (potential) opposites—words and silences, faith and doubt—that I think Ingmar Bergman is most compelling. In his works, forces are set in motion and play themselves out not in a dualistic manner but rather in a dialectical fashion, so that they constantly seem to mirror and test each other (those "ifs") instead of becoming fixed in static positions. If nothing else, it is a fine irony that those dialectics and oscillations between faith and doubt in Bergman's works so often are delivered by a man of the church, and of the Lutheran persuasion. That is, by men who by definition are on the side of the Word, but who at the same time speak in the vernacular, in the language of common people—words composed with small letters. Or to cite Jacob once again: "Don't say the word 'God'! Say 'the Holy One.' The Sanctity of Man. Everything else is attribute, disguise, manifestations, tricks, desperation, ritual, cries of despair in the darkness and silence."[28] This view most likely comes close to Bergman's own view, for in an interview at this time, on his production of Euripides's drama *The Bacchae*, he said: "This play lays bare something that I call 'the sanctity of man.' "[29] Regardless, it is such vernacular language that most us of can understand, believers and nonbelievers—this insistence on human sanctity—and it is here that one may find grace of sorts, which (as we have had reason to note by now) is never a fixed state but always fleeting and momentary. If I have understood Martin Luther at all, this is central to his thinking—namely, that it is all about a constant coming to knowledge.

Perhaps it is this kind of knowledge that is expressed in the final scene of *The Silence*, in which we see the ten-year-old boy with his mother on the train on their way back home from their troubled journey abroad. He has just unfolded a piece of paper with some words in a strange language, which his aunt has jotted down for him. We see him read those few words while his mother is looking at him, probably realizing that she has lost him to something new in his life, of which she is no longer part. In the very final shot of the film, we see the boy mouth the words in a concentrated fashion—but silently. This scene becomes a secularizing counterpart to the Word that is (still) performed in the echoing church by Tomas the parson, and in that case it is a decisive movement from the Word to words, from "God" to "the holy," from the past toward a possible future. Redemption, if it exists, lies not in the finalized, capitalized Word, but rather in words—in all those small words that we try to interpret, translate, and comprehend, in ever-renewed regenerations.

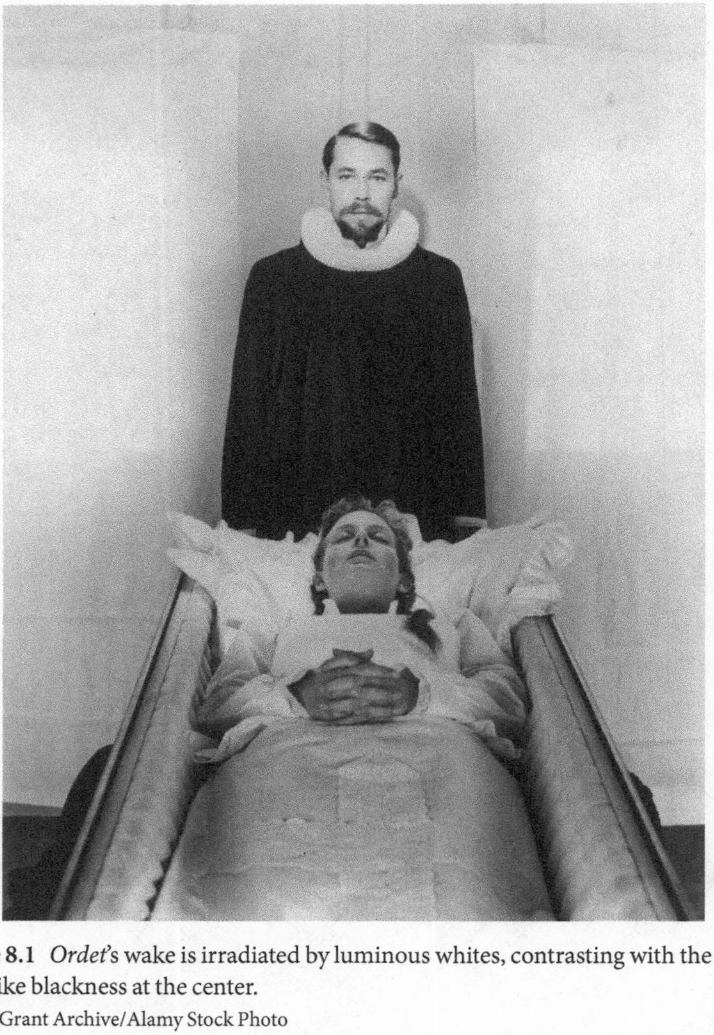

Figure 8.1 *Ordet*'s wake is irradiated by luminous whites, contrasting with the deathlike blackness at the center.
Ronald Grant Archive/Alamy Stock Photo

8
Protestant Miracle in Dreyer's *Ordet*

Mark Le Fanu

The landscape of Scandinavia, like that of the British Isles, is littered with small parish churches that continue to function much as they have always done: they constitute a living tapestry. Under a certain light, it is quite easy to believe that Christianity has not given up here. Nor has it. But these visible manifestations of tradition are also quite illusory. Scandinavia is as secular and multicultural as anywhere else—perhaps more so. From the time of Ibsen and Strindberg, Swedes and Danes (and Norwegians, too) have delighted in championing the modern in all its forms. Pioneers of secularism—in art, in design, and in social thought—the citizenry exude an easy tolerance born of the fact that, on the whole, democracy reigns, and the social-political system functions efficiently.

Just as Strindberg and Ibsen can be said to stand for a certain kind of theater that revolutionized stagecraft at the end of the nineteenth century—and not merely stagecraft, but the whole notion of where theater stands, or may be said to stand, in terms of a spiritual enterprise—so, too, in the twin figures of Ingmar Bergman (1918–2007) and Carl Theodor Dreyer (1889–1968) Scandinavia gave birth to two cinematic giants who have come to epitomize the potential of film as a medium of spiritual-poetic exploration. Naturally they are quite different in many ways (just as Ibsen is different from Strindberg), but in both cases, if from very different angles, God is somehow part of the equation.

In Dreyer's case, how God came to be there, and what allegiance He occupied in the soul of the artist, have always been something of a puzzle. Neither of the director's adoptive parents was a church-goer. Carl senior was by profession a typesetter, traditionally one of the most radical branches of trade working in nineteenth-century Copenhagen. Sunday, the day of rest, was reserved for the activities of the cycling club, of which he was chapter president, rather than for any form of worship. Carl junior was baptized and confirmed, but these concessions were merely administrative: during his childhood he never set foot in a church. When, as an adolescent, the future director occasionally attended services in the French Reformed Church, it was primarily to improve his language skills; according to biographer Maurice Drouzy, he enjoyed, and profited from, listening to the pastor Clément Nicolet preaching in French.[1] The secondary school he attended for six years in Frederiksberg was Lutheran in origin,

Mark Le Fanu, *Protestant Miracle in Dreyer's* Ordet In: *Protestants on Screen*. Edited by: Gastón Espinosa, Erik Redling and Jason Stevens, Oxford University Press. © Oxford University Press 2023. DOI: 10.1093/oso/9780190058906.003.0009 but under the charismatic direction of the writer and journalist Carl Ewald it had moved in the direction of progressive secular liberalism. It is fair to say that the spirit of Georg Brandes rather than that of N. F. S. Grundtvig reigned there. In the years following his graduation, when Dreyer worked as a journalist (eventually specializing in the field of aviation, in which he became a national pioneer), there were no signs of piety or conversion. As far as we can see he was a modern secular freethinker: clever, energetic, admired by his contemporaries, and something of a rebel.

The move from journalism to scriptwriting was accomplished between the summers of 1912 and 1913. Established at Ole Olesen's Nordisk Film Kompagni, Dreyer went on to write nineteen film scripts before signing his first directed movie, *Præsidenten* (The President) in 1918. The example of D. W. Griffith was vitally important to Dreyer's developing interest in religion as a cinematic subject. Dreyer's second directed film, *Blade af Satans Bog* (Leaves from Satan's Book, 1919) follows the method of Griffith's great epic *Intolerance* (1916) in pinning much of the unhappiness of recorded history on the quarrels of established religion. Yet Griffith himself was a Christian of an idiosyncratic stripe. *Intolerance* distinguishes between what religion becomes in the hands of rulers and fanatics, on one hand, and something else that one might call true religion, exemplified above all in the teachings and deeds of the Savior, on the other. At some point, though we cannot say exactly when, this distinction got established in Dreyer's own worldview. It penetrated deeply, becoming the intellectual and moral basis of a handful of his own greatest masterpieces.

A handful of his masterpieces—but not all: that also needs to be borne in mind. A number of Dreyer's films, defined by subject matter, seem remote from the concerns of religion. Among these we ought to include such works as *Mikaël* (1924), from Herman Bang's novel (a piece of delicate expressionism); *Du skal ære din Hustru* (Master of the House, 1925), a comedy; *Vampyr* (1932), a tale of horror; *Två Människor* (Two People, 1944), a sort of filmed radio play made in Sweden; and finally *Gertrud* (1964), the erotic melodrama that served as his swan song. All five of these possess spiritual power and authenticity without ever entering into the vocabulary of faith. Yet three other great films do confront Christianity directly, and it is to these films that I now direct our focus.

The Road to *Ordet*

The first of the films in question, *La Passion de Jeanne d'Arc* (1928)—one of the most famous and beautiful of all silent films—has a Catholic saint, Joan, as its heroine. Yet Dreyer's treatment of Joan is doubtless Protestant in its way, if we use Protestantism here as a shorthand for severe spiritual discipline and an interiorized relationship to God. Once seen, who can ever forget the face of Falconetti playing the beleaguered spiritual warrior in relentless close-up, and who could fail to respond to the way that Dreyer manages to bring out in such graphic detail the torments of her Christian conscience? The great film came out at more or less the same time as a native French version of the story, *La Merveilleuse Vie de Jeanne d'Arc*, directed by Marco de Gastyne, with Joan's role taken by the very young (seventeen-year-old) actress Simone Genevois. It was this version that enjoyed popular success, and one can see why. It is full of pageantry and action. It paints a vast patriotic canvas, in the course of which Joan's gallantry as inspired leader at the head of her troops is given proportionally far more weight than the later (but still affecting) scenes outlining her trial and abandonment. I wouldn't say that de Gastyne's film is a "Catholic" movie or that it isn't, but it certainly isn't a Protestant one: its essence is flamboyant and spectacular. In Dreyer's unfolding of the same life story, on the other hand, the dominating tone is sobriety.

Day of Wrath (Vredens Dag, 1943), too, we must surely mention on our way toward *Ordet*. It is one of the greatest-ever films about witchcraft. No question here but that the ambience *is* Protestant, since we are in Denmark at the beginning of the seventeenth century, in the midst of mass spiritual paranoia. Much more is now known about early modern witch hysteria than was known in Dreyer's day; indeed, since the late 1960s it has become something of a scholarly industry.[2] Yet Dreyer's drama, released a good decade or so before Arthur Miller penned *The Crucible*, gives among other things a remarkably subtle and cogent account of the psychological tensions—the rivalries, the petty hatreds, the easy recourse to spitefulness—that enabled these kinds of accusations to flourish in the narrowly hierarchical environment of the time. The performance of Lisbeth Movin as the tender young bride in love with her stepson (and for this reason accused by jealous elders of witchcraft) is one of the glories of classical Scandinavian cinema. Without ever losing her virtue, or even her modesty and demureness, she maintains the sovereignty of the erotic. Her forthright espousal of sexual love gradually brings home the truth of the contention—it surely only adds to our admiration of her—that in some way she really *is* a witch. How can this be? The loose or metaphorical meaning of the word "bewitchment" contains the ambiguity: the film concentrates on the eyes as the organ of entrapment. Her lover praises Anne's eyes as "deep and mysterious," and they are described at other times as burning and ardent. Are they, limpid and innocent, the window to her soul? Or are they, as her enemies believe, the godless weapon of female destructiveness? In some wonderfully ambivalent way, miraculously confirmed by Dreyer's lighting of Movin's close-ups, they are *both*. Nothing is more beautiful in the film than the way it conveys that Anne's powers are the source of as much fear and mystery to her as they are to everyone else. Because she is noble and forthright, the question of whether she *did* cause her elderly husband's death is a growing burden on her conscience, and she is not aided in her troubles by the fact that Martin, her lover, slowly gives signs of ceasing to believe in her. Courageous to the end, she will not relinquish her inner faith in the validity of passion. Anne's affirmation of erotic, individual happiness—*jusqu'au bout*: she will die at the stake for it—points to an antinomian energy that is intrinsic to Protestantism: an energy that can be turned against religious law, even when that law is legitimated by Protestant authority.

Ordet and Miracles

Day of Wrath was to be the last film Dreyer made in his homeland for ten years. He had always had an uncomfortable relation with the Nazi occupiers of his country, and the release of the film seemed to act as a catalyst. The banning of his new movie—the censors having evidently found something allegorical and pointedly contemporary in its meditation on persecution and torture—led to Dreyer seeking refuge across the water in neutral Sweden, where he remained for the duration of the war.

When, back in Copenhagen in the early 1950s, Dreyer felt he was able to return to feature-length filmmaking, his choice fell upon the adaptation of a drama by one of Denmark's most important anti-Nazi resisters, the pastor-playwright Kaj Munk, murdered by the Germans in 1944 after a series of publicly dissident sermons. *Ordet* (The Word), written in 1925 and first performed in Denmark in 1932 in an opening night that Dreyer attended, is a nonpolitical drama from early in the poet-priest's career (Munk was only twenty-seven when he wrote it). It tells the story of two warring families in rural western Jutland who are kept apart by sectarian differences. The Borgen family belongs to the branch of reformed or liberal Lutheranism that came into being in the nineteenth century, largely under the influence of the philosopher N. F. S. Grundtvig (his portrait, in Dreyer's film, hangs prominently in the family parlor), whereas the family of Peter Skraedder—Peter the tailor—belong to the much more restrictive and puritanical Inner Mission (little beer or coffee on *their* table!). Though neighbors, the families would in the ordinary course of events have kept their differences to themselves, but Anders, Borgen's youngest son, has fallen in love with Peter Skraedder's daughter and wishes to gain permission to marry her.

All of Dreyer's films are literary adaptations (fundamentally different in this respect from Ingmar Bergman's approach), but each of them—and none more than this work, perhaps—conveys the feeling that by paring down the source \ and working it over, he has made the material profoundly his own. *Ordet* ends with one of the greatest single fictional scenes that has ever been recorded on camera, and the question I have sometimes found myself asking is whether the impact of this ending (which we will discuss presently) *could* ever have been as powerful in the original stage production. The key thing is that Dreyer himself had been struck by the potential of the play and had given thought to what would be needed (in terms of light, movement, gesture, music—the music by Nielsen's pupil Poul Schierbeck is marvelous) to turn it into a movie. Dreyer told a radio interviewer in 1954: "My approach to working with Kaj Munk's *Ordet* has, therefore, been this: first to possess myself of Kaj Munk, and then to forget him!"[3] In every important sense, we would have to say, it is *his* version of the interaction of the earthly and the divine that has come down to us.

The film is about a miracle, which brings us back, inevitably, to Catholicism. Some may feel that Catholics are more open to the possibility of the "miraculous incident" than Protestants are. The wonder-working of the saints through the ages belonged to the part of credulous popular culture to which Luther and his successors were unremittingly hostile. On the other hand, there is the authority of the Bible, and the attested miracles performed by Christ himself in the Gospels, to the meaning and truth of which Protestants are formally committed. And, of course, there is what might be called an additional strain of Protestantism that can be traced back to Tertullian and the *credo quia absurdum*, and which could be said to find its culmination in the mind-bending paradoxes of Kierkegaard. "I believe *because* it is absurd": the challenge today would be to remove this aphorism from the ambit of a literary teaser like Lewis Carroll in the Alice books and to place it instead where it should be placed—where Dreyer places it: at the heart of the Christian mystery.

In *Ordet*, then, it is the ending that demands our attentiveness, the unfolding of the impossible event. At the same time, the ending cannot be appreciated without taking into account the episodes that have led up to it, since the film is all of a piece. Shot partly in the studio and partly on location in Jutland—in Vedersø, the very parish where Munk had practiced his ministry—the movie imposes from the start a profoundly sustained level of realism. There is a seamless blending of outdoors and indoors; for example, it strikes our ears not as an effect but, rather, as part of the film's documentary grittiness that every so often and at exactly the right moment the cows can be heard mooing in the barnyard. Those who have seen *Ordet* will not forget either the gravity of the sound of the horses' hooves over the cobbles as, toward the film's upshot, the stately hearse enters the farm's courtyard or, earlier on, the noise of the flapping linen on the clothesline as the Borgen family seeks out among the sand dunes their lost and mad prodigal son, Johannes.

Bearded Johannes (Preben Lerdorff Rye, the same actor who plays Martin in *Day of Wrath*) is a central figure in the narrative, though at first he seems marginal enough to the main thrust of the story, which is the dispute between the

Borgens and the Skraedders. We are struck by his strange way of speaking, as also by his handsomeness, his distracted manner, and the oddity (and informality) of his wardrobe. One of old Borgen's three sons—the middle one, dedicated to the church—Johannes has lost his wits, we are led to believe, while studying theology in Copenhagen, and now believes himself to be, in some strange way, an avatar of the risen Jesus Christ. The family puts up with him, but only just. He disappears from the story, as mentioned above, only to reappear sometime later in the midst of another fearful crisis, associated this time with Borgen's beloved daughter-in-law Inger (Birgitte Federspiel), who, pregnant from the beginning of the film, is going through the travails of childbirth.

In the long night that follows, periods of relative calm alternate with episodes of anguish. The summoned doctor, a seemingly trustworthy fellow, seems to think all will be well, and leaves, offering old Borgen a cigar. The beam from the headlights of his departing motor vehicle casts a strangely ominous arc of light over the parlor's walls and ceiling. Meanwhile, Johannes has been occupying himself elsewhere in the house by comforting his little six- or seven-year-old niece Maren (daughter of Inger, who in turn is married to Borgen's eldest son, Mikkel): she has seated herself on his lap to be closer to him. Yet Johannes's comfort includes words that seem to be stranger than ever: he speaks of the child's mother as being "in heaven" and even offers the option of bringing her back from the dead!

Johannes it is, then, who rightly discerns, in his own mad way, that the crisis of childbirth is far from over and that its upshot will be tragic. The bitterness of Mikkel's suffering as he reports back to old Borgen first the death of the infant, then the death of the mother, is unforgettably conveyed by the blond actor who plays him (Emil Hass Christensen) in episodes of overwhelming emotional might. That mournful night comes to an end with Johannes quitting the farm by the window while the others are sleeping. He leaves behind a note with these words from the Gospel: "Ye shall seek me and shall not find me. Whither I go, ye cannot come." The following day, after fruitless searching for the errant son, brings preparation for Inger's funeral, and in due course, with neighbors gathered, the horse-drawn hearse that has already been mentioned clatters nobly into the courtyard.

The sequence that follows has several slow stages, and the accretion of these different narrative elements builds up to overwhelming force. First, there is the reconciliation, on the human plane, between the Borgens and the Skraedders. Old Peter the tailor has come to see that his behavior has been harsh. He remembers the Gospel's injunction to turn the other cheek, and in a beautiful gesture of Christian generosity he publicly endorses, in front of Inger's coffin, the engagement of his daughter Anne to the young Anders Borgen. Next, there is the prayer of the priest, a handsome, worldly man, whom we have met earlier in conversation with the doctor, swapping urbanities. Nonetheless, the words that he now speaks at the head of the open coffin, with Inger's beautiful face in front of him, are appropriate and heartfelt. They are, as it were, the right Christian words, reminding his listeners that "death is the gateway to eternity." "You two," he says, turning to Mikkel, "will meet again and be united, never to part." And Mikkel—casting aside his previous bitterness—shakes the priest's hand and thanks him for this conventional solace.

Yet before the lid can be placed on the coffin, Johannes appears through the door. He seems a changed man, his voice and his gait normal again, a certain health radiating from his features. Still, if there is hope among the assembled gathering that the erstwhile theology student has found his wits again, the words he speaks bring nothing but consternation. "None of you has asked God to return her to you," he avers to the assembly, in all seriousness. Silence follows. "Now you mock God!" expostulates old Borgen. "No," Johannes replies, "it is *you* who mock God with your halfheartedness!" And taking the child Maren's hand—she has quietly stolen up to her uncle, and looks at him with silent encouragement—he proceeds to utter the prayer, the invocation to Christ, that will bring Inger back from the dead.

Figure 8.2 "Do you believe I can do it?" "Yes, uncle!" Johannes Borgen encouraged by his little niece Maren toward the final moments of *Ordet*.
Positif Archive by arrangement of Mark Le Fanu.

The "resurrection" of Inger—registered first as a brief movement of the hands, then, seconds later, in the infinitely slow opening of the eyelids, along with a wisp of a smile as she turns to look up at her husband's face poised above her—is, it needs to be repeated, one of the most sublime moments in the whole of world cinema, leading as it does to the couple's final embrace and some few incandescently noble fragments of dialogue. First, Skraedder, an old man himself, turning to old Borgen, embraces him with rapture: "He is still the God of old—the God of Elijah, eternal and the same!" "Eternal and the same," concurs Borgen in amazement, embracing him back. The camera shifts back to Inger, her face pressed closely to Mikkel's. "And the child, is it alive?" she asks. "It is alive, it lives with God." "With God?" "Yes, Inger, I have found your faith. A new life is beginning for us." "Ah, life," she echoes contentedly, and repeats the word again. And then again, finally and softly.

If the viewer doesn't weep at this moment, when would they ever weep? I include within our hypothetical audience people of all faiths and none. Yet it is fascinating to try to work out why this should be so. We know—or at least we think we do—that resurrection is impossible, so what exactly is happening here, at the film's climax? Of course there is the *desire* for resurrection when we

Figure 8.3 "Alive with God." Inger Borgen and her husband, Mikkel, miraculously reunited at the climax.

Positif Archive by arrangement of Mark Le Fanu.

love someone who is precipitately taken away from us: the scene we have just witnessed in this sense enacts a common fantasy. At the same time, it is a fact of life (though a rare one) that people do indeed come back from the dead; one thinks of the "lucky ones" rescued from earthquake and other natural perils, or even, on a lesser scale of miracle, those who recover from some deadly disease or survive an intricate hospital operation. On an absolutely naturalistic level, it happens that people have been pronounced dead and found later to be alive after all—they have "pulled through," miraculously, even in the depths of the morgue. So once we have adjusted our tears and the lights have gone up, Dreyer's film allows itself, perhaps, to be rationalized in this manner.

The need for an "escape clause"—seeing it as a criticism of the movie that none is provided explicitly—was the substance of a complaint tendered in a newspaper *feuilleton* written by the critic Knud Sønderby shortly after the film's Danish premiere. The accusation here (so Casper Tybjerg tells us in an illuminating account of *Ordet*'s reception) is that Dreyer has omitted a line from the original play where the doctor sums up the events that have been collectively witnessed with the vehement remark: "The *ligsynsmand* system must be abolished!" The *ligsynsmand*, Tybjerg informs us, "was a locally appointed layman who inspected dead bodies, ascertained that signs of death were indeed present, and signed death certificates." Tybjerg continues: "Because these people were not trained professionals there was considerable worry... that they might overlook [patients] in deep coma."[4] Hence the expostulation of the doctor—the omission of which by Dreyer, according to Sønderby, "castrated" Kaj Munk's text and intentions.

It is easy enough to see why Dreyer dropped the line in question, if indeed it was there in the first place (there seems to be confusion about whether Munk himself omitted it from an earlier draft): its would-be inclusion introduces an extraneous level of sociological realism that serves only to bring the scene down to earth in the wrong way. Bathos, absolutely, needed to be avoided, and the omission is simply a question of artistry. Art and illusion have always gone hand in hand, and Dreyer was straightforward about the psychological state of mind that the audience, in this kind of affair, had to be subjected to if the plot revelation was to come off. "To make themselves receptive to the miracle," Dreyer wrote in an unpublished note on the screenplay unearthed by Tybjerg, "the audience must be placed in that peculiar mood of sorrow and melancholy in which people find themselves when they attend a funeral.... They must be made to forget that they are watching a film and induced or, if you will, hypnotized to believe that they are witnessing an act of the divine." It is obvious that what is being talked about here is artistic strategy rather than the literal truth: being "induced" to believe is different from believing. Still, the mild controversy stirred up by the *ligsynsmand* business raises the question of what Dreyer *did* believe concerning the possibility of miracles in the modern age: did he himself harbor an escape clause?

It happens that we know quite a lot about his views. Challenged by certain "uncomplimentary" remarks in the wake of *Ordet*'s outing at the Venice Film Festival by the Marxist critic Guido Aristarco, who accused the director of "rejecting science for the miracles of religion,"[5] Dreyer defended himself in an essay praising what he referred to as recent "discoveries" of psychic research. The relevant passage goes as follows: "The new science brings us toward a more intimate understanding of the divine power and is even beginning to give us a natural explanation to things of the supernatural. The Johannes figure of Kaj Munk's play can now be seen from another angle. . . . I have not rejected modern science for the miracle of religion. On the contrary, Kaj Munk's play assumed new and added significance for me, because the paradoxical thoughts and ideas expressed in the play have been proved by recent psychic research."[6] "Proved" we might think of as being rather a strong word under the circumstances, but this appears to be what Dreyer truly thought about the matter. Did it make him any less of a Christian? It is certainly an interesting question. Tybjerg provides fascinating further information about the extent of Dreyer's wide reading in the subject of paranormal phenomena—it had evidently become something of an obsession with him.[7]

The separate confessions (Protestant, Catholic, Eastern Orthodox) each have their orthodoxy, yet it remains true that, within the broad corpus of available beliefs, each professing Christian faces the demands of faith in their individual way. No one (not even the Pope, one is tempted to say) can escape idiosyncrasy. For belief in the end is a cultural, historical, and personal matter. It encompasses a settled allegiance of heart as much as an attachment to minute points of dogma. What Dreyer "really" thought about the miracle of resurrection can, ultimately, only have been known to himself. There is a limit to what commentators can say on the matter. The trouble with the intrusion of science (or pseudoscience, in the case of psychic research) into our consideration of *Ordet* is that it takes us too far away from the experience of the film, which is predicated, of course, on profound ambiguity. Miracles, by definition, *are* mysteries. The Christian says at Easter, "Christ is risen again, hallelujah!," and who shall gainsay this profound affirmation? We need not, at this stage, attempt to spell out the relevant contradictions—beyond venturing to observe that faith *is* extravagant, faith *is* impossible, and always must be. Few enough artists in the twentieth century have been able to dwell here, not in the realm of necessity and science (how can any modern person avoid respecting *science*?) but, grandly and boldly, within the pure realm of scripture and spirit. Dreyer, in the field of cinema, is surely among the greatest of them.

Figure 9.1 Babette (Stéphane Audran) handling grapes, alluding to the Holy Communion, in *Babette's Feast*.
Entertainment Pictures/Alamy Stock Photo

9

Babette's Feast: Protestant Pietism, the Conflict of Spirit and Flesh, and Reconciliatory Grace in the Danish *Babette's Feast*

Kjell O. Lejon

The Danish drama film *Babette's Feast* still fascinates and charms audiences, yes, even beguiles them.[1] The origin of the film is a short story written in English and published in 1953 by Danish author Karen Blixen (1885–1962) under the pseudonym Isak Dinesen.[2] In 1958, the story appeared in Danish translation, holding a place in the last anthology published during Blixen's lifetime, entitled *Skæbne-Anekdoter* (*Anecdotes of Destiny*).[3] Almost three decades later, in 1987, Danish filmmaker Gabriel Axel (1918–2014) directed the film adaptation of the short story, *Babettes Gestebud* (*Babette's Feast*).[4] The acclaimed film received an Academy Award for Best Foreign Language Film in 1988.[5]

Grace at the Heart of *Babette's Feast*

Even though commentators such as Priscilla Parkhurst Ferguson argue that *Babette's Feast* "inaugurated . . . a veritable cinematic genre—the food film," the food is neither the beginning nor the end of the film.[6] Neither is an extraordinary culinary experience its central message. Instead, I argue that, behind its deceptive simplicity, slow-moving intrigue, and Nordic visual scenery, the film offers deep, complex, and enthralling perspectives on a most central theme in Lutheran theology—namely, the biblically grounded notion of *grace*, a notion deeply embedded in the Scandinavian soul during the era in which the story is set.[7] Consequently, *Babette's Feast* is primarily a religious film, but as such a truly human story of the vital need for mercy and grace in the reconciliation process of understanding the circumstances of life.

The film starts with a description of two pious sisters in a group of Scandinavian Pietists longing for Jerusalem (i.e., a symbol of heaven) and ends in

Kjell O. Lejon, *Babette's Feast: Protestant Pietism, the Conflict of Spirit and Flesh, and Reconciliatory Grace in the Danish* Babette's Feast In: *Protestants on Screen*. Edited by: Gastón Espinosa, Erik Redling and Jason Stevens,
Oxford University Press. © Oxford University Press 2023. DOI: 10.1093/oso/9780190058906.003.0010

a sort of vision of paradise (another picture of a heavenly future). In addition, a quote from Psalms 85:10, already used by the pastor at the beginning of the short story and the film, both starts and ends the crucial speech at the feast: "For mercy and truth have met together, and righteousness and bliss shall kiss one another." (The character General Löwenhielm uses the Swedish word *nåd*, which in the context is closer to "grace" than "mercy.")

In fact, Psalm 85 can be seen as a key entry to the essential tone of the short story and film. The psalm is about the restoration and forgiveness of God with reference to his people. The overarching theme of reconciliatory and restoring grace and the centrality of the Bible quotation, not least as the beginning and end of the crucial speech, point at the end of the psalm (85:12), which provides a point of entry to the quintessential character to the film as a whole: "The LORD will indeed give what is good" (NIV). Grace is at the very heart of the film—and not only the possibility but the actuality of reconciliatory grace in times of temporal disjunctions or conflicts between spirit and flesh—both within self-examining individuals and among a group of Scandinavian Lutheran Pietists. Grace also overcomes subtle legalism and joins the Lutheran Pietists and the two Catholics in the film. Spiritual longing and self-giving actions connect the two traditions despite doctrinal differences. Thereby, the film becomes a social and religious commentary about the risks of legalism or dogmatism and the estranging separation of spirit and flesh in a world created by God as a whole. But the commentary is gentle, slow, and in several respects delightful.

Moreover, aesthetic beauty helps to overcome estrangement. This is highlighted in several forms: Mozart's opera *Don Giovanni* and visual links to the Scandinavian art tradition (such as Danish artist Paul Bjerre's *The Prayer Meeting*) and to the Skagen painters (such as Peder Severin Krøyer).[8] The film also alludes to Scandinavian literature, such as Søren Kirkegaard's works, "on the struggle between duty and sacrifice and the contrast of faith with the aesthetic."[9] Not least, the film also presents artistic and gastronomic beauty through the film character of Babette, the former famous French chef of the Parisian Café Anglais.

The Story Behind the Story

The story behind the story is in *Babette's Feast* an indispensable interpretative context in order to shed light on various significant theological and social dimensions and implications of the film.

The Lutheran Protestant reformation in Scandinavia had an immense effect on all aspects of cultural, societal, educational, and religious life. Eventually, Lutheran orthodoxy was implemented and the state and church were unified. However, the stress on correct Lutheran doctrine that was supported by the state church did not satisfy some groups that were in search of individual Christ-centered Christian living. Ideas from Pietist and Moravian groups in Germany continuously reached Scandinavia; these stressed devotional life, sincere and in-depth study of the Bible in private meetings, the necessity of a new birth (John 3:3), a personal relationship with Jesus, and practical Christianity showing good fruits.[10] It was common to stress simplicity and the importance of rejecting so-called worldly amusements.[11]

Through the German August Hermann Francke (1663–1727), biblical revivalism and social activism became hallmarks of Pietism. The ideas made large impressions on groups of both laypeople and clergy in Scandinavia, resulting in revivals but also, at times, in conflicts with the orthodox leadership within the state churches, since some Pietists from time to time openly ignored the organized church's orders and laws, which forbade religious meetings without the presence of the local (Lutheran) pastor. In the long run, the Pietist cultural impact was substantial because it helped give birth to other revival movements during the 1800s. In many cases, the Pietist revivals were encouraged and spread by "awakened" Lutheran pastors.

The stress on simple and moral living took a somewhat strict or even legalistic form among certain Pietist groups. The pleasures in what "the world" could offer were seen as temptations, something that was in conflict with the spirit and drew attention away from a true godly life. It might be that the unconditional grace of God had become conditioned in their thinking, at least to some degree—that is, stipulated by certain behaviors and moral living in a certain tradition. However, in Luther's teaching, grace was the fundamental beginning point, originating in God's unconditional love, and good behavior was the consequence, something that flowed out of the life of the believer, the person who had received grace and faith. Among some Pietists, however, the consequence had in some sense fatefully become a prerequisite.

In addition to being theologically astute about Pietism, *Babette's Feast* is also historically sensitive to the movement's impact on Scandinavian nobility. The film uncovers how the aristocrat General Löwenhielm, from a more or less outside position, discovers spiritual truths during the feast and in the midst of the elderly Pietists. It is therefore noteworthy that many influential aristocrats became attracted to, involved in, and also protectors of the Pietist movement in Scandinavia during the 1800s, which is the time in which the short story and film are set. It is underlined that piety was in fashion at the Swedish royal court.[12]

Brief Character Analysis

Flashbacks in *Babette's Feast* establish the past of the two unmarried sisters, Filippa and Martine. Their father was a pastor who led a small group of Lutheran Pietists and, at the same time, served as regular pastor of a local geographically defined Lutheran congregation. He was even called a prophet, a man with a message from God. He was well respected, and his collected sermons were a favorite of the queen.[13] The pastor knew French and had studied the works of the Catholic French theologian d'Etaples (1460–1536) in his youth, even though his theology was molded in a German Lutheran Pietist tradition.[14] In this tradition, also manifested for centuries in Scandinavian constitutions and national codes of law, Roman Catholics (or "papists," as they were called) were seen as grave heretics, holding fast to unbiblical teachings. No wonder the narrator describes that the pastor "turned pale" when Achille Papin, Filippa's onetime suitor, declared himself a papist.

The pastor's strongly held tradition is manifested in the names of the daughters: Martine and Filippa, named after Martin Luther and his fellow professor and reformer Philipp Melanchthon. Throughout the film, these two sisters are portrayed as pious and warmhearted, devoted and dedicated to the cause of their father: a life in Pietist fashion. Faith, simple living, and social work for the poor and the elderly characterize their lives. What this world could offer, worldly ties and even marriage, is not important in comparison to what could be reached in the life to come, in "Jerusalem, my heart's true home" (as sung by the Pietists). Thus, they are depicted as somewhat otherworldly (i.e., willing to give up temporal pleasures). Spiritual matters hold priority over worldly matters, the soul priority over the body. However, they are still socially concerned and active in their everyday life.

In their youth, two men appear in their lives, and the sisters clearly have very passionate feelings for them. First, a handsome young Swedish aristocrat and officer, Lorens Löwenhielm, who was sent to the home of a rich aunt in this desolate area of Denmark to reflect on his life and debts, falls in love with Martine. He joins the small Pietist revival group and their Bible and prayer meetings in the pastor's home. He listens to the pastor reciting Psalms 85:10. These words stayed with him. However, he is never able to affect Martine with his love, and so he eventually leaves the place, presumably forever, pondering that life is "hard and cruel . . . that in this world there are things that are impossible." After that, his career becomes the focus. He marries a lady-in-waiting to the queen, uses pious vocabulary at the Pietist-influenced court, and goes on military missions to Russia and France. When he returns later on in the film, he does so as a sophisticated and decorated general. However, when he is back at his aunt's, haunting memories are brought to light. He perceives his younger self, his ambitions, and the goals he has reached in his career from a new perspective.

The Parisian Achille Papin is a somewhat unexpected French visitor in the remote fishing village. But on a recommendation, this was the place where he seeks silence and solitude after a special two-week performance at the Royal Opera in Stockholm. In deep melancholy, he visits the parish church and hears an angelic voice, the voice of Filippa. Papin, successful but at the end of his career, is amazed and excited, and gives her lessons, seeing in her a potential new diva for Paris—a new beginning for a renewed career? The congregation sings the Norwegian Petter Dass's famous hymn: "Lord, our God, Thy name and Glory / Should be sung throughout the world / and every soul Thy humble subject / And every wayfarer shall sing aloud Thy praise." The congregational hymn ends with "The Lord's Glory shall rise in a thousand hearts," while the camera focuses on the large crucifix in the church.[15] Something transcends transitory temporal matters and fame. There is hope. However, Papin's affection for Filippa overflows, as shown in the *Don Giovanni* duet scene. The father and Martine worry about Filippa's relationship with Papin. However, Filippa decides to end the singing lessons. Papin receives her note about her decision and leaves for Paris deeply disappointed.

Life goes on, memories remain. Thirty-five years pass, and then something unexpected happens. On a stormy evening in September 1871 Babette knocks on the door of the sisters' house. In her hand she has a letter from Papin. He asks the sisters to help Babette, who has fled from her home in Paris searching for refuge after the repression led by General Galliffet following an insurrection in Paris against the French government in 1871. But something else is revealed in the letter: he has for many years regretted that Filippa's voice was never heard in at the Grand Opera in Paris. He envisions her, in light of his own miserable loneliness (echoing Ecclesiastes 1:2, "all is vanity"), sitting honored and loved among her children, and writes that "she may have chosen the better part in life" while describing himself as "a lonely, graying old man forgotten by those who once applauded and adored me," adding, in his melancholy: "What is fame? The grave awaits us all." But, he continues, referring to the Don Giovanni duet: "And yet, my lost Zerlina, and yet, soprano of the snow! As I write this I feel that the grave is not the end. In Paradise I shall hear your voice again. . . . There you will be the great artist that God meant you to be. Ah! how you will enchant the angels."[16] Papin, a Catholic, has a longing for the life to come, like the Pietist Lutheran sisters do.

Now another papist, Babette, has entered their home. The sisters tremble a bit. Who is she? A refugee? True. But also a *pétroleuse*, a supporter of the Paris Commune who uses gasoline to burn down the city? They decide to open their home to her, "a hard-tried fellow creature," and do not want to worry her with catechization. Instead, "they silently agreed that the example of a good Lutheran life would be the best means of converting their servant."

Babette serves as a maid for years. According to Dinesen's story, she became the dark "Martha" of the house, and the two sisters could flourish as two fair "Marys" (see Luke 10:38–42). The Pietist revival group, with the members growing older, add Babette in their evening prayers and thank God for her. And the story concludes: "The stone which the builders had almost refused had become the headstone of the corner," putting her in a biblical light, almost as a sort of Christ figure (Psalms 118:22, Acts 4:11).

The Feast

Eventually Babette wins ten thousand francs in a lottery. She plans a "real French dinner" at the pastor's centenary celebration, which comes as a great surprise to the sisters. Yet they are willing to go along with Babette's wishes. At the same time, the sisters are saddened by the discord and dissension among the old believers. Old sins are brought up, and some have turned "testy and querulous." They are Pietist, but not without faults. They are Christian—forgiven and made righteous by God—but still sinners: *simul justus et peccator* (at the same time righteous and sinners), in the words of Luther, and always in need of grace.

Babette prepares the meal, and the flock of believers has new worries. Will the anniversary meal be spiritually harmful? Are they not to avoid apparent sins? Nightmares of devilish sensuality appear. Is Babette a temptress?

The marvelous feast begins. The believers are initially, and in a humorous way, portrayed as suspicious and avoiding the pleasures of the dishes and drinks, but the mood changes and becomes by turns cheerful and celebratory. Wrongs are forgiven, trust is restored, and the skepticism of the body and worldly goods, here represented by an extraordinary culinary experience, is conquered. However, it is not the food that conquers all. This becomes clear in General Löwenhielm's speech. The earthly gifts point at deeper biblical and spiritual truths. For those familiar with biblical history, the centerpiece of the dinner, quail in sarcophagus—quail being a form of manna, and the word "sarcophagus" meaning "flesh-eater" (Gk. *sarx*, "flesh," and *phagein*, "to eat")—might intend two allusions. First, the centerpiece recalls the quails and manna given by God during the Hebrews' time in the desert (Exodus 16:13-16), between the time of slavery in Egypt and the settlement in Canaan, the land of honey and milk. Second, it recalls the words of Jesus: "I am the bread of life. Your ancestors ate the manna in the wilderness, yet they died. But here is the bread that comes down from heaven . . . Whoever eats this bread will live forever. This bread is my flesh, which I will give for the life of the world" (John 6:48-51, NIV).

General Löwenhielm is surprised and overwhelmed by the food presented. It reminds him of a dinner at Café Anglais in Paris, hosted by General Galliffet. The feast evolves, becoming a reconciliatory tool and a culinary love affair that resembles the Last Supper/Holy Communion and brings forward the hope of a perfect world to come, "Jerusalem."[17] Löwenhielm clinks his glass and raises his voice: "Mercy and truth have met together. Righteousness and bliss shall kiss one another" (Psalms 85:10). This biblical verse, once voiced by the pastor, echoes.

Figure 9.2 General Löwenhielm meets Martine for the last time; old choices as well as the future are placed in the hand of God, under God's mercy.
DVD screen capture, fair use

Löwenhielm speaks of weakness and shortsightedness and of our choices. But "there will come a day when our eyes are opened. And we come to realize that grace is infinite. We need only await it with confidence and receive it with gratitude. Grace imposes no conditions." The speech ends as it began, with the words from Psalm 85:10. Theologically, grace is at the center of a reconciled life. By grace, the general seems to experience a miraculous moment in which mercy has overflown and he is reconciled with his choices in life. He understands his career, with all its choices and accomplishments, in a new light, and his skepticism of the spirit dissolves. In the midst of the feast among the elderly Pietists, Löwenhielm is able to acknowledge a spiritual truth that had eluded him: the love of God is unconditional, and God's grace is greater than any misjudgments and choices made.

The celebratory feast ends. General Löwenhielm speaks with Martine for the last time, revealing his feelings: "I shall be with you every day that is left to me. Every evening I shall sit down, if not in the flesh, which means nothing, in spirit, which is all, to dine with you, just like tonight. For tonight I have learned, dear sister, that in this world anything is possible." Martine replies: "Yes . . . in this world anything is possible." Old choices as well as the future are placed in the hands of God, under God's mercy. They can go on and live reconciled. The groups of believers sing and dance around a well outside the sisters' house in the night, under bright stars, and greet each other joyfully with a "Bless you!"

After the feast Martine and Filippa speak with Babette, who wears an eye-catching cross. Babette reveals her background as a chef at Café Anglais, that all ten thousand francs are gone, and that she had been a Communard on the barricades: "Thanks be to God, I was a Communard!" She had given all, and there was no way back. Economically she is poor again, but she has revealed herself as a great artist, and with all this artistic and gastronomic knowledge, she will never feel poor.[18]

At the end of the conversation Filippa turns to Babette, saying, "This is not the end! . . . In paradise you will be the great artist that God meant you to be!" A French Catholic is included in the longing for paradise, along with the Pietist Lutherans. Blixen and Axel seem to underline that the gap between the traditions is thereby somewhat closed, a thought strange to many at the time when the short story was written. Therefore, the story and film reveal the notion of dogmatic tolerance before the main era of ecumenism.

Releasing Grace Through Earthly Means

The manifold biblical allusions and intricate theological dimensions of the dialogue in the short story and film imply that they are not primarily about food or art but rather are concerned with God's grace and reconciliatory actions. If one adopts the redemptive perspective of Löwenhielm, then God is restoring His people. Thus, the portrait of the feast is not a goal in itself, but a means to underscore the centrality of grace in order to be reconciled with one's past, present, and future, and with God. Thus it is simply not "a culinary tale for all times and places, for all those cooks who transform eating into dining, and for all those diners who come away from the table transformed."[19] Instead, it is a story about the need for grace in human life, of the enormous impact the revelation of grace might have, especially in a (Lutheran) context and tradition, which has as its motto *sola gratia*, or "grace alone." Faith through grace is not a fixed matter in Luther's teaching, but something that needs to be renewed day by day in order not to be distorted through legalism and self-righteousness. In this way, the short story and film can be seen as critically commenting on legalistic ideas of faith. Supping together releases grace, which overcomes restrictive formalism—secular (i.e., careerism) and religious (legalism)—and shortcomings (choices and wrongdoing and sinfulness) in the individual lives of the participants as well as in the fellowship among the followers of various denominations.

The feast can be understood as an analogy for the sacraments in the Christian tradition (i.e., spiritual gifts through earthly means). By emphasizing earthly means and spiritual gifts, *Babette's Feast* rejects a misleading dichotomy between body and soul and indicates the need for a reconciliation of the two in times of conflict. This implied message corresponds with John 1:14: Jesus "became flesh

Figure 9.3 The feast becomes a reconciliatory tool and a "culinary love affair" that resembles the Holy Communion.
DVD screen capture, fair use

and made his dwelling among us . . . full of grace and truth" (NIV). In Jesus, God became man. Flesh and spirit were truly united, as bread and wine are united with Jesus Christ in the Holy Communion, as Lutherans (and Catholics) understand it. Thus, God has not abandoned His creation, but is to be found (also) in the midst of it, most clearly in the Bible and in the sacraments (baptism and Holy Communion in the Lutheran tradition). Earthly means, like the feast, might reveal the grace of God.

The feast might even be interpreted as a symbol of the Holy Communion, a blissful sign of the future heavenly feast in the midst of gray everyday life, worth longing for and singing about: "Jerusalem, my heart's true home." The two sisters, Martine and Filippa, come to understand that worldly pleasures do not necessarily contradict spiritual truths. Instead, they can provide a foretaste of heaven and, enjoyed communally, become means of divine grace and reconciliation: "For mercy and truth have met together, and righteousness and bliss have kissed one another."

Conclusion

In *Babette's Feast*, a solution to the commonly portrayed general conflict between the flesh and the spirit is revealed, and it is revealed in grace-infused biblical faith. According to the Bible, God wants to restore his people (Psalm 85).

Reconciliation processes start within individuals and between people. The grace of God can be reached through earthly means. Thus, at least indirectly, the film can be viewed as a critique of a faith that more or less expels God from the physical sphere and establishes a clear dichotomy between the spirit and the body/flesh. This critique of otherworldliness is normally formed from the perspective of incarnation theology, which holds that God became man in Jesus Christ.

Thus, at the very heart of the film is not food or art or simply a possibility of renewed friendship or grace, but releasing and life-reconciliatory grace. Löwenhielm is able to go on, reconciled with all the choices made; he has finally found peace, channeled through the Bible's message of mercy and truth. Martine is able to embrace her past choices, her present, and, as it seems, her future from the perspective of mercy. Additionally, the believers in the revival group are spiritually renewed and reconciled through worldly means; the spirit is reconciled with the flesh. God has used an opportunity at a feast to reveal biblical truths.

Moreover, the theological conflict between the Pietists (not least the sisters) and the Catholics (Papin and Babette) is settled: paradise is open for all of them. Thus, the short story and the film intervene in the several-centuries-long theological dispute between Lutherans and Catholics, sending a message that reconciliatory grace transcends temporal disjunctions.

God's grace, as formulated in the concept of *sola gratia*, is at the heart of the short story, the film, and Lutheran theology. In the last, it is accompanied by the concepts of *sola scriptura* (scripture alone) and *sola fide* (faith alone). It is therefore characteristic that quotes from the Scripture are at hand, both explicitly and implicitly. The quote from Psalm 85 points at the centrality of God's restoration of his people, that God gives what is good.

Of course, *Babette's Feast* film brings the inspiration of French cuisine and notions of Scandinavian light and art. Certainly it gives hope and inspiration to artists. But first and foremost it brings insight to Scandinavian Protestant Pietist Lutheranism, not least to the centrality of grace in Lutheran thinking. It gives the message that reconciliatory grace is needed both among plain pious people in remote places and among seemingly successful careerists. God's grace might flow in the midst of self-examination and heart-searching reflections.

To modern secular and religious people, *Babette's Feast* communicates the possibility of self-reconciliatory and bridge-building grace and a foundational understanding of the compatibility of body and soul, of art and faith, of people from various social backgrounds, and of two different Christian traditions—they may exist together without conflict. It brings into the cinema theology and hope for truth, mercy and grace to unreconciled people and traditions. In this film, when God is at hand, conflicts are resolved when truth and mercy meet.

Figure 10.1 In this scaffold scene from Wenders's *The Scarlet Letter*, a guard roughly turns Hester's face toward the Puritan patriarchs who will judge her.
Photo 12/Alamy Stock Photo

10
Protestant Ambivalence Toward Allegory in Wim Wenders's *The Scarlet Letter*

Erik Redling

The Reformation period saw an outright resistance to allegory. The reformers professed a deep skepticism toward the rhetorical trope and the fourfold hermeneutic method used in Roman Catholic scholasticism. Foremost among these critics was Martin Luther. A statement about allegory found in his lectures on the book of Genesis illustrates his view:[1]

> Allegorias esse inanes speculationes et tanquam spumam sacrae scripturae. Sola enim historica sententia est, quae vere et solide docet. Postquam haec tractata et recte cognita est, tunc licet etiam Allegoriis ceu ornamento et floribus quibusdam uti, quibus illustretur Historia seu pingatur.

> Allegories are empty speculations and like the spume of the sacred scripture. Only a historical evaluation teaches truthfully and factually. Only after the evaluation has been applied and recognized as being correct may ornamentations or flowery language be added, which illustrate and embellish history.[2]

Luther's resistance to allegory stems in part from his rejection of the medieval fourfold allegorical exegesis that allowed Catholic theologians to create overly elaborate interpretations of the Bible.[3] Regarding allegory as an inessential "supplément" (to use Jacques Derrida's term) to the literal or historical sense, he called for a return to the actual text, the Bible. Hence the central doctrines that guide the Protestant Reformation are *sola scriptura* (by scripture alone), *sola fide* (by faith alone), *sola gratia* (by grace alone), and *sola historica sententia* (by historical view only)—or, as Brian Cummings puts it, "solus sensus litteralis."[4]

Luther's distaste for allegory was shared, as Cummings points out, by his fellow collaborator and friend Philipp Melanchthon, who argues in his *Elementa rhetorices* (1531), "Nam oratio quae non habet unam ac simplicem sententiam nihil certi docet," or "Any discourse which does not have a single and simple meaning teaches nothing for certain."[5] Other reformers, like Huldrych Zwingli, Martin Bucer, and John Calvin, followed in the footsteps of Luther and

Erik Redling, *Protestant Ambivalence Toward Allegory in Wim Wenders's* The Scarlet Letter In: *Protestants on Screen.* Edited by: Gastón Espinosa, Erik Redling and Jason Stevens, Oxford University Press.
DOI: 10.1093/oso/9780190058906.003.0011

Melanchthon and adopted the doctrine of the literal sense, which also came to govern English Protestant thought.[6] For instance, the English cleric and theologian William Perkins (1558–1602), who was one of the foremost leaders of the Puritan movement in the Church of England during the Elizabethan age, reiterates the reign of the literal sense in his treatise on preaching entitled *The arte of prophecying* (posthumously published in 1607). He argues that "there is one onelie sense, and the same is the literall"; an allegory, he continues, "is onely a certaine manner of uttering the same sense."[7]

Despite the strong anti-allegorical stance in Protestant England, English literature beginning in the mid- to late sixteenth century saw the rise of allegory, as Edmund Spenser's *The Fairie Queene* (1590), John Milton's *Paradise Lost* (1667), and John Bunyan's *Pilgrim's Progress* (1678), just to name the most prominent examples, document. Several reasons may account for the emergence of what Cummings has called "Protestant allegory," which, for him, seems to be a paradoxical expression. He claims that "Protestant literalism" included allegorical readings: "Once a figurative reading was subsumed as part of the act of interpretation demanded by the literal, the literal sense was encountered as already rich and complex."[8] Thomas Luxon argues in *Literal Figures* (1995) that English Protestant culture professed an anti-allegorical attitude that, behind the official façade, was accompanied by a deep commitment to allegory.[9] More specifically, Protestant literature also drew on classical and medieval frames of reference, which included allegory; and, last but not least, allegory indicated a vertical upward movement, that is, from the material realm to the immaterial realm, from the concrete to the abstract, from earth to heaven. The ambivalent Protestant attitude toward allegory can perhaps be seen best in *Pilgrim's Progress*, in which "Bunyan appends an 'Apology' for allegory in the form of a verse preface. He never meant to write an allegory: it just came into his head—he accidentally 'fell into allegory.' "[10] Bunyan's apology for using allegory clearly exhibits the ambivalent interdependence between Protestant resistance to allegory and the need for it.

This peculiar development from an anti-allegorical stance (Luther, Melanchthon, Perkins) to the rise of allegory in Protestant literature up to the eighteenth century serves as a necessary foundation of this chapter. The first part introduces Angus Fletcher's concept of "allegorical mode" and illustrates its explanatory power with a brief discussion of John Bunyan's *Pilgrim's Progress* and especially Nathaniel Hawthorne's *The Scarlet Letter* (1850). The second part demonstrates the allegorical mode in the 1926 American silent film *The Scarlet Letter*. The third part focuses on Wim Wenders's German-Austrian film adaptation of Hawthorne's novel and his ambivalent attitude toward the allegorical mode in *Der Scharlachrote Buchstabe* (1973). I specifically argue that Wenders uses a plain camera style as a "Protestant" reaction against the allegorical camera mode found in the 1926 *Scarlet Letter* and yet, at the same time, is attracted to the allegorical mode at the end of his movie in order to give it a trans-literal dimension of meaning.

The "Allegorical Mode" in European and American Literature: John Bunyan's *Pilgrim's Progress* (1678) and Nathaniel Hawthorne's *The Scarlet Letter* (1850)

Since antiquity, the concept of "allegory" has been the subject of critical discussions and a plethora of critics have analyzed allegories in literature, art, and film.[11] Angus Fletcher's *Allegory: The Theory of a Symbolic Mode* (1964, 2012), which paved the way for allegorical readings of visual art, provides a usefully flexible definition of allegory by claiming that it can be regarded as a "mode":

> In the simplest terms, allegory says one thing and means another. It destroys the normal expectation we have about language that our words "mean what they say." . . .
>
> In this sense we see how allegory is properly considered a mode: it is a fundamental process of encoding our speech. For the very reason that it is a radical linguistic procedure, it can appear in all sorts of different works.[12]

In each of the six subsequent chapters, Fletcher identifies a central feature of the "allegorical mode" that guides literary texts and visual art. Aside from what Fletcher calls "allegorical causation" (magic and ritual) and "psychoanalytic analogies" (obsession and compulsion), he introduces four aspects of the allegorical mode, which will be briefly discussed below. He calls the first feature "daemonic agency" (the term "daemonic" can denote either good or evil) and claims that

> personified abstractions are probably the most obviously allegorical agents, whether virtues and vices in a *psychomachia* or chivalric ideals in a medieval romance or magic agencies in a romantic epic. Whatever area the abstract ideas come from, these agents give a sort of life to intellectual conceptions; they may not actually create a personality before our eyes, but they do create a semblance of personality.[13]

The second feature of the allegorical mode is the "cosmic image." "The type of allegorical imagery is . . . an isolated emblem," such as an astrological sign, a banner or a signet ring.[14] "Each image," he argues, "tends towards a *kratophany*, the revelation of a hidden power."[15] Fletcher's third feature is a "symbolic action," which "can be formed into progresses or battles, and that fictions of this type necessarily have double meanings, and necessarily have daemonic agency and cosmic imagery."[16] The (real or ideal) "allegorical progress" can be "a questing journey," and the allegorical battle can take the shape of a *psychomachia* or an "ideological warfare."[17] Finally, the allegorical mode comprises the feature of "thematic effect" (which may involve semantic ambivalence; e.g., "theological dualism," that is, "the opposition of Absolute Good and Absolute Evil," "emotive ambivalence," irony, the sublime, and the picturesque).[18]

Fletcher's model, though only rudimentarily sketched above, allows for a brief comparison between Bunyan's *Pilgrim's Progress* (1678) and Nathaniel Hawthorne's *The Scarlet Letter* (1850) that will highlight the allegorical mode in both works, introduce Hawthorne's novel, and explain a few differences between the two allegorical texts. *Pilgrim's Progress* not only evinces what Fletcher calls "daemonic agency," as the names of the characters, such as Christian, Evangelist, Faithful, Simple, Sloth, Help, and Mr. Worldly Wiseman, represent abstract qualities, but also displays a string of isolated emblems (with "hidden power"), that is, cosmic images, such as the Wicket Gate and the "shining light." The symbolic action centers on Christian's journey from the City of Destruction, where he and his family live, to the Celestial City, where all the true believers live, and the "thematic effect," which involves allegorical dualism and semantic ambivalence, is achieved through the two dimensions of meaning: the literal and the allegorical meanings of the text.

The allegorical mode also governs *The Scarlet Letter* by Hawthorne, who, as many critics and biographers have pointed out, was familiar with Bunyan's *Pilgrim's Progress*.[19] However, the allegorical mode in his novel is much more diffuse at times: the names of the main figures hint at the flattened, personified abstractions (as in the older allegory) and thus retain their daemonic agency, but the characters are much more rounded and multifaceted. The last names of Hester Prynne, Roger Chillingworth, and Arthur Dimmesdale allude to abstract ideas ("Prynne," for instance, rhymes with "sin"; "chilling" refers to the "cold" personality of Roger Chillingworth; and "dim" indicates a feeble character in body and mind), and yet their figures go well beyond personifying these abstract ideas alone. Hester Prynne, for instance, cannot be reduced to the embodiment of sin, for she is also portrayed as a strong and "good" (even holy) woman who, on the one hand, accepts the sentence and punishment of the Puritan community (she is imprisoned and has to wear the letter *A* for "adultery") and, on the other hand, challenges her role as a woman in a patriarchal society. Fletcher identifies and discusses the other aspects of *The Scarlet Letter*'s allegorical mode in his book. Hester's letter is a classic example of a cosmic, universally controlling icon. The flaming red embroidered letter worn by the accused Hester motivates her whole story, since the *A* stands for "angel" and "adultery," the absolute or the ambiguous, any or all things, the abandoned or the accepted.[20] Fletcher views the symbolic action of Hawthorne's novel in terms of a battle (rather than in terms of a journey) and claims that

> *The Scarlet Letter* is an anti-Romance, which enables Hawthorne to question the absolute principles and rituals of atonement of Puritan religion, and this questioning is one typical method by which the greatest allegorical writers introduce a skeptical view of their idealizing interests.[21]

As for the thematic effect of the novel, Fletcher mentions once more the letter *A* with its semantic ambivalence. It comes as no surprise that he regards Hawthorne's *The Scarlet Letter* as a perfect example to illustrate the (skeptical) allegorical mode in nineteenth-century American literature.

Hawthorne's novel continuously serves as a source for film adaptations, such as Victor Sjöström's 1926 silent film *The Scarlet Letter* (with Lillian Gish) and Wim Wenders's 1973 film *Der Scharlachrote Buchstabe* (with Senta Berger). The question then arises of how those filmic versions of *The Scarlet Letter* render the allegorical mode in the visual medium. My starting point for the exploration of this question in the final part of this chapter is a remark made by Angus Fletcher in the afterword to his study on allegory, in which he contends that filmmakers of the 1950s and 1960s, such as Ingmar Bergman, Federico Fellini, and Michelangelo Antonioni, still work in the tradition of the allegorical mode and "reflect the continuing need of the emblematic mode."[22] Their films, he states, "spell out an iconographic intention" or, in other words, an iconographic impulse, which derives from the "cosmic image."[23]

The Iconographic Impulse in the American Silent Film *The Scarlet Letter* (1926)

The iconographic impulse that gives expression to the allegorical mode in film is not limited to the films of the 1950s and 1960s. It can be also detected in movies from the silent era, such as the 1926 version of *The Scarlet Letter*, starring Lillian Gish.[24] On the level of the plot, the film embellishes the love story between Hester Prynne and Arthur Dimmesdale and, displaying influences of melodrama, which Fletcher considers to be "modestly allegorical," depicts the allegorical struggle (Gk. *agon*) between "good" lovers and the "evil" villain Roger Chillingworth.[25] The semantic ambivalence of the letter *A*, however, is reduced to "adultery"; that is, the cosmic image becomes merely a single-purpose signifier in the movie.[26] On the level of the camera work, the allegorical mode is conveyed through a string of isolated iconographic images that point to a higher realm and, at times, through vertical camera movement.

The first indication of an allegorical mode occurs at the very beginning of the movie. After the initial intertitle prepares the audience for a tragic "episode in the lives of a stern, unforgiving people" and the second one introduces the setting ("Puritan Boston on a Sabbath Day in June ---"), the camera tilts upward from a close-up of a white rosebush to a nearby small window with a grate affixed to the wooden wall of the house and a young boy who looks out through the window bars, thereby connecting the symbol of purity and innocence (the white roses) with the symbol of a restrictive, "imprisoning" Puritan society (the boy behind the window bars). Cutting directly to a low-angle shot of chiming church bells, which become a recurring leitmotif for the first part of the movie and stand for the heavenly realm, the camera moves gradually downward to show an imposing and even threatening scaffold positioned in front of the church, underneath which a young mustachioed man, a sinner destined for hell, has been incarcerated. This series of symbolic images (white roses, young boy behind bars, church bells, and young man imprisoned underneath the scaffold) together with the bottom-up and top-down movements of the camera leave no doubt about the film's religious allegorical dimension—innocence versus sin, heaven versus hell.

The next three scenes reinforce the allegorical mode of the movie. After showing people flocking to church (with the scaffold moving into the center of the picture) and a procession of stern-looking Puritan families also on their way to the service, the camera perspective shifts from the outside to the inside of the church and focuses on one of the protagonists of the movie: the Reverend Arthur Dimmesdale. A medium shot of Dimmesdale's profile shows him reading and meditating on what he just has read shortly before the beginning of the service; the light source is situated behind his head to create the impression that his head is surrounded by a saintly halo. The same technique is used in the subsequent scene to endow Hester Prynne, the other protagonist, with an angelic radiance. A wooden sign with the inscription "Hester Prynne / Ye Seamstress" announces the ensuing scene in which Hester, dressed in white, holds two white bonnets in her hands and cannot decide which bonnet to wear to church. She walks over to a mirror and hesitates for a moment upon reading "Vanity Is an Evil Disease," which is embroidered on a piece of cloth covering the mirror, before she removes the cover to look at herself in the mirror and tries on one of the bonnets. The next shot shows Hester wearing the bonnet, and the light emanating from behind her bathes her in a saintly luminosity.

A third instance of using backlighting to emphasize a spiritual dimension happens shortly afterward. Hester uncovers a cage to check on her songbird, which immediately starts to sing; as soon as it is taken from the cage, it flies outside into the woods. Trying to catch the bird, Hester follows it into the woods and loses her bonnet on the way. Unable to find the bird, she abandons her search after hearing the final tolls of the church bells; she picks up and puts on her bonnet, and belatedly enters the church to attend the service. Meanwhile, a few elders, who heard the bird sing and witnessed Hester's foray into the woods, report her transgressions to Dimmesdale ("'Tis against the law to run and skip on Sabbath. The minister must be told"). After Hester has quietly taken a seat in a pew toward the back of the church, Dimmesdale points at her and orders her to step in front of his pulpit. The low-angle shot and the radiating light behind him give a visual boost to his saintliness as he severely chastises Hester for her misbehavior: "Hester Prynne, thou hast profaned God's holy day!" The circle of light still engulfs him as he looks down into the blinking eyes of Hester (a subjective point-of-view shot from Dimmesdale's vantage) and, feeling a sudden, strong sympathy for her, discontinues his hardhearted speech. As a way of regaining control over his emotional turmoil and his budding love for her, he continues with his reprimands ("Take heed, therefore! If ye sin, ye must pay—there is no escape!"), but he has been visibly shaken and barely manages to cover it up. Thus, the light that surrounds Dimmesdale serves not only as a saintly gloriole but also as a connecting (heavenly) bridge between the godly minister and the angelic Hester, who wears a white dress and whose white bonnet looks similar to a saintly halo as well.

The allegorical mode reaches its peak in two central scenes of the movie, which both take place at the scaffold. In the first scene, Dimmesdale returns from a trip to England in the summer of the following year and learns that Hester, with whom he had a secret love affair before his departure, has given birth to their baby. He implores her to share the punishment with her ("I—I am the guilty one, Hester! I must share thy punishment"), but without success: she wants to protect him, and requests that he atone for both of them. After Hester has been led to the scaffold, Dimmesdale, standing above her on a balcony, reluctantly performs the Puritan minister's duty and asks her to tell him the name of "the fellow sinner." Hester refuses. Then she looks up at Dimmesdale and delivers a powerful statement that increases Dimmesdale's agony: "I will never betray him. I love him—and I will always love him!" As a consequence, the magistrate orders her to reveal her brand of shame, the letter *A*, which is embroidered on her dress. The carefully composed tableau that ends this scene—a long shot—shows Hester standing on a pedestal in the middle of the scaffold, holding her baby in her arms with her eyes looking heavenward. The upward movement of her gaze is underscored by the spearheads of the lances carried by the guards who are positioned in a regular pattern around the scaffold, the triangular shape of Hester's profile, and the letter *A* itself.

Figure 10.2 Tableau from Sjöström's *The Scarlet Letter* (1926): the heavenward movement of Hester's (Lillian Gish) gaze is underscored by visual motifs.
PictureLux/The Hollywood Archive/Alamy Stock Photo

The final image of the movie—again a tableau—shows both Dimmesdale and Hester on the scaffold. Having met in the woods after the abovementioned scene, the two lovers decide to flee together, but Hester's long-lost husband, Roger Chillingworth, who is portrayed as a beastlike villain in the movie, overhears their conversation. Later on in the church, after he notices Dimmesdale's painful suffering, he torments Dimmesdale by declaring that he will always stand between them and their happiness ("Dost think thou shalt ever have happiness? *I shall always follow thee!*"). Dimmesdale sees no other way to escape the evil persecutor and end his physical and mental suffering than to step onto the scaffold, openly acknowledge his sin to the whole community, and bare his chest to reveal the letter *A* branded there. Exhausted by this effort, Dimmesdale dies in Hester's arms. The movie ends with a final tableau that is reminiscent of a pietà (a depiction of the Virgin Mary cradling the dead body of Jesus) and that highlights—together with the low-angle shot, the spearheads of the lances, and especially the triangular shape of the church in the background—the allegorical mode of the silent movie.

The string of symbolic images, the camera work, and the stylized tableaux bear witness to an allegorical mode that visualizes the movie's "higher" realms of spirituality. Only traces of this mode, however, can be found in Wim Wenders's adaption of Hawthorne's novel, as the 1973 movie has at its core a secular topic: a woman's rebellion against male oppression in a patriarchal society.

"*A* for America": Wim Wenders's Ambivalence Toward Allegory in *The Scarlet Letter* (1973)

Instead of moving along a vertical axis to indicate a spiritual realm, the camera work in Wim Wenders's 1973 film *Der Scharlachrote Buchstabe* (*The Scarlet Letter*) avoids such bottom-up or up-down movements and abstains from a religiously oriented allegorical camera mode. Although the movie includes shots or scenes that carry symbolic meaning (e.g., a panorama shot of an isolated cabin where Hester and Pearl live indicates their isolation from the Puritan community), its symbolism mainly refers to a sociopolitical realm rather than a religious one. The camera remains fixed and only a few times moves on a horizontal axis, panning from left to right or from right to left, to follow, for instance, processions; however, there are no tilts, no tracking shots, no zoom shots, or other typical camera techniques. Wenders's abstinence from camera movement, I argue, derives in part from his Protestant leanings. In an interview conducted in 2008 (that is, thirty-five years after the release of *Der Scharlachrote Buchstabe*), he answered the question on the influence of his Catholic background on his work as follows:

> Yes, sure. Catholicism is all about mysticism, imagery, imagination. It wouldn't be hard to guess that Bergman is a Protestant. . . . As much as I have come to respect (and prefer) the sobriety of Protestantism, I can still easily detect the romantic Catholic boy in myself. Anyway, I don't consider myself belonging to any denomination. As a Christian, I can go to a Catholic service or to a Baptist one. I've come to accept my Catholic "roots" and my Protestant tendencies as part of one and the same faith.[27]

Based on his professed "Protestant tendencies," I draw an analogy between Wenders's camera work in his filmic adaption of Hawthorne's novel and the "plain style" of Puritan or Protestant writing; furthermore, I claim that Wenders employed a plain camera style to resist the allegorical mode evident in the novel and its previous 1926 film adaptation. Instead, he highlights the (literal) political dimension of the narration. Pointing out that Wenders's adaptation is a child of the seventies, the critic Michael Dunne elaborates on its political agenda, claiming that, "as would be appropriate at that time, Hester's situation takes on gender-inflected counter-cultural resonances. Wenders's Hester is a young, sexy, independent woman opposed by older, repressed male authority figures."[28] Three scenes will illustrate Wenders's focus on the gender conflict and his use of a plain camera style.

Wenders's avoidance of the allegorical mode comes to the fore at the beginning of his movie. Looking down on a scaffold and an assembly of Puritan men and women, the camera cuts to a procession and shows a clergyman leading Hester Prynne (Senta Berger) to the scaffold amid a hostile crowd repeatedly cheering the word "whore" (Ger. *Hure*). The camera perspective then switches from a moderate high angle to a medium shot of a group of men, who sit on benches on a platform directly across from the scaffold. The next sequence of medium shots shows Hester, wearing a blue dress with the embroidered red letter *A* and a shawl draped around her red hair, climbing up the stairs to the scaffold and a guard who roughly turns her face toward Governor Fuller, Reverend Dimmesdale, and Reverend Wilson. Adopting a subjective point-of-view shot, the camera puts the audience into the perspective of Reverend Wilson, who has to stand up to read a proclamation, and from his POV looks at Hester from a slightly elevated angle. The image of Hester standing on the scaffold surrounded by a crowd of Puritan men and women is strikingly similar to the two tableaux of Hester in the 1926 silent film, but the former fails to convey the upward (heavenward) movement of the latter: no low-angle shots create an upward movement, no spearheads point skyward, and Hester does not look up to heaven. Instead, the camera takes on a patriarchal gaze (that is, the camera angle and position encourage the audience to view Hester from the imaginary spatial vantage of the Puritan elders who are judging her) and establishes a clear opposition between the blue-dressed, red-haired Hester, who looks downward in anticipation of her punishment, and the oppressive régime of Puritan men, who are predominantly dressed in black. Wenders's camera work alternates between long and extremely long shots (e.g., of the beach or of the house on the peninsula where Hester and Pearl live), medium shots, and close-ups (e.g., of the faces of people engaged in a conversation), and it also includes a few panning shots. Yet, significantly, it eschews vertical camera movements of any kind to avoid a visual allusion to a religiously oriented allegorical mode.[29]

Likewise, Wenders's changes to the novel's characters and plot serve to reinforce the political themes of female oppression and gender conflict, rather than highlight the allegorical underpinnings of the source. For one, he makes Mistress Hibbins the daughter of Governor Bellingham instead of his sister, places the black slave Sarah at her side, and turns her into "an eerie *doppelgänger* for Hester."[30] According to Dunne, Wenders strengthens the bond between Hibbins and Hester, which, in turn, allows him to establish a "female world" that is set

Figure 10.3 Wenders's image of Hester (Senta Berger) standing on the scaffold is similar to the tableaux of Hester in the 1926 silent film, but fails to convey heavenward movement.
DVD screen capture, fair use

apart from the male one: "Since Mistress Hibbins alone among the Puritans sympathizes with Hester, Wenders creates opportunities to show at least some form of female solidarity by filming Hester, Hibbins, and Sarah together in scenes cut contrastingly against shots of the joyless, sexless, Puritan male elders."[31] Other alterations of the novel, such as giving a political meaning to the letter *A*, also fit into the overall design of the movie. When a musician looks at Hester and asks her for the meaning of the letter *A*, Pearl, who is playing on his flute, answers him, "Aaaaaamerika," to which the musician replies, "Aaaach so" (I see). Wenders thereby reduces the ambiguity of the cosmic sign to the single meaning of "America," which, as it is said by Pearl, carries the hopeful note that future generations will experience a different America, an America that is no longer governed by a "theocratic order" that subdues women.[32]

Wenders's twofold strategy of dramatizing the repressive Puritan society, on the one hand, and offering a positive outlook for America, on the other hand, finds its epitome at the end of the movie. Standing inside the church rather than on the scaffold (as in the novel), Reverend Dimmesdale delivers a powerful sermon that resembles what Sacvan Bercovitch has called an "American jeremiad" and then confesses his sin to the assembled Puritan men and women before he reveals the letter *A* on his breast.[33] Weakened, Dimmesdale falls to the ground, and Governor Fuller and Reverend Wilson carry him to an adjoining room where he regains consciousness and states that now he can live together with Hester and Pearl. In order to prevent the two lovers and sinners from continuing their romance under the eyes of the Puritan public, Governor Fuller—sanctioned by Reverend Wilson—strangles Dimmesdale to death with his two black-gloved hands.

However, the final scene of the movie ends with a positive outlook, which, somewhat surprisingly, draws on the allegorical mode. It shows Hester and Pearl sitting together in a boat on their way to Providence, Rhode Island (not to England, as in the novel): Hester looks out to the sea and thus forward to a new future while Pearl sings the end-rhymed lines "Mein Vater ist gestorben, ich freue mich auf morgen" (My father has died, I'm looking forward to tomorrow). Wenders's change of their destination from England to the theologically punning Providence underscores the hopeful end of the movie and, in fact, rekindles the allegorical mode, as the term refers not only to a geographic place but also to God.

Conclusion

These two film adaptations of Hawthorne's novel *The Scarlet Letter* feature two different ways of approaching the allegorical source text. While Sjöström picks up the allegorical mode already inherent in the genre of melodrama and translates it into a striking visual style in his 1926 silent film, Wenders adopts a restrained, plain camera style, which works against the allegorical visualizing practices found in silent-era Hollywood movies such as Sjöström's. At the end of *Der Scharlachrote Buchstabe*, Wenders, however, introduces allegory only at the point when the heroine is breaking off from Puritan society, exhibiting his ambivalence toward allegory: on the one hand, he favors a more sober camera work that radicalizes his Protestant influences, avoiding vertical camera movements that would indicate any allegorical dimension at all, but, on the other hand, he is drawn toward Hawthorne's allegorical mode to enhance his heroine and his ending with a transliteral meaning. Would it have been a riskier strategy for his largely secular and feminist interpretation to employ allegory any earlier in the narrative—to employ allegory as Hawthorne and Sjöström do, to both express and criticize the mentality of Puritanism? Most likely it would have detracted from his decidedly realist approach to the allegorical source and his harsh critique of the patriarchal Puritan society. Yet this decision comes with a significant drawback: Wenders chooses not to express the allegorical mode of the Puritan mind, as Hawthorne and Sjöström did in their work. Wenders's allegorical impulse at the end of his movie nevertheless adds a glimpse of hope to the heroine's new destiny: Providence.

PART IV

PROTESTANT EXPERIENCE IN AMERICAN MOVIES

Figure 11.1 *The Tree of Life*'s family reunited in a vision of eternity.
AF archive/Alamy Stock Photo

11

"Where Were You?" The Problem of Evil in Terrence Malick's *The Tree of Life*

Mark S. M. Scott

Christian theology posits God's cosmic ubiquity as the Creator, Sustainer, and Redeemer whose benevolence underlies all reality.[1] When disaster strikes, however, God's goodness and power come into question, and God's presence in the world seems doubtful at best.[2] In the darkest moments of life, when our worst fears materialize, God seems conspicuously and culpably absent: *deus absconditus* (the hidden God).[3] C. S. Lewis, a famous convert from atheism to Christianity, vividly describes his agonizing experience of God's absence in the aftermath of his wife Joy's death: "Meanwhile, where is God? . . . [G]o to Him when your need is desperate, when all other help is vain, and what do you find? A door slammed in your face, and a sound of bolting and double bolting on the inside. After that, silence."[4] Lewis particularizes in his grief the global question of theodicy: why does God permit evil, and why does God seem to vanish in our most desperate times? Terrence Malick's *The Tree of Life* (2011) explores the perennial problem of God's absence and silence in the face of evil in a way that reflects the auteur's theological sensibilities and personal experiences of loss.[5] Malick's youngest brother, Lawrence, a gifted guitarist, committed suicide, so the film, which wrestles with the loss of a brother and son, functions both as a semi-autobiographical artistic tribute to him and as a profound theological meditation on the meaning of suffering. As Peter Leithart argues: "*The Tree of Life* is a cinematic homage to Larry Malick, a celluloid requiem."[6]

In this chapter, I will argue that Malick's impressionistic film offers a poignant and stylized[7] reflection on suffering that rejects glib answers to the mystery of evil.[8] Rather than construct a theodicy, *The Tree of Life* traces the subjective experience of suffering against the vastness of the universe and asks: is personal meaning possible in a world of unrelenting struggle, violence, and death?[9] The opening frame indicates the cosmic scope of the film: "Where were you when I laid the foundations of the earth? . . . When the morning stars sang together, and all the sons of God shouted for joy?" (Job 38:4, 7). These divine words, written in

Mark S. M. Scott, *"Where Were You?" The Problem of Evil in Terrence Malick's* The Tree of Life In: *Protestants on Screen.* Edited by: Gastón Espinosa, Erik Redling and Jason Stevens, Oxford University Press.
DOI: 10.1093/oso/9780190058906.003.0012

white script against a black backdrop, announce the film's primary motifs: suffering, meaning, and the mystery of existence. As the epigraph of the film signals, Malick's epic cinematic engagement with the problem of evil draws explicitly from the classic biblical treatment of it in the Book of Job, and Job's fictional analogues in *The Tree of Life* wrestle with God's absence as Job does. "Where were you?" softly reverberates as the driving theological question of the film. As in Job, however, the question never receives a definitive answer, but rather invites deeper faith and anticipates its ultimate resolution individually and cosmically, although the precise nature of that resolution remains as unspecified in the film as it does in the Book of Job.

The problem of evil impacts all branches of Christianity—Catholic, Orthodox, and Protestant—with equal force, but the primacy of the Book of Job in Malick's film gives it a distinctly Protestant valence, despite the ecumenical nature of the problem and his Catholicism.[10] While perhaps not a Protestant film *per se*, it explores a Protestant question in a Protestant way, especially in its explicit employment of scripture as an authoritative source for theological questions. In what follows I will discuss the problem of evil, the futility of theodicy, and the possibility of personal felicity amid individual and cosmic misfortune in dialogue with the Book of Job, the film's primary interlocutor, as well as with major philosophers of religion who situate the mystery of suffering within a wider intellectual framework.

Figure 11.2 Malick traces the subjective experience of suffering against the vastness of the universe.
DVD screen capture, fair use

Divine Absence: The Problem of Evil

In theological and philosophical discourse, the problem of evil signifies the logical friction between divine goodness and omnipotence, on the one hand, and the reality of suffering, particularly innocent suffering, on the other.[11] Typically, the problem appears as an inconsistent set of theological affirmations, often framed syllogistically. John Hick, a leading twentieth-century philosopher of religion, expresses the standard willing/able formula: "If God is perfectly good, He must want to abolish all evil; if He is unlimitedly powerful, He must be able to abolish all evil: but evil exists; therefore God is not perfectly good or He is not unlimitedly powerful."[12] The problem becomes most acute in the suffering of children, as Jürgen Moltmann remarks: "It is in suffering that the whole human question about God arises; for incomprehensible suffering calls the God of men and women into question. The suffering of a single innocent child is an irrefutable rebuttal of the notion of the almighty and kindly God in heaven. For a God who lets the innocent suffer and who permits senseless death is not worthy to be called God at all."[13]

In *The Tree of Life*, the problem of evil surfaces first through the premature death of R.L. O'Brien, the nineteen-year-old middle child of the O'Briens, whose first names we never learn. His mother collapses when she learns of his death. His father turns inward and expresses regret over the things left unsaid between them, especially his failure to atone for his abusive behavior, as we will discuss momentarily. For the O'Briens, the personal experience of evil creates a crisis of meaning because, as Peter van Inwagen notes, "evil threatens meaning. Evil threatens our ability to regard the world in which we find ourselves as comprehensible."[14] As Mrs. O'Brien reels and sinks into despair, she encounters theodicies ("theodicy" is "the technical term widely used to refer to an intellectual defense of God's goodness or existence in the face of the presence of evil and suffering").[15] The theodicies—or, put simply, theological explanations of evil—foisted on her by her priest and mother neither alleviate her grief nor allay her theological crisis, but they expose the types of specious explanations the film problematizes.

Empty Answers: The Failure of Theodicy

In a futile effort to bring comfort and meaning, Father Hayne appeals to the afterlife: "He's in God's hands," he assures Mrs. O'Brien. In other words, her son now enjoys the bliss of heaven, free from the trials and tribulations that assail human life. But the priest's assurance of heavenly beatitude, which has always been a cornerstone of Christian theodicy—hope of the resurrection of the dead—falls

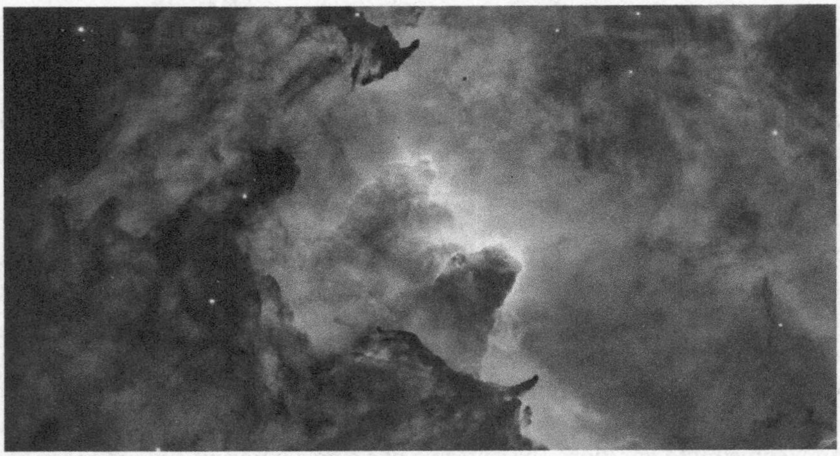

Figure 11.3 The frequent skyward shots visualize Mrs. O'Brien's search for God's presence and her questioning of God's justice in the midst of despair.
DVD screen capture, fair use

on deaf ears. "He was in God's hands the whole time, wasn't he?" she retorts.[16] She implicitly blames God's inaction, the failure to intervene, for R.L.'s death. Why were God's hands withdrawn when their son needed them most? The frequent skyward shots in the film, which Mrs. O'Brien earlier identifies as the place "where God lives," visualize her search for God's presence and her questioning of God's justice in the midst of despair.[17] The film's first theodicy—an appeal to the afterlife, where divine felicity engulfs and transforms human suffering—falls flat in the face of her joy-crushing, life-ruining grief.

Next, her mother spews a series of insidious platitudes, textbook examples of inept and unhelpful consolation: "You have your memories of him," "The pain will pass in time," "Life goes on," and, most egregiously, "You've still got the other two."[18] Mrs. O'Brien winces at the words of cold comfort, even as her mother proceeds to invoke the Book of Job: "The Lord gives and takes away; that's the way he is," she opines.[19] Her characterization of God echoes Job's famous words of fidelity in the aftermath of his affliction: "Naked I came from my mother's womb, and naked shall I return there; the Lord gave, and the Lord has taken away; blessed be the name of the Lord" (Job 1:21).[20] Like Job's infamous three friends, Mrs. O'Brien's confidants employ easy and empty answers that fail to ameliorate or illuminate her loss.

The film's invocation of the Book of Job at the outset and at several key junctures, including here, invites theological analysis of how the biblical book inflects the film. At a fundamental level, both explore the question of unjust suffering, represented by Job in the Bible and by the death of R.L. as the major chord and as the minor chords that anticipate and echo it in the later flashbacks. Both texts, then, wrestle with God's absence and silence in the midst of suffering. Job, for example, never learns why he suffers: God never reveals the cosmic backstory. Moreover, those closest to him, his wife and friends, compound his pain rather than alleviate it. His wife enjoins him to "curse God and die" (Job 2:9), which does not assuage his agony, and his friends blame him relentlessly for his plight. Similarly, in the film, Mrs. O'Brien remains in the dark about God's possible providential designs, and her husband and friends are also ineffective in their attempts to succor her grief and allay her anger toward God.

Nicholas Wolterstorff's poignant and powerful book *Lament for a Son* serves as an instructive analogue to the film, both in its expression of grief and anger toward God and in its invocation of the Book of Job.[21] Wolterstorff is a professor emeritus of philosophical theology at Yale Divinity School and of religious studies at Yale University. In 1983, his son Eric died in a mountain-climbing accident in Germany at the age of twenty-five. Wolterstorff wrote *Lament for a Son*, which consists of his journal entries in the subsequent weeks, to honor his son and to express his grief.[22] Although a notable philosopher of religion and a devout Christian, he finds that his intellect and faith are unable to reconstruct his fractured world, to give it coherence. In a beautiful passage, he describes his faith and experience of loss as incompatible puzzle pieces: "I cannot fit it together at all. I can only, with Job, endure. I do not know why God did not prevent Eric's death. To live without the answer is precarious. It's hard to keep one's footing."[23] His wording here alludes to the manner of his son's death and to the theological crisis it elicits: Eric's fall from the mountain takes his father to the edge of his faith.

Continuing the theme of unfitted puzzle pieces, he broods over the failure of theodicy to solve the problem of evil, that is, to reconcile his faith with his confounding experience of loss:

> I have no explanation. I can do nothing else than endure in the face of this deepest and most painful of mysteries. I believe in God the Father Almighty, maker of heaven and earth and resurrecter of Jesus Christ. I also believe that my son's life was cut off in its prime. I cannot fit these pieces together. I am at a loss. I have read the theodicies produced to justify the ways of God to man. I find them unconvincing. To the most agonized question I have ever asked I do not know the answer. I do not know why God would watch him fall. I do not know why God would watch me wounded. I cannot even guess.[24]

Wolterstorff's confusion and plaintive cries echo Mrs. O'Brien's anger and despair at the failure of "God's hands" and her interrogation of God. Malick sets

Mrs. O'Brien's theological questions, spoken in an interior voice-over, against a cosmic relief, an artistic depiction that parallels the Book of Job.

Later in the film, the focus shifts from Mrs. O'Brien to her boys, specifically Jack, and his experience of abuse and injustice.[25] Mr. O'Brien, an ambitious, narcissistic, conflicted character, torments his boys with subtle abuses, not only violence. Through various forms of control and manipulation, he erodes and ultimately destroys the sense of glory and wonder that their mother instills, which he later regrets when he says he made them feel shame, his shame for his personal failures. His domineering presence suffocates the family's joy and raises the problem of evil in a new register: the suffering of children, which has been a central facet of theological reflection on suffering. Jack asks God why he allows their dad to hurt them, expressing his confusion and anger. After a boy drowns, Jack confronts God with the injustices of the world in voice-over narration: "Was he bad? Where were you? You let a boy die. You let anything happen. Why should I be good if you aren't?"[26] These questions haunt him as he begins to internalize his father's violence and to externalize it through his own destructiveness.

"Where Were You?"

On the surface, the cosmological interlude between Mrs. O'Brien's grief and Jack's complicated childhood years might strike viewers as out of place or disruptive to the narrative thread, but it serves a deeper theological purpose. It takes the subjective experience of suffering and the individual instantiation of the problem of evil and recasts it onto a cosmic canvas. To Mrs. O'Brien's question "Where were you?" when her son died, and to Jack's question "Where were you?" when the boy drowned (both asked in voice-overs), the film retorts, "Where were you when God set into the motion the chain of events that eventuated in a cosmos?"[27] By transposing the problem to a cosmic key, it broadens the scope of the question, reframing the particular problems of evil that punctuate the film within the larger context of existence in a world that constantly interweaves life and death in every moment. Through its cosmogentic imagery and non-linear narrative it asks: where is God amid the interminable interplay of life and death?

In the Book of Job, God turns the tables on Job.[28] Rather than answer Job's sometimes indignant questions about God's justice in the face of his personal misfortune, he confronts Job with a series of questions: "Where were you when I laid the foundations of the earth?" (Job 38:4) and "Have you comprehended the expanse of the earth?" (Job 38:18). The long-anticipated theophany in chapters 38–41 does not dispel the mystery of suffering. Quite the contrary, it ignores Job's subjective experience and instead expands the horizon of the question to the point where it completely overwhelms him. Job says: "See I am of small account; what shall I answer you? I lay my hand on my mouth. I have spoken once, and I will not answer; twice, but will proceed no further" (Job 40:4–5). It is not, as chapter 42 makes clear, that Job deserved to suffer or that he was wrong to question God. Rather, God invites Job to trust in his power to subdue chaos, symbolized by the Leviathan, and to recognize his own epistemological limitations. Ironically, then, Job functions not as a theodicy, as most interpreters have rightly noted, but rather as a literary meditation on the mystery of suffering and the limits of human knowledge.[29]

In the epilogue, God restores the fortunes of Job (Job 42:7–17). According to the text, God gives Job "twice as much as he had before," presumably as compensation (Job 42:10). The ending, with Job's vindication and restoration, has troubled many interpreters. For some, it seems to blunt the theological point of the story: that the innocent sometimes suffer unfairly. For others, it is simply a narrative device devoid of theological significance: everyone loves a happy ending, after all, even the ancients. In any case, the picture of restoration centers on Job, not the cosmos, which was the focus of the theophany in Job 38–41. So while the Book of Job reframes the problem of evil from the personal to the cosmic, it moves from the cosmic to the personal in its resolution of the problem through the vindication and restoration of Job. *The Tree of Life*, similarly, modulates its focus from the personal to the cosmic and back to the personal. The subjective experience of suffering, then, serves as a microcosm of the macro or global problem of evil, the resolution of which it locates in personal, not cosmic, narratives.

Like the Book of Job and the film, Marilyn McCord Adams focuses on subjective restoration over global theodicies. Traditionally, theodicies would conclude with an account of the cosmic defeat of evil, appealing to heaven and hell, universalism, or some other vast eschatological vision where God destroys evil and restores creation. Adams, on the contrary, argues that the tenability of theodicy hinges not on cosmic resolution but on personal reconciliation and restoration: "I have forwarded, as criterial for solving the problem of horrendous evils, the idea that God guarantee to created persons lives that are great goods to them on the whole (in which good at least overbalance evils by a wide margin) and in which any participation in horrors is defeated within the context of the individual's life."[30] The success of theodicy, she avers, rests not on a cosmic balance-tipping toward divine goodness at the expense of lost souls but on the absolute defeat of evil in the life of each person in the beatific vision. Only the personal restoration of every soul in its particularity can outweigh and engulf the global problem of evil, she argues.

In the final narrative sequence in the film, the O'Brien family reunites amid the gently lapping waves that represent eternity, as the title of the film chapter reveals. As they walk together on the shore, the waters of chaos have been tamed, the Leviathan within Mr. O'Brien and Jack has been subdued, and wonder, glory, hope, life, and love have been restored for all. Here the focus lies not on cosmic renewal but on interpersonal and communal restoration. They look up in wonder, overwhelmed. They laugh, cry, smile, embrace, caress, kiss, and walk hand in hand, all gestures of reconciliation, unity, healing, and love, key elements of Christian eschatology, or the "last things," but framed in personal, subjective terms, rather than in impersonal theoretical categories.[31] The reunited O'Briens do not, however, speak, which perhaps suggests that no explanations or apologies are necessary in the afterlife. As Job's suffering stunned his friends into silence (Job 2:13), perhaps our future beatitude will also take our breath away, negating the need for words and explanations, theological or otherwise. Both the depths of misery and the heights of bliss defy expression, and their ineffability unites them in their profundity and singularity.[32] The reunion, then, is both solemn and celebratory.

Conclusion

The Tree of Life explores the interplay between cosmic beauty and chaos as well as between individual joy and sorrow, which raises the theological problem of God's presence and absence in a world of wonder and woe. In the boundlessness of the universe, where life and death constantly collide, what is the significance of subjective experiences of suffering? Are they minute blots on the vast canvas of the universe, discordant notes in a cosmic symphony that eludes our unhallowed ears? Or, rather than contribute to its beauty, are they impersonally absorbed by the cosmos, so that the despondent cries of the afflicted simply evaporate in the silent expanse of space, without any empathy or answer? Put in theological terms, where is God when the dreaded day of disaster comes, when the valley of the shadow of death appears? While the film avoids definitive answers, the pitfall of theodicy, it nonetheless suggests the possibility of meaning in the personal integration of suffering, either emotionally, psychologically, or eschatologically, depending on the viewer's interpretation of the O'Briens' reunion. Is it a dream? Is it a symbolic depiction of emotional and psychological acceptance? Is it a vision of the afterlife, of the future joy and harmony of heaven? That remains a mystery, as does the problem of evil. That mystery, as *The Tree of Life* and the Book of Job suggest, invites silent wonder and trust, not facile theological solutions or global theodicies.

The Tree of Life creatively employs the Book of Job to frame the problem of evil in terms of the painful mystery of God's absence in the face of evil, and to shift the perspective away from the certitude of theodicy to the possibilities of faith. Malick employs narratives of brokenness to probe into the depths of incomprehensible suffering with unflinching honesty while positing that the God who grounds all reality will ultimately put the cosmic Humpty Dumpty back together again and refit the incompatible puzzle pieces of our lives in ways that outstrip our present noetic and imaginative capacity. In this way, Malick presents an artistic entryway into the problem of evil that invokes classic Christian sources and symbolism while expanding the discourse beyond the rarefied rationalism of traditional treatments to include emotion, experience, and imagination. When submerged in the mystery of suffering, we can either opt for Stendhal's view that "God's only excuse is that he doesn't exist" or for Kallistos Ware's view that "it is not the task of Christianity to provide easy answers to every question, but to make us progressively aware of a mystery. God is not so much the object of our knowledge as the cause of our wonder."[33] Malick, in his cinematic theological artistry, opts for wonder.[34]

Figure 12.1 Robert Duvall as Sonny (Reverend E.F.) performing a self-baptism in *The Apostle*.
RGR Collection/Alamy Stock Photo

12
"Holy Ghost Power!" in Robert Duvall's *The Apostle*

Gastón Espinosa and Jason Stevens

In the post-credits of *The Apostle* (1997), Pentecostal evangelist Sonny Dewey pulls his car over to the side of the road, grabs his Bible from the dashboard, and briskly walks through a field of tall grass and crosses the yellow police tape at an accident scene. A young woman lies lifeless next to her paralyzed boyfriend, who has blood lightly streaming down the side of his mouth and tears welling up in his eyes. Seeing death on the young man's doorstep, Sonny lifts his hands in the air and prays for the young man's salvation. Then he leans through the driver's-side window and asks the young man if he wants to accept Jesus Christ as his personal lord and savior, and the young man indicates yes. Espying him, a police officer orders away Sonny, who persists. Arms crossed, the officer wryly comments, "I guess you think you accomplished something in there." Sonny retorts, "I did not put my head through that window in vain. I'd rather die here today and go to heaven than live a hundred years and go to hell." "Is that right?" the officer says with a smirk. "*Yes*, sir. *Yes*, sir," Sonny declares. As he walks away, Sonny lifts his hands in victory and prays ecstatically, "I believe in the Lord God omnipotent.... Glory!"

This powerful scene sets the tone of the film's main motifs: finding redemption, the spirit overcoming the law, and the hope, love, and salvation of Jesus breaking into a broken and hopeless world. The flashing lights of a squad car open and close the film. Despite the law seeming to eclipse hope, director Robert Duvall shows Sonny overcoming the law in the first scene with a dying young man's last words and in the final scene with another young man's decision to come forward for salvation at Sonny's last altar call before he's hauled off in handcuffs for murder. Not only do both young men find redemption, but so too does Sonny, who, with the love and support of his new multicultural congregation, musters the courage to stop running from the law and God. We see Sonny in the epilogue on a prison chain gang continuing to preach and call on his fellow prisoners to chant about "Jee-sus!"

Through its key motifs and its flawed protagonist's story arc, *The Apostle* perceptively depicts the spiritual rebirth of a man and the birth of an independent

Gastón Espinosa and Jason Stevens, *"Holy Ghost Power!" in Robert Duvall's* The Apostle In: *Protestants on Screen*.
Edited by: Gastón Espinosa, Erik Redling and Jason Stevens, Oxford University Press.
DOI: 10.1093/oso/9780190058906.003.0013

Pentecostal church in Deep South in Louisiana bayou country. Throughout, it also shows Pentecostals striving to embody the Word of God in their dress, piety, worship, music, and direct use of scripture: spoken, performed, and displayed. The film's optimistic portrayal, which contradicts decades of movies skewering evangelicals and Pentecostals, has earned both praise and harsh criticism. In a review of *The Apostle*, Amy Taubin charges that Duvall paints a utopian vision of Pentecostalism, which she deems fundamentalist and associated with the religious right, despite the fact that most Black and Latinx Pentecostals are staunch Democrats. She further claims that Duvall's decision not to portray or comment on the politics of race, abortion rights, and doctrinal purity indicates that he is masking a white racist agenda to co-opt the Black church in the South. While Taubin acknowledges Black agency and diversity, she seems unwilling to acknowledge the historical multicultural experiences of white, Black, and Latinx Pentecostal leaders and churches in American society.[1]

We argue that Duvall paints a much more complicated and nuanced portrayal than Taubin admits. Contrary to her claims, we argue that Pentecostalism differs from and should not be reduced to a form of fundamentalism, that Black, white, and Latinx Pentecostals have a long if checkered history of interracial cooperation and integration. While some segments of Pentecostalism allowed for racial separatism in the Deep South and later became associated with the religious right in the 1990s, other equally large segments of the movement did not—especially the vast majority of Black, Latinx, and working-class white Pentecostal churches and denominations, who often participated in joint special city-wide services, revivals, Bible schools, camps, and other activities. By highlighting the movement's interracial, egalitarian character and its healing redemptive power, *The Apostle* corrects a history of critical misunderstanding and cinematic misrepresentation of Pentecostalism.

Background

Writer, director, producer, and star of the film, Duvall had a long-standing interest in this project because of his identification with the region and culture. Though a Christian Scientist by upbringing and hailing from Maryland rather than the Deep South, Duvall has a longstanding interest in the southern milieu that extends back through his screen-acting career. He made his film debut playing Boo Radley in the classic *To Kill a Mockingbird* (1962), set, like many of his films, in the rural South. In addition to his roles in expensive epic films (*The Godfather*, *Apocalypse Now!*), he has taken many roles in smaller movies (*Tomorrow*, *The Great Santini*, *Rambling Rose*, *Convicts*, *Sling Blade*) because they have afforded him the opportunity to play multidimensional southern characters. He began writing the screenplay for *The Apostle* shortly after winning his Best Actor Oscar for the movie *Tender Mercies* (1983), in which he plays a country-western singer in Texas who recovers from alcoholism through the love of a Methodist woman, her son, and her church, where he is baptized. Moved by the religious themes of *Tender Mercies* and encouraged by the film's positive reception, Duvall himself undertook the writing of an original story of a southern Pentecostal evangelist because he believed this type of character had never been fully explored and represented in a mainstream film with sufficient depth and emotional texture.

His seed idea for the project came in 1970, after stumbling across a Pentecostal church during his travels through Arkansas. Tantalized by what he saw in the pulpit that evening, Duvall harbored the dream that he would someday play a dynamic preacher. With the success of *Tender Mercies* backing him, he fully immersed himself in research, conducting firsthand interviews with Penteostal ministers and on-site visits to churches throughout the region.

Duvall poured his insights into a 160-page script in which the character he had dreamed of playing in 1970 took shape as Eulis F. "Sonny" Dewey. It took Duvall nearly fourteen years to bring this story to fruition. He spent $13 million creating and marketing the film and grossed $21 million in theaters across the globe.[2] To lend authenticity and conviction to the material, Duvall recruited many Pentecostals and evangelicals to appear in the film, the most famous of them being June Carter Cash (Johnny Cash's wife), who plays Sonny's mother. Sonny's buddy Joe is played by gospel singer Billy Joe Shaver. All of the ministers seen in the film, except for Reverend Blackwell (John Beasley) and an unnamed Latina evangelist, are played by actual preachers. The blind Black evangelist preaching in the prologue is the Reverend Daniel Hickman, with whom Duvall consulted in preparation for the film. The famous Pentecostal evangelist T. D. Jakes from Alabama has a cameo as a minister preaching "Jesus power" to a congregation of Black men. Even the Black fisherman in Bayou Boutte, who let Sonny sleep in a tent on his property, is played by Brother William Atlas Cole. Duvall's own character, Sonny, is a composite of many Black and white ministers, but especially J. Charles Jessup, a white Texan radio preacher of the 1950s who ended his career in prison. Several of the parishioners in the film were non-actors recruited from local Pentecostal churches, including Zelma Loyd as Sister Johnson and Joyce Jolivet Starks as Sister Delilah, who, according to Duvall, effectively played themselves.[3] He also actively drew ideas and a song from Black Pentecostal leaders.[4]

Although the film is suspenseful, has a captivating central character with a dynamic story arc, and includes a romantic subplot (with actress Miranda Richardson as Tootsie), it is episodically structured to give the narrative sufficient breathing room to include regional details from the on-location shooting in Lafayette, Louisiana. These details do more than add "local color." They create a credible environment in which the behaviors on-screen seem to belong to a habitus, the casual practices and idioms of the everyday. This semi-documentary approach naturalizes a portrayal of southern Pentecostalism as fraternal, interracial, and salutary.

Sonny's story arc follows his spiritual journey from powerful megachurch evangelist to brokenness to redemption. The white male protagonist in *The Apostle* is seriously flawed. Sonny in some of the film's early scenes comes across as a calculating, egocentric, temperamental, and sometimes womanizing pastor who whips his Bible-belt Texas congregation into a frenzy to build his own little empire. His powerful status contrasts with his humble interracial origins, as shown in the opening credits sequence: we see Sonny as a child attending a Black-led multiracial Pentecostal church with his African American nanny (the minister is played by Reverend Hickman). As an adult, Sonny has become a spiritual prodigy and a soul-winning evangelist who preaches in white, Black, and Latinx churches and tent missions. Though he has sought to live up to the standards of the Holiness-Pentecostal movement and married the church pianist, he confesses to God and his close friends his struggles with liquor, anger, and a wandering eye. The character's moral and spiritual ambiguity are connoted by his mode of dress: on the one hand, his flashy white coat and dark sunglasses suggest a Jim Jones–style pastor, but on the other hand, they call back to the working-class Reverend Hickman's costuming in the opening credit sequence. Unlike white churches where people dress down on Sunday, in Black and Latinx Pentecostal churches people (often working class) dress up to show respect and because it was historically the only time in the week where many could wear a coat and tie and colorful dress.[5]

Story Arc

The inciting incident that sets Sonny on his spiritual journey in search of hope and redemption is his discovery that his wife, Jessie (Farrah Fawcett), and her lover, the youth director, are taking over the church and expelling him. The point of no return takes place after Sonny in a fit of drunken rage, after he gets in an argument with his wife and the lover tries to intervene, fatally smacks the youth pastor in the head with a baseball bat at his son's Little League game and flees the scene. Sonny's life now appears broken beyond redemption. Rather than face the consequences of his homicidal action, Sonny runs away and becomes a fugitive from society and God.

Like Moses fleeing to a foreign land after his killing of the Egyptian in Exodus 2:11–15, Sonny disappears into the swamps of Bayou Boutte country, Louisiana. Rather than Sonny finding his own way and saving himself, there

God speaks to him through the interactions with an African American pastor named Reverend Blackwell, whose kindness and deep spirituality reorient Sonny's life and sets him on the path to redemption. Reverend Blackwell supports Sonny's decision to pursue redemption the only way Sonny knows how: by building a church. His church's name captures his vision and Pentecostal mindset—One Way Road to Heaven Pentecostal Tabernacle. But unlike his wealthy church in Texas, his Louisiana congregation is made up of poor and working-class Blacks and whites, mostly women, children, and social misfits. In his journey to redemption, he seeks to build a congregation that embodies the same authentic Pentecostal spirituality that first drew him to the faith as a boy.

After he and his congregation stop a local racist (Billy Bob Thornton) from destroying his new church with a bulldozer, it seems like Sonny has completed his redemptive journey. In the film's climax, however, Sonny must finally face the law. At the christening of the new church, police officers arrive to haul a now compliant Sonny off in handcuffs. He buys enough time to finish his sermon and bring one more young man to salvation—someone he was mentoring, and then submits to the officers' custody. In a final shot, Duvall pans out to show Sonny leading Christian chants on a chain gang of Blacks and whites—thus keeping the spark of hope alive and the Spirit triumphing over the law.

The Apostle's great narrative feat, if it succeeds, is to persuade us that Sonny ultimately finds redemption and that Pentecostalism is not a tool of the religious right or white racist agendas, but rather a restorative influence wherever it takes deep and sincere root. The film adopts an internal point of view that observes what Pentecostals seek—not *religion*, but an experiential encounter with the Holy Spirit that serves as a catalyst for living a sincere, holy, and sanctified life, however broken or varigated—even in the Deep South, where racial strife, economic inequality, and societal divisions have been especially intense. The story shows how even a seriously flawed and broken man can be redeemed and reflect the Holy Ghost's healing power.

The Historical Context of the Holiness-Pentecostal Movement (Pentecostalism)

The larger historical and religious context for *The Apostle* is the Pentecostal movement in America. As noted in the Introduction, all Pentecostals are evangelical because they believe in having a personal, born-again relationship with Jesus Christ and affirm historical Protestant beliefs. They are not classified as fundamentalists by most experts on American religions because fundamentalists view Pentecostals as a "menace" to Christianity for promoting speaking in tongues, divine healing, prophecy, the ordination of women, and the spiritual sign gifts.[6]

Pentecostalism in the United States traces its origins back to a variety of nineteenth-century Protestant evangelical movements, including Black slave religion, revivalism, the Keswick movement, the Reformed idea of power for Christian living, dispensational premillennialism, divine healing, and especially the Holiness movement. Pentecostals stress evangelism, revival camp meetings, divine healing, and living a holy, sanctified life free from drug abuse, smoking addictions, drunkenness, immorality, and other harmful worldly practices. Two of the main founders of classical American Pentecostalism are Charles Fox Parham and William J. Seymour, former Holiness leaders. In January 1901, Parham taught the distinctive beliefs that speaking in tongues is the physical, initial evidence of baptism in the Holy Spirit (the initial evidence theory) and that the Holy Spirit wanted to restore to the modern church the spiritual gifts once practiced by the Apostles in the New Testament church (Acts 2:4; 1 Corinthians 12 and 14; Ephesians 4:11; Mark 16:17). These spiritual gifts did not cease with the death of the Apostles (cessationist theory), as fundamentalists claim, but were for all born-again, Spirit-filled Christians. These spiritual gifts include divine healing, working miracles, prophecy, words of knowledge, speaking in tongues, casting out evil spirits, and others listed in 1 Corinthians 12 and 14.[7]

Parham moved to Texas, where he set up the Houston Bible School in 1905. Seymour attended the school for less than two months but was forced to sit in the hallway due to Texas segregation laws. Seymour embraced Parham's teachings about the Holy Spirit, the spiritual gifts, and speaking in tongues, but rejected Parham's affirmation of white supremacy, eighth-day creationism, British Israelism, annihilation (the soul is extinguished after death and there is no hell or eternal punishment), and the notion that miscegenation between the races had caused God's judgment on the world via Noah's flood.

In April 1906, Seymour moved to Los Angeles and began an interracial prayer meeting that erupted into the multiethnic Azusa Street Revival, which ran daily from 1906 to 1909. People from more than twenty nationalities attended, along with foreign missionaries and other people from over fifty nations, including many Mexican Americans and Mexican immigrants. At the revival, eyewitnesses reported that the Holy Spirit possessed the participants and gave them an extra abundance of love for God and humankind and power for Christian service. They were literally filled and embodied by the Spirit and sought to act out God's words in their daily lives. Seymour's revival was appealing because he created a Christian transgressive social space where people could overcome racism, racial segregation, and unbiblical class, gender, social, and theological differences. Above all, he stressed the importance of getting people saved (born again) and helping them to identify and use their spiritual gift(s) in the service of others.[8]

Parham criticized Seymour and his revival as a "counterfeit revival" and "darky camp meetings."[9] In response, Seymour rejected Parham's leadership and created his own church and unique vision and version of Pentecostalism, one that simultaneously promoted traditional Protestant evangelical Christianity and racial integration and equality. Seymour spread his views by sending missionaries and four hundred thousand copies of his *Apostolic Faith* newspaper across the U.S. and around the world. By 1914, Pentecostalism had spread to every U.S. city with more than three thousand people and to fifty nations. Today there are more than 610 million Pentecostal, charismatic (people who believe in the spiritual gifts and tongues in traditional Protestant or Catholic denominations), and independent born-again, Spirit-filled Christians around the world, but especially in Africa, Latin America, and Asia.[10] While it is true that some churches and denominations later practiced de facto segregation (primarily in the South), others always kept Pentecostalism's original interracial character alive, especially racial-ethnic and independent churches like the ones that Sonny attended as a boy and led as an adult. In 1994, the Assemblies of God and other white Pentecostal leaders came together with Black leaders from the Church of God in Christ and other Black denominations in what was called "the Memphis Miracle," publicly apologizing for past racial biases and engaging in a foot-washing service of Black leaders. Today, Pentecostal churches are on average among the most racially diverse and integrated Protestant churches in America.[11]

Pentecostals have historically been apolitical because they believe politics is a worldly pursuit that is hopelessly corrupt. To this day, the vast majority of working-class Pentecostals who are Black, Latinx, female, immigrant, and poor white are Democrats because of their views on civil rights, economic justice, and race, class, and gender equality, though a growing number are becoming Republican after the Democratic Party switched from being pro-life or neutral on abortion to being explicitly pro-choice. Organizations like Jerry Falwell's Baptist-origin Moral Majority were not very appealing to Pentecostals because many Baptists questioned and in many cases rejected Pentecostal practices like speaking in tongues and the ordination of women.

Duvall's Departure from Prior Cinematic Representations

In its sensitivity to the historical and religious contexts of Pentecostalism, *The Apostle* corrects a long practice of cinematic misrepresentations. From the silent-film period through the post–World War II era, Hollywood had regionalized both Black and white evangelicals and Pentecostals and depicted them, with a mixture of sentiment, humor, gothic horror, and ethnographic curiosity, as simple folk. In the 1960s, beginning with Richard Brooks's Oscar-winning *Elmer*

Gantry (United Artists, 1960) and Stanley Kramer's *Inherit the Wind* (United Artists, 1960), American cinema outside the Christian film industry had begun to transform its image of white evangelicals, from being figures of rural virtue or communal conscience to hucksterism and bigotry corrupting American religion.[12] Kramer's film of *Inherit the Wind* adds a sequence absent from the original play in which local evangelicals led by their demagogic pastor follow up a "prayer meeting" with a pogrom in the town square, replete with torches and a burning effigy of the town's schoolmaster. E. K. Hornbeck (Gene Kelly), a character based on H. L. Mencken, who covered the Scopes trial for *The Baltimore Sun*, bursts into a hotel room wearing a Klansman's white hood in mock solidarity with the demonstration outside. *Elmer Gantry* features a scene in which a farmer, overcome with conviction of his sin, grasps a tent pole and begins barking like a dog to God. The film also includes Jean Simmons's Oscar-nominated role as Sharon Falconer, a character inspired by Pentecostal preacher Aimee Semple McPherson and killed off, in a stroke of poetic justice, during a fire that destroys her Angelus Temple (a double for McPherson's Foursquare Church).[13] An enduring set of cinematic motifs evolved from this period, traversing social problem films, exploitation movies, and even documentaries: the evangelist as silver-tongued bunko artist, the vigilante quoting the Bible, the southern Christian mob defending its *herrenvolk* honor, and crazed Holiness people sweating from repression.

The evangelical huckster/charlatan/hypocritic motif from *Elmer Gantry* was picked up and affirmed in a string of smaller movies like *Marjoe* (1972), *Wise Blood* (1974, from Flannery O'Connor's 1949 novel), *Oh, God!* (1977), *Fletch* (1985), *Leap of Faith* (1992), and Sacha Baron Cohen's Oscar-nominated mockumentary *Borat* (2006). Paul Thomas Anderson's frontier gothic epic *There Will Be Blood* (2007) adds to the satiric figure of the dynamic but fraudulent evangelical leader an element of Nietzschean self-deception and will to power. Pastor Eli Sunday (Paul Dano) of the Church of Revelation is the treacherous shadow self of the film's ruthless oil baron Daniel Plainview (Daniel Day-Lewis).

The image of the white southern evangelical as bigoted and hysterically, even psychopathically repressed was even transposed into genres not ostensibly connected with the region or its religion, as in Robert Aldrich's World War II actioner *The Dirty Dozen* (1967). The Bible-quoting degenerate Maggot (Telly Savalas) nearly skewers the mission when he murders a sexually alluring fräulein and gratuitously opens fire on a Black member of the team. Scriptures tattooed on his body, Robert De Niro's "white trash" ex-convict in Martin Scorsese's bayou-set thriller *Cape Fear* (1991) is the ne plus ultra of Hollywood's southern gothic rendition of evangelicals. Parodying both glossolalia and river baptism, the character dies in a swampy whirlpool while babbling "in strange tongues," his eyes, just above water, glinting like God's sword of vengeance.

Documentaries have entrenched rather than overturned these figures. Peter Adair's *Holy Ghost People* (1967) blends the southern gothic with ethnography as it immerses viewers in a Pentecostal service at Scrabble Creek Church, West Virginia, where ecstatic worshipers demonstrate their faith by handling deadly rattlesnakes.[14] Sarah Kernochan and Howard Smith's Best Documentary Oscar-winner *Marjoe* uses a modern-day Elmer Gantry, Marjoe Gortner, to debunk and demythologize his own Pentecostal ministry and practices, including the faking of miracles and tongues.[15] Heidi Ewing and Rachel Grady's *Jesus Camp* (2006) exposes the ideological indoctrination techniques at Kansas City's Pentecostal Christ Triumphant Church. It interprets Becky Fisher, a layperson who runs the youth camp, as a frightening authoritarian figure. In neglecting to distinguish the broader Pentecostal movement and evangelicalism more generally from militant and radical fundamentalism, the filmmakers seem, in the words of one commentator, "less interested in understanding evangelicals than in making secular viewers wet their drawers."[16] Indeed, the tone of the film is one of ratcheting psychological horror.

Departing from simplistically sentimental films as well as the satirical, polemical, and gothic depictions that trended after 1960, *The Apostle* redresses oversights and misinterpretations of Pentecostalism in several ways. With the exception of a four-minute segment in Robert M. Young's *Alambrista!* (1977; rereleased 2004), it is the first fiction film to acknowledge the interracial qualities of these churches and their histories. It acknowledges how much white evangelical preaching, worship style, and music have taken stylistically from Black churches. *The Apostle* goes some way to remind us of Ralph Ellison's comment that America has "a mulatto culture"—that in so many areas, especially in the popular arts and in popular religion, its culture is the result of a mingling of Black and white experiences.[17] In the film, these experiences are also formalized into bonds of religious community, and the Pentecostal quest for a Spirit-filled life fosters interracial friendships, support systems, and community. In all of this, Duvall takes the Holy Ghost theology of Sonny seriously even when the character himself falters in his spiritual vocation. He portrays the religious way of life that Sonny imperfectly though vigorously embodies, a way of life hitherto largely unknown to mass audiences and film critics.

The Apostle puts forth an implicit argument, at times problematically, that Pentecostal churches have the capacity to subdue racism; promote hope, racial integration, and healing; and promote individual and societal redemption—though sometimes this redemption is just out of reach. Duvall provides a more balanced and healthier portrayal of Pentecostals, like those depicted by African Americans themselves, such as T. D. Jakes, Denzel Washington, and Tyler Perry (the last of whom is carefully analyzed by Melanie Johnson in this book).

Reviews, Criticisms, and Rebuttal

The Apostle omits some important and distinctive features of Pentecostalism: no one in the film speaks in tongues or receives the baptism of the Holy Spirit, and there are no scenes of miraculous healing. Moreover, with one key exception that we discuss below, the film does not highlight the active roles that Pentecostal women have taken as ministers and evangelists. Three women (mother, wife, and girlfriend) are given prominent screen time, but their agency is limited and mixed; they serve in the narrative mainly to inhibit or support Sonny's personal story arc. These omissions aside, several critics praised Duvall for offering a fair and sympathetic interpretation of Pentecostalism.[18] Robert Ebert gave *The Apostle* a 4/4: "*The Apostle* is like a lesson in how movies can escape from convention and penetrate the hearts of real characters."[19] Carl Grenier argued that Duvall's movie challenges the idea that religion cannot offer resources and power to overcome everyday challenges.[20] Ed Cohen stated, "All along, the powerful spirit and flavor of the Pentecostal church are well portrayed."[21] In an interview with Mark Moring, Duvall noted that religious leaders like Billy Graham and James Robison liked the film because it promoted understanding rather than stereotypes. Duvall lamented, "But they [Hollywood] mock the interior of the United States of America, the heartland. They don't go out of their way to understand what's really there."[22]

As we have seen, perhaps the sharpest criticism came from *Village Voice* film columnist Amy Taubin.[23] She inaccurately conflates fundamentalism and Pentecostalism and argues that Duvall's *The Apostle* promotes a veiled white political agenda from the religious right to win over Blacks with a false interracial and religious narrative, even though there is not a single reference in the film to the religious right or anyone associated with it. She argues that it is absurd that any Black minister would willingly cooperate with a white evangelist. She seems completely unaware of the interracial and multicultural history of Pentecostalism and its largely apolitical nature. Furthermore, Duvall's film explicitly repudiates racism and white supremacy, promotes full racial integration, and says absolutely nothing about abortion or right-wing political issues. Taubin also misremembers the movie when she claims that Duvall has Reverend Blackwell asking Sonny for help to raise up his church after his retirement, when just the opposite is true—Sonny asks Reverend Blackwell to support and assist him in creating a new church.

Taubin reflects a long-standing history of criticism of Protestant Evangelical and Pentecostal Christianity that misunderstands the movement. We have already shown that Pentecostals are not fundamentalist, their origins are biracial and shortly thereafter multiracial, and there has always been a tradition of interracial equality, integration, and unity that ran alongside separationist and segregationist traditions in certain periods of the movement's history, especially among independent churches. We have also shown that Pentecostalism has largely remained (and still remains to this day among most segments of the movement—especially among minorities, poor whites, single working-class women, and immigrants) apolitical, and that when ordinary Pentecostals did go out to vote, they voted Democratic. Ignoring these facts makes Taubin's review come off as uneven, uninformed, and biased. In response, Duvall himself had a terse and punchy reply: "People in New York, stop reading your provincial rags and do some traveling below the Mason-Dixon line."[24]

Aside from history, the best riposte is an attentive reading of the film itself. We have selected three key scenes in the narrative. They underscore *The Apostle*'s implicit argument—that Pentecostalism is capable of subduing racism and promoting individual and societal healing—while also fully acknowledging how the film occasionally stumbles in making its case.

The scene in which the members of One Way Road to Heaven Church convert a white southern bigot (Billy Bob Thornton) is pivotal because the character embodies a history of racial violence. He and his posse have come to wreck the church, as members of the KKK destroyed Black churches in acts of terror throughout Black history even to this day. Sonny and the congregation's capacity to quell the bigot's hatred and bring him to contrition and redemption carries a lot of symbolic import for *The Apostle*'s portrayal of Pentecostalism's healing and restorative role in southern history. The scene, and a prior one in which the bigot fights Sonny hand-to-hand, gains much of its conviction from Billy Bob Thornton's choice not to condescend to the character he is playing, which could have easily been stereotyped. The "redneck" or "cracker" racist is a familiar southern trope, from classics like *To Kill a Mockingbird* and *In the Heat of the Night* through more recent films like *Mississippi Burning*, *A Time to Kill*, or *Ghosts of Mississippi*.[25] Thornton's interpretation manages to suggest that there is something tentative and self-tormenting about the bigot's attack on the church; the character clearly has a prior relationship to religion and perhaps Pentecostalism. When he is offered the chance to become reconciled to God, he is able to show his brokenness, tears running down his face, to Blacks as well as whites without being inhibited by pride or shame.

While provocatively suggesting that the love of a multiethnic Pentecostal community with faith in Jesus Christ can overcome racial hatred, the film resolves the bigot's crisis too easily. After his reconciliation, Thornton's character disappears from the narrative, introducing a story gap that awkwardly raises the possibility that he is a recidivist. Moreover, in giving attention to the spiritual quandary of the white bigot, the film misses an opportunity to show how Black Pentecostals have reckoned—socially, morally, theologically—with historical wounds of racism. The racial rift within Pentecostalism's own checkered past produced scars, which the film does not acknowledge. Indeed, the conclusion of the bigot's conversion and other moments showing racial integration and unity, in the absence of any countervailing conflicts, could lead some to inaccurately believe that southern Pentecostalism was racially integrated when there was in fact a long history of separation and in some cases segregation in some segements of the movement.

If *The Apostle* falters by minimizing the past racialization of Pentecostalism, it is more effective at portraying how Pentecostals have practiced racial integration, reconciliation, and cooperation. Early in *The Apostle*, Duvall contrasts Sonny's megachurch ministry with a Black congregation in a church and a small gathering of Latinx Pentecostals meeting in a tent. In both scenes, Sonny coleads with another preacher, T. D. Jakes in the first case and a Latinx evangelist in the second. The bridge between the scenes is Psalm 23:4, which describes the Lord (Jesus) as the Good Shepherd leading his flock through the valley of the shadow of death, a valley with which Blacks and Latinxs have been all too familiar in American history. While membership in liberal churches has waned, Pentecostalism has burgeoned, in large part because of African American and Latinx participation. The two scenes and their common verse allusion hint that Jesus as the Good Shepherd has empowered Blacks and Latinxs through their faith traditions to overcome racial injustice and socio-economic insecurity through divine love and interracial community.

In the first scene, Sonny and T. D. Jakes take turns asking questions from Bible verses, while members of the congregation, in a call-and-response pattern,

Figure 12.2 Sonny and a Hispanic evangelist march with Jesus and stomp on the Devil.
DVD screen capture, fair use

chant the name of Jesus. The camera alternates between close-up shots of the two ministers and long shots that show upturned fists thrusting into the lower part of the frame to powerfully punctuate "Jesus." Duvall captures here how Pentecostals who promoted Seymour's integrationist transgressive social space have worshiped together across racial lines throughout the twentieth century.[26]

The next scene following the "Jesus power" sermon shows Sonny and a petite but electrifying Latina evangelist offering bilingual interpretations of the 23rd Psalm.[27] With the words, "Though I walk through the valley of the shadow of death, I will fear no evil," Sonny and his female counterpart march in sync, miming a walk with Jesus that also stomps on the Devil. In this scene, Duvall captures the raw enthusiasm, power, and hope that Latinx evangelists offer immigrants living in the shadows of U.S. society. It also captures the critical role that women have played in Pentecostalism, ever since Susie Villa Valdez, Abundio and Rosa López, and countless other female and male Latinx evangelists took Seymour's Azusa Street Revival message to the urban barrios and migrant farm labor camps in the Southwest and beyond throughout the twentieth century.

The Apostle's finale summarizes its case for Pentecostalism's redemptive power to mend souls and knit together interracial communities. Sonny gives an altar call wherein his car-mechanic-turned-helper Sammy (Walter Goggins) comes forward to kneel with Sonny in a prayer for salvation. From Sammy's entry into the story, their destinies are providentially yoked. Yet Sammy's conversion is still a startling moment upon a first viewing, for he is led to God by Sonny despite having overheard the night before that he killed a man months earlier. Sonny's past sin does not break Sammy's tender faith in Sonny, as one might have expected.

Theologically, Sammy's conversion is a testament to the love of the Spirit of God radiating from Sonny and his multicultural congregation: grace operating reparatively through a broken vessel—indeed, a broken community. As Sonny exits the church, Reverend Blackwell moves toward the pulpit in a shot that mirrors him on the right with a framed picture of Jesus hanging on the wall behind him. Blackwell's face is nearly level with Jesus's, and the shallow depth of field in the shot collapses the distance between picture and foreground, enhancing the mirroring effect. Symbolically, Blackwell has become the Good Shepherd: he is coming out of retirement, assuming the leadership of the flock that Sonny—however broken and wounded—founded. One Way Road to Heaven Church will clearly survive Sonny's departure. Contrary to Taubin's interpretation, the congregation does not need a white patriarch to continue, but it does need a Christlike figure, embodied by Reverend Blackwell. The finale also mirrors the film's opening scene, in which little Sonny exits a church where another Black minister stands in the pulpit. The Black minister at the story's beginning and at its end registers authenticity; the redemption Sonny has always

Figure 12.3 Reverend Blackwell (John Beasley) moves toward the pulpit in a shot that mirrors him on the right with a framed picture of Jesus.
DVD screen capture, fair use

sought, he has found once again. And what he has found the film's final shot shows him passing on. The contrast between the white and Black convicts' compulsory labor (a prison detail reclaiming a field) and their full-throated "Jesus" chant reminds us that grace is not only freely given but freeing.

If *The Apostle* were less convincingly detailed in its depiction of present-day Pentecostal communities, its optimism—especially in light of its faulty handling of the bigot character's subplot—would seem disingenuous. Throughout, the film shows Pentecostals' fervent commitment to the priesthood of all believers, as Seymour had radically understood it. Sonny's bouts with God early in the narrative could be misunderstood on a first viewing. Shouting at God in his upstairs bedroom loudly enough that he awakens the neighbors, Sonny prays, pleads, and even argues: "I'm mad at you, God!" Yet Sonny is not being irreverent or delusional (like *The Night of the Hunter*'s mad preacher, Harry Powell, addressing the Almighty). He is living out Pentecostals' belief that a person can honestly speak to God anywhere and anytime regardless of their social station. Just as there is no human institution standing between God and the individual, whomever they may be, so too there should be no institution or color line standing between those who seek and love Jesus Christ. Duvall is careful to underscore that belief in the egalitarian polity of the churches and revivals we see in the film.

Figure 12.4 Sonny, Bible in hand, standing by his church bus painted with the inscription, One Way Road to Heaven.
RGR Collection / Alamy Stock Photo

Throughout, *The Apostle* also shows Pentecostals striving to embody the Word. They do so in their dress (Sunday-best clothing at church), music (hymns from "I Have Decided to Follow to Jesus" to "Victory Is Mine" to "I'll Fly Away"), piety (in the congregation's prayers, charity, and self-discipline), worship (call-and-response; ecstatic dancing, clapping, and exclamations of rejoicing during Sammy's conversion), and direct use of scripture, both spoken (on the radio, in the pulpit, in revival) and performed (Sonny and his fellow evangelist marching as they enunciate the 23rd Psalm). They also proudly display scripture: "Jesus" is stenciled on a banner stretching between Sonny and T. D. Jakes, and "One Way Road to Heaven," alluding to John 14:6 and Matthew 7:13–14, is painted on the side of the church bus and on a big, skyward-pointing wooden arrow affixed to the church front. It is often noted that Protestants use the Bible devotionally, moving from the text to inward contemplation. Pentecostals, however, also want to make the Word, as witnessed by the Spirit, tangibly felt and present in the world. This is no more powerfully demonstrated than when an African American member (Sister Johnson) of One Way Road to Heaven Church places her Bible in the path of the bigot's bulldozer. "That book," as she and the congregation call it, is not functioning as a magical talisman against evil; it is a physical symbol of the Gospel (*evangelion*, "good news"—the notion that Jesus can save even the most horrible of sinners) that Bibles contain, and which hate cannot eradicate.

Conclusion

In this chapter we have made two key arguments. First, we argue that the main motifs in *The Apostle* are finding redemption, the spirit overcoming the law, and Pentecostal spirituality breaking into a broken and hopeless world with love, hope, healing, and salvation. Second, we argue that Duvall paints a complicated and nuanced—if at times incomplete—portrayal of interracial Pentecostalism, accentuating its long history of interracial cooperation and integration. In fact, when compared to other Protestant traditions, Pentecostalism has a much longer history of promoting racial equality, integration, women in ministry, and voting Democratic than most realize.

The Apostle was a watershed for cinematic representations of evangelicalism and Pentecostalism. In 1997, Duvall became the first actor in thirty-seven years to be nominated in the category of Best Actor for playing an evangelical minister. The last such nominee was winner Burt Lancaster for *Elmer Gantry* in 1960. While the images that *Elmer Gantry* and *Inherit the Wind* imprinted still persist, *The Apostle* helped to effect a change in American movies comparable to what scholar Harvey Cox's *Fire from Heaven* accomplished for Pentecostalism in academic studies.[28] It opened the gates for a much fuller, more nuanced, and more complicated picture not only of Pentecostalism but also of popular religiosity and a global religious movement. *The Apostle*'s critical and financial success began to pry open Hollywood's eyes to a renaissance and resurgence in evangelical filmmaking that has since developed the movie capital's serious interest in faith-friendly production and marketing. The best and perhaps the most moving films are yet to come.

Figure 13.1 Martin Luther King Jr. (David Oyelowo) leads a religious coalition to the Edmund Pettus Bridge in *Selma*.
AF archive/Alamy Stock Photo

13

Sinner or Saint? Martin Luther King Jr. and the Civil Rights Movement in *Selma*

Julius H. Bailey

Previous portrayals of Martin Luther King Jr. have often elevated the civil rights leader to an almost saintlike status, with written accounts usually reading more like hagiographies. The director of *Selma* (2014), Ava DuVernay, an African American woman and a Catholic, strikingly departs from these idealized representations in her reenvisioning of the pivotal events that took place in Selma in 1965. Like no other previous film, DuVernay's *Selma* depicts King's human flaws and engages the range of viewpoints of those in his inner circle. In her artistic interpretation of the history leading to the Selma-to-Montgomery march (1965), DuVernay rearranges the order of events and casts President Lyndon B. Johnson in an adversarial role that may belie his actual position on the issues but nonetheless propels the narrative forward with King as the imperfect but courageous protagonist of the story.

However, in her efforts to humanize King, DuVernay provides only fleeting glimpses of the powerful place that Christianity played in King's life and so thoroughly informed his leadership of the movement. The film shows little to nothing of King's own personal spiritual life. He is never shown privately praying, singing, or reading the Bible. His religious life is seemingly conflated with the public performance of marches, sermons, and speeches. In many ways, religion itself remains on the periphery of the broader narrative of *Selma*. Its inclusion in the film feels more like a prerequisite that must be included rather than an integral part of the plot and an essential aspect of who King was. Despite its best intentions, the film, as W. E. B. DuBois put it years earlier, catches the "jingle but not the music, the body but not the soul" of Black Protestantism.[1]

Historical Context

Although the topic is sometimes a matter of debate, most scholars argue the civil rights movement was sparked by the 1954 *Brown v. Board of Education* Supreme Court decision to desegregate public schools on the basis of race

Julius H. Bailey, *Sinner or Saint? Martin Luther King Jr. and the Civil Rights Movement in* Selma In: *Protestants on Screen.* Edited by: Gastón Espinosa, Erik Redling and Jason Stevens, Oxford University Press.
DOI: 10.1093/oso/9780190058906.003.0014

and by Rosa Parks's refusal to give up her seat on a segregated bus to a white man in Montgomery, Alabama, in 1955. Parks's courageous actions led to the Montgomery bus boycott, which ran from December 5, 1955, to November 14, 1956. Although accounts often highlight the spontaneity of Parks's actions, it is important to note that she was a longtime member of the National Association for the Advancement of Colored People (NAACP, founded in 1909) and was no stranger to activism. The Montgomery bus boycott thrust a young Black preacher, Martin Luther King Jr., onto the national stage as the spokesperson for the civil rights movement.

Martin Luther King Jr. was born in Atlanta in 1929. Both his father and grandfather had been Baptist preachers and community leaders. It was within this legacy that King developed his own oratorical style, which became known for its powerful tones and inflections, and sermons that could intricately interweave Christian scriptures and patriotic imagery to call Americans to live up to their better selves. His spiritual, educational, and intellectual journeys were intimately intertwined. After studying sociology at Morehouse College, he prepared for the ministry at Crozer Theological Seminary before proceeding to earn his Ph.D. in theological studies from Boston University. King studied Walter Rauschenbusch's writings on the Social Gospel (e.g., *A Theology of the Social Gospel*, 1917), Protestant theologian Reinhold Niebuhr's critique of pacifism in *Moral Man and Immoral Society* (1932), as well as Mahatma Gandhi's belief in nonviolent resistance (satyagraha). It was the last perspective that shaped King's own understanding of the ways that nonviolently protesting unjust laws could awaken the consciousness of the broader American public and lead to change.[2]

Though primarily taking place in the 1950s and 1960s, the civil rights movement was within a long history of the efforts of African Americans to gain equal rights in America. The Fourteenth and Fifteenth Amendments to the Constitution gave African Americans equal protection under the law as well as the right to vote. However, the rise of Jim Crow segregation laws in the southern United States prohibited Blacks from realizing those rights, especially after the 1896 *Plessy v. Ferguson* Supreme Court decision, which upheld the constitutionality of racial segregation laws for public facilities provided that the facilities were equal in quality ("separate but equal"). President Woodrow Wilson caved to pressure from fellow southerners to segregate government offices across the nation. Southern segregationist practices created "whites only" facilities, businesses, and schools and often implemented arbitrary requirements for African Americans to vote, such as literacy tests, poll taxes, and voter vouchers—all of which are depicted in *Selma*. In 1954, the *Brown v. Board of Education* Supreme Court decision made segregation illegal in public schools, but there was resistance to implementing the ruling. For example, in 1957, the Little Rock Nine, a group of

African Americans seeking to attend a formerly all-white school in Arkansas, were turned away by the Arkansas National Guard. It was not until President Dwight D. Eisenhower ordered federal troops to escort them in that the African American students were able to attend the school. In the 1960s, young African Americans led by Ella Baker, Diane Nash, John Lewis, and many others sat in at lunch counters and other facilities to protest segregation in restaurants. These efforts and their leadership led to the formation of the Student Nonviolent Coordinating Committee (SNCC).[3]

Selma addresses a particularly violent moment in the history of the civil rights movement sometimes referred to as "Bloody Sunday." In the effort to spur the passage of a voting rights act, protesters planned to march from Selma to Montgomery, Alabama, on March 7, 1965. Those who marched were met on the Edmund Pettus Bridge with a large contingent of police officers who prevented them from moving forward and viciously beat and teargassed the protesters, as depicted in the film. While some of these events are placed in a different order to heighten the drama, *Selma* eloquently captures the tenuousness of life that many African Americans faced during that historical moment.

It is also important to note the central role of Black churches in the civil rights movement. From the arrival of African slaves on the shores of America in 1619, African Americans have had a complicated relationship with Christianity. For some it was the religion of the slave masters and should be shunned at all costs, but for other African Americans the Christian message of obedience and subservience propagated by slaveowners was transformed into a message of hope and deliverance, especially after the Second Great Awakening of Christianity from upstate New York to the Deep South. Racism and segregation were not only a part of secular American society. Many nineteenth-century churches remained either whites-only or relegated Black congregants to a separate seating section. Accounts from the era describe white preachers refusing to hold Black babies during baptism, making Black congregants wait until all the white members had taken communion before being able to take it themselves, and in some cases even creating separate cemeteries based on race. However, there was also a small group that defied the racial conventions of the South and created interracial churches and fellowships where the color line was reported to have been "washed away by the blood of Jesus."[4]

This generally hostile climate toward African Americans led to the formation of African American churches completely independent of white control and leadership. In November 1787, Richard Allen and other Black lay leaders of St. George's Methodist Episcopal Church in Philadelphia were pulled up off their knees during prayer for being in a whites-only section of the church and directed to pray in the back of the church. As a result, they and their followers left the church as a body and formed the African Methodist Episcopal Church in 1816. Like the AME Church, the African Methodist Episcopal Zion Church emerged in the 1790s as a response to discriminatory treatment in Methodist Episcopal churches in New York; the "Zion" was added to their denominational name much later, in 1848, to distinguish them from the AME Church. The Colored Methodist Episcopal Church was formed from the Methodist Episcopal Church, South in 1844 after disagreements over doctrine and the slavery issue. The first African American Baptist churches were established even earlier with the African Baptist, or "Bluestone," Church in Mecklenburg, Virginia, in 1758 and the Silver Bluff Baptist Church, founded in South Carolina by George Liele between 1773-1775[4]. Today, the National Baptist Convention, U.S.A. remains the largest Black denomination.

Many other Black Protestant churches in turn spun off to create their own small denominations and traditions. In 1906, the former Louisiana native William J. Seymour moved to Los Angeles and led the Azusa Street Revival, which attracted Blacks from across the country, including Charles M. Mason, who founded the largest Black Pentecostal denomination in America, called the Church of God in Christ (COGIC). Seymour's revival helped birth not only COGIC but also the American and global Pentecostal movements—the legacy of which we see portrayed in Robert Duvall's movie *The Apostle*. Key civil rights leaders came out of this Pentecostal tradition, including James Baldwin. In fact, the last place King spoke before his assassination was Mason Temple, the headquarters of the Church of God in Christ, where he gave his famous "I've Been to the Mountaintop" speech. Although many contemporary people are surprised to learn about the critical role in the Civil Rights Movement that the Black church played in the Civil Rights Movement, they shouldn't be. Due to a lack of economic investment and glass ceilings in politics, education, law, and media, the Black church provided one of the few Black-owned and -led spaces where it could nurture future Black leaders, engage in advocacy, and create capacity-building skills that could easily be transferred into the political and civic arena. So it was with Martin Luther King Jr.[5]

Given this history, it is not surprising that Black churches played such a central role in the civil rights movement. However, the boundaries between the sacred and the secular varied between African Americans. While many in the civil rights movement saw themselves as engaging in faith-based activism, others saw themselves as strictly advancing racial and human rights. The march from Selma to Montgomery was a key moment in the civil rights movement. With Blacks having secured access to public accommodations, the passage of the Voting Rights Act would give unprecedented access to voting for African Americans. The Selma march would be one of King's last mainstream efforts for racial equality as he turned his attention to economic issues and the Poor People's Campaign.

Plot Summary and Narrative Analysis

The film opens with Martin Luther King Jr. (David Oyelowo) practicing his speech for the Nobel Peace Prize award ceremony in Oslo in December 1964 with his wife, Coretta Scott King, and closes approximately three months later in Montgomery, Alabama. This is a key moment in the civil rights movement as King continues to emerge as a national figure. The dialogue between husband and wife is significant because it raises a number of issues about the perception of Black preachers and foreshadows King's assassination. King is concerned that "people back home" will think that he is living "high on the hog" because he will be wearing an ascot onstage during the award ceremony. King and Coretta speculate about their possible life in the future after leaving the leadership of the movement. King plans to be the pastor of a small church in a college town where he would teach a class, with "maybe the occasional speaking engagement." Coretta says that she will pay all of the bills, including the mortgage on their very own house. King replies, "Perfect." Both quickly snap back to reality as each seemingly realizes that this quiet, peaceful future that they dared to imagine, if only briefly, would almost certainly never come to be.

The narrative goal of the film is achieving the Voting Rights Act, and DuVernay makes the challenges facing African Americans seeking to vote in the South tangible through the experiences of individuals. An older African American woman, Annie Lee Cooper (Oprah Winfrey), demonstrates the courage that it took for many African Americans to try to register to vote. As she summons her strength to go to the window to register, Cooper has to endure the white clerk saying, "Get on up now. I ain't got all day" and accusing her of "stirring up a fuss." The clerk tells her to recite the preamble to the Constitution, and when she has successfully completed that task, he asks her how many county judges there are in Alabama. Once she has addressed that question, he asks her to name them. This scene powerfully exemplifies the arbitrary nature of the barriers that many African Americans faced when they sought to vote as well as the lengths to which white gatekeepers would go to prevent them from doing so.

After the stage is set with these powerful scenes, Martin Luther King Jr. is established as the protagonist who seeks to have the Voting Rights Act passed. There are a number of obstacles in his way, including President Lyndon B. Johnson; J. Edgar Hoover and the FBI; Governor George Wallace of Alabama; Sheriff Jim Clark of Dallas County, Alabama; state troopers; the legal system; members of SNCC, particularly James Forman; and dissenting members of his own inner circle, including Diane Nash, Ralph Abernathy, Andrew Young, C. T. Vivian, James Bevel, Hosea Williams, and James Orange. While some historical accounts portray King as the saintly leader of the civil rights movement, *Selma* depicts a flawed figure who in some ways is his own worst enemy, with varied vices and weaknesses including smoking, snapping at his wife, jealousy, insecurity, indecisiveness, and adultery.

Equally revealing are the depictions of the meetings between Martin Luther King Jr. and President Lyndon B. Johnson (Tom Wilkinson). It is in these exchanges that King urges Johnson to support the civil rights movement, particularly the rights of African Americans to vote. In these conversations in the film, King points out that though there are laws on the books giving African Americans the right to vote, their enforcement is another matter, with Black voters being kept off the voting rolls through, as he says in the film, "systematic intimidation and fear." King presses Johnson to allow African Americans to "vote unencumbered." In response, Johnson is intent on seeing how the current legislation plays out before addressing other civil rights issues: "Let's not start another battle when we haven't even won the first." Johnson seeks to direct King's attention to the eradication of poverty. However, King will not be deterred. He counters that the issue of voting cannot wait. Here the film accurately portrays King's historical position. Because thousands of racially motivated murders continued to take place in the South without the white murderers being held accountable, perhaps most dramatically illustrated by the case of the Birmingham church bombing, King felt action could not be delayed. Those who perpetuated the violence, King asserted, were protected by a white electorate and all-white juries because African Americans were prevented from registering to vote. In the film, when Johnson remains unmoved, King says after the meeting, "Selma it is." As a Black Protestant minister, King is seemingly obligated to respect and seek the sanction of the earthly leaders that God has put into power, such as the president. However, after making the attempt, King appeals to a higher divine law that he believes will lead to justice for oppressed African Americans.

King's perspective and approach continued to evolve as the civil rights movement grew. As a Protestant, King believed in the "priesthood of all believers," a person's individual standing before God, and he placed an emphasis on the Bible as the central source of authority in one's public and private life. King was also influenced by Protestant thinkers like Walter Rauschenbusch, whose Social Gospel theology resonated with King's father's teachings in his church. The Social Gospel sought to transform society for the better, and King was drawn to Rauschenbusch's prophetic emphasis on social issues and Jesus's teachings about addressing the needs of the less fortunate. King wrote that "Rauschenbusch gave to American Protestantism a sense of social responsibility that it should never lose."[6] As Taylor Branch observed in his book *Parting the Waters*, Rauschenbush's *Christianity and the Social Crisis* was among the few books that "King would ever cite specifically as an influence on his own religious beliefs."[7] King also considered theological positions that he was previously unfamiliar with, like those in Reinhold Niebuhr's *Moral Man and Immoral Society*, which King said made him "aware of the complexity of human motives and the reality of sin on every level of man's existence."[8] King modeled his vision of nonviolent resistance after Mahatma Gandhi's work in India. He wrote, "As I delved deeper into the philosophy of Gandhi, my skepticism concerning the power of love gradually diminished, and I came to see for the first time that the Christian doctrine of love, operating through the Gandhian method of nonviolence, is one of the most potent weapons available to an oppressed people in their struggle for freedom."[9] King was also influenced by African American Protestant philosophers like the ordained Baptist minister Howard Thurman. Thurman mentored several young ministers, including King. King brought Thurman's *Jesus and the Disinherited* (1949) with him during the Montgomery bus boycott because he was spiritually edified by the book's argument that Jesus preached to the oppressed and called them to a faith and unconditional love that would allow them to overcome their oppression.[10]

Unfortunately, in the film we see little to none of this vibrant and complex Black Protestant legacy that informed King's thinking. Instead there is often a more Catholic rendering of his viewpoints. After the church bombing that killed four African American girls, in the film King's sermon does not address the role of God or Jesus but focuses on the encouragement that the children provide to continue on in the movement. "We see children become victims of one of the most vicious crimes ever perpetuated against humanity within the walls of their own church. They are sainted now. They are the sainted ones in this quest for freedom. And they speak to us still. They say to us, to all of us, all colors and creeds, that we must do this." The ecstatic call-and-response characteristic of many Black church services is also largely absent, although this might be due to the somberness of the moment. The Black congregations portrayed in the film remain mostly quiet and reserved in a high-church fashion.

Although President Johnson signed the Civil Rights Act of 1964, which prohibited segregation in public places and banned employment discrimination based on race, color, religion, sex, or national origin, he is depicted as a conflicted figure. While he continually asserts that civil rights are a priority of his administration, he appears torn about how to make that a reality without upsetting various constituencies such as southerners and Governor Wallace. Given the choice between King and someone he sees as more militant, like Malcolm X, Johnson is portrayed as seeing King as the lesser of two evils.[11] The closed-door meetings between President Johnson and various white advisors demonstrate how many directions he was being pulled in and the various perspectives he was considering. When King insists on moving forward with the march from Selma to Montgomery, President Johnson says that he is tired of King's demands and calls for FBI director J. Edgar Hoover, presumably to have him put into motion his plan to discredit King. Although Hoover did have King under surveillance, it is unclear whether Johnson actually sanctioned the actions. In one exchange, Hoover calls King a "political and moral degenerate." He tells Johnson that he "can shut him down permanently" or go after his wife. Since there is already tension in the home, he estimates that he can "weaken the dynamic" and "dismantle the family."

The collective nature and divergent perspectives of those involved in the civil rights movement are conveyed throughout the film. As King and his fellow activists arrive in Selma, the typed words appear on-screen: "King arrives in Selma, AL with Abernathy, Young, Orange and female agitator, Diane Nash. 10:12 am. LOGGED." This is a striking way of demonstrating the ways participants in the civil rights movement were surveilled by the United States government, but it also communicates information to the audience about the movement's activities and the role of participants other than King in furthering the cause. Rather than being the sole leader of the movement, King arrives in Selma with much of the necessary groundwork already in place, done by other people. For example, one way of testing the waters is the plan for King to attempt to register at a whites-only hotel, which leads to him being violently punched by a white bystander. In the meetings of the civil rights activists, the film shows the varied viewpoints within the movement as they consider the present situation and future directions to take. The most pressing issues, they decide, swirl around obstacles to voting, such as people having their name and address published in the newspaper if they try to register to vote, poll taxes extending back several years, and voting vouchers requiring the support of a currently registered voter.

One of the ongoing tensions in the story is between the Southern Christian Leadership Conference (SCLC) and the students in the Student Nonviolent Coordinating Committee. Diane Nash and other students had staged sit-ins and other nonviolent protests. Ella Baker had directed a number of branches of the NAACP. While King had encouraged the students to organize, some in SNCC felt that the older activists were now trespassing in their territory and swooping in to take all of the glory after they had already done the hard work of laying the foundation. Although both SCLC and SNCC fought for civil rights, *Selma* shows that SNCC pushed to raise Black consciousness over time, while King, as quoted in the film, sought to "negotiate, demonstrate, and resist." As the film illustrates, King pressed for a public confrontation in which the drama of the injustice would be broadcast to large audiences over television, raising white consciousness.

While some accounts of the civil rights movement emphasize its spontaneity, *Selma* demonstrates just how well planned the marches were. While "Bull" Connor, the commissioner of public safety for the city of Birmingham, had opposed the civil rights movement by violently controlling the streets, King was confident that Sheriff Jim Clark's control of only the courts provided "clear avenues of approach to a defined battle zone." Concentrating on one building, the Selma courthouse, King believed, offered the "perfect stage." Although nonviolent resistance required strict discipline, the outcomes of the demonstrations were impossible to predict, as evidenced in the film by the scene at the courthouse that witnesses one older African American gentleman being shoved to the ground while Annie Lee Cooper hits the sheriff with a rock and is violently wrestled away.

In the aftermath of the protest, King and other activists are arrested. Far from the unflagging leader he is often memorialized as being, the film shows King as conflicted and at times almost despondent. In the jail, King again struggles with the moral implications of placing people in harm's way as well as the effectiveness of the movement. He shares with Ralph Abernathy (Colman Domingo), a Baptist minister, co-founder of the Southern Christian Leadership Conference, and a close friend and advisor, the dilemma that while African Americans can fight to have a seat at a table and eat at a lunch counter, it may not matter if they cannot read the menu or do not have the money to buy the burger. King asks, "Is that equality?" In this way, King grapples with the intersectionality of race, socioeconomic status, and education—all of which served as obstacles for African Americans seeking to have the same opportunities as other Americans. King describes a string of racially motivated assassinations: Medgar Evers, who was murdered in his driveway; George Lee and Herbert Lee, who were not related, were killed six years apart for their involvement in SNCC and their efforts for Black voter registration; and Lamar Smith, who was shot and killed on a courthouse lawn by a white man because he had encouraged Blacks to vote in a recent election. King states, "Man stands up only to be struck down. What happens to the people they led? What are we doing, Ralphy? They are going to ruin me so that they can ruin this movement." King is painted as a man in despair and unsure of the moral basis for the movement and the way forward. It is Ralph Abernathy who in that moment ministers to the minister by encouraging King with scripture: "Look at the birds of the air, that they do not sow nor reap, nor gather into barns, yet your Heavenly Father doth feed them. Are you not worth much more than they? And who of you by being worried can add a single hour to his life?" King immediately recognizes the passage as Matthew 6:27. Abernathy comforts him with the understanding that while King may not know what the future holds, his Heavenly Father does and will take care of him. Falling short of the iconic assurance conveyed by his famous "I Have a Dream Speech," King is portrayed as the one who needs to be comforted in his time of need. When Coretta comes to visit him in jail after her meeting with Malcolm X, King snaps at her that she sounds "enamored" with Malcolm X. King apologizes, but the image fittingly captures the depiction of him as a determined but flawed individual.

With King out of town, the protesters stage a night march, and with no cameras filming, the police take advantage of the situation and savagely beat the civil rights activists. In one of the most violent scenes in the film, Jimmie Lee Jackson is shot and killed by a white trooper in a restaurant after seeking refuge from the beatings there. Rather than dying on the floor of the diner, as depicted in the film, accounts describe Jackson making it back to the street, where he was beaten further; he died a week later in the hospital. In any case, Jackson was seen as a martyr whose sacrifice galvanized the civil rights movement. As James Baldwin has shown, those who died to advance the cause were often seen as being in the lineage of Jesus and the early first-century martyrs of the Christian church.[12] Here again it is striking that it is not King who is portrayed as Christlike but Jimmie Lee Jackson. Once back in town, King has recovered from his despondency and has returned to the role of comforter meeting with Jackson's grandfather and consoling him. King returns to the theme of sacrifice in his sermon at Jackson's funeral service in the film. "Our lives are not fully lived if we are not willing to die for those we love and for what we believe," he says. "We will not let your sacrifice pass in vain, dear brother. We will not let it go! We will finish what you were after! We will get what you were denied!" And "We will win what you were slaughtered for!"

Selma thus seeks to illustrate just how violent the 1960s were and how precarious life was for many African Americans, including Martin and Coretta King. Even with the film's attention to white violence and to the harassment of King and his family, it still portrays King as an inherently flawed and "sinful" leader of the movement. One of the tensest scenes in *Selma* shows Martin and Coretta listening to a tape, presumably sent by Hoover, of King allegedly having sex with another woman. While Coretta believes it is not King on the tape, she asks him if he loves her, and then she asks, "Do you love any of the others?" King says no, but by answering the question implicitly admits to having affairs. Recently released FBI recordings from the time period allege that King had affairs with multiple women. However, no one woman has been directly identified as being on the tape. With this, the film returns to the theme of the recurrent government efforts to undermine the civil rights movement. However, even with that acknowledgment, King remains a humanly flawed prophet.

While the film attributes King's absence from the first Selma march to his having to address marital issues at home, there is no indication in the public record that this was the case. Rather, there was a series of logistical issues that arose and prevented his attendance. In King's absence, the other leaders are shown moving forward with the first attempted march from Selma to Montgomery. In the aftermath of a violent encounter between the marchers and law enforcement officers on the Edmund Pettus Bridge, divergent perspectives within the movement are once again displayed. Some suggest getting guns and fighting back that way, but others urge calm over fears of a broader retaliation against African Americans. While some in the civil rights movement were engaging in faith-based activism, others in the movement self-identified as secular humanists who focused on ethics, empiricism, and humane living without necessarily embracing the supernatural aspects of Christianity. This perspective is demonstrated by Andrew Young telling those seeking to use weapons, "I ain't talking about the Bible. I ain't talking what's right by God. I am talking facts. Cold, hard facts!" This appeal is not to the authority of the Bible or a divine law but to a secular and rational way of approaching the situation. Embedded in this scene is seemingly DuVernay's critique of those who embraced the supernatural rather than a pragmatic solution in the natural realm.

In the wake of the first failed attempted march, King calls for white Americans, particularly white clergy, to join the movement. White clergy like Boston Unitarian Universalist James Reeb, who is played in the film by Jeremy Strong, answered the call. The FBI log that again appears on the screen provides the exposition: "King leads march against Wallace's orders. Clergy present. One-third Caucasian participants. 9:35 am. LOGGED." With the white presence, the troopers stand down and withdraw. When King kneels, the entire group follows suit until he stands up and makes his way back through the crowd returning to Selma. The leadership team meets together after the aborted march to express their opinions. Many of those present are angry with King. James Forman from SNCC insists that it was the wrong move to make—especially for not taking advantage of the white presence, because "they are not going to be around here for long. They never are." The student derisively refers to King and his associates as "De Lawd and his disciples." For King, the central issue was the potential violence that might have ensued on the march, and this is his apparent concern in the movie as well. Some of the white clergy are shown feeling misled by King. One says, "He betrayed trust. He called and we came, and he didn't fulfill his own call." James Reeb responds that King may have "tapped into what's higher. What's true [when] God is guiding you." Shortly after giving this response, Reeb and his fellow clergy are depicted in the film being attacked and killed by white Klansmen. For the most part, white ministers are portrayed as unerringly good liberal servants for the cause, as highlighted by the film's concluding description of Unitarian Universalist Viola Liuzzo's death at the hands of white supremacists. Liuzzo (who was killed on her way home from Montgomery) is thus granted martyrdom alongside the central figures in the movement even though her character only appears briefly in the film. Archbishop Iakovos, a Greek Orthodox leader, is also depicted as walking arm-in-arm with others across the bridge in Selma.

Despite the fractured depiction of Black Protestants, the film ultimately shows King's inner circle rallying and coalescing around him, particularly in moments of crisis. This time it is John Lewis, who served as chairman of the Student Nonviolent Coordinating Committee starting at the age of twenty-five.

Figure 13.2 King kneels and prays at the Edmund Pettus Bridge before deciding to turn back, a decision that divides the leadership team.
DVD screen capture, fair use

Lewis reminds King of what he said in a speech shortly after a particularly violent encounter with whites during the SNCC Freedom Rides: "We would triumph because there was no other way. Fear not. We have come too far to turn back now."

The conclusion of the film ties up the remaining plot points. The final battle is a legal case, *SCLC v. State of Alabama*, over the right to march from Selma to Montgomery. After a judge approves the five-day march from Selma to Montgomery, the activists make their preparations at Brown Chapel, highlighting the Black church as a key site of planning for the movement. President Johnson's redemption occurs in his final meeting with Governor Wallace. Johnson requests that Wallace allow Blacks to vote undeterred, but the governor remains entrenched in his position, insisting that Blacks would never be satisfied. Johnson uses a line that King had used on him, asking Wallace whether he wanted people to remember him saying, " 'Wait,' or 'I can't,' or, 'Uh, it's too hard.' " When Wallace is unmoved, Johnson concludes, "I'll be damned if I'm going to let history put me in the same place as the likes of you." Johnson is next shown speaking about the new law that was passed. King's penultimate scene is a discussion regarding his security detail during the march, in which he states, "I'm no different than anybody else. I want to live, love, and be happy. But I'll not be focusing on what I want today. I'm focused on what God wants." Because King's heirs did not allow his speeches to be used in the film, this is a rough paraphrasing of the final sermon that King gave before his assassination in which he spoke of having been to the "mountaintop" and looked over to see the promised land but stated, "I may not get there with you." The film concludes with historical footage of the march intercut with brief biographical synopses of the main individuals, but the final image of Oyelowo as King shows him standing before the Alabama state capitol,

Figure 13.3 Oyelowo as King preaching
Pictorial Press Ltd / Alamy Stock

his eyes closed and his right hand swung heavenward, shouting, "Glory, glory! Hallelujah!" This introduces the film's Oscar-winning song, "Glory," which plays over the end credits.

Throughout the film, music plays an important role in communicating King's spirituality and that of the larger movement. When Coretta takes issue with Martin's seemingly casual statement that Selma is "as good a place to die as any," King seeks comfort by calling the famous gospel singer Mahalia Jackson to sing to him over the phone, as he wishes to "hear the voice of the Lord." Jackson sings Thomas A. Dorsey's hymn, "Take My Hand, Precious Lord," which she would later sing at King's funeral.[13] Jackson was an active participant in the civil rights movement, including the March on Washington, and was known to sing to King after particularly hard days. John Legend and Common's song "Glory" bridges R&B and rap with the gospel music of the civil rights era (portrayed so eloquently in George T. Nierenberg's Oscar-winning 1982 documentary, *Say Amen Somebody*). As "Glory" is played over the ending credits, Common's lyrics proclaim, "Freedom is like religion to us," which gains resonance from Common's role within the film as SCLC leader and preacher James Bevel. From the outset, DuVernay wanted to emphasize "B-sides and underground hits." When Black Selma residents are walking to the courthouse to attempt to vote, Sister Gertrude Morgan's "I Got the New World in My View" (1957) can be heard. Like so many spirituals, the song operates at a number of levels and holds multiple meanings. The song signals an anticipation of a "new world" here on earth with new opportunities, but it also foreshadows the eventual return of Jesus and a new world with him, as promised throughout the New Testament. For the violent confrontation on the initial Selma march on the Edmund Pettus Bridge, Martha Bass's "Walk with Me" is playing in the background. This spiritual also has multiple meanings, as the activists are literally walking across the bridge, but the lyrics allude to Jesus walking alongside and protecting and guiding them, as described in Psalm 23:4: "Even though I walk through the darkest valley, I will fear no evil, for you are with me, your rod and your staff, they comfort me." At the close of the film, DuVernay included a medley of "This Little Light of Mine/Come by Here," which was taken from an actual mass for Jimmie Lee Jackson during that time period.[14] Music is an important element of *Selma* because it played a number of functions in the movement: promoting unity, speaking words aloud that invoked God's aid, stimulating defiance, and soothing the brokenhearted.

Criticisms

Although some depictions of the civil rights movement, like *King: A Filmed Record . . . Montgomery to Memphis* (1970), emphasize the spontaneity of the movement and King as its central leader, *Selma* displays the close bond that he had with his leadership team and his skill as a thoughtful tactician. While other films, like *Mississippi Burning* (1988), *Ghosts of Mississippi* (1996), *A Time to Kill* (1996), and *Lincoln* (2012), focus on white protagonists, DuVernay puts the efforts of African Americans advocating on their own behalf on full display in a way that no previous civil rights feature film had done with the exception of Spike Lee's *Malcolm X* (1992). Lee provides a romantic portrayal of Malcolm X (Denzel Washington) that depicts his rise, despite the obstacles of systemic racism, to become one of the most powerful orators and leaders in American history. Lee makes Malcolm X, a character whom many Americans viewed as a controversial outsider because of his Muslim faith and advocacy of Black self-defense, into one of us and someone to emulate; the film concludes with various people proclaiming "I am Malcolm X" to the camera. In contrast, while DuVernay humanizes King, she provides no inspiring redemptive arc comparable to Malcolm X's personal and religious transformation in Lee's film. King begins the film flawed and ends just as flawed. Without the pressure placed upon him by people like Nash, Abernathy, and Lewis, *Selma* seems to suggest, King would have continued to wallow in self-doubt, causing the movement to languish. The film shows King being rude to his wife, smoking, and being a philanderer, which might be jarring to some viewers still holding on to an idyllic image of the leader. However, others may find that this acknowledgment of King's frailty makes him movingly accessible.

The film as an interpretation of an incredibly important historical moment seeks to revise history, broaden the list of players covered in the narrative, and capture voices that have too often gone unheard. *Selma* recovers female leaders from the shadows by including the experiences of Annie Lee Cooper, Diane Nash, and Coretta Scott King. However, *Selma* does not go quite far enough in capturing the pervasive and influential role that Black women played in the movement. Although SNCC and SCLC are mentioned in the film, *Selma* does not fully explore the varied strategies that they and other organizations like the NAACP, Congress for Racial Equality (CORE), and the Urban League employed to advance change.

While it is always challenging to satisfactorily address historical accuracy, some of the characterizations in *Selma* have been tailored for dramatic and ideological emphasis. Much has been written about the portrayal of President Johnson as not only hesitant to support the civil rights movement but also antagonistic to King's efforts.[15] While it is difficult to know precisely why DuVernay made this choice, it may partly have come out of a need to overcorrect for previous films like *Mississippi Burning* and *Ghosts of Mississippi*, which emphasized the efforts of whites to uncover and correct misdeeds in the South without fully acknowledging the long history of African Americans advocating on their own behalf. Given the vast area that the film seeks to explore, there may have been some concern that examining the nuances of Johnson's position would cloud King's clear role as the protagonist of the story. The artistic and ideological decision to make President Johnson one of King's antagonists points toward the complexities of exploring and portraying the dynamics facing the movement while acknowledging Black agency.

Conclusion

Selma complicates the static image of Martin Luther King Jr. that lives on in the often too brief coverage of the civil rights movement in school textbooks. These portrayals seemingly seek to memorialize King on the steps of the Lincoln Memorial delivering his "I Have a Dream" speech as the lone voice of the civil rights movement. DuVernay rightly challenges this one-dimensional portrayal of King, depicting a complicated and conflicted figure whose perspective was one of many within the broader movement, which itself was often rife with tensions. She also provides a glimpse of King as a sinner and not simply as a saint. However, as with many revisionist histories, DuVernay may be guilty of overcorrection. It is one thing to point out the flaws of a historical figure. It is another to include them without fully capturing the exceptional qualities that empowered and motivated that figure to achieve the great heights they did. For King, among those exceptional qualities were his relationship with God and his lineage within Black Protestantism. While no film can cover everything, their omission seems to be too great an oversight for a historical film about an avowedly religious leader. What emerges is an engaging and complex but incomplete depiction of King that fails to fully capture his personal religious life and the Black Protestant legacy that propelled his role in the civil rights movement.

Figure 14.1 Tyler Perry, Hollywood's most successful independent producer, makes films imbued with messages that connect with African American Protestants.
Image Press Agency/Alamy Stock Photo

14

The Religious Motif of Mountains in Tyler Perry's *Why Did I Get Married?*

Melanie Johnson

In her groundbreaking work *Hollywood Be Thy Name: African American Religion in American Film, 1929–1949,* Judith Weisenfeld explores film depictions of African American religion beginning in the early sound era of motion pictures.[1] In addition to Hollywood films that replaced whites in blackface with all-Black casts, such as King Vidor's *Hallelujah* (1929) and Marc Connelly's *The Green Pastures* (1936), Weisenfeld unearths Black church films (made by and for African Americans) that form a marked contrast to their Hollywood counterparts.[2] For example, *Sunday Sinners* (1940), based on a story by Black actor Frank Wilson, does not represent Black theology and worship as childlike or exclusively rural.[3] Instead, the film suggests a thoughtful, moderate theology through the character of one Reverend Hampton, who agrees to relinquish his campaign to shut down a nightclub after the owners agree to close the club on Sunday nights. Through the compromise, the film also suggests the importance of the continuance of all aspects of Black life and culture, not only the church.

Much has changed since the introduction of films about African American religious experience. The past decade saw a spate of Black church videos and films specifically developed to appeal to African American audiences. Productions such as *Pastor Jones: Preaching to the Choir* (2009), *Cheatin' Hearts* (2011), *Saving Grace* (2011), *The Sins of Deacon Whyles* (2013), and many others have explored a variety of themes: marriages recovering from adultery, ministers questioning the authenticity of their calling, ministerial misconduct, and pastors attempting to maintain church relevance and save failing congregations.[4]

In the twenty-first century, one screenwriter-director dominates the landscape of feature films containing religious messages produced by and for African Americans. With the release of *A Madea Family Funeral* (2019), Tyler Perry has written and directed nearly two dozen features since the release of his first film, *Diary of a Mad Housewife* (2005). Perhaps best known for films starring his iconic character Madea, Perry has produced several films depicting African American Christianity that emphasize forgiveness, compassion for those fallen from grace, and love demonstrated through practical service. These films employ

Melanie Johnson, *The Religious Motif of Mountains in Tyler Perry's* Why Did I Get Married? In: *Protestants on Screen.* Edited by: Gastón Espinosa, Erik Redling and Jason Stevens, Oxford University Press.
DOI: 10.1093/oso/9780190058906.003.0015

common religious motifs, such as ministers, church mothers, and gospel music within an African American context, in dramas about struggles within marriage, family, and community life.

This chapter specifically examines Tyler Perry's interpretation of Jesus through the motif of mountains in *Why Did I Get Married?* (2007). Perhaps the least common of the motifs referenced in Perry films, the mountain motif is pervasive in African American spirituals and gospels: "Rough Side of the Mountain," "Move On Up the Mountain," and "Climbing Up the Mountain."[5] In the context of these songs, the mountain is an obstacle, a place of struggle, or a challenge. Yet the mountain in the biblical text and Christian religion is also a place of revelation and of the call to share the good news of the Gospel, as in the African American gospel song "Go Tell It on the Mountain" and Martin Luther King Jr.'s last sermon on April 3, 1968, "I See the Promised Land."[6]

Apart from occasional musical references in their soundtracks, the mountain motif is not used in other Perry films as clearly as it is used in *Why Did I Get Married?* Whereas most Perry films involve the layering of two or three of his oft-used motifs, *Married* has no ministers, no mothers, and very little music. In this film, screenwriter-director Perry interprets Jesus as an ever-present help almost exclusively through employment of the mountain motif as part of the mise-en-scène, as a site of divine encounter outside of the familiar religious contexts of African American churches and their ministers. *Married* serves as a particularly strong example of Perry's Jesus as ever-present help to Black people in trouble, specifically because Perry's Jesus is present outside of institutional religious settings yet remains consistent with the tradition of the biblical text as referenced by African American historians, scholars, theologians, and writers, particularly of the liberation theology tradition.

In the Gospels, Jesus is often found outside of the temple, as his itinerant ministry goes into the homes of his followers, such as Zacchaeus, Mary, Martha, and Lazarus; to sea with fishermen; in the fields of farmers; and upon the mountains.[7] Likewise, in the African American tradition, Jesus's ministry through the minister goes outside the church. Slave preachers preached in the fields where believers toiled. During the civil rights era, ministers, such as Martin Luther King Jr., invaded both the economic and political realms. Storefront preachers and street evangelists took the message of the Gospel into blighted and impoverished communities. The Pentecostal movement led by African American William J. Seymour began as a home-based prayer group on Bonnie Brae Street in Los Angeles, California.[8]

In *Married*, Perry likewise presents a Jesus present to and for hurting African Americans outside of formal religious settings: a personal Jesus, a constant Jesus, a Jesus ever-present everywhere. In the mountain motif, Perry's Jesus is transfigured from a figure associated with religion into one who is a reality in any context where hurting Black people may be found.

In the Old and New Testaments, those who ascend mountains are closer to heaven and in this place encounter God. Mountains are sites of new visions and revelations of God and of self. God declares his name to Moses on Mount Sinai.[9] On Mount Sinai God also gives Moses the Ten Commandments and establishes the covenant that transforms a throng of former slaves into a nation. Mount Zion became the site of the Temple in Jerusalem, the highest place of worship and communion with Israel's God. The prophet Isaiah declares "how beautiful on the mountains" are the feet of those who proclaim the good news of peace, salvation, and the reign of God.[10] The Apostle Paul references Isaiah's proclamation in his Letter to the Romans proclaiming the Gospel of salvation through Jesus Christ.[11]

In the New Testament, it is on a mountain that Jesus delivers the Beatitudes and instructs his disciples on the ethics of the kingdom of God.[12] He uses mountains as metaphors for great obstacles that can be defeated with the smallest seed of faith. Jesus is transfigured on a mountain, has his last fellowship with his disciples on the Mount of Olives, is crucified outside the gates of Jerusalem on Mount Zion on a hill called Golgotha, and delivers the Great Commission on a mountain before ascending to heaven. The Book of Revelation records that Jesus will return to Mount Zion in the Second Coming to establish his millennial reign. For these reasons, mountains play an important role in the Christian story generally, in African American religious traditions, and even in the names of Black churches, such as Mount Zion, Mount Sinai, Mount Olive, and many others.[13]

In keeping with the biblical tradition, African American theologians and writers have referenced mountains and mountaintops as sites of struggle, new visions, and revelations, and as locations on which to carry the message of liberation to African Americans. In his semi-autobiographical novel *Go Tell It on the Mountain*, African American James Baldwin chronicles the coming of age spiritually, sexually, and socially of the young stepson of the pastor presiding over a "fire-baptized" Pentecostal church in Harlem during the 1930s.[14] After reconciling his homosexual identity with his Christian faith, Baldwin's protagonist John is free, as the scriptures and spirituals say of those who spread the gospel on the mountain, to go forth declaring his own salvation: "I'm saved and I know I'm saved."[15] Baldwin's tale of a youth coming to grips with his identity has been reinterpreted by womanist theologians to apply to African American women struggling with their identity within a religious context. Carol Henderson appropriates Baldwin's *Go Tell It on the Mountain* and suggests that it is a story equally applicable to the African American woman who struggles to "refigure a 'self' " apart from traditional religious or patriarchal roles and expectations.[16]

Carol Henderson's notion of refiguring the self is applicable to the character Sheila in Perry's *Why Did I Get Married?* In this film, Sheila is an African

American woman who is challenged to refigure her self-image and her image of God when she is confronted with the reality of an unfaithful and emotionally abusive husband. Perry's film employs the hermeneutical motif of mountains as sites of struggle, new vision, and ultimately transformation consistent with the biblical tradition as interpreted in the context of Black liberation theology and relatedly womanist theology. As Sheila embarks upon the journey to see herself and God anew and become the woman that she desires to be in the setting of the Colorado mountains, Perry's conception of Jesus, an ever-present help, is revealed through the analysis of the mountain motif.

The film opens with pediatrician Terry (Perry) and his attorney wife, Diane, driving into the Colorado mountains to meet three other couples, all best friends since college, for an annual marriage retreat. Their marriages have a variety of mountainous challenges: infidelity, death of an infant child, and the demands of professional schedules have strained intimacy and compromised trust. For purposes of highlighting the interpretation of Jesus through the mountain motif, this chapter focuses on one of these couples, Sheila and Mike, and particularly Sheila. It is important to note that these couples are highly successful professionals, generally not the demographic Perry targets in his films. However, Sheila has been a wife and homemaker and has no marketable skills or job experience. She has defined herself by her marriage to Mike.

In addition to Mike's infidelity and abuse, Sheila suffers from low self-esteem consequent to (or caused by) being significantly overweight. She is left to drive alone to Colorado because she has not paid for an extra seat on the plane. She suffers the further humiliation of her husband's refusal to go with her. Naive Sheila is unaware that Mike is having an affair with her friend Trina, whom Sheila has invited along for the trip. This situation is admittedly problematic as a plot element: it is unlikely that a single friend would be invited to a marriage retreat. This implausible element, however, does not affect the validity or analysis of the hermeneutical motif of mountains as they apply to Perry's interpretation of Jesus.

Initially, the mountains symbolize a site of struggle. Sheila's prayer as she commences the drive from Missouri reflects her perceived mountain—a marriage in trouble: "Lord, help me up this mountain to save my marriage. I am going up this mountain to save my marriage. You are the ruler of all things. Jesus, make it all right."[17] Sheila already perceives Jesus as a present help in her floundering marriage and in the difficult drive. Stephanie Mitchem describes Black women's relationship with God through prayer:

> Black women often report some sense of interactive prayer. One woman might say: "I took my problem to the Lord, and left it there," with another black woman's response: "Don't pick it up again." God is understood as a partner in

> life rather than a distant observer. Black women report experiencing a sense of openness to God's guidance: they expect response, whether in the form of a sign or a problem resolved.[18]

This interactive prayer partnership is reflected in Sheila's petition for the Lord's help up the mountain. She expects that he is ever-present to guide her and resolve both the challenge of the drive and the problems of her marriage. Due to a fallen tree on the road, she is forced to spend the night at the jail/office of Sheriff Troy, where she sleeps in a holding cell. Here Sheila's personal mountain of poor self-worth related to negative body image manifests when Troy asks if she would like some dinner. Sheila replies, "Don't I look hungry? Don't tell me you can't see I am a big girl." Troy, who will become Jesus's agent of change for her while on the mountain, blows off her self-denigration, stating that everyone needs to eat. Among a variety of marginalized populations, Perry advocates for overweight African American women, who often play significant roles in his films.

Escorted by Troy, Sheila arrives at the mountaintop cabin in the morning. Met by her friends, who criticize Mike to Sheila for his lack of concern and protection, Sheila again denigrates herself: "Mike is not that bad; I just need to lose some weight and things will get better for us. It's me [*over protests of her friends*]. It is me. I'm trying to lose weight. . . . Sometimes he looks at me like I disgust him. . . . It'll get better. I know this." She is further humiliated and wounded when Mike laughs at her for wearing a sexy nightgown to bed in hopes of sparking romance.

Figure 14.2 Sheila's prayer as she commences the drive from Missouri: "Lord, help me up this mountain to save my marriage."
DVD screen capture, fair use

Sheila has yet to see that her real mountain is not her physical weight but the weight of self-blame and excusing Mike's abuse. She has come to the mountain retreat, she believes, to save her marriage; but Perry's Jesus, as interpreted through the mountaintop experience, wants to save Sheila's sense of self-esteem.

After Sheila's friend Angela observes Mike sneaking into Trina's bedroom at night, she exposes their affair at breakfast the following morning. At this point, Mike reveals the secrets he knows about each of the other marriages, and the retreat falls apart. Mike informs Sheila that he wants a divorce. At this point, the transformation begins—with properly directed, if unhealthily expressed, anger: Sheila strikes Mike's head with a wine bottle. After breakfast and after Terry (Perry) attends to Mike's injuries, everyone leaves the mountain except Sheila. There is a picture of the Colorado mountains in the rearview mirror as they drive away. Perry thus frames the site of Sheila's forthcoming transformation.

Troy checks up on Sheila, who has gone to a hotel room. Thinking she may be arrested, she tells Troy, "I should have killed him. I gave him my life. He emptied out my bank account. I don't know what I'm going to do." Troy invites Sheila to a high vista at the top of the range, where God (Jesus) is present to invite Sheila to the journey of transformation:

TROY: I come here to pray, scream, clear my head—it's just me and God.
SHEILA: Come here to cry?
TROY: Yeah, that too.
SHEILA: I can't even describe to you the way I feel. I keep trying to understand—what did I do so wrong? Why he betrayed me. It hurts. I have no life without him. I can't even pray about it.
TROY: You know, Sheila, it's a great time for a new start if you want to stay.

It is in Sheila's deep sorrow that Jesus, through the agency of Troy, comes alongside Sheila to comfort her. Jacquelyn Grant says of Jesus's presence and accessibility in the sadness and sorrow that is to be a Black woman: "In the experiences of Black women, Jesus is ever-present; he has commonly been perceived as present in 'times of trouble.'"[19] The same Jesus that Sheila sought in prayer when she began to drive up the mountain is especially near in her brokenness on the mountain to help her on the journey toward a new life.

New starts require new visions of self and hope of a better future, and mountaintops in scripture and African American religious history have been these sites of vision and hopeful futures. In one of his most famous speeches, "I See the Promised Land," Martin Luther King Jr. poignantly conveys the image of the mountain as the place of hope, promise, and vision of life yet to come.[20] King references Moses's mountaintop view of the promised land from Mount Abarim (Nebo) in Numbers 27:12 when he states:

Figure 14.3 Troy invites Sheila to a high vista at the top of the range. "I come here to pray, scream, clear my head—it's just me and God."
DVD screen capture, fair use

> Well, I don't know what will happen now. We've got some difficult days ahead. But it really doesn't matter with me now, because I've been to the mountaintop. And I don't mind. Like anybody, I would like to live a long life. Longevity has its place. But I'm not concerned about that now. I just want to do God's will. And He's allowed me to go up to the mountain. And I've looked over. And I've seen the promised land. I may not get there with you. But I want you to know tonight, that we, as a people, will get to the promised land![21]

The mountain in *Married* transitions from a site of obstacle and struggle to one of revelation and new vision as Shelia stays there in Jesus's presence. Sheila's and Troy's experience of the mountaintop as that place of "just me and God" references lyrics from the Negro spiritual "Every Time I Feel the Spirt," which sings of mountains as the place of encounter with God: "Upon the mountain, my Lord spoke, out of his mouth came fire and smoke."[22] In Sheila's case, the Lord is present on the mountain speaking through the fire and smoke of her pain to invite her to a journey of self-liberation. The apocalyptic revelation for Sheila is the end of life and self-definition as she has known it. Her faithful response to God on the mountain is to simply allow Jesus to help her in her journey to redeem her own life.

Stephanie Mitchem writes, "Redemption is a journey that begins by daring to care for self in the face of repeated assault on dignity and value. Salvation is born of the struggle to reconcile some assigned place in the world with a self-determined identity that springs from hope and is grounded in faith."[23] In Sheila's case, the mountain is the site of her redemption journey, as she is invited to redefine herself apart from her marriage to an abusive husband and a general "disgust" of herself that she has internalized consequent to being overweight. Sheila's transformation is facilitated primarily by her faith. Coupled with the hope that Troy offers and facilitated by his inspirational presence, she comes to believe that she can transform her self-image.

Sheila (on a conference call with her friends) owns her part in the process and explains why she must stay on the mountain: "I spent too much time letting other people take care of me. Gotta find my own way. Gotta do this on my own." But Sheila is not on her own. Jesus is present on the mountain through the struggle and the self-confrontation, through the invitation to become transformed, and through her new friend, Troy. In this film, Troy serves not as a type of Jesus but rather as an agent. Jesus is present with Sheila through her faith and through the agency of one who views her as Jesus does. Troy, like God/Jesus, views her as a person of value and worthy of esteem. (Sheila does not recognize this initially but does by the end of the film/parable.) Such self-liberatory transformations, womanist theologian Jacquelyn Grant contends, are a result of encounters with Jesus. Referencing a sermon from Sojourner Truth, who described a joyful encounter with Jesus, Grant describes the Jesus whose love propelled Truth to liberating action: "This love is not a sentimental, passive love. It was a tough, active love that empowered her to fight more fiercely for the freedom of her people."[24]

Through Troy, Jesus offers Sheila the same tough, active, and empowering love that confronts the internalized oppression evidenced in her negative self-view. This love empowers Sheila to love and liberate herself. Troy has a tough-love confrontation with Sheila while at lunch one afternoon. This is the second time Troy challenges Sheila's self-denigration through the offering of a meal, which symbolizes loving nurture rather than Sheila's punitive self-denial and self-denigration. It is not unlike Jesus redeeming Peter over a meal of fish in John 21. In this passage, Peter's self-view has so diminished after his betrayal of Jesus that he, along with other disciples, has abandoned his true calling. Jesus restores Peter's relationship with him and Peter's call to ministry as they commune together over a meal. Likewise, Jesus, through the agency of Troy, begins to restore Sheila's sense of herself and her potential as they have lunch.

TROY: This man tried to break you down and every day I see you make it. You are an amazing, intelligent, spiritual, sexy, strong, and beautiful woman.

SHEILA: Not as big as I am.

TROY: If you are not happy about the way you look, change it. Stop downing yourself. It's not attractive and it makes me uncomfortable for you.

Consistent with Grant's description of Jesus's "tough love," Troy's tough-love encounter with Sheila confronts her and demands self-agency on her part. He then kisses her. His kiss, like his words, are a loving contradiction to Sheila's self-perception. More than romantic, the connection is redemptive. Troy's admiration of and obvious attraction to her say that she is not "disgusting," as Mike saw her. Troy finds (as does Jesus) a woman who is beautiful inside and out. Sheila is now challenged to see the same in herself.

Sheila is again provoked to pray for aid in processing her feelings in the light of this confrontation. "Oh, Jesus, Lord have mercy, God. I haven't done that in a long time. I need to pray. Can we pray?" In this case, Troy (as the agent) is rightly invited into Sheila's "interactive" prayer space with the ever-present Jesus. If she is to embrace what both Jesus and Troy see in her, she will need divine aid. Pastor and Black theologian James T. Murphy Jr. asserts, "Praying is the strength of Black worship. The pain predicament of both historical and contemporary struggles has maximized the glory and the power of Psalm 112:1–2; 'I will lift up my eyes unto the hills from whence cometh my help. My help comes from the Lord.' "[25] Sheila needs Jesus's help to see the woman Troy sees. As she lifts up her eyes unto the mountain through prayer, she can access the help available for her transformation. On the mountain, Sheila begins to move her greatest obstacle—her poor self-image (not her weight)—and prayer is key to her doing so. Murphy continues, "Black people know first-hand that some mountains can only be moved by fasting and prayer."[26]

It is important to note that Troy is not simply a replacement for Mike, a new man in whom Sheila can submerge herself. Troy is an agent of God/Jesus present to facilitate the self-liberatory journey that Sheila must take for herself. Any romantic relationship that ensues is secondary to her self-liberation.

Months later, Sheila, with new husband Troy, reunites with the other couples (all of whom have tackled the respective mountains affecting their marriages) to celebrate a great achievement of one in their group. Now fifty pounds lighter, she shares with her friends the revelation *on* the mountain and *of* the mountain that led to her transformation.

SHEILA: I thought—I prayed that God would save my marriage. It wasn't built on the right things anyway. I thought if Mike got right, if I lost the weight, that everything would be okay. It's been hard [*crying*]. It's been hard. But it's me. I did it. I'm doing it. And it feels so good. It feels so good. Ah! I thought that God had given up on me because here I am in this marriage and it don't work. He don't love me, he don't like me. But he brought me somebody. He is an amazing man. He is supportive, he doesn't criticize me. He walks with me and he loves me through all of it, you understand what I'm saying? I didn't have that, and I do now. I wake up, I wake up with so much joy in my heart.

ANGELA: Oh God; help us, Jesus. [*Then, hugging Sheila:*] Oh, he already has.

Angela's statement summarizes the matter: it was through Jesus, present when Sheila needed him most, that she was transformed. But there is a final step to complete Sheila's self-liberation.

Sheila has confronted her greatest obstacle on the mountain—her own poor self-image. She has been to the mountaintop, where she began to embrace a new vision of herself, and by the end of her self-liberatory journey she is transformed spiritually, psychologically, and physically. On the mountain, she was invited to love herself in response to Jesus's loving presence. For Sheila, loving herself means to count herself worthy of love whatever her size. She divorces her abusive husband and embraces Troy's love as a reflection of her newly embraced self-love.

According to Madea's Big Scholarly Roundtable panelist E. Patrick Johnson, Black Americans are in an aesthetic crisis, not yet recognizing our beauty. Referring to Perry, he commented that "certain people have been able to pimp American pop culture and win." Referring to Madea, Johnson then states, "What we are really doing is playing with this trope of ugliness."[27] He contends that Perry uses the Black actors and actresses that we dream of looking like because we have not yet been persuaded of our own beauty; Black audiences pay for the fantasy to see "beautiful Black people" (in contrast, for example, with the "ugly" Celie, played by Whoopi Goldberg in Stephen Spielberg's *The Color Purple*) because they have been so desperate for beautiful Black images on the screen.[28] However, through the character of Troy, Perry is not simply "pimping" American pop culture. He is also commenting on the beauty of the overweight African American woman.

The Black female body, particularly the overweight body in *Married* and other Perry films, also serves as text. In response to scholars participating in Madea's Big Scholarly Roundtable, I suggest an alternative way of viewing Perry's use of the large female body, one that draws upon Black feminist and womanist Christologies. In this reading, obesity can be symbolic of unrecognized, unacknowledged beauty and the embodiment of divine love through self-love. For this symbolic purpose, Perry intentionally and unapologetically uses overweight Black women in *Married* and other films—consistently so in the person of Madea in his comedy films, but also in *Daddy's Little Girls* and *The Single Moms Club* (2014).

Pursuant to Mona Sahyoun's 2016 discussion of subversion of Black female stereotypes, Perry's use of the overweight Black woman in *Married* is arguably subversive. According to Sahyoun, the white, patriarchal image of the fat Black body is exemplified by the subjugated, servicing mammy who is not sexually desirable.[29] In *Married*, the stay-at-home, submissive wife in the character of Sheila is sexually desirable to Troy. Yet she is not a "jezebel" or "hoochie" because, as a devoted wife, she is neither aggressive nor unfeminine. A part of the transformation Sheila undergoes is a sexual liberation in addition to the liberation from an abusive husband, who himself represents oppressive patriarchy. Here on the mountain of Sheila's transfiguration, Troy, as an agent of Christ, is very present to help Sheila experience wholeness, which includes liberation of her self-image and sexuality. For Perry, this parable does not function to perpetuate stereotypes of Black women, such as the "mammy"; rather, in the person of Sheila, Perry demonstrates that fat women are not excluded from femininity or sexuality as part of their identity. On the mountain, Jesus is present to affirm the beauty and desirability of Black women, who have suffered under the negative stigmatization, born of white patriarchy, of being considered unfeminine and undesirable.

The hurting person in *Married* is an emotionally abused, soon-to-be-divorced, overweight African American woman with limited marketable job skills. She might, in fact, be an embarrassment to certain African Americans. As Perry states:

> The [critics] were saying . . . the people that I was talking about didn't deserve to have their stories told because they were an embarrassment to a certain level of Black people. . . . Headlines, shocking, "Why did he put these fat Black people on TV?" when "House of Payne" came out. "Tyler"—this is the title of one of the articles I saw—"Tyler Perry hates Black women." I was blown away. I thought, how can these intellectuals with these degrees—they are so smart—how can they not see what I am doing here? How could they not get the power of what was going on here for people that everybody else had given up on?[30]

For Perry, fat, large, or overweight is not the same as "ugly." The character of Sheila embodies love, forbearance, and endurance (the endurance of Mike's ugly abuse and infidelity). Through Troy's response to her as desirable, Perry uses the romance trope to suggest that Black women, regardless of size, have the right to be loved. Likewise, in *Single Moms Club*, the full-figured Lytia is hotly pursued by Branson, who finds her voluptuousness appealing. Interestingly, Perry uses the ugliness of Madea's brother Joe's often lecherous conduct to undercut Joe's comments about his own sister's ugliness. It is not possible to find Joe attractive, appealing, or sensible (even if some may find him comical). Thus the audience can dismiss what he says about his sister, Madea. For Perry, ugly is as ugly does, and beauty is found within the fullest of figures and the most abundant of curves.

Another area of Perry's work targeted for criticism is "Perry's overuse of the knight-in-shining-armor trope" as a means of countering any speculations about Perry's own sexual identity or a means of creating "alternate happy places" for himself.[31] In the case of *Married*, the marriage between Sheila and Troy may seem to present the same happily-ever-after as some of the sanitized evangelical films created by the Kendrick brothers and to convey the heterosexism with which these critics also charge Perry. This would be the case if Troy simply replaced Mike as the source of Sheila's identity. But that is not what happens, as we discover with the message of the parable behind the romance plot. As the agent of Jesus, Troy is primarily the one who confronts Sheila's internalized abuse and walks with Sheila through her journey of self-liberation. Sheila owns and assumes responsibility for the journey, as she stated in the conference call with her friends and as she shares with them at their reunion toward the end of the film. Thus, the relationship between Sheila and Troy is not consistent with the patriarchal oppression portrayed through Mike that womanism seeks to counter, nor is it the simple "happily ever after." In keeping with liberationist and womanist theologies, Troy and Sheila's primary relationship is linked to Sheila's self-liberation. Moreover, *Married* further suggests that Black women (including overweight Black women) are worthy of love and sex, and that Black men and women are capable of healthy romantic love. As Shayne Lee states, "With Sheila's story, Perry's message to Christian women suffering in bad marriages is that it is easier for God to bring them new loving partners than it is for God to change the hearts of husbands who have already checked out of their marriages."[32] By embracing the large Black woman in his films and by portraying them as desirable and placing them in romantic storylines, Perry transgresses Hollywood notions of thinness as a requisite for beauty, desirability, or lovability.

Conclusion

By employing the mountain motif, Perry fashions a parable that focuses on struggle, revelation, new vision, and ultimately transformation, in keeping with the biblical symbolism of mountains and African American hermeneutical motifs. By reading through the storyline and discerning the mountains as a site of struggle, vision, and transformation, women who can identify with Perry's character can have hope for such transformations as well, because Jesus is ever-present in times of trouble. Through film parables such as *Married*, Perry broadens the film representation of Christians to include other "shades" of Christianity and of Christ through storylines contextualized in marginalized African American experience.

Figure 15.1 Corinne (Vera Farmiga) and Annika (Dagmara Domińczyk) seeking the Spirit in *Higher Ground*.
AF archive/Alamy Stock Photo

15

A Tender View of Conservative Evangelicalism in *Higher Ground*

Paula M. Kane

Like many motion pictures, *Higher Ground* (2011) began as a book. In this case, the inspiration is an American woman's 2002 memoir of her journey in and out of various expressions of conservative Protestantism. As a contemporary spiritual autobiography, the memoir narrates the facts of the author's life, but it also discloses how the genre itself has undergone mutations over time since its arrival on New England's shores in the seventeenth century. As documented by historians, the English Puritans who colonized North America kept obsessive records of their spiritual status via scrupulous journal entries about their moral failures. Their purpose was to calculate, as best they could, whether they had been chosen by God to be among the elect who would be saved. Their efforts at moving from sinful guilt to near-assurance of election have been supplanted in the twenty-first century by very different stories. Recent narratives of female self-actualization such as the bestselling *Eat, Pray, Love* are less concerned with sin and retribution and more with pleasure and renewal.[1] *Higher Ground* seemingly combines both types of soul-searching, offering a traditional conversion tale grounded in one woman's search for certainty, but with a contemporary twist that steers her away from Christian religion and toward self-culture and gender assertion.

This chapter addresses the treatment of a spiritual memoir in its transfer to screen, especially as it engages the impact of religious patriarchy upon women in conservative Protestantism. The specific denominational connection is not specified, yet the groups that the author had joined in real life included the Jesus movement of the 1970s, followed by various conservative Protestant congregations. The film's star and director, Vera Farmiga, is not focused on parsing those differences; instead, she aims to show how the warm but controlling house-church group gradually became stifling for the protagonist. Patriarchal values dominated each of the religious groups that the author joined.

Paula M. Kane, *A Tender View of Conservative Evangelicalism in* Higher Ground In: *Protestants on Screen*.
Edited by: Gastón Espinosa, Erik Redling and Jason Stevens, Oxford University Press. © Oxford University Press 2023.
DOI: 10.1093/oso/9780190058906.003.0016

Eventually the controlling impulses of the male leaders pushed her out of the church altogether.[2]

For *Higher Ground*, which debuted at the Sundance Festival in January 2011, Farmiga was determined to create a scenario that ends up neither valorizing nor rejecting faith. She thus presents the viewer with sincere questions about religious belief while offering a neutral outlook on its truth claims. Although the screenplay had no obligation to be rigidly faithful to the author's life, the memoir and the motion picture share a theme of rejecting religious exclusivity and the self-righteousness that characterizes some cultish Christians. The result on-screen is a tender and subtle but highly natural look at the role of faith across several decades in the characters' lives, which accompanies the female protagonist's path away from Christian affiliation.

The motion picture takes its inspiration from *This Dark World: A Memoir of Salvation Found and Lost*, written by Carolyn S. Briggs.[3] Briggs's text is the source for the screenplay (written by her and Tim Metcalfe) and for its gender dynamics. Briggs (b. 1955) wrote it as part of her academic training in creative writing, which then led to a teaching position in the English department of a community college in Des Moines, Iowa. As the subtitle suggests, Briggs's life reverses the expected sequence of events in a religious autobiography, in which a young person usually arrives at a stable adult faith after facing and overcoming a series of challenges during childhood and adolescence. Briggs's experiences of masculine control of women and of the strongly marked barriers between believers and outsiders were among the negative forces that propelled her to challenge her religious community and to eventually leave her husband and her church behind. But mostly, she confided of her departure from a fundamentalist faith, "I grew tired of all the hating we had to do."

Throughout this chapter I argue that *Higher Ground* offers heartfelt insight into a young woman's subjectivity, shown against the backdrop of American society from the 1960s to the 1980s, and represents her search for authenticity in those turbulent decades, which for a time was satisfied by traditional Protestantism.[4] The Christian quest for perfection and the metaphysical quest for the "really real" converge in interesting ways in *Higher Ground*. The search for truth and the rejection of false wisdom undergirds the path of author Carolyn Briggs, who welcomes her experiences but learns over time to reject those that are detrimental to her humanity. At the end of both the book and the film, she has become more autonomous and less constrained by religious norms, with an open-ended future. She comes to abandon "extreme religion" because of its toll on her identity, but she also realizes that a life without Christianity need not degenerate into its extreme opposite—a world of savagery, she recalls, such as depicted in the novel *Lord of the Flies*.[5]

A Memoir of Extreme Religion

Carolyn Briggs opens her memoir in Iowa with her first experience of being saved: her family's rescue from carbon monoxide poisoning in their rented farmhouse during a bitterly cold winter.[6] When her father did not show up at work one morning, her grandmother became worried and asked a neighbor to check on the family. He axed down the door, finding everyone in the home unconscious from the toxic fumes, but was able to resuscitate the family by opening all the windows. This astonishing "salvation" precedes chapters describing an utterly mundane family life that was not in the least religious. Cleanliness, not Christianity, was "the first principle in our home," Carolyn recalled, because the Briggs family moved thirteen times, residing always in rental properties.[7] Early in her life, Carolyn discerns a family hierarchy based on unfair rules. Her older sister was the family beauty: tall, blond, bosomy. By contrast, Carolyn, called "Squirt" by her father, was flat, bony, and hard, even in high school. She offers a pithy portrait of her parents: "My dad had tattoos and my mom got a suntan every summer."[8] Her mother, glimpsed in brief recollections, is flirty, freckled, and fun, and dresses differently than the "church moms."[9] Her father liked to drink and play cards on Friday nights with the large extended family of his in-laws. The parents "just didn't pay much attention to God" but sent the kids to Sunday school anyway, where Carolyn cheated on her Bible tests in order to look smart and gain approval.[10] Parental surrogates, such as the local public librarian who was a prudish Baptist, monitored Carolyn's book choices; in a memory duplicated in the film, Carolyn is steered away from *Lord of the Flies*. Briggs's parents separated when Carolyn was fifteen (suggested on-screen by episodes where her drunken father menaces her mother), and during that difficult time Carolyn took up with Eric, a musician in a local rock band.[11] Both of her parents then remarried.[12]

Carolyn becomes pregnant at age seventeen, and shortly after her engagement to Eric, she has her first encounter with the "Jesus freak people." After the couple's wedding and the baby's birth, the new family lives in a trailer. Through Carolyn's friendship with a woman named Katherine, she reads the Bible and comes to believe in God at age eighteen.[13] The young parents' faith is confirmed when they survive a bus crash on the band tour bus, in which their daughter escapes drowning, a second salvation story. The print memoir discloses the type of Christianity that Carolyn embraces, through her descriptions of watching *The PTL Club* on television and reading Hal Lindsey, author of *The Late Great Planet Earth*, a 1970 bestseller that predicted an imminent apocalypse based upon reading the signs of the times as predicted by dispensational theology.[14] Carolyn was also moved by a film about the end times called *I Wish We'd All Been Ready*.[15] She and her husband, Eric, join a nondenominational evangelical church in Des

Moines that shared these apocalyptic concerns—namely, "the experience of being primed, of being ready to go at any minute."[16]

By 1980, Carolyn's positive experiences of evangelical religion led her to describe her contented life as "a decade-long family reunion."[17] The film portrays this comforting world through shots of the earnest preaching of their pastor, communal hymn singing, and the ordinary routines of household life undertaken by a wife who does not question her God-given role. Dispensational theology, however, will lose its charm for Carolyn and become a stumbling block instead. She confessed, "I realized how judgmental I had become, how ready to throw the first stone."[18] Fortunately, a free-spirited friend, Pauline, enters her life. Pauline, who has six children, is comfortable with her sexuality, seen in her fondness for making drawings of her husband's penis, a detail faithfully recreated on screen in a moment of bonding and laughter between the two women. Carolyn's questioning sharpens when she experiences an unwelcome third pregnancy and the notion of living "by faith" starts to seem absurd to her. Her marriage falters as she no longer desires Eric anymore, experiencing their married relationship as companionable but not passionate—an emotional shift that makes her husband fearful.[19] Further trouble surfaces when Carolyn's sister, who comes to visit for a while, hides drugs in the garage. The family's fate shifts again when Eric receives a job offer in Arkansas. Although his church pressures him to stay in Iowa, the family chooses Arkansas, where unfortunately Carolyn has "no fellowship, no real friends."[20] The couple joins Mount Olive Church, but Carolyn tires of the negative views they are obliged to uphold through attending a constant round of Christian anti-abortion, anti-left, and anti-gay demonstrations. She becomes bored with religion and attends community college, graduating Phi Beta Kappa in 1994 at age thirty-eight, followed by her admission to the MFA program at the University of Arkansas. She leaves her husband, enduring harsh letters and comments from the church. Following a trip to Ireland, she returns to America, resolved to end the marriage.

Film Adaption as Faithful Witness

The film's title suggests Carolyn's/Corinne's (the main character is named Corinne in the film) personal search for a better way to live in "this dark world" through ascent to "higher ground." When Vera Farmiga was presented with the script, she recalled her own lifelong debates with the Ukrainian Greek Catholic roots of her immigrant parents: "We've all struggled with disenchantment and conflict." In an interview about the making of *Higher Ground* she calls her film a "token of affection" for her staunchly faithful father, suggesting that she found kindred feeling between the Protestant narrative of Carolyn Briggs and the Christianity of her own family, a feeling perhaps made even stronger since the Farmigas had converted to Pentecostalism when Vera was a child.[21] Five months pregnant while acting in and directing *Higher Ground*, Farmiga put her relatives to work producing the film. The teenage Corinne is played by Farmiga's younger sister, Taissa, reportedly bribed by the offer of a new pickup truck to accept the role.[22] Numerous family members are in the cast and production crew.

The Iowa setting of Briggs's early life was transposed to southeastern New York State, around the towns of Poughkeepsie, Kingston, New Paltz, and Woodstock. This largely rural locale, in and near the Catskill Mountains, differs from Iowa but is perhaps a good substitute for the rural Arkansas of the latter part of *This Dark World*.

The change of setting from the Great Plains to the Catskills allows Farmiga to take advantage of the primal beauty of the Hudson Valley, where the pristine natural setting evokes the innocence of the church members. In the film's opening scene, for example, a young bearded man testifies that standing up for Jesus is not an easy thing, "but he saved my life!" Young persons listening intently to him are seated on the rocks around a scenic riverbed. Other moments in the film establish the Edenic motif as the Christian congregants witness to their faith, sing together, and swim in the river.

In addition to establishing the change of locale without compromising the mood of spiritual purity, the film adaptation had to make choices about how to represent the significant religious events of the characters' lives, such as baptisms, vacation Bible school, home Bible study groups, speaking in tongues, and church services—events that in Briggs's book are seen only from a first-person perspective. The film tends to follow this lead of privileging Corinne's inner experience. Corinne's baptism, for instance, is treated from her point of view: she awaits the ceremony dressed in a white gown and seated on the rocks of a riverbank. The pastor arrives. The subsequent baptism ritual presents Corinne gazing up from under the river's surface at the beaming faces above her—reassuring, welcoming, joyful. A later scene hints at the divisions between Protestants over the practice of speaking in tongues, sought by charismatic Christians but regarded as satanic in Corinne's fundamentalist church. When her friend Annika speaks in tongues while boating with Corinne, Corinne, amazed at the sounds coming from Annika's lips, responds, "*I* want it. *I'm* gonna get it." There is humor in Corinne's determination to "get" Annika's spiritual gift by practicing alone in her bathroom mirror. "Come on, Holy Spirit," she urges over and over, while outside the closed door, her sister eavesdrops with a skeptical face. Such devices simultaneously grasp the humor and oddness of the desire of a would-be charismatic Christian.

Even Corinne's final moments in a church, which come during a service with her family, are from her perspective. She keeps the microphone after her children and husband have performed the sentimental hymn "In the Garden," best-known for its chorus, "And he walks with me, and he talks with me." Although Pastor Bill motions for her to stop speaking, Corinne describes giving her heart to God as a young child but now feeling only His absence: "I feel like I live in an empty place. . . . I'm wrestling something nameless, without form and void,

Figure 15.2 In a humorous scene, Corinne tries to get the gift of tongues by practicing in her bathroom.
DVD screen capture, fair use

and I just want it to be solid so bad," she tells the congregation, regretful that she cannot share the pastor's faith. After completing her remarks, she kisses her husband, Ethan, on the lips and exits the church to the sound of the congregation singing "How Great Thou Art," marking her determined departure from that congregation and from her former life.

Music and Worship

Hymns and communal singing are at the heart of much Protestant evangelical experience, as the film's musical moments make clear. The camera builds empathy for the church congregation with camera close-ups of church members as they listen to the preacher with interest or sing with enthusiasm, but the remarkable soundtrack brings the memoir alive on-screen. In an interview segment entitled "The Substance of Things Hoped for: Making *Higher Ground*," Farmiga notes the importance of music's ability to unite people and her intention to capture that fellowship.[23] Her husband (Renn Hawkey), the film's musical director, created a soundtrack that perfectly accompanies its themes and provides some of its most touching and heartfelt moments. Hymn singing at the church services ranges from the contemporary guitar music and banjo accompaniment of the neo-charismatic "Jesus freaks" at their house church to traditional hymns that form background music to set the emotional tone of a scene or to contrast with it. The latter technique is especially effective in a scene near the end as Corinne pays a nostalgic visit to her former church to the accompaniment of a female voice singing the intimate nineteenth-century hymn by a female lyricist, "I Need Thee Every Hour." The plaintive lyric keenly echoes Corinne's loss of reliance upon God and her church. In other worship scenes, the use of contemporary instruments like electric guitar, as well as the more folkish arrangements with the banjo, signals that the "Jesus people" are akin to the era's rebellious hippies. Both groups shared the same countercultural norms and mistrust of institutions, albeit with different ultimate goals.[24]

Beginning in 1970, as attested by Billy Graham in *The Jesus Generation* (1971), the humanity of Jesus enjoyed a cultural revival in America, and music played a large part. The Broadway hit musical *Godspell* (1970), composed by Stephen Schwartz, its film adaptation in 1973, and the 1970 rock opera *Jesus Christ Superstar* were three manifestations. According to a 1971 cover story in *Time* magazine dedicated to the Jesus movement in the United States, another result was the springing up all over the nation of numerous independent Christian communities that espoused a simple lifestyle of communal living and countercultural values that were combined with attempts to restore the practices of the first Christians, including signs and wonders, faith healing, and speaking in tongues.[25] These "Jesus people" or "Jesus freaks" appeared within numerous Protestant denominations and even among Roman Catholics, who launched their own charismatic revival. Even after the moment waned in the 1980s, due to the rise of the religious right, the Jesus movement had left its mark within growing Christian right- and left-wing movements and upon Christian music. Likewise, in *Higher Ground*, the Jesus people are a kind, nature-loving, seemingly innocent manifestation of the counterculture, although not immune to the larger culture's gender ideologies, which assumed the necessity and rightness of male leadership. Despite Farmiga's efforts to portray Corinne's congregations empathically, each one ultimately reveals the contradictions of its assumptions about the lesser role of women.

Repression of the Self

Several changes made to the memoir on-screen serve to engage the themes of female friendship and sisterhood in a more concise way than the memoir, such as the portrayal of two women, Pauline and Delia, renamed Annika and Wendy in the film. Unlike Pauline of the memoir, Annika is funny and earthy. She is a good friend to Corinne but suffers a serious seizure. Although she survives a dangerous surgery, during which the church members assemble at the hospital to pray for her, she is left mute and wheelchair-bound, leading Corinne to further question God's mercy. At the church service following Annika's "successful" surgery, the pastor sings the hymn "It Is Well with My Soul," which rings false with Corinne. Scenes with Corinne's sister Wendy, a bleached-blond "bad girl" who scoffs and yawns through services at Corinne's church and takes advantage of her sister's hospitality, allow the viewer to glimpse Corinne's experience of love, loss, and betrayal from women.

Higher Ground suggests ways in which the close-knit Protestant church limited the behavior of women through group pressure and small mortifications. Early in her married life, Corinne speaks at church about praying recently with another mother in the congregation. The minister rebukes her publicly, noting that women should not take this initiative and that good women should pray with the church elders, not with each other. In the kitchen a few moments later, the pastor's wife echoes him by reminding Corinne that she cannot presume to teach the men. These two scenes anticipate further humiliations visited on Corinne in her church by both men and women who will not tolerate challenges to patriarchy. The churchwomen prove to be the enforcers of their own submission. In one scene, after a home communion service, Deborah tells Corinne that her maternity dress is inappropriate because it is too revealing. "You don't want to make a brother stumble," Deborah warns her. This mostly psychological cruelty about gender roles reaches a climax in the film's only overtly violent scene. Corinne has not welcomed her third pregnancy and grows emotionally distant from Ethan, who never challenges the church's norms and gender hierarchies. After Ethan yells at his wife during their child's softball game, Corinne runs to hide in the car in embarrassment. Her angry conversation with her husband there leads him to try to strangle her, his anger reaching the boiling point after being primed in earlier scenes where she had rebuffed his kisses.

When the couple attends marriage counseling to save their fifteen-year marriage, the sexism of their minister-therapist parallels that of the male pastors, who assume that women, following an oft-cited Pauline verse, should remain silent. The counselor introduces himself by saying that he "considers himself a prophet of God." When he isolates Corinne to speak with her alone, he diagnoses the fault as entirely hers: "You are worshiping at the altar of yourself!"

The film's conclusion is more decisive than the memoir's. In the latter, Carolyn makes a solo trip to Ireland while her husband remains behind, still hoping to save their marriage. We do not know if Carolyn, without God and her husband, finds her higher ground in her new artistic pursuits. Do they provide "salvation" from the closed-minded Protestants who mean well, yet remain wedded to an oppressive gender ideology? Does her apparent choice to seek her own fulfillment align with other self-searching (and globe-hopping) contemporary women, notably Elizabeth Gilbert in *Eat, Pray, Love*? The film's tidier finale displays Corinne's independence in a sequence of scenes that show her decorating her own apartment, taking her children to a contemporary art exhibit (presumably

Figure 15.3 Corinne's husband begins to sense her waning affection when she rebuffs his kiss.
DVD screen capture, fair use

off-limits to the narrow-minded congregants because of its nude sculptures), and experiencing the joys of making her own choices without fear of judgment from church members and criticism from her husband.

The chapters in Briggs's memoir carry titles such as "Lost," "Quitting the World," and "Travail." In the film, analogous phrases appear throughout the film as five on-screen titles. In order, these are "Summons," "Renegade," "Consumed," "Wilderness," "Wrestling Until Dawn," and "The Book of Life." The terms convey the potential for spiritual growth through rebellion, conflict, and struggle that has long been central to Protestant spiritual narratives, following John Bunyan's 1678 allegory *The Pilgrim's Progress*. The screen titles may even suggest conflicts as well as similarities between the journey experienced by Briggs as an everywoman and that of Bunyan's everyman. The sinner, burdened by sin, faces adversity and danger en route to the Celestial City. But Briggs's narrative ends quite differently: instead of securing "salvation" in Jesus and the reward of unshakable faith, she achieves her own subjectivity without losing her Christian concern for her children and other family members. On-screen, Corinne leaves her husband and the constricting church but does not abandon them. Rather, we see her flourishing anew in an environment free from the limits imposed by autocratic church elders.

Ultimately, Corinne tallied the ways in which her spiritual life was not contributing to her happiness and well-being. When she dared to speak at a prayer gathering, she was put down by the pastor and rebuked by his wife for trying to teach the men. She is chastised for wanting to enjoy a pretty dress, because it might draw attention from men. When she sought professional help to salvage her marriage, the therapist blamed her. In this closed world of spiritually defended patriarchy, she has learned that no one honors the opinionated woman. Corinne joined churches that represented an ideological approach to morality in American fundamentalism similar to that noted by theologian Rosemary Ruether: "It is as if the Bible endorses a version of the late Victorian, Anglo-Saxon patriarchal family as the model of family life proposed in the Scriptures."[26] This model was wholly unprepared to meet the cultural transformations of the 1960s.

Farmiga's treatment of Corinne's spiritual pilgrimage remains sympathetic and nonjudgmental. During the movie, Corinne has three pregnancies, in line with her community's embrace of the biblical command to be fruitful and multiply, and she is shown as a fun-loving and attentive mother. Her community is not opposed to sexual expression and enjoyment within marriage—an area of overlap with hippie culture—and this produces humor during a scene of the men's weekly meeting in which they listen with growing unease to cassette tapes urging them in increasingly explicit terms how to please their wives sexually. The "Jesus people" in Corinne's circle have large families and are shown to be caring parents. But while the community has strict norms for moral and faithful marriage, temptation lurks everywhere. Even Corinne's attempt at Bible study with a male friend holds the potential for flirtation, which her husband observes from across the room. Ethan's growing anxiety about his wife's lack of interest in him drives the latter half of the film, yet he fails to defend her against the sexist treatment she has received. Corinne reveals her feelings of being let down during a women's Bible study and prayer meeting. As the housewives share refreshments, including carob brownies made by the pastor's wife, Annika and Corinne chat on a sofa while the rest of the group help themselves to food. "Do you know what carob tastes like?" Corinne asks Annika. "Chocolate?" Annika suggests. "Disappointment," Corinne replies. As Corinne's regret infects her marriage, she looks for answers outside of the church community to overcome her feelings of emptiness and isolation.

History: The Film's Silent Character?

The backdrop to Briggs's life and *Higher Ground* is one of the most conflicted and tumultuous eras in American history: the three decades from the 1960s to the 1980s. Following World War II, the Cold War decades saw the positive developments of rising prosperity, increasing access to higher education, and an expanding middle class, followed by the rise of social movements supporting antinuclear and antiwar causes, Black power, ecology, feminism, free speech, and sexual liberation. Corinne, however, caught up in the Jesus movement in rural

New York, seems rather isolated from these concerns. Yet the Cold War and the threat of nuclear war did in fact influence many Christian groups, who by the 1970s began to embrace apocalyptic rhetoric and prepare for the end times. Corinne's community seems to choose the apolitical approach of restoring spiritual innocence through their communalism, which nonetheless rests upon the acceptance of patriarchy. Other Protestant Americans took a deadly path, such as those who embraced the extremist apocalyptic Branch Davidian cult in Waco, Texas, in the 1980s. While *Higher Ground* neither engages these larger cultural conflicts nor names them specifically, they form the background to the Jesus people movement, which at times found evangelicals, fundamentalists, and Pentecostals overlapping in their approach to Christian faith and in their urgency about the world's end. On an intimate plane, Corinne's story is one of affectionate engagement with the Jesus people, followed by disenchantment with the men who controlled her life inside those congregations. In a sense, her gradual evolution toward self-confidence and self-assertion stands in contrast with the immediate and revolutionary impact of the moral revolutions of the 1960s, but it could not have occurred without them.

Conclusion: Expression of the Self

Higher Ground is a fine instance of the "Christian movies for the rest of us" that have surfaced since 2010 and which by now form an identifiable corpus, including such titles as *Tree of Life*, *Of Gods and Men*, *The Way*, *Calvary*, *Last Days in the Desert*, *Risen*, *Silence*, *The Confirmation*, and *First Reformed*.[27] These films are a different sort of "religious" film than, say, the explicitly Christian prophesies enacted in the Left Behind series, or the heavy-handed variations on the rapture by evangelical filmmaker Donald Thompson. While also calling to mind other earlier films about American Protestants, such as *Tender Mercies* (1983) and *The Apostle* (1997), *Higher Ground* is nonetheless different because it dramatizes an actual memoir.[28] The film successfully establishes the atmosphere of joyfulness and wonderment experienced by Corinne and her congregation, which is gradually contested. The wisdom that Corinne acquires does not prompt her to remain inside the faith as a reformer, but neither does it lead her to attack it or to forget its benefits. She can recognize her former life inside its separatist citadel but regards her departure from it as a step forward. Throughout the film, Farmiga eyes with affection the landscape of Protestant culture inflected by biblical literalism, showing its closely bonded communities and loving families, its singing and sermonizing, its modest dress codes and earnest scripture study, while challenging its narrow insistence on biblical interpretation by masculine authority and its dampening effects on the psychic and social lives of women. Following its source in the genre of spiritual autobiography, *Higher Ground* successfully portrays a contemporary woman's struggle to become an individual by developing interests outside marriage and motherhood. The film presents a life with faith and hints of one without, gracefully raising questions about the conflicts between personal autonomy and psychological health, on the one hand, and group belonging and patriarchal authority, on the other, without requiring answers.

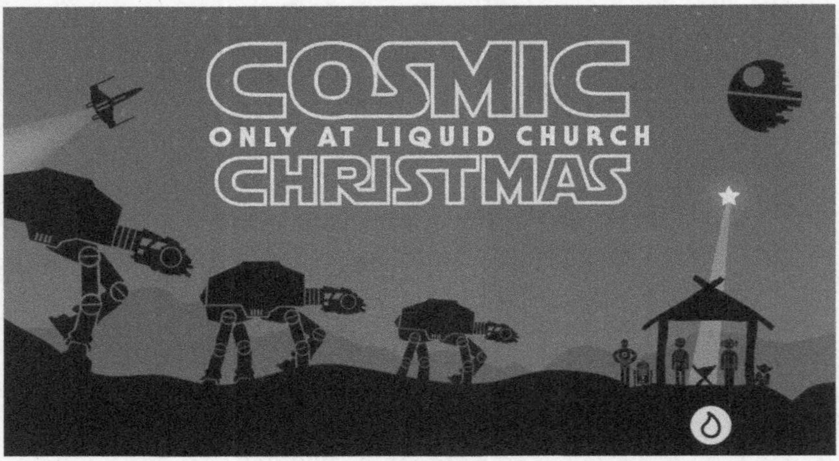

Figure 16.1 *Star Wars*–inspired advertisement (December 2015) for the Liquid Church, a New Jersey evangelical megachurch.
Courtesy Liquid Church

16

Evangelicals and *Star Wars*: Appropriating a Culture from a Galaxy Far, Far Away

Alex Wainer

December 18, 2015, saw the return of one of modern Hollywood's most resilient film franchises. Trailers for *Star Wars Episode VII: The Force Awakens* had excited fans who awaited returning to the faraway galaxy with old and new characters. The celebration was happening, among other places, in a northern New Jersey megachurch. Liquid Church, meeting at five campuses, was planning a "Cosmic Christmas" event for Christmas Eve, a week after the premiere of the new film. A page on the church's website, featuring images of four-legged Imperial AT-AT assault vehicles approaching the Christ child's stable like giant metal camels, described the event:

> - NJ's only LIVE Star Wars Nativity Scene! You'll wield a lightsaber and join the Nativity Scene with Leia, Han Solo & Chewy.
> - Sit on "Darth Santa's" knee and take a selfie.
> - Plus Jolly Ol' Stormtroopers and fun Star Wars giveaways.
>
> This family friendly event culminates in a message of hope that tells the story of Jesus' birth in a way you've never heard before![1]

The conflation of the star of Bethlehem with *Star Wars* points to the current state of many evangelical churches, which is the culmination of a two-track journey: evangelicals experiencing, on the one hand, qualms about aspects of the blockbuster film series's Eastern-philosophy-inflected Jedis and the Force and, on the other hand, an eagerness to co-opt the movies for evangelism and teaching opportunities. While in an earlier time evangelicals were theologically wary of popular amusements, the modern church appropriates all things *Star Wars* as a strategy for marketing the Gospel.

Alex Wainer, *Evangelicals and* Star Wars*: Appropriating a Culture from a Galaxy Far, Far Away* In: *Protestants on Screen*. Edited by: Gastón Espinosa, Erik Redling and Jason Stevens, Oxford University Press.
DOI: 10.1093/oso/9780190058906.003.0017

Evangelicals, *Star Wars*, and Cultural Change

The relationship between American evangelicals and mass culture is a tortured one. As far back as the nineteenth century, congregations heard warnings from the pulpit against "worldly amusements" such as card playing, theater attendance, and novel reading. "'I cannot believe that a person who has ever known the love of God can relish a secular novel,' a famous evangelist of the period, Charles G. Finney, remarked. 'Let me visit your chamber, your parlor, or wherever you keep your books. What is here? Byron, Scott, Shakespeare and a host of triflers and blasphemers of God.'"[2] The separatist stance, corresponding to the "Christ against culture" position that Richard Niebuhr defines in *Christ and Culture* (1951), would have enduring consequences for evangelical churches.[3] Much of the evangelical church took its cues from such dire exhortations, staying away from the consumption, not to mention the production, of much popular culture. With the arrival in the twentieth century of consecutive waves of new media—film, radio, and then television—the antagonism was sorely tested. Other churches besides evangelical ones made common cause in the 1920s against racy conduct on- and off-screen by Hollywood actors and directors. Frank Walsh, among other chroniclers, describes the film capital's conflict with churches, which led to the enforcement of the Production Code of 1930.[4] Television, though initially broadcasting innocuous content for the widest possible postwar audience, in the latter 1960s became a purveyor of permissive values that were restrained mostly by whatever advertisers and the FCC would tolerate. Televisions proliferated into almost every household, with few to no exceptions in evangelical homes.

William Romanowski has described varying attitudes held by evangelicals toward the popular arts. *Condemnation* characterized many churches from the nineteenth century well into the twentieth. The ever more ubiquitous media of the last fifty-plus years saw a gradual shift toward *appropriation* of the wider culture, exemplified by the rise of contemporary Christian music (CCM), which had no inherent musical distinctiveness, preferring to retain the forms of popular musical style while changing the content to be safely Christian, "infusing them with a spiritual justification."[5] The adoption of "worldly" musical styles in the service of evangelically appropriate lyrical content and the rise of a CCM recording industry helped evangelicals acclimate to more mainstream styles, leading to a greater openness to cultural products that might have been viewed warily or avoided outright in an earlier time. The adoption of media habits, says Romanowski, led to the *consumption* approach, which "tends to downplay the spiritual conflict in human affairs."[6] Thus, we see a transition from Niebuhr's "Christ against culture," promoted in nineteenth-century evangelical pulpits, to something more like "Christ transforming culture," a position that embraces the forms of popular culture while seeking to redeem them by filling them with Christian content. This accords with Augustine's (in *On Christian Doctrine*) and other early Christian writers' concept of "plundering the Egyptians"—that is, finding the golden or true elements of human culture and converting them to serve God's redemptive purposes. To be sure, there were earlier instances of evangelicals using popular media to attract potential converts "into the tent," but the rise of CCM was a broader, more influential, and more lasting effort.[7]

Evangelical resistance to the surrounding culture gradually declined through the era of television's dominance and then the rise of the blockbuster film as the central support system for a revived Hollywood film industry. In the late 1970s, when *Jaws* (1975), *Rocky* (1976), and *Star Wars* (1977) were all immensely successful while avoiding the scandal of an R rating, a new generation of evangelicals more willingly embraced popular culture.

This warming to popular culture had occurred against the backdrop of a shift in cinema that had begun in 1968, when Hollywood replaced the Production Code with the MPAA rating system. Whereas the former had been an all-ages entertainment strategy, the rating system afforded far more room for adult experimentation with movie content. In the films of the late sixties and early seventies, the antihero was both protagonist and antagonist, having questionable or obscure goals, questioning authority and traditional values, and exhibiting nothing like the moral code of Hollywood's studio era. When *Star Wars* arrived, its impact reverberated across the culture. After years of films created in the long shadows of Vietnam and the Watergate scandal, as described by Peter Biskind among others, George Lucas's epic hit felt like a happy return to the simpler stories of classic Hollywood cinema, with clear demarcations between good and evil.[8] The most distinctive element was the addition of the Force, a metaphysical concept that functioned as a sort of unseen character throughout the film. Aging Jedi knight Obi-Wan Kenobi described it as "an energy field created by all living things. It surrounds us, penetrates us, and binds the galaxy together." The addition of a mystical component that could determine the outcome of an interstellar conflict updated the classic Hollywood adventure film into the Age of Aquarius, and many Christians, seeing something like faith in an unseen entity, were attracted and intrigued.

By the time the first three *Star Wars* films had been released, ending with *Return of the Jedi* (1983), two evangelical stances toward the films had emerged. Writing in *The Religion of the Force*, Norman Geisler and Richard Howe had taken on the task of comparing and contrasting Christianity with the numerous Eastern and occult influences that are found within the films' concept of the Force. In contrast to the impersonal energy field of the Force, "Christianity understands God as a personal being who is the transcendent Creator and upholder of all things whose will for everyone is to have a personal relationship with him."[9] Geisler and Amano take an apologetic approach, using the analysis of the Force to point readers toward Jesus Christ as the ultimate fulfillment of what many find attractive about Lucas's galactic metaphysical entity.

Following the release of the original *Star Wars* film, now known *as Episode I: A New Hope*, evangelist and Bible teacher Winkie Pratney wrote perhaps the first book to harness for Christian allegory the wonder and delight audience members had found in the two burgeoning fantasy/science-fiction properties: *Star Wars, Star Trek, and the 21st Century Christian.* Avoiding any condemnation of the Force as a disguised lure to Eastern mysticism, Pratney instead sought to stir the imaginations of readers, writing in free-verse style, to suggest that there is a greater truth prefigured in *Star Wars.*

> You think it is just pure fantasy don't you? . . .
> Ah, but great fairy tales have a way of telling the truth/Snow White/Cinderella/Pinocchio/Sleeping Beauty
>
> *Star Wars*,
>
> My friend, it's too good not to be true.
> Come with me and I will tell you the story again.[10]

The various characters of the movie are presented as allegorical stand-ins for the sweeping cosmic drama of God's salvation in Jesus Christ. Deftly interpreting movies and fairy tales as allusions to the great biblical narrative of spiritual warfare, Pratney seeks to inspire the reader to join the reality that *Star Wars* can merely intimate, by coming to faith in Christ. Pratney's book and Geisler and Amano's set the dueling patterns of the two approaches evangelicals would exhibit up to the present.

Perhaps no single evangelical publication focused on the movies as did the August 1983 issue of *Contemporary Christian Magazine*, nor did another publication so closely track the opening of evangelicals to American entertainment production. Originally founded as *Contemporary Christian Music*, for a time the magazine dropped the word "music" from its title to better frame its engagement with not only the Christian music industry but also popular culture generally. The August issue featured an illustration from the recently released *Return of the Jedi* on its cover and contained four articles on the film and the *Star Wars* franchise. The coverage led with "The Gospel of Lucas," by publisher and editor in chief John Styll. Citing comments by George Lucas from numerous sources, Styll sought to capture Lucas's stated intention that the series was a vehicle for teaching moral values to young people. Styll cites Lucas's statement in one interview: "For better or worse, the influence of the church, which used to be all-powerful, has been usurped by film."[11] In a *Time* interview cited in the article, Lucas boiled down his message: "I was trying to say in a very simple way, knowing that the film was made for a young audience, that there is a God and there is both a good side and a bad side. You have a choice between them, but the world works better if you're on the good side. It's just that simple." Styll then proceeds to examine the concept of the Force: "Pantheistic—identifying God as a force of nature—and dualistic, the Force also bears elements of Zen Buddhism, Taoism, Islam, and Judaism. . . . These ingredients are a matter of concern for many Christians." He also notes that the phrase "May the Force be with you" resembles the traditional blessing "May the Lord be with you." But Styll cautions that Lucas's potpourri of religious and philosophical fragments cannot add up to a complete religion: "If there is a danger in his 'gospel,' it is that it's incomplete and could lead people astray from the gospel of Christ."[12]

In the same issue, Stephen R. Lawhead positively analyzes the film in terms of its storytelling and cinematic achievement while highlighting the Force as the metaphysical entity of the film. Countering critics who complained that *Return of the Jedi* lacked mention of God, Lawhead noted the tendency of some writers to link "the character of Luke Skywalker with the Antichrist, Darth Vader with Satan or the Beast, or—perhaps worse—trying to interpret the Force as the God of the Bible," and he judged that "one ought not to spend too much time allegorizing non-allegorical works."[13]

Following *Return of the Jedi*, there was a lull in the *Star Wars* universe as Lucas turned to other projects. By this time, an article in the *Christian Science Monitor* could observe that evangelicals' discomfort toward the erstwhile "worldly amusements" had dramatically declined. Citing the example of a traditional Presbyterian church having transitioned to a megachurch "with video screens, rock music, and an upbeat tempo," the article noted that evangelicals had incorporated marketing principles to improve their outreach efforts.[14] "The shift here, as in pews across the country," commented writer Robert Marquand, "signals a new attitude by evangelicals toward popular culture. More than ever, experts say, evangelical churches are using formerly disavowed ways of the world to preach the Gospel—touching off an internal clash over the identity and direction of the church." This embrace of pop culture as a means to presenting ancient doctrine became an established practice in church growth strategies. Whereas in times past an assumed biblical literacy allowed sermons to employ scriptural language, stories, and references, the new approach no longer assumed such familiarity. Marquand pointed out that a survey by the Alliance of Confessing Evangelicals had shown "that 71 percent of the Christian bookseller community . . . could not name half of the Ten Commandments." The new assumption was that recipients of church sermons were more familiar with the content of popular culture than with the Bible, and thus forms, stories, lyrics, and characters from film, television, and rock music were the starting place to garner the attention of target audiences.

Underlying this attraction to pop culture as a means of proclaiming the Gospel were certain historical attitudes shared by evangelicals. "American evangelicals and the surrounding culture," wrote communication scholar and frequent analyst of evangelical culture Quentin Schultze, share four essential traits: "*a disinterest in tradition, a faith in technology, a drive toward popularization, and a belief in individualism.*"[15] The first three traits especially explain the willingness of evangelicals to adopt new media and popular art forms uncritically in the pursuit of attention from believers and nonbelievers alike. Just as contemporary Christian music had adopted the forms of pop and rock music while substituting sometimes raucous lyrics with "safer," more faith-oriented words, so many evangelical churches sought to exploit familiarity with ubiquitous mass media content by adopting the idioms of popular culture to draw in greater numbers.

By 1997, there having been no new *Star Wars* films for over thirteen years, George Lucas released the three films in theaters as special editions, using the occasion to experiment with newer CGI technology to add or improve effects not possible in the original releases. A new generation was able to experience in theaters what had only been available on television broadcasts and home video, thus sustaining and widening interest in the franchise. The experiments encouraged Lucas to pursue a new trilogy of prequels released between 1999 and 2005. By now, *Star Wars* was a multimedia phenomenon that included video games, novelizations, and animation, not to mention the ever-proliferating varieties of merchandise. With the franchise now clearly a cultural institution, it was practically impossible to grow up unaware of *Star Wars*.

Early after the turn of the twenty-first century, *Time* magazine's Richard Corliss could observe how much popular culture was being co-opted by evangelical churches: "Clergy of all denominations have commandeered pulpits, publishing houses and especially websites to spread the gospel of cinevangelism."[16] His article features a typical approach to drawing lessons from numerous films, showing pastor Erwin McManus cinematically sermonizing:

> "Peter Parker gives us all a chance to be heroic. . . . The problem is, we keep looking for radioactive spiders, but really it's God who changes us." What's the big idea behind *The Village*, according to the website movieministry.com? "Perfect love drives out fear." Behind *The Notebook*? "God can step in where science cannot." And, gulp, *Anchorman*? "What is love?"

As evangelicals became ever more comfortable with popular culture in the sanctuary, it was reflected not only in references but also in the use of multimedia, skits, concerts, costumes, and other tie-ins to churches' ministries.

The prequel trilogy ended in 2005 with *Episode III: Revenge of the Sith*, and that year saw the publication of articles and numerous books by evangelicals that examined the *Star Wars* franchise from a faith perspective. The books included such 2005 titles as *Finding God in a Galaxy Far, Far Away*, *The Star Wars Trilogy* (Connect Bible Studies), *A True Hope: Jedi Perils and the Way of Jesus*, and *Star Wars Redeemed: Your Life-Transforming Journey with Jesus and the Jedi*, the back cover of which features this description:

> The Cross Gave You "A New Hope" But What if the Devil Strikes Back?
>
> Is your Christian life like Luke's disappointed gaze to the horizon? Do you find your lack of faith disturbing? When you read the Bible, is it as confusing as the plot of *The Phantom Menace*? Well, go strap yourself in and get ready for a *biblical blast off!*[17]

One book, *Christian Wisdom of the Jedi Masters*, by writer and radio host Dick Staub, sought to meet the needs of young Christians, like a young man who had just watched one of the *Star Wars* films with him and had expressed frustration that he could not pursue a deeper spiritual experience outside Lucas's mythology. Staub responds to the youth, "It's like you want to be a 'Jedi Christian' and my generation didn't produce a Yoda."[18] Using the films as an interpretive platform, Staub's book takes on the task of transmitting Christian wisdom drawn from many sources such as C. S. Lewis, Søren Kierkegaard, Thomas Merton, and others. Advice at the end of each chapter takes the form of Christian Jedi teacher Staub addressing the pupil with sage counsel: "Aspiring Jedi, your success in seeking the Lord of the Force requires putting down your guard and allowing the Lord of the Force to find, know, and love you, just as you are."[19]

The trend continued beyond 2005 with *Star Wars Jesus—A Spiritual Commentary on the Reality of the Force*, and of course *The Gospel According to Star Wars: Faith, Hope and the Force*.[20] In *Star Wars Jesus*, author Caleb Grimes uses the iconic scene in *A New Hope* when Luke Skywalker, longing to escape his mundane existence on the desert planet Tatooine, gazes at the binary sunset as the soundtrack swells to connect the reader to C. S. Lewis's concept of *Sehnsucht*, the "inconsolable longing" for a greater unseen reality: "Is this a subconscious hunger to know the Force, which is similar to our desire to know a personal God?"[21]

Figure 16.2 Yoda is the model of a "Jedi Christian."
DVD screen capture, fair use

Figure 16.3 This iconic scene from *Star Wars: A New Hope* evokes a cosmic yearning that is perhaps akin to humanity's need for a personal God.
DVD screen capture, fair use

The Audience Awakens to More *Star Wars*

In 2009, George Lucas sold Lucasfilm to the Walt Disney Company for over $4 billion, and soon there was talk of new *Star Wars* films. Star director/producer J. J. Abrams was chosen to direct the next film, eventually titled *Star Wars: Episode VII: The Force Awakens*. The saga would continue with characters from Episodes IV–VI while adding a new generation of younger figures picking up the story decades later. Shrewdly blending familiar elements from a desert planet, spacecraft, a resurgent empire, and now older but still beloved characters, the film updated the franchise with a young female protagonist experiencing the same call to adventure as had Luke Skywalker originally.

Again, evangelical media responded with two strategies. The critical apologetics approach is exemplified in an article by Robert Velarde, "May the Force Bewitch You," published in the Christian Research Institute's print journal and on its website. Despite the films' heroic morality and other positive qualities, Velarde states: "In reality, however, Star Wars is replete with non-Christian worldview concepts, including elements of Gnosticism, Taoism, Hinduism, Buddhism, Eastern meditation, occultism, and moral relativism."[22] In the article, Velarde notes that the series has been "overly praised," with a footnote listing several of the books mentioned above that used *Star Wars* to point readers toward Christianity. "When it comes to questions of truth and knowledge," he writes in the concluding paragraph, "Christianity calls us to test evidence, using the intellect to understand and critically investigate. Faith is involved, but it is not a blind faith. In contrast, the world of Star Wars encourages individuals to 'feel' rather than 'think' and to search inside themselves for answers."

Perhaps the most detailed attack on the franchise's Eastern content comes from an article by Tal Brooke, "Creating a New Mystical Religion," published in the Spiritual Counterfeits Project's journal. For the evangelicals wary of syncretism, the Spiritual Counterfeits Project's publications were a response to the spread of Eastern and other non-Christian philosophies into popular culture beginning in the early 1970s. Tracing Lucas's Force concept through Joseph Campbell's Jungian study of myth and the collective unconscious, *The Hero with a Thousand Faces* (1949), Brooke argues that the *Star Wars* films' mysticism contributes to the development of a "shared mythology," for a world that "needs a unifying, nondivisive planetary religious experience—and a more universal creed from this awakening."[23] At the website of Ligonier Ministries, a conservative Bible-teaching organization in the Reformed tradition, Peter Jones discussed the "neopagan" aspects of the Force in the article "Star Wars and the Ancient Religion," in which he describes the monism of the movies' belief system, which he terms "Oneist," wherein all in the universe is one.[24]

There seemed to be significantly more force to the other strategy, that of using *Star Wars* uncritically to point back to biblical figures and stories. *Relevant* magazine, aimed at a Christian young adult demographic, published an article, "The Gospel of Star Wars," noting the good meanings of the series despite the unbiblical cosmology:

> We shouldn't just avoid the franchise because of its deeply embedded pantheism—essentially the view that the universe itself is god—as long as we recognize it for what it is. *Star Wars*' mystical force that binds all things together does not equate with the personal triune god of scripture who is intimately involved with his creation (while also remaining definitively distinct from it).

Still, those of us who firmly believe in the supernatural shouldn't dismiss or discourage the proclivity to see life as divinely charged.[25]

Another article, "A Force for Good? How Star Wars Explores Big Questions About Faith, Power, and Morality," published on the site of Newspring Church, a South Carolina megachurch, adopted the now familiar tack of illustrating principles of Christian living through examples from the films, thereby redirecting *Star Wars* into advice literature:

> Luke came to a moment of decision: leave home and risk his life, or stay comfortable and safe, never to discover who he really is or what life is like beyond his predictable existence. . . . That's not so different from the Bible's account of Abram, whom God called not with a fully formed plan or even a destination, but with the simple invitation to leave all he had ever known and He would provide something beyond his imagination (Genesis 12:1–4).[26]

Just as preachers in generations past employed literary and historical references as well as biblical ones, based on the assumption that the congregants knew Scripture, many of today's evangelical pastors know that they are not likely to stir the interests of the average listener without resort to the content of popular culture. In a Vimeo online video recorded in November 2016, Pastor Petey Bingham delivers the sermon "Functional Fulfillment" as part of the Florida-based Celebration megachurch's "At the Movies" series. Dressed in jeans and a black T-shirt and sporting a tattoo on his biceps, Bingham opens the sermon by generously sprinkling in humorous comments, like a seasoned comedian. After screening the scene from *The Force Awakens* where Kylo Ren kills his father, Han Solo, to complete his journey to the dark side of the Force, Bingham notes that though Kylo is very gifted in the Force, he is misusing his talents. Bingham then shifts to a discussion of how Christians can best find fulfillment in using their gifts to serve others.[27]

Production values at another megachurch's "At the Movies" event demonstrated the commitment that the church, Christ Fellowship of Palm Beach County, Florida, has made to employing the latest technology and stagecraft to capture the audience/congregation's attention. Christ Fellowship shot footage of an on-screen "Darth Vader" threatening a campus pastor in a pre-sermon sketch. Assembling a "trailer" from various *Star Wars* films, complete with the green-band MPAA opening, a YouTube video (since removed) announced the upcoming event with a message urging viewers to "invite a friend," in the classic *Star Wars* yellow-on-black-star-field font.[28]

Conclusion

The two tracks described above share the general assumptions of the "Christ transforming culture" position. Those critics who warn about Eastern elements in the films usually grant that the franchise can speak to the audience's longing for traces of spirituality and transcendence, and none condemn outright Christians' attendance at movies, as the nineteenth-century advocates of "Christ against culture" did when they condemned any cultural participation as worldly distractions from godly living. Twenty-first-century evangelical use of popular culture is marked by a more uncritical approach to cultural engagement unimaginable in earlier generations.

Mark Noll, a historian of evangelicalism, notes in an online interview that one of the strengths of the movement has been its ability to pursue its mission by adapting its methods to changing times. "The positive side of that motivation is that the Christian message is brought to newer groups of people," he remarks. "In our day, the negative danger is that a thin kind of Christian message will be brought that is adjusted more for popular cultural norms than by the norms of the Christian gospel."[29] An extreme example of this danger is the Liquid Church's *Star Wars* Christmas celebration, displacing traditional members of the Nativity scene with heroes from the dazzlingly popular space opera. The question of whether using popular culture narratives to promote a Gospel message undermines and distracts from the ancient Gospel message itself is a question with which the modern evangelical church is yet to fully reckon.

Conclusion

PART V
PROTESTANT THEMES IN FILM GENRES

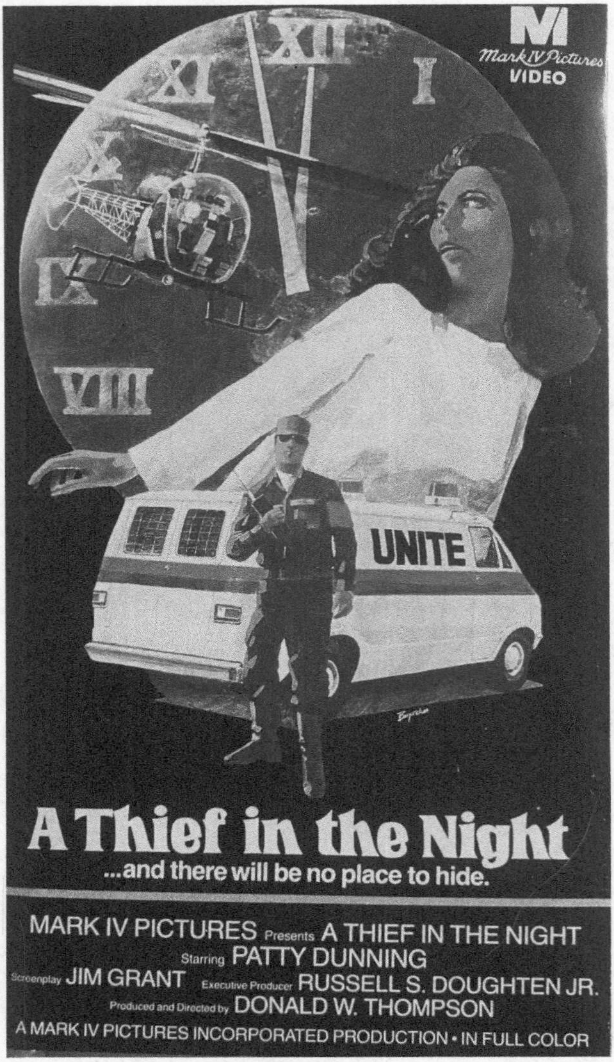

Figure 17.1 Original poster for Donald Thompson and Russ Doughten's *Thief in the Night* (Mark IV Pictures), the most influential evangelical feature film of the 1970s.
Used with permission of Timothy Doughten, director, Russ Doughten Films

17

The Rise and Fall of Evangelical Protestant Apocalyptic Horror: From *A Thief in the Night* to *Left Behind* and Beyond

Timothy Beal

The late 1960s and early 1970s were big years for American Protestant evangelicalism generally and evangelical youth culture specifically.[1] Emerging since the 1940s out of and in some ways over against the fundamentalist movement, which had become increasingly sectarian in the wake of the Scopes trial and other embarrassments, the parachurch movement of neo-evangelicalism, as it was then known, made American youth culture its mission field, and sought to make its Gospel popular by the world's standards. In the perennial evangelical dilemma of preservation versus popularization—protecting and preserving the sanctity of the tradition versus getting the Word out by whatever means necessary—the new evangelicals leaned hard toward popularization, taking as their motto Paul's declaration "I have become all things to all people, so that I might by any means save some."[2]

Central to their approach were parachurch organizations such as Youth for Christ, Campus Crusade for Christ, and Young Life, which explicitly targeted the most popular kids with the expectation that others would follow, and whose weekly club meetings included wild and crazy games and skits along with more serious (if brief) Bible study and prayer. Youth for Christ had actually begun as a series of Saturday night youth rallies that attracted hundreds of thousands of young people in big cities across the United States. These rallies were led by young, energetic preachers like Billy Graham (the first full-time employee of Youth for Christ) and were modeled on the big shows popular in the emerging secular entertainment industry. Organizers produced slick ads and created mainstream radio and television tie-ins. Some of the evangelists went so far as to adopt the voices and styles of celebrities like Frank Sinatra. Others, like Graham, soon found their own distinctive star power.[3]

By the early 1970s, neo-evangelical rallies were looking less like a Frank Sinatra show and more like an Aerosmith concert. In 1972, Campus Crusade for Christ hosted Explo '72, a weeklong gathering of high school and college

Timothy Beal, *The Rise and Fall of Evangelical Protestant Apocalyptic Horror: From* A Thief in the Night *to* Left Behind *and Beyond* In: *Protestants on Screen*. Edited by: Gastón Espinosa, Erik Redling and Jason Stevens, Oxford University Press. © Oxford University Press 2023. DOI: 10.1093/oso/9780190058906.003.0018 students in Dallas, Texas. The event culminated in what was later dubbed the Christian Woodstock, an eight-hour-long Christian rock concert in the Cotton Bowl that drew over a hundred thousand people.

A Thief in the Night

At the same time, a robust Christian film industry was emerging to produce, promote, and distribute evangelical feature films in the familiar styles of Hollywood and B movies to show in local churches, libraries, school gyms, and community theaters.[4]

One of the more successful of these companies in the early years was Charles O. Baptista's Scriptures Visualized Institute, which not only produced dozens of evangelistic films for wide distribution but also sold its own movie projector, called the Miracle Projector, which had a label guaranteeing that it would be "good until the second coming of Christ." In 1941, Baptista produced a movie called *The Rapture*, which was to the best of my knowledge the first evangelistic rapture movie.

In documentary newsreel style, and no doubt haunted by the thousands of soldiers disappearing in the battles of World War II every day, this twelve-minute short includes many shots, cuts, and special effects that would become standard fare for nearly all rapture movies to follow: unconductored trains and other unpiloted vehicles crashing into each other, people disappearing while perplexed others are left behind, and empty cradles, all interspersed with an antiphonal text message in the sky, asking, "Are you ready?" Baptista's *The Rapture* was screened in churches and at youth rallies across the United States for years.

But no rapture movie has been more widely watched and more influential on American youth culture or on the emergence of evangelical horror culture than the 1972–1973 movie *A Thief in the Night*. Its production company, Mark IV Pictures (a reference to Mark 4:33, "With many such parables he spoke the word to them, as they were able to hear it"), was a collaboration of Russell S. Doughten Jr., a longtime Christian, and Donald W. Thompson, a new and zealous convert to the faith. Both had extensive experience producing and directing secular films, including B-movie horror and action features (famously, Doughten had produced the 1958 drive-in horror hit *The Blob*), and their ambition was to make Christian action-adventure movies for young people. *Thief* was shot entirely in Des Moines, Iowa, where Doughten and Thompson lived, on a budget of about $60,000, and was promoted only by word of mouth. Its success exceeded their wildest expectations: at the peak of its popularity, they were booking fifteen hundred rentals per month. Some local libraries held as many as fifteen copies in order to keep up with demand from churches and other organizations. And many groups rented it regularly (e.g., for annual Halloween or New Year's Eve showings). In all, *Thief* generated an unprecedented $1 million-plus in rental revenues, and by 1984, including video sales, it had reportedly grossed $4.2 million. Estimates as to how many people have seen the film range from 100 million to an astounding 300 million.[5]

Given those numbers, it's not surprising that the movie had a tremendous influence on innumerable American teens, including myself. It scared the hell out of many, who started getting themselves ready by converting at the end of the movie (Doughten and Thompson intended this, and included a scene in which a little girl, terrified of being left behind by her mom, says a very scripted prayer to ask Jesus into her heart, thereby providing viewers with the words they would need for conversion). Still other kids, equally traumatized, ran the other way. Satanic rock performance artist Marilyn Manson, for example, recalls being terrified by the movie, which ultimately helped push him in a more Nietzschian *Beyond Good and Evil* direction.[6]

Thief also had tremendous influence on the emergence of evangelical horror. Its financial success not only paved the way for Mark IV's sequels (*A Distant Thunder* [1977], *Image of the Beast* [1981], and *Prodigal Planet* [1983]) but also opened the door to other kinds of Christian B-movie horror, most notably the hellfire-and-real-maggots splatter films about what happens to you in hell by Ron and June Ormond, who converted to Christianity after cutting their teeth making sexploitation movies in the sixties; some of their best-known movies, like *The Burning Hell* (1974) and *The Grim Reaper* (1976), sent overwhelmed viewers running from church basement screenings to throw up and/or cry and/or get saved.

A Thief in the Night of the Living Dead

Part of what distinguishes *A Thief in the Night* from these later, far more violent, and often more expensive films is the weirdly slow-paced, down-home Iowa, lo-fi banality that seems to drive its vision of a world in the wake of God. Some of that was unintentional: Doughten and Thompson were working with a very small budget; the actors were all local Des Moines residents with little or no experience in the film industry; The Fishmarket Combo, which performs the movie's theme song, Christian rocker Larry Norman's 1968 hit "I Wish We'd All Been Ready," was a local group of Young Life student volunteers; and there was no money to create cinematic spectacles of crashing planes and trains, people being swept up into the heavens, and demonic world leaders marking the foreheads of frightened left-behinds. In fact, the actual depiction of the moment of rapture doesn't take place until more than halfway through the movie. And when it does, what we get is a series of cuts between the lead singer of The Fishmarket Combo mowing his suburban lawn and a lonely little puffy cloud in the sky. The next cut is back to the lawnmower, now with no one pushing it but still running in the middle of the lawn. Though eerily effective, this puffy little cloud was not what Doughten and Thompson were aiming for. They wanted theophanic thunderclouds to depict the dramatic scene of the Second Coming described in some biblical passages. Throughout the shooting of the film, however, there were no clouds in the Des Moines sky. Thompson happened to have a little footage of this one cloud, and they were stuck using that.

But it fits with the rest of this lo-fi Des Moines–style rapture. When the world organization UNITE (United Nations Imperium of Total Emergency) institutes a mark—a stamped image of zeros and ones that digitally represents the number 666—to indicate conformity with their rule, we see elderly locals sitting at card tables politely smiling and pointing to their hands or foreheads to indicate where they would prefer to take it.

Indeed, in many respects, the film is reminiscent of other early low-budget, lo-fi horror movies from the 1960s and early 1970s. Take, for example, the scene

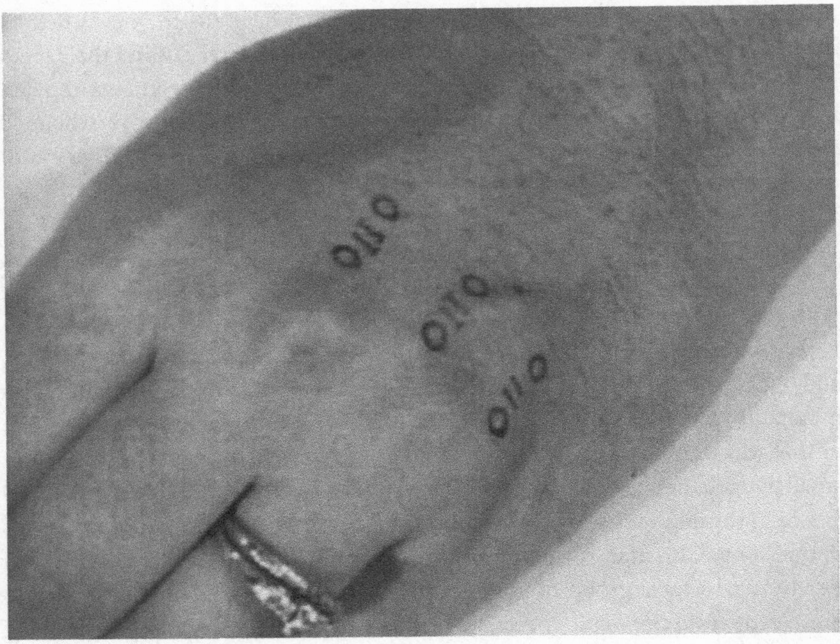

Figure 17.2 In *Thief in the Night*, the world organization UNITE institutes a mark—a stamped image of zeros and ones that digitally represents the number 666.
DVD screen capture, fair use

immediately following the opening performance, in which a series of quick cuts between shaky handheld shots of carnival images in saturated color is accompanied by a soundtrack of oddly demonic funhouse laughter created by sound director Ralph Carmichael (who has sometimes been called the "Bernard Herrmann of Christian cinema," Herrmann being best known for the screeching violins in Alfred Hitchcock's 1960 horror movie *Psycho*).

Most traumatically memorable for many viewers is the scene of a young girl who, having just heard a sermon on the rapture by the "good" pastor (played by none other than American religionist Randall Balmer's father), comes home to find her house empty and fears that she's been left behind. Here again, as in the opening scene we saw earlier, the barely acting, lo-fi slowness, overlain with escalating disharmonious sound, is suddenly interrupted by a burst of short cuts with wild angles.

Likewise, the film's narrative framing strategy, which begins and ends with the exact same footage depicting our main character, Patty, waking up to being left behind by her husband and God while the radio explains what has happened, recalls the equally slow-moving and creepy 1962 film *Carnival of Souls*, a low-budget horror movie (shot by a guy known for industrial films and commercials) that has a similarly surprising ending that loops back to the beginning.

Much of what lends *A Thief in the Night* this lo-fi vibe of end-times banality is particularly reminiscent of George Romero's lo-fi *Night of the Living Dead* from 1968, which was shot in rural Pennsylvania outside Pittsburgh on a very low budget ($114,000) with nonprofessional or first-time actors. Beyond the similar graininess and hollow sound of both movies (probably due to budget constraints as much as anything), they also share some narrative elements. Both, for example, use radio and TV emergency broadcasts in order to provide the broader global context of the personal and local crisis. In fact, both movies begin with a radio suddenly turning on by itself (Patty's bedside radio in *A Thief in the Night* and a car radio in *Night of the Living Dead*).

Most strikingly living-dead-like, however, are the scenes related to Patty's arrest by UNITE, her escape, and the ensuing chase through the strangely empty city and nearby woods. First, as Patty sits alone in her darkened house at night, watching the news, zombie-like UNITE police lurk outside. Then, after her arrest, she escapes and keeps easily slipping away from her slow, speechless, easily eluded, but ultimately relentless pursuers. At one point, she stumbles in horror into a zombie-like elderly couple with marked foreheads.

At the same time, the movie is very effective in encouraging viewers to identify with Patty, who by the middle of the movie is the only character who has been left behind without taking the mark (her liberal pastor, Reverend Turner, was also left behind, but he was executed by UNITE). Two common film strategies work together to create this identification with Patty in her post-rapture godforsaken isolation. First is the long, dreamlike series of flashbacks that explain what's happened (i.e., the saved have been raptured). These include a sermonette by the lead singer of The Fishmarket Combo; sermons by and conversations with the "good" pastor that lay out the rapture and tribulation to come and that explain how to be saved by accepting Jesus Christ as one's personal lord and savior; a long video montage of pictures of Patty and her husband's first few months of happy marriage before the rapture, overlain with a mournful instrumental version of the movie's theme song, "I Wish We'd All Been Ready"; and the conversions of Patty's husband and one of Patty's friends, who, along with God, have left her behind.

The second means of encouraging identification with Patty is the film's use of shot–reverse shot sequences, which involve an initial shot facing a character looking at someone or something, immediately followed by a shot turned roughly 180 degrees around, so that viewers see what that character sees (often followed by a third shot that returns to the original point of view). The effect of such sequences is to identify or "suture" the subjectivity of the viewer with that of the character in the first shot. There are several shot–reverse shot sequences in *A Thief in the Night* that build subjective identification with Patty in her alienation from everyone and everything else. During the flashback scenes, they often involve Patty reacting in disbelief and doubt to a pastor's preaching or to her husband's acceptance of that message. In other cases, they involve Patty confronting and evading UNITE's thugs and zombie-like old people who have taken the mark. With each of these shot–reverse shots, the world of the viewer, like that of Patty, grows more hostile and isolating—until, trapped by her former friends, she jumps off a bridge, presumably to her death, only to wake to her alarm and find herself exactly where the whole thing started: left behind.

Finally, the placement of Revelation-related mythemes within the movie's broader pre-tribulation rapture narrative also contributes to its disturbing lo-fi horror vibe. In fact, although the presumption of the film is that the biblical Book of Revelation is the blueprint for the scenario of the saved being raptured before a period of tribulation under demonic rule, there is in fact no such scenario—indeed, no rapture at all—in that text. The rapture scenario is built from other texts, especially a couple of passing references to saints being taken up into the clouds in 1 Thessalonians and 1 Corinthians, as well as other biblical and nonbiblical media, including, for this movie, Hal Lindsey's 1970 bestseller *The Late, Great Planet Earth* and the poignant lament of being abandoned by loved ones and God in Larry Norman's "I Wish We'd All Been Ready."[7] That said, there are three places in which mythemes of Revelation embed themselves in this film in cryptic and, to many viewers, disturbingly scary ways.

The first and most obvious is the use of the number 666 as the mark people must take to show their submission to and alliance with UNITE, most often represented by a makeshift van that was hastily customized by Doughten's son. Oddly, the number is never explicitly identified as the mark of the beast of

Revelation, which his minions must take on their right hand or forehead in order to be able to buy or sell (Revelation 13:16–18), and UNITE is never explicitly linked to the beast or its demonic dominion over the godforsaken earth. These undeciphered symbols likewise leave Patty, and most of the viewers identifying with her, inexplicably uncertain and in the dark.

The second Revelation mytheme derives from the armored locusts with human faces that are released to torture those who do not have the seal of God on their foreheads (Revelation 9:1–11). In the early 1970s, thanks largely to Hal Lindsey, these locusts were identified with Cobra attack helicopters. That is the only explanation for this cut.[8]

Third and most obvious is the reference in the title and throughout the film to the biblical warning (given in Revelation 3:3 and 16:15 as well as in several other New Testament passages [Matthew 24:36–44; cf. Luke 12:39; 1 Thessalonians 5:2, 4; 2 Peter 3:10]) that Christ will return like a "thief in the night." Having become commonplace in evangelical discourse, this idea is usually taken simply to mean that it will happen when you least expect it. But placed in the context of this movie, a more horrifying, if largely sublimated, sense emerged: the divine as a threat, which might at any time invade your home and steal you or, worse, your loved ones. Which is exactly what happens. Not that you would want to give your life to such a threatening invader, let alone love him; but would that he had taken you, too, so that you could at least be with the ones you do love.

Combine these film strategies with the ritual context in which the film was typically experienced by a viewer—as part of a captive congregation of young people in a Christian youth group meeting, opened and closed with prayer, in the evening, in a church or similar religious space—and you might even prefer it if it was the night of the living dead instead of the day after the rapture.

From Apocalyptic Horror to Apocalyptic Adventure

Lindvall and Quicke and others have traced the rather dull but lucrative path from *Thief* through the many rapture and tribulation movies and video shorts of the 1980s and 1990s that led to Cloud Ten Pictures' *Left Behind* movies, all based more or less on the bestselling series of apocalyptic fantasy-action novels by Tim LaHaye and Jerry B. Jenkins: first the trilogy (*Left Behind: The Movie* in 2000; *Left Behind II: Tribulation Force* in 2002; and *Left Behind III: World at War* in 2005), and then the single *Left Behind* movie starring Nicolas Cage in 2014.[9]

As the titles suggest, and as authors LaHaye and Jenkins readily acknowledge, their series drew much inspiration from *A Thief in the Night* and its sequels. Indeed, there's not a lot that's both new and interesting in the *Left Behind* movies (or the books, for that matter). They are chock full of now stock images and motifs from the evangelical apocalyptic mythosphere, drawn from early dispensationalist diagrams, *Scofield Study Bible* notes, Baptista's early rapture short film, and of course *A Thief in the Night*: unpiloted planes, trains, and automobiles; weeping mothers clutching blankies and teddy bears of disappeared babies; wifeless husbands or husbandless wives; pets lingering over the clothes of raptured owners (apparently children go but pets don't); and, of course, remorseful pastors left behind in their chapels, only realizing after it is too late that they have betrayed their faith.

And yet, although cinematographically unremarkable, I do think that the *Left Behind* trilogy and the most recent *Left Behind* redux with Nicolas Cage are worth our attention as symptoms of the changing face of evangelical apocalyptic culture. Perhaps most significantly, we see a shift away from the horror and toward the thrill. Apocalyptic dread becomes apocalyptic anticipation. In *A Thief in the Night*, being left behind really was a living nightmare, abandoned in a creepily dull, godforsaken Iowa wasteland. The withdrawal of God highlights the absence of loved ones, and the withdrawal of loved ones highlights the absence of God.

In the *Left Behind* movies, on the other hand, as in the novels and videogame, left behind is where all the action is.[10] Here we have all the makings of an apocalyptic thriller, as our heroes, the "tribulation saints," lead the ultimate resistance movement against the ultimate bad guy, the Antichrist, Nicolae Carpathia, whose name and Bela Lugosi–like accent suggest that he is intended to represent some kind of diabolical descendent of Bram Stoker's original diabolical invader from the Carpathian Mountains. In these movies, unlike in *Thief*, you really have to feel bad for the ones who got raptured, because they're not there when the shit starts to go down.

Perhaps Cloud Ten Pictures planned to unpack those details in a sequel or two, once audiences were hooked. In the last scene of *Left Behind*, Buck gazes on the city skyline in flames, shakes his head, and says, "It looks like the end of the world." To which Chloe responds, "No, not yet. I'm afraid this is just the beginning."

Neither is it to be continued, as Cloud Ten does not appear to have found sufficient underwriting, and its grassroots Indiegogo.com fundraising campaign failed miserably, reaching only 16 percent of its goal of $500,000 before closing in May 2015, with Indiegogo's standard notification, "No Time Left," ringing with peculiar irony.

From Apocalyptic Adventure to Zombie Apocalypse

In the wake of the *Left Behind* flop, Cloud Ten's co-founder Paul Lalonde has found something new to do with his time. He has left behind the Christian

Figure 17.3 Nicolae Carpathia, the Antichrist in *Left Behind: The Movie* trilogy. His name and Bela Legosi–like accent suggest that he is a diabolical descendant of Bram Stoker's Dracula.
DVD screen capture, fair use

Revelation-inspired rapture story world inaugurated by *A Thief in the Night* and left in ruins after the most recent *Left Behind* movie for another end-times cultural treasure trove: zombies.

In 2019, Lalonde co-produced a remake of David Cronenberg's 1977 sci-fi zombie thriller, *Rabid*, which is about a woman who, after undergoing plastic surgery, develops a taste for human blood, turning her victims into bloodthirsty zombies who in turn infect others. Lalonde was especially excited about the movie's directors, the Soska sisters, who are best known for horror flicks like *American Mary* (2012), about a young woman who pays her way through medical school by working with clients from the extreme body modification community, and *Dead Hooker in a Trunk* (2009), which is a sort of gory morality play that begins when Badass and Geek, played by Jen and Silvia Soska themselves, pick up their friend Goody Two-Shoes from a church youth group meeting.

No doubt this news confirms what the authors of the *Left Behind* books, Tim LaHaye and Jerry Jenkins, had strongly suspected: that Lalonde is more

Nicolae Carpathia than tribulation saint. But I doubt Lalonde cares. He's following the money. Rapture movies seem to be played out, at least for time being, whereas zombie culture is still trending. And although Lalonde's move from the unraptured to the undead does appear to be dramatic, even an act of apostasy, perhaps the post-rapture story world has more in common with the post-zombie-infestation story world than we might initially think. I suggest five points of comparison that might begin to draw the story worlds of tribulation saints and zombie hunters closer together.

First, both story worlds are especially popular in times of war, terrorism, and mass death (maybe seen as a means of dealing with the collective trauma of all that meaningless violence and death). Is it any accident that Baptista's rapture movie was released during World War II, and that *A Thief in the Night* (as well as Harold Lindsell's *The Late, Great Planet Earth*) and *Night of the Living Dead* came out during the Vietnam War and the Cold War, and that the second rounds of both came out during the wars on terrorism and in the wake of 9/11?

Second, both story worlds emerge in some sense after God—in the wake of divine presence, in the theological vacuum of the perceived withdrawal of God from the world.

Third, both the raptured story world and the zombied story world are built on a dynamic of "us versus them," in which the "us" is a community of individual souls, still conscious of what's going on and trying to save themselves, and the "them" is the undifferentiated, unindividuated, brainwashed or brain-dead masses. The monstrous threat that the others outside pose to us inside is above all the threat of losing our individual subjectivity—literally losing one's soul. In the post-rapture story world, Patty and I are at risk of losing our souls under the pressure to conform to the dominant order of UNITE, whose very name signifies the homogeneous subordinated oneness of its marked subjects. Similarly, in the zombie-infested story world, the survivors and I are at risk of losing our souls under a relentless deluge of unindividuated, mindless bodies, an entropic heat bath of animated death.[11]

Fourth, both story worlds are constructed to scare the hell out of us. Imagining myself in the evangelical post-rapture story world, I am terrified into denouncing the powers of evil and accepting Jesus Christ as my personal (emphasis on personal) Lord and savior. Imagining myself in the world of zombies, I am compelled to pull close to my companions, to build a safe and secure community over against the forces of chaos impinging on all sides (think gated communities, think Homeland Security). In both scenarios, those on the outside are already lost, forsaken, and their lostness, their forsakenness, is experienced as a direct threat to my power to remain among the living, in the Book of Life.

Fifth and finally, both of these story worlds draw on Revelation. In fact, some evangelical Christians are way ahead of me on this. Presuming, as evangelical

Christians tend to do, that the Bible anticipates and answers every question that might possibly ever emerge, there are several websites that answer the question "What does the Bible say about zombies?" Lo and behold, a lot of what they find comes from—you guessed it—the Book of Revelation, especially its description of people seeking death but not finding it ("death will flee from them"; Revelation 9:6) and its description of the so-called first resurrection in Revelation 20, in which the dead who had not taken the mark and had been beheaded are brought back to life, and then the rest of the dead are reanimated later, after the thousand-year reign.

Taken together with the rapture and tribulation themes in evangelical apocalyptic horror movies, this zombie connection, I believe, speaks to the range of ways that Revelation feeds into deep, largely repressed correspondences between religion and horror in contemporary culture. Whereas the post-rapture story world dwells on the fear of being left behind, in the time of tribulation, in the wake of divine presence, I suggest that zombies climbing out of their graves speak to our mostly sublimated sense of horror and repulsion at the Christian vision of the resurrection of the dead, a vision drawn largely from Revelation and then elaborated in later Christian commentaries and creeds.

That zombies are the return of the theologically repressed in the Christian vision of the resurrection of the dead is probably not what the evangelical Bible-answer webmasters have in mind. Then again, Protestant evangelicalism on-screen has been full of surprises. Perhaps the next big thing will be evangelical zombie movies.

Figure 18.1 Delilah (Anna Thomson) and a reborn Will (Clint Eastwood) discuss new life in *Unforgiven*.
DVD screen capture, fair use

18

The Western: Radical Forgiveness in *Unforgiven*

Sara Anson Vaux

Clint Eastwood's *Unforgiven* (1992) bundles everything a viewer might want to know about the prolific and profitable genre called the Western into a two-hour exploration of America's past. If every society needs a foundational myth around which to organize its aspirations, memory, and political, religious, and cultural conflicts, then French critic André Bazin was right: America has the Western.[1] *Unforgiven* stands in a long line of iconic Westerns that comment upon the American experiment, but its complex and rich text engages as well the nature of storytelling, the vicissitudes of aging, and Eastwood's own history as an iconic star of Westerns. It also offers a case study that explores the relationship between the cinema and Protestantism, one that demonstrates and critiques the Western's role to shape the ways viewers "remember" and enshrine the country's history.

Unforgiven tackles the contradictory relationship within Protestantism between its broad belief in conversion, forgiveness of sins, and commitment to a new life, on the one hand, and a theology, rooted in Calvinism and the Reformed tradition, that posits a deterministic universe, on the other.[2] *Unforgiven* exposes the contradiction—at the core of both Protestantism and the Western genre whose ideology it supports—through a severing of its vengeance plot from its portrayal of individuals trying to "make do," and through its nested and provisional narrative construction, in which no single perspective has absolute narrative authority. The film reveals the seemingly providential design of Manifest Destiny to be an effect of selective storytelling, strategic elisions, and processes and actions.[3] The revelation holds promise for the possibility that individuals and societies might change, while forcing a confrontation with the bloody basis of westward progress.

The Western and Protestantism

Because *Unforgiven* so acutely critiques the Western genre of which it is a part, it is necessary first to explore the genre and its importance to American

Sara Anson Vaux, *The Western: Radical Forgiveness in* Unforgiven In: *Protestants on Screen*.
Edited by: Gastón Espinosa, Erik Redling and Jason Stevens, Oxford University Press. © Oxford University Press 2023.
DOI: 10.1093/oso/9780190058906.003.0019

self-identity. It is nearly impossible to overstate the central position of the Western in cinematic history and in the creation of an American mythology. Since nearly the beginning of cinema, American audiences turned to Western movies for adventure, entertainment, and comforting tales about the country's history. The first example, *The Great Train Robbery*, directed by Edwin S. Porter (1903), appeared alongside the rise of the cinema itself and provided many of the classic motifs: a train, mighty symbol of progress; bad men with guns; a heroic defense of valuables; a chase; and a final shoot-out. From there on, the genre took its place among still earlier tales of the vanished frontier that circulated through Wild West shows, novels, and dime Westerns since at least 1860. America in the nineteenth century *had* trains, guns, and shoot-outs, but the Western strips the concrete facets of nineteenth-century life of their rootedness in specific experiences, instead granting them symbolic weight. In this way, the Western functions as myth, defined by historian Richard Slotkin as "a complex of narratives that dramatizes the world vision and historical sense of a people or culture, reducing centuries of experience into a constellation of compelling metaphors."[4] Specific experiences yield to narrative tidiness.

Following the genre's 1903 cinematic debut came some 7,600 Westerns that initially created reassuring worlds where good vanquished evil, heroes triumphed, and the American experiment received continual validation. For Slotkin, the underlying language of the myth was "regeneration through violence," a theme that, even before the Western proper, threads through three centuries of American sermons, tales, songs, rituals, and propaganda.[5] That is, if white settlers took land that belonged to indigenous peoples, cleared the wilderness, and broke treaties, the bloodshed was justified to serve a higher purpose: to rid the land of heathens and make it safe for white people and their children. America itself, by this logic, became a "redeemer nation," one chosen by God.[6]

Puritan clergyman Increase Mather provides an early articulation of the link between land seizure and Christian redemption. He starts off his *Brief History of the Warr with the Indians in New-England* (1676) with an unmistakable point of view that seems odd and yet familiar. Mather describes "the Heathen People amongst whom we live, and whose Land the Lord God hath given us in rightfull Possession," and refers to the wilderness as "land not sown," as though it were lying dormant in anticipation of its colonization.[7] Throughout the essay, the fault lies continually with the Indians; he credits victories to God. The structure of what would become the Western myth developed from the retelling of events of New England's first century, when preachers like Increase and Cotton Mather, John Winthrop, William Bradford, and John Cotton imagined a paradise blessed by God that would not involve blood sacrifice, drought, failed crops, and deaths of warriors who resisted the settlers' land thefts.[8] Westward settlement was to realize this paradise, self-evidently given to the colonizers, who could then exploit the purportedly uninhabited land for profit.[9]

Protestantism, then, infuses the Western films at all levels: from the earliest settlers' religious identities (largely Puritan, Quaker, Methodist, and Congregational) to those deliberately excluded (Indians and their religious practices, French Catholics, and Blacks, free or enslaved) to the range and scope of their theological groundings to symbolic systems such as the "city on a hill" upon which Calvinists and evangelicals drew. The ideology that drove the settlements itself arose from a view of history in which all events are determined by God, driving toward the eschaton, or end times. Movement, progress toward a goal, characterizes the Protestant worldview. Western films perfectly capture the sense of a people who are part of a divine plan in motion, even if the particulars of character and place during film's formative decades require a heroic white male with six-gun to reestablish peace in a beleaguered community.[10]

Terry Lindvall notes the links between nineteenth- and early twentieth-century Protestant sermons and Western films. "As popular culture was steeped in Protestant rhetoric and symbols," he writes, "silent film maintained continuity with the habits of Protestants to appropriate culture for their own ends. Threads of a conservative Puritanism . . . found itself translated into the visual sermons of western cinema."[11] A similar influence is found in classical Westerns of the sound era. Consider, for instance, the Protestant pieties that lace films like *My Darling Clementine*, directed by John Ford (1946), and *High Noon*, directed by Fred Zinnemann (1952): Be nice to your parents and children; ease tensions with your neighbors as long as they are Protestant like you. Resolve tensions without violence, but if you do not protect yourself, it is a moral failing. Community is good; the settlement needs a lot of shops, a good restaurant, a barber shop, and a few saloons (some towns along the cattle routes had dozens).

My Darling Clementine in particular infuses the making of a new community with Protestant music—"Shall We Gather by the River?," "The Cuckoo Waltz," "My Darling Clementine," and "I Dreamt I Dwelt in Marble Halls"—that displays the Protestant work ethic. The Others are excluded, pointedly: drunk Charlie the "Injun," anyone who does not work, and the drunk Doc Holliday. Music expresses the ideal community, and the community has a role in determining the chosen.[12] The thousands of Westerns that filled screens all over the country for so many decades (particularly the 1920s through the end of the 1950s) thus assumed as natural the seizing of land from its original inhabitants, obscuring the crime beneath a veneer of a Protestant morality that was portrayed, here through song, as self-evident.[13]

That is, underneath each Western's story world, in which the march of "progress" was destined and thus not open to challenge, lies a disturbing historical background that needs to be remembered and analyzed. Yet the genre's success required that it be obscured. As Kent Jones has written, in Westerns "the landscape remained blissfully depoliticized while the 'moral conflicts' wrote themselves upon it."[14] The white settlers' ownership of the land was providential, an assumed precondition for Western conflicts between good guys and bad guys, rather than the subject of conflicts itself.

Thus, Westerns in large part shaped the ways the centuries-long expansion of white settlement was perceived, absorbed, and sanitized. The territory's indigenous inhabitants had never been systematically exterminated, according to plot logic, for God had given the land to white people, and the settlements in the West that the movies represented were all part of progress. The Western genre functioned to elide the contradiction at the core of Protestant ideology: the destiny was *manifest*, foregone, except that manifesting it was a process that took time, cost lives, caused violence, held risks. Even capitalism itself, rooted in speculation and risk, was less inevitable than the logic might lead one to believe. In the Western, conflicts were temporally bounded, to be solved by the end of act three or at the close of the final chapter. The myth of progress became stronger and stronger, its heroes having endured ever more threats, from Indians (*Stagecoach*, directed by John Ford [1939]; *Fort Apache*, 1948), rustlers, thieves, murderers (*Clementine*), and homegrown criminals (*The Man from Laramie*, directed by Anthony Mann [1955]; *Winchester '73*, also directed by Mann [1950]).

Many films of the Western genre critique the ideology of the genre and the moral rot that lies beneath its happy endings. In these films, often described as "revisionist" rather than "classical," music—used to highlight the Protestant basis of the genre, as discussed above—can hold myth and critique together. John Ford's *The Searchers* (1956) illuminates land theft, race hatred, and the tight link between religion and violence throughout its labyrinthine plot, which echoes Puritan captivity narratives but rejects their sense of Providence.[15] The protagonist, Ethan Edwards (John Wayne), seems to step out of a sermon: the (Confederate) "Lost Cause" he vows to avenge confuses nostalgia for a lost way of life with a "righteous desire" to reclaim land from the heathens who pillage and burn homesteads; scalp, kidnap, and rape white women; and despoil the whites' sacred lands. Ford sets a sympathetic theme song, "What Makes a Man to Wander?," as a counterpoint to Ethan's crazed actions. The Methodist hymn "Shall We Gather by the River?," which in other Westerns signals the singleness of the frontier mission, is not inserted by Ford as religious solace or unity for the isolated settlers but rather to underline Ethan's savage hatred.[16] Early on, he wrenches the grieving survivors of a Comanche raid away from sorrow and sets them off to exact blood vengeance. Later in the film, the crazed searcher disrupts a wedding performance of "Shall We Gather" to insist on death for his "polluted" niece Debbie and her kidnappers. His fury exposes the racism even in the most sympathetic character, Laurie, who, dressed in wedding white, spews poison that

Figure 18.2 In *The Searchers* (1956), John Ford inserts a Methodist hymn to underline Ethan's (John Wayne) savage race hatred.
DVD screen capture, fair use

infects the entire settlement operation. Music facilitates the shifts in the movie between murderous hatred toward the Comanche for occupying lands that belong to whites and the film's struggle to define justice.[17]

Other revisionist films, like Howard Hawks's *Red River* (1948), Ford's *Fort Apache* (1948) and *The Man Who Shot Liberty Valance* (1962), Sergio Leone's "Fistful" trilogy of spaghetti Westerns, and recent revelations like *Dead Man*, directed by Jim Jarmusch (1995), and the Coen brothers' version of *True Grit* (2010), keep the historical truth alive even as the surface events seem to skirt over them, using not only music but also the whole gamut of filmmaking tools.[18] Clint Eastwood's oeuvre is central to any discussion of the Western's mythmaking and its potential for facilitating a critical perspective. *High Plains Drifter*, *The Outlaw Josey Wales*, and *Unforgiven* each mark a valuable step forward in the probing of the genre's lacuna-strewn past.

Unforgiven: The Seduction of Vengeance and the Dream of Forgiveness

Any of the films mentioned above could easily sustain a long discussion of the relationship between Protestantism and the Western. *Unforgiven*, however, differs from other Westerns in part because its critique is woven into each strand of the plot sequences and also belongs to the ways the story is told—diegetically and narratologically. As a work of narrative art, *Unforgiven* simultaneously tells a story (Will Munny's return to gunfighting) and is a story *about* stories (replays of the myth embodied in Western tales). Each register considers and exposes the contradictions or nuances of Protestant worldviews.

The plot of *Unforgiven*, upon first glance, seems simple: a retired gunslinger and widower, Will Munny, is enticed out of retirement to avenge the maiming of a prostitute and claim a reward that will rescue his failing farm and feed his young children. Munny, his longtime partner Ned Logan (notably played by African American actor Morgan Freeman), and the Schofield Kid, who recruited him, travel to the town of Big Whiskey and succeed in killing the cowboys who disfigured the woman, Delilah. The town's villainous sheriff, however, whips Logan to death, and Munny kills the sheriff and his men and leaves town.

The film does not gallop from Will's trials through a "mighty Redeemer" script and a providential rescue to put the world back in moral and political order. Rather, each sequence reveals what economic and social forces brought about the events and persons before us. We are given the years and places of the prostitute's assault as well as of Claudia Munny's death: 1880 in Wyoming and 1878 in Kansas, respectively. The Munnys' farm, seen at the beginning of the film, shows the effects of market forces and the curse of living on a land that belonged to Native peoples, which have combined with droughts and plagues of locusts during the 1870s to destroy the fragile economies of Kansas as well as of Missouri, barely emerged from bloody border raids and the Civil War. Further, the states during the years before and after the war were flooded with cattlemen and their herds seeking railway passage to markets in the East.[19]

Though rooted in historical trauma, *Unforgiven* demonstrates keen awareness of the ways in which history changes as it is written and rewritten. The film takes the myths of the West (grand, in which all historical events are Providential) and says that these are stories, repeated and altered and romanticized until their layered connection with war trauma is but an occasion for cathartic violence or even a distant memory. In this light, consider the film's opening text scroll, laid against a peaceful tableau of sunset's glow, which immediately questions the definitiveness of all that viewers think they will come to know about the characters:

> She was a comely young woman and not without prospects. Therefore it was heartbreaking to her mother that she would enter into marriage with William Munny, a known thief and murderer, a man of notoriously vicious and intemperate disposition. When she died, it was not at his hands as her mother might have expected, but of smallpox. That was 1878.

The few sentences set the tone for a film rooted in diffident and provisional truth-telling. For each statement of seemingly self-evident truth ("Therefore"), there are hesitations—the participle "known," without specifying by whom, the double negative of "not without prospects," and especially the speculation of "as her mother might have expected." And of course, the viewer does not know who narrates the lines.

The opening frame situates the film as a palimpsest of alleged events, stories about events, dime comic allusions to events, allusion upon allusion to rough towns that must be beaten to be silenced or ruled, endless saloons stewed in whiskey, and untethered men with or without guns, gambling, or jobs. The names of Kansas, Missouri, Texas, and Wyoming and their famed towns, notably Abilene, Kansas, spill out of the mouths of the prostitutes, deputies, the sheriff Little Bill, train passengers, English Bob (another aging gunslinger), Ned, Will, and the damaged Kid who rides into Kansas expecting to burst right into the famous gun battles that supposedly lit up the nights with glorious exploits. Even the epithets attached to the characters—"English," "Little," "the Kid"—attest to mythmaking as fundamental to the characters' self-presentation, but in a mannered, obvious way that undercuts that mythmaking's persuasiveness.

In addition to positioning the narrative in the realm of storytelling, the opening frame establishes the first of two worldviews, one of which searches for a way for humans to live together in harmony with the natural world and each other. This view, evident in the first visual and what immediately follows, offers peace, care for the earth, and openness to strangers and the vulnerable—a theme that runs counter to the poverty, despair, and violence that tarnished settlements all over the West. Even with the death of Claudia, the young woman referenced in the opening, her love for her children and her husband provides a powerful example of ways to live well, ways to live within forgiveness. Her mother, we assume from the scrolled text, judges. Claudia forgives. Hers we might name "radical forgiveness" a theme that threads throughout the scriptures, Old Testament and New, to counter the figure of a vengeful God who appears to limit divine action to judgment and destruction, not love.

The second worldview, positioned inside the film's outer frame, presents in thirty-eight sequences a perverted paradise that did not turn out the way the land companies and preachers promised. Sequence after sequence exposes the ravaged earth as the end point of a logic in which "everything in the West was a commodity or a resource—something that could be mined, cultivated, or exploited for profit."[20] The mythologized view looks to heaven to save its creatures from disasters natural and human-made. Each mini-drama, grounded in violence, opens not in peace but with rutting noises punctuated by a young woman's screams as her sex partner slashes her face. A nervous camera and a partially blocked lens, violence heard but not seen, a fragmented back story, memories partially cued, and the frantic opening minutes of the sequences inside the outer frame simultaneously replay versions of older Western movies and undercut any assumption of righteousness in the supposed histories that these movies recount. The disoriented viewer becomes aware of the film's immersion in land theft, mass murder, sale of human bodies in slavery and prostitution, and a horrible, gaping wound in America's body politic: the Civil War.

Yet *Unforgiven*'s structure allows each event to be measured against the transforming, humanizing ideal imaged in the initial meditative visual and sonic tableau, returning repeatedly to the unfolding inner plots to counter their linear, violent histories. "Claudia's Theme" enfolds the opening scene, its plaintive melody rising and falling with the burial shovel's rhythm. The theme returns at film's end to embrace the palpable, human evidence of lived life—clothesline, evening ritual in front of the grave, quiet progression of a single melodic line into full orchestration. Vanished are the fragmentary, chaotic bits of banjo riffs from the inner sequences that evoke rowdy dance halls, minstrel tunes, and folk songs used in earlier Westerns to evoke a fictional, violent, and romanticized frontier.

Unforgiven's power, and one feature that differs from other Westerns, lies in the ways that the film keeps the two visions separate but interposed: it does not present the latter vengeful path as a prerequisite for achieving the peace implied in the former. Rather, it presents the peace as antithetical to the ravages of Western vengeance, precisely *because* peace requires true care for the earth, the Other, and the vulnerable, not merely a veneer of peace that obscures an ideology of conquest. The plot bits in the primary narrative sequences present contrasting visions of what the New World might have been and might still become. The version of apocalypse that races through so many Westerns, inspired by the cinematic Book of Revelation, need not be the final story, nor does apocalyptic violence lead inexorably to a peaceful stasis. Revenge and its mechanics, so appealing to storytellers, are balanced by another way of viewing the moral obligations all humans owe each other.

Hence the ambiguous appearance in *Unforgiven*'s climactic sequence of a common figure in Westerns, the avenging angel, a *deus ex machina* that acts with a swift finality that suits the genre's ethos. Munny storms the saloon, guns blazing, but the character's brokenness and the ways in which the film juxtaposes violent catharsis against the quiet harmony of the initial narrative frame rob the final shootout of the restorative weight of similar climaxes in earlier Westerns and provide merciful distance from the explosive inner tales. Instead, the film ends on a note of ambiguity: Will is rumored to have moved even farther west, achieving prosperity selling dry goods. Here, too, westward movement is intrinsically linked to capitalism, but it is merely suggested, couched in rumor. He may or may not have ended up in San Francisco; such a movement does not emerge as an ordained and inevitable conclusion to his enactment of avenging violence. Rather, it is rooted in a human, conditional impulse.

Unforgiven and Conditional Storytelling

The insistent ways the film undermines the authority of its own storytelling contributes to the contrast between a determinist view, in which each action inevitably begets another, and a conditional or ad hoc view, in which individuals attempt to live in harmony with each other. Here, Protestant/Western mythmaking is constantly revealed as exactly that—continuously denaturalized and thus stymied, for myths' functioning relies on their seeming naturalness. This is most evident in the character of Will (if he ever was a "damned killer"), who is thoroughly grounded on the earth. He is no creature of legend or a conscious fabricator of legend but "just a fella now." The film's images reinforce this: since Eastwood shoots with natural light and on location and rarely uses stunt doubles, Will's spills into the mud or his struggles with his horse feel natural, even personally painful. The pace of the editing reinforces a sense of weariness: it is slow, giving time for situations (the falls, the target practice, the missed mounts) to play out his aging and desperation.

The first conversation between Will and the Schofield Kid takes place in the sad, tight space of the poor man's remote cabin, not in the grand wide open. Similarly, campfire scenes in *Unforgiven* do not induce romance (e.g., Anthony Mann's *The Naked Spur* [1953]) or even the vicious, mordant offhand humor when Ethan Edwards shoots a thief in the back (*The Searchers*). Rather, in *Unforgiven*, the campfire sequences are shot tight, the image blurred by rain, the "hero" suffering from unconfessed guilt, war trauma, and grief over the death of his wife—not all that heroic. Later, a sick, miserable Will huddles in a darkened corner of a saloon, beaten nearly to death by the local representative of law and order, and cast into the darkness of a bloody street. Here, too, his suffering feels *inhabited*, rather than iconic.

Throughout the film, Will never excuses his past actions or justifies them as inevitable or necessary steps in the service of a greater cause—the Increase Mather argument. Rather, he repeatedly admits, without boastfulness, that he has committed at least some of the acts ascribed to him in legend. In the main portion of the film's narrative, he reflects upon the acts in the context of religious belief and the law: they were wrong. Specifically, he implicitly refuses the labels "redeemer," "avenger," and "judge," as when he says of one of his past victims that "he didn't do anything to deserve" death at Will's hands. The killings were not only wrong but disgusting, defiling, foul. "I seen the error of my ways . . . the sins of my youth," he says, reflecting upon the concrete effects of pulling the trigger. Will *changed*, in other words, even experienced a complete conversion, and in his redeemed self has abandoned whatever superiority would attach to a hero of legend.

The film, then, turns a mythic redeemer-gunslinger figure into a human being whose (alleged) past murders torture him.[21] Will has been endowed with no superhuman qualities, given no star lighting or image boosting to urge spectators to desire that he stain himself with revenge murders. That Munny is played by an aging Eastwood adds poignancy and power to this characterization, as viewers can imagine his earlier, iconic roles such as Harry in 1971's *Dirty Harry* (directed by Don Siegel) or Blondie in 1966's *The Good, the Bad, and the Ugly* (directed by Sergio Leone).

The film's overall aesthetic contributes to a deglamorized effect. It displays few of the well-lit, expansive shots that distinguished much of the glorious landscape in earlier Westerns like Ford's *Stagecoach* or *My Darling Clementine,* shots that seductively but falsely established the landscape as open for the taking. Will and Ned ride through golden wheat fields; Will, Ned, and the Kid cross a desert expanse; and a reborn Will and Delilah, the young woman whose mutilation sets the plot in motion, discuss new life in a setting laid against a sky of radiant blue and mountains bathed in fresh snow. That's it. There is no thrilling chase across the plains, through the mountains, across Texas. No guns blazing. No Apaches in pursuit, as in *Stagecoach.* Only brief glimpses of natural beauty, overshadowed by saloons and muddy trails and the stench of a horrific Civil War not really over.

Further, Will, Ned, English Bob, and Little Bill are men of a "certain age," totally unlike themselves as figures in their legends. Heroes do not age, and heroes do not reflect upon the morality of their actions. Legends are static: they stop time and defeat aging and death. The characters in *Unforgiven* endure through time, aging, and reflection upon the past. In the plot of the film, the character of the Kid functions to juxtapose the legendary figures of Western stories against the aging men who appear on the screen. His vivid and insistent narratives fix time precisely. Notably, when Will first spots him, he is riding out of the distant landscape like the apocalyptic punisher of *Revelation* (with a nod to the beginnings of *Shane* and *Pale Rider*). English Bob, apparently still a roving six-gun, does not trust the public to spread his legends but travels with a personal chronicler, who takes a "certain artistic liberty" with the facts, just as Bob embellished his own history, remolding his Cockney self into an English aristocrat.

Little Bill, by contrast, insists upon the truth about written accounts of the West's history and about the human condition: all men (in this film, also all women) are violent. If civilization is to continue in America, he reasons, it can only do so if men such as himself hold absolute power. Little Bill's universalizing stance—his belief that *all* people are violent, his belief in *absolute* power—is merely a more evident version of a determinism that characterizes Western mythology generally. To establish law and order in a chaotic land, you need sanctioned killings.[22] *Unforgiven* counters the mythos of Western heroes' self-baptized righteousness: that story worlds inherently accept the inevitability of murder to enforce the law. It acknowledges layers of storytelling, the romanticizing discourses that turn history into myths to make westward expansion seem like divinely inspired fulfillment.

In contrast to mythic figures—static, iconic—*Unforgiven* reveals humans in all of their messiness and contingency. *These* are the characters in *Unforgiven*: everyone is humanized, even the villainous Little Bill, who is a zealot but a deranged and needy one. He looks back uncertainly after he beats English Bob, for instance, in a shot that could have demonized him but instead reduces him. The prostitutes are named within the body of the film, but more critically, they are individualized in age, size, looks, ethnicity, and moral awareness, as evident in their varied responses to the assailant Davey-Boy's attempt at restitution. The deputies are not hardened but rather tremble with fear. In each scene in Big Whiskey, the camera explores the characters' space, lingering upon terrified faces. Such an approach deprives the viewer of immersive and unreflective identification with any side in violent, painful, unbearable events—as when English Bob and Will are kicked nearly to death, and Ned is whipped to death while the horrified deputies and women watch.

Viewers live in the moment, these lived moments, not in a superhero cartoon. The characters succeed and fail, do good and evil, live and die, but they do all of these as living, suffering humans, not to fulfill a destiny or adopt a mythic mantle. By virtue of his humanity, the character of Will is able to convert from the gunslinger of legend to husband and farmer, then reluctantly to a man who kills, then back again, accepting the consequences. It is on the basis of the distinction between human and legend, determined and provisional, static and changing, that the film achieves its power.

Conclusion: Converting the Western

Motion and change define the Western, as historian Garry Wills writes, with its "racing, overlapping new technologies—the stagecoach, the Conestoga wagon, the telegraph, the cavalry, the railroads, barbed wire, successively improved firearms, and new breeds of horses."[23] Ironically, the structure and themes of Western movies present such changes through the static figure of the Western hero, resulting in so many conflicts between good and evil presented in propulsive narratives of divine fulfillment that mirror powerfully influential strands of Reformed theology in American history. *Unforgiven* provides such a story of movement (Will's final, rumored journey west) and one of seemingly providential vengeance (in the climactic shootout). On first consideration, the vengeful shootout may seem to reflect a logical and satisfying cleansing of an evil world by a redeemer figure, and the suggested but uncertain conclusion of Will's story something outside this belief system.

But what if the final, guns-blazing revenge inset functions only as an interpolated tale, mythmaking at its most intense and damaging, manufactured expressly to provide cathartic and easy release where humans need to heal and move forward? The provisional ending with the sorrowing man, a white-strung clothesline that witnesses continuing domestic life, and Claudia's grave laid against a golden sunset all testify to a worldview that characterizes the film's opening moments: one rooted in the ways people find to live with one another, with themselves, and within forgiveness. Although the lifegiving perspective seems removed from the determinism of much American Protestantism and the Western itself, it too is rooted in Protestant beliefs.

Unforgiven opens up radical forgiveness, an alternative way to approach Protestantism and the American West—not one based upon the obscuring of historical trauma in the service of American mythmaking, but rather one that comes to terms with the historical specificity, the moral failings and strivings, the humanness, of America's history. The apocalyptic view of history, the pursuit of blood vengeance to respond to suffering and loss, makes big box office but does not provide sustenance after the deaths of dearly loved friends, or sons, or daughters. The images and music that begin and end *Unforgiven* speak not to judgment and hatred but to love, to the embrace of the marginalized, the vulnerable, the ones abandoned in a brothel or alone in the wilderness or with their conscience. Will Munny was forgiven, his eyes now turned inward at death itself, as his friend Ned and the frightened Kid embrace him. He is reborn in the sunlight, in kindness to the lonely prostitute, whom he does not dominate but affirms.

Figure 18.3 *Unforgiven*'s provisional ending, with the sorrowing man and Claudia's grave laid against the sunset, rejects vengeance.
DVD screen capture, fair use

Will's final message as he rides out of town: do not abandon Adam and Eve, creatures of the earth, but take their hands and protect them. Take responsibility for past violations. Embrace the earth and its peoples in all their colors and cultures and rituals. Move past war. Radical forgiveness, too, is Protestant, and free, and full of hope.

Figure 19.1 Desmond Doss (Andrew Garfield) holding his Bible in a promotional photo for *Hacksaw Ridge*.
Entertainment Pictures/Alamy Stock Photo

19

Protestant Pacifist: War and Pacifism in Mel Gibson's *Hacksaw Ridge*

Matthew S. Rindge

Hacksaw Ridge (directed by Mel Gibson, 2016) depicts the story of Desmond T. Doss (1919–2006), the first conscientious objector to receive the Medal of Honor.[1] President Harry S. Truman presented Doss, a U.S. Army medic, with this medal for saving the lives of about seventy-five fellow servicemen during the World War II battle on Okinawa. Among the many remarkable elements of Doss's story—and what makes his narrative cinematic—is that he accomplished this extraordinary feat while maintaining his pacifist commitment to not carry or even touch a weapon throughout his entire Army service. In addition to examining Doss's pacifism within the broader context of his religious identity as a Protestant Christian, this chapter also frames *Hacksaw Ridge* within Mel Gibson's broader cinematic oeuvre, and explores how the film relates to Gibson's penchant for redemptive violence.

Reconfiguring Pacifism as Courage

The film's primary narrative conflict is the juxtaposition between Doss's enlistment in the U.S. Army and his refusal to touch, let alone fire, a weapon. Doss (Andrew Garfield) wants to serve his country, but he insists on doing so in a nonviolent manner. These twinned desires elicit immense bewilderment and persecution from those (almost everyone except Doss) who cannot imagine how a person might serve in the military and not engage in violence against the enemy.

Playing a formative role in the nascent development of Doss's commitment to pacifism are two violent episodes in his youth. When he is ten, Doss hits his brother in the head with a brick. He recalls, "I could have killed him," and Doss's mother (Rachel Griffiths) at the time tells him, "Murder is the worst sin of all. . . . To take another man's life. That is the most egregious sin in the Lord's sight." On another occasion, Doss's father (Hugo Weaving) is physically assaulting Doss's

Matthew S. Rindge, *Protestant Pacifist: War and Pacifism in Mel Gibson's* Hacksaw Ridge In: *Protestants on Screen.* Edited by: Gastón Espinosa, Erik Redling and Jason Stevens, Oxford University Press.
DOI: 10.1093/oso/9780190058906.003.0020

mother, and a young Doss intervenes by pointing a pistol directly at his father's face. Doss recounts to a soldier, "And that's when I made my promise to God I ain't never gonna a touch a gun again."

Doss is introduced to healing as a possible alternative to violence when, as a young adult, he witnesses an automobile accident and fashions a tourniquet on an injured boy. He is told at the hospital that this act likely saved the boy's life. Looking around him, Desmond absorbs the sight of the doctors, nurses, and injured patients as though he is witnessing a potentially new vocational opportunity. It is also here where he first meets his future wife, Dorothy, a nurse. While later reading the *Manual of Practical Anatomy*, Doss exclaims, "I have to enlist. . . . I want to be a medic. . . . I figure I'll be saving people, not killing." Doss then finds his vocational dream, which involves the unique blend of nonviolence and military service.

The multiple conflicts Doss experiences in basic training are presaged by a discussion he has with his girlfriend, Dorothy (Teresa Palmer). On a date at a movie, the two discuss ethics related to violence. Desmond asks her, "What about His commandment?" Dorothy replies, "It's not killing if it's war." Here she echoes a conventional perspective that ending a life is acceptable if carried out in wartime. War, in other words, provides an ethical cover for killing. Doss, however, refuses to accept that war justifies killing. He is committed to acting in a way that exemplifies healing and helping. In his words, "With the world so set on tearing itself apart, it don't seem like such a bad thing to me to want to put a little bit of it back together."

Basic training is the setting for the crux of the conflict between Doss's refusal to touch a weapon and the military's insistence that he do exactly that. Doss enlisted with 1-A-O status, meaning that he is willing to serve but unwilling to carry a weapon. Since no one in the Army seems to understand this paradox, Doss tries to explain: "I was told I didn't have to carry a weapon. I can't touch a gun." When confronted by his commanding officer and other Army soldiers, Doss refuses to relent: "Sorry, but I will not bear arms." His pacifist commitment results in various forms of persecution. He is verbally mocked by Sergeant Howell (Vince Vaughn), who exclaims to the other enlistees, "Private Doss does not believe in violence. He will not even deign to touch a weapon. So I plead with you, do not look to him to save you on the battlefield because he will undoubtedly be too busy wrestling with his conscience to assist." Doss is beaten by fellow servicemen one night, but declines to identify them when asked about the incident by his superior officer. Doss's refusal to touch a rifle leads him to be placed in a cell while awaiting a court-martial. He tells Dorothy that he is being treated like a criminal "just because I won't kill." At the subsequent trial, Doss is eventually declared not guilty of disobeying orders and officially declared a "legitimate conscientious objector."

The film shifts to the May 1945 battle at Hacksaw Ridge on Okinawa, a site of omnipresent and relentless carnage. A truck of dead bodies illustrates the grim and stark reality of death's haunting and pervasive presence. The camera lingers on a gruesome scene of severed limbs and corpses littering the ground, soldiers' intestines, and rats climbing on bodies. With nonstop explosions, bullets, and fire, the battle epitomizes chaos. One soldier after another is shot. Flame-throwers light men on fire. As in Steven Spielberg's *Saving Private Ryan* (1998) and in Gibson's previous films, violence is served with a certain realistic relish.

It is within this grisly context of slaughter that Doss displays the heroic actions that would earn him the Medal of Honor. In the midst of the nonstop chaos from Japanese artillery fire and shelling by the U.S. Navy, he begins looking for (and finding) wounded soldiers to treat. He carries one of the injured soldiers to the cliffside (which the Americans had ascended to fight) and there constructs a makeshift rope harness, which he uses to belay the wounded soldier to the ground. Doss finds a second injured soldier, carries him on a stretcher to the cliffside, and lowers him to the ground below as well. Thus begins a cycle Doss repeats about seventy-five times. Doss is eventually injured and rescued by fellow soldiers. Upon realizing Doss's bravery, his fellow soldiers are in awe of the man they once mocked.

On one level, the film is thus a story of a man who triumphs by holding steadfast to his personal convictions, at great personal cost, and despite immense pressure. *Hacksaw Ridge* offers a notable contrast with an Oscar-winning World War II film from Hollywood's Golden Age. Howard Hawks's *Sergeant York* (1941) is based on the true story of evangelical convert Alvin C. York (Gary Cooper), who received the Medal of Honor for an extraordinary feat in World War I in which he killed twenty-five German soldiers and captured 132 more. In the film, York applies for conscientious objector status since he believes that "war is killing," according to the Bible. His request is denied, however, and York ends up carrying and using a weapon triumphantly. Pragmatic killing prevails over the virtue of pacifism. *Hacksaw Ridge* thus offers a more robust commitment to, and embrace of, pacifism than that in *Sergeant York*.

Hacksaw Ridge inverts the conventional expectations that a pacifist on the battlefield would be of no help, or even a liability. As Christopher Nolan's 2017 film *Dunkirk* explored what heroism looks like when one fails, and how one can be a hero in failure, *Hacksaw Ridge* examines how a pacifist commitment to nonviolence can be of benefit and service to fellow soldiers. Both films reconfigure what constitutes a hero and what heroism entails. Unlike Clint Eastwood's *American Sniper* (2014), in which heroism involves eliminating enemy soldiers, *Hacksaw Ridge* offers pacifism as a viable heroism. Unlike Don "Wardaddy" Collier, who proclaims in David Ayer's *Fury* (2014), "Ideals are peaceful. History is violent,"

Doss demonstrates that the ideal of pacifism can be embodied in a meaningful and helpful way, even in the unlikely setting of war. And unlike Captain Glover (Sam Worthington), who tells Doss, "You don't win wars by giving up your life," Doss demonstrates that he can do precisely this very thing. The film also counters—as Martin Luther King Jr. often sought to do—the common misconception that pacifism is tantamount to passivity. In these and other ways, *Hacksaw Ridge* reimagines pacifism as courage.

Sola Scriptura: The Bible as Moral Authority

The Protestant nature of Doss's faith is primarily evident in the significant role that the Bible plays in his faith commitment generally and in his pacifist worldview more specifically. Apart from *The Passion of the Christ*—a film based partly on the Gospels—the Bible plays a more prominent role in *Hacksaw Ridge* than in any other of the five films Gibson has directed; this emphasis on the biblical text may well be due to Doss's Protestant identity. The film opens with Doss quoting from the text of Isaiah:

> Have you not heard? The Lord is the everlasting God, the Creator of the ends of the Earth. He will not grow tired or weary, and His understanding no one can fathom. He gives strength to the weary and increases the power of the weak. Even youths grow tired and weary, and young men stumble and fall. But those who hope in the Lord will renew their strength. They will soar on wings like eagles. They will run and not grow weary. They will walk and not be faint. (Isaiah 40:28–31, NIV)[2]

Accompanying this biblical citation is a series of visual images detailing the gory nature of the war on Okinawa. Scenes are dominated by men's burning bodies, and an injured Doss lies on a stretcher and is carried by fellow soldiers on the battlefield. This juxtaposition at the film's outset is a classic example of the compatibility in Catholic cinematic imagination between religion and violence. In the works of many Catholic filmmakers such as Martin Scorsese (*Mean Streets*, *Raging Bull*, *Cape Fear*, *Silence*) and Francis Ford Coppola (*The Godfather*, *The Godfather II*), religion and violence are intimate bedfellows. Gibson's films also demonstrate, perhaps to an even greater degree, a high level of comfort with the coexistence of religion and violence. Gibson's identity as a particular kind of ("traditional") Catholic makes his portrayal of a particular kind of (Seventh-day Adventist) Protestant striking, and it raises questions that are not easily answered about the degree to which *Hacksaw Ridge* is a "Protestant" film, a "Catholic" film, neither, or some blend of the two.[3]

The English translation of Isaiah 40 that Doss cites at the film's opening is significant, since Gibson uses the New International Version (NIV), which since 1978 has been the preferred translation for many evangelical Protestant churches and individuals. It is telling, for instance, that Gibson does not use here the New American Bible, one of the most common English translations used in the Catholic Church.

Doss's quote from Isaiah 40 is the first of dozens of biblical citations or allusions in the film. Even more significant than these multiple uses of the Bible is the way in which the Bible functions for Doss as the principal authority that shapes his religious and moral identity. Doss views the Bible primarily as a guide for how to live. The Bible is for Doss a moral or ethical blueprint. Chief among the values Doss gleans from the Bible is his commitment to nonviolence. In addition to his mother's influence and two childhood memories (cited above), it is the Bible that Doss refers to more than anything else in his effort to explain his steadfast devotion to pacifism. His childhood memory of hitting his brother with a brick includes recalling a picture hanging on their wall illustrating the Ten Commandments. The sixth command, "Thou shall not kill," accompanied by a visual image of Cain and Abel, captivates Doss. It is this same commandment that Doss apparently references when he and Dorothy discuss the ethics of killing in warfare. "What about His commandment?" Doss replies when she suggests that killing is acceptable in warfare. Doss refers to this same command yet again when the Army psychologist asks him if it was God who told him not to touch a rifle. Doss responds, "God says not to kill. That's one of His most important commandments."

It is significant that the vast majority of the biblical allusions and citations in the film are from the Hebrew Bible. There are only two biblical references to the New Testament in the film.[4] In addition to texts already mentioned, the Bible that Dorothy gives Doss is bookmarked at 1 Samuel 17 (the story of David and Goliath). This almost exclusive focus on the Hebrew Bible is noteworthy since it is quite common when proffering defenses of pacifism to quote from the New Testament. In Tim Robbins's *Dead Man Walking* (1995), for example, Helen Prejean and other opponents of the death penalty refer several times to Jesus's statements (e.g., John 8:7) to support their stance against violence, and it is proponents of the death penalty who quote from the Hebrew Bible (citing Genesis 9:6 and the *lex talionis* principle in Exodus 21:22–25 and Deuteronomy 19:16–21; cf. Leviticus 24:17–22).[5] In this way, Gibson inverts a common (yet uninformed and inaccurate) stereotype that imagines a false dichotomy between the Hebrew Bible's support of violence and the New Testament's advocacy of peace and nonviolence. This reliance on the Hebrew Bible for Doss's faith—and his commitment to pacifism—is especially noteworthy in light of the criticism

Gibson received for what many considered to be antisemitic elements in *The Passion of the Christ*.

In addition to its internal content, the Bible also plays an important role as a physical object in the film. While Doss is in basic training, tucked in his Bible is a picture of Dorothy with a note reading, "Come home to me, D.D. I love you." A link is established here between Doss's two great loves—the Bible and Dorothy. When she first gives him the Bible, she says, "You keep it right here [indicating his heart], where I'll be." It is perhaps unsurprising that the Bible is a chief source of comfort for Doss. He reads it at night when he is in his cell awaiting court-martial and also before the battle on Okinawa. At the end of the film, as he is carried on a stretcher from the battlefield, a distraught Doss utters, "My Bible, my Bible, my Bible." A soldier leaves and returns, having retrieved Doss's Bible from the battlefield. He hands it to Doss, who clutches it gratefully. As Doss is lowered from the cliff on a stretcher, the camera lingers on him holding his Bible on his chest.

Martin Luther's dictum *sola scriptura*, although never cited in the film, captures the spirit with which Doss views and relates to the Bible. Nothing is more authoritative for him than certain biblical texts. Doss adopts his nonviolent stance not because of official church teaching, church tradition, mystical visions, academic study, critical thinking, or logic but rather because of his focus on certain biblical texts. The film fails, however, to address or wrestle in any real substantive way with the conflicting perspectives in the Bible regarding pacifism and violence. *Hacksaw Ridge* is somewhat selective in its reference to biblical texts that oppose violence. Unlike *Dead Man Walking* or *The Mission* (directed by Roland Joffé, 1986), the film does not illustrate the contested nature within Christianity of the use of pacifism and violence.

In *Sergeant York*, the Bible also plays a formative role in shaping York's opposition to violence and his commitment to pacifism. York exclaims at one point, "I ain't a-goin' to war. War's killin', and the Book's agin' killin'! So war is agin' the Book!" He elsewhere remarks, "You see, I believe in the Bible, and I'm a-believin' that this here life we're a-livin' is something the Lord done give us and we got to be a-livin' it the best we can, and I'm a-figurin' that killing other folks ain't no part of what He was intendin' for us to be a-doin' here." After his request to be a conscientious objector is denied three times, York again turns to the Bible, but now he does so to justify his military service, citing Jesus's remark to "render unto Caesar the things that are Caesar's, and unto God the things that are God's."[6] Thus, in the best-known instance of Christian pacifism in an American war film prior to *Hacksaw Ridge*, some of the Bible's internal tensions regarding violence are recognized, although the filmmakers, under the advisement of the Office of War Information, ultimately resolve this tension in order to support U.S. intervention in the war. Gibson's film is more selective with the Bible than its classic

Figure 19.2 In *Sergeant York* (1941), the classic counterpart to *Hacksaw Ridge*, the Bible also plays a formative role in shaping the hero's opposition to violence.
DVD screen capture, fair use

counterpart, but both the film and its protagonist strive for a more consistent morality with respect to repudiating violence. As we will see, the ramifications of Doss's actions, and what the film makes of them, are ultimately not as clear as they appear to be regarding their rejection of violence.

Personal Interpretation as Ultimate Authority

The second main way in which the Protestant nature of Doss's faith is evident is in the authority that his own interpretation carries in his understanding (and application to his own life) of the Bible. It is, again, not the church's teaching nor church tradition but rather Doss's own personal perception of the meaning of the biblical text, along with his experiences, that shapes his belief that pacifism is God's will for him. In this regard, it is significant that Seventh-day Adventists are not one of the three main historical peace churches in the Protestant tradition. Unlike Mennonites (including the Amish), Quakers, and the Church of the Brethren, Seventh-day Adventists do not have a denominational policy of pacifism. If they had, then Doss's commitment to pacifism could be understood as a result of his conformity, or obedience, to Church teaching. Doss's vegetarianism (illustrated in two brief scenes) and his unwillingness to work on the Sabbath (Saturday) do stem from the official teaching of his Seventh-day Adventist church. Yet since pacifism is merely an option for Seventh-day Adventists, Doss's commitment to nonviolence is due not to his acceptance of church teaching but rather to his own personal conviction that this is God's will.

This elevation of the powerful role of Doss's conscience in interpreting the biblical text is a chief characteristic of his Protestant identity. When Doss declares, "I believe in this Book . . . I wrestle with my conscience," he (perhaps unknowingly) reflects the powerful role that his own personal moral compass plays in interpreting and making sense of the biblical text. Doss's father also recognizes the influential role of Doss's conscience when he describes his son's commitment to pacifism as "whatever beliefs you have in your crazy head now." Similarly, as we have seen, Sergeant Howell says of Doss in front of other soldiers, "Do not look to him to save you on the battlefield because he will undoubtedly be too busy wrestling with his conscience to assist." Doss himself recognizes the importance of his conscience when he says to Dorothy, "I don't know how I'm going to live with myself if I don't stay true to what I believe." Doss's beliefs are so powerful that they function as a sort of vicarious belief for his fellow soldiers. As Captain Glover tells Doss, "Most of these men don't believe the same way you do, but they believe so much in how much you believe."

In what may be one of the more insightful critiques of the potential dangers of Doss's position, Dorothy warns him, "Don't confuse your will with the Lord's." She offers here a valuable reminder of the risk Doss (and all Protestants) face when they rely so heavily and exclusively on their own personal interpretation of the Bible. Of course, for Doss and many Protestants, the unexamined and operative assumption is that they are not interpreting the biblical text at all but merely recognizing and doing what the text "clearly" says.

Doss's own interpretation of the Bible is integrally connected to the personal nature of his relationship with God. Doss relates directly to God without relying upon any interlocutor (priest or pastor). He thereby illustrates to a certain degree Martin Luther's notion of the priesthood of all believers. Doss's relationship with God is so important to him that it raises questions about his mental fitness. During an interview, an Army psychologist says to him, "I understand God talks to you." "I'm not crazy," Doss replies. "I pray to God—I'd like to think he hears me." The personal nature of Doss's faith is also exemplified during his repeated prayer to God during the final battle scene when he ends up rescuing and saving the lives of seventy-five servicemen. "Please, Lord, help me get one more" becomes a mantra Doss repeats in a form of prayer to God at least four times; it is suggested that he says this every single time after he rescues a fallen companion.

If *Hacksaw Ridge* illustrates something about Protestantism, it is that the Bible plays a primary role, if not *the* primary role, in shaping one's moral framework, and that this framework is primarily the result of the individual's own personal interpretation of the biblical text. The individual conscience becomes the most powerful authority. This motif is at home with an elevation and celebration of the individual in aspects of American culture. Gibson also promotes the authority of the individual, a theme that is paramount in films such as *Braveheart* and *The Patriot*, in which men remain committed to personal values, despite immense pressure, and often at great personal cost.[7]

Mel Gibson, Violence, and the Bleeding of Truth and Fiction

As with any film based on actual events, *Hacksaw Ridge* occupies a strange liminal space between truth and fantasy, fiction and nonfiction, history and myth. The film opens with the note "A True Story." The film ends by cutting immediately to historical footage of Doss receiving the Medal of Honor from President Truman. A series of other images of Doss and his wife, Dorothy, leads into a brief video of the historical Desmond Doss speaking about his famed battle experience. The film thus ends in a quasi-documentary mode.[8] Contributing to the sense of realism are the film's first visual images of the war on Okinawa: corpses littering the ground, blood, explosions, soldiers on fire, and so on. These explicit efforts to enhance the film's realism are familiar to viewers of Gibson's other films such as *Braveheart* and *The Passion of the Christ*.

One potential function of this merging of fiction and reality is to invite viewers to imagine that they are viewing history itself unfolding on the screen. (A "real" portrayal might have included attention—as is provided in Clint Eastwood's 2006 movie *Letters from Iwo Jima*—to the perspectives of the Japanese soldiers.)[9] Yet what is the intent or motive behind this effort at capturing and conveying verisimilitude? One of the possible results of this type of storytelling is to remind viewers that the radical views and commitment of Desmond Doss are not relegated to fantasy but are possible to enact in the real, concrete world. If the story of Doss is "true," then viewers might imagine the realistic possibility of committing themselves fully to their own personal convictions.

Gibson's films are well known for relishing violence on a grand and detailed scale, and for locating violence against the male body as the epicenter of redemption.[10] In *Braveheart* (1995), *The Passion of the Christ* (2004), and *Apocalypto* (2006), the male protagonist undergoes horrific torture and suffering that are nonetheless potentially redemptive, if not meaningful, for others. Gibson has also starred in several films that feature violence (often in the form of torture) against his own body as infused with redemptive power and potential salvation.[11]

Hacksaw Ridge might represent a shift for Gibson from a former view in which violence is inherently redemptive to a new perspective where violence is still central but what constitutes redemption has shifted from violence to a person's courage to remain committed to one's convictions. Violence clearly remains essential in *Hacksaw Ridge* (one of the first and final visual images of the film is of the wounded Doss being carried on a stretcher), but it is not *the* center; that space is occupied by the courage and conviction of Doss, who rescues and saves lives not by suffering or dying but instead by living for, serving, and rescuing others.

The Crucifixion of Jesus has imparted to Christianity a central symbol that has a complex and ambiguous function regarding violence. On the one hand, the cross can be understood as a locus of redemptive violence, of an act that carries within itself the potential for redemptive or salvific activity on behalf of others. On the other hand, the cross can be interpreted as a rejection of any type of violence as grotesque, dehumanizing, and therefore unjust. Gibson's films (e.g., *Braveheart* and *The Passion of the Christ*) typically align with and illustrate the former view, but in *Hacksaw Ridge*, Gibson might want to have it both ways: the cross (and Christianity as an extension) as both violent redemption and also a repudiation of violence.

Conclusion: A Critique of Violence or Violent Ends?

As with many other cinematic genres, Hollywood war films do far more than retell history; they reveal insights and myths about American culture.[12] In the same way that Kathryn Bigelow's *The Hurt Locker* (2008) proposes that war is an addiction, and Coppola's *Apocalypse Now* (1979) depicts war as psychosis, *Hacksaw Ridge* also offers its own arguments about America and its culture of war. By

Figure 19.3 Gibson might want to have it both ways—the cross (and Christianity) as simultaneously both violent redemption and a repudiation of violence.
DVD screen capture, fair use

portraying the violence exhibited by Doss's father as a result of his experience as a soldier in World War I and the subsequent PTSD he endured, the film suggests that America also suffers from a collective trauma due to its previous violence, and that the violence America visits upon others is both a symptom of previous violence it has endured and also a cause of future violence. Along with 2005's *A History of Violence* (directed by David Cronenberg) and Showtime's *Dexter* (2006-13), *Hacksaw Ridge* imagines that America will inevitability return to its violent impulses. Although the film illustrates Desmond Doss's ability to end the cycle of violence within his own family, such hope for the domestic sphere is not extended to the nation itself. The film might also imply that, like Doss's father, who is accused by Doss's mother of hating himself, America's violent tendencies are birthed from trauma and a particular form of self-hatred.

It is worth probing further if *Hacksaw Ridge* represents a shift for Gibson away from his previous embrace of violence as redemptive and toward a new paradigm in which violence is rejected.[13] Some have suggested that *The Passion of the Christ* (2004) also illustrates an interest in pacifism.[14] Despite its embrace of pacifism as a valid personal value, however, *Hacksaw Ridge* illustrates how pacifism, far from a liability, is not only compatible with warfare but even potentially beneficial in its service. Far from repudiating violence, *Hacksaw Ridge* reconciles pacifism and violence and illustrates how they can be symbiotic. Such a vision seems to co-opt pacifism and baptize it so that it is fit for serving the nobler and holier purposes of (just?) war. Doss's personal pacifism can be accepted precisely because, although perhaps inconvenient, it fails to pose a serious threat to the broader system of American warfare. Personal ethics become subordinate and subservient to the national ethic at the heart of American civil religion, in which the state insists on the right to use violence against whomever it deems a threat to its own safety.

Doss reflects—perhaps unconsciously—this assimilation of pacifism to the purposes of militarism when he replies to a question during his court-martial about his refusal to touch a weapon by explaining, "I need to serve. I got the energy and the passion to serve as a medic, right in the middle with the other guys. No less danger, just . . . while everybody else is taking life, I'm going to be saving it. With the world so set on tearing itself apart, it doesn't seem like such a bad thing to me to wanna put a little bit of it back together." The historical Doss's preference for the term "conscientious cooperator" (over "conscientious objector") also reflects a similar understanding of how his pacifism can serve broader military ends. Captain Glover, who derided Doss's pacifism throughout basic training, ends up praising him at the end of the film for saving so many lives. "All I saw was a skinny kid. I didn't know who you were. You've done more than any other man could've done in the service of his country. Now, I've never been more wrong about someone in my life, and I hope one day you can forgive me." Doss's pacifism is ultimately accepted because, far from threatening America's military ends, it actually supports them.

Perhaps more important than whether Doss is Protestant is his identity, first and foremost, as a loyal devotee of American civil religion. In an American culture in which the dominant religion is neither Christianity nor Judaism but America itself (Americanism), the divine right of giving and taking life is a sacred prerogative America reserves for certain circumstances such as war.[15] Far from being an antiwar film, *Hacksaw Ridge* raises pointed questions about whether Doss's presence at Okinawa makes him complicit in the violence unleashed against the Japanese there, even though he personally does not carry or fire a weapon. To what extent does his presence baptize or condone the violence of the American military machine?

Figure 20.1 "My damnable pride!" Jake van Dorn (George C. Scott) confronts his runaway daughter—and himself—in *Hardcore*.
Pictorial Press Ltd/Alamy Stock Photo

20

Film Noir, Calvinism, and Self-Surveillance in Paul Schrader's *Hardcore*

Jason Stevens

Hollywood cinema has typified Calvinists in one of three ways: heroic Puritan settlers, witch-finders and bigots, or the legalistic patriarchs of silent film melodramas. In each of these guises, they are emblems of the virtues or ills of America's Protestant errand. The movie that concerns this essay, Paul Schrader's New Hollywood film noir *Hardcore* (1979), remains, even after thirty-five years, a compelling break from these cinematic depictions of Calvinism.[1] It is the story of a contemporary Dutch Reformed father and his harrowing collision with a version of secular society that seems alien to him. Unfolding in the present tense, the film displaces Calvinism from familiar, legendary settings to the movie-making West Coast, where crime, commerce, and pornography are interlinked. The character's interiority remains enigmatic, and his contradictions multiply over the course of the narrative. He emerges as a sincere man of devout principles, a pilgrim undergoing a spiritual trial, a disturbing figure of aggrieved manhood, and a potent vigilante.

The film's director, Paul Schrader, turned to film criticism and screenwriting at age twenty-six in rebellion against his very strict upbringing in the Christian Reformed Church, a branch of the Dutch Reformed Church in America.[2] He has returned to his Calvinist roots explicitly in two of his films. The second time, *First Reformed* (2018), owes its cinematic pedigree to different sources than *Hardcore*. The contemporary story of an alcoholic pastor (Ethan Hawke) of a Dutch Reformed church in upstate New York, *First Reformed* is a drama of spiritual crisis that nods to classic European art films about faith and God's silence—Bresson, Bergman, Dreyer, and Tarkovsky—rather than film noir.[3] Seeing an impending apocalypse that modern Christianity cannot avert, the minister in *First Reformed* experiences a loss of vocation, if not complete loss of belief. *Hardcore*, in contrast, has at its center a man of unwavering faith whose certainty is the source of his self-deception and his monocular vision.

Hardcore does not imply an attitude that is either for or against the protagonist's Calvinist faith. Instead, the movie's narration draws on the style and discourse

Jason Stevens, *Film Noir, Calvinism, and Self-Surveillance in Paul Schrader's* Hardcore In: *Protestants on Screen*. Edited by: Gastón Espinosa, Erik Redling and Jason Stevens, Oxford University Press. © Oxford University Press 2023. DOI: 10.1093/oso/9780190058906.003.0021 of film noir, a mode of anti-classical Hollywood cinema that Schrader helped to conceptualize, in order to expose its protagonist's failure to take seriously enough a problematic common to Calvinism: the split within the soul of the spiritually elect between the justified and natural selves, and the resulting burden of monitoring the soul for the struggle of good and evil within it. The protagonist's lapse of self-scrutiny is both underscored and supplemented by the narration, which channels the spectator to judge the character as well as align with them.

Film noir is a fusion of elements from America and Europe, vernacular and high modernisms. The category, referring initially to pessimistic Hollywood thrillers produced in the 1940s and 1950s, was invented in France after World War II and subsequently adopted in Anglo-American film criticism. Not a distinct genre so much as a deviant mode in the Hollywood cinema, film noir names a constellation of visual styles, themes, motifs, and narrative devices that filmmakers applied to established genres, darkening the mood and look of these forms and the ways they told their stories. Reflecting the influence of hard-boiled crime fiction, European émigrés, and American directors like Orson Welles and Alfred Hitchcock, film noir brought to American cinema an exceptionally grim view of the modern urban world as well as a preoccupation with the unseen, the forbidden, or the hidden made visible. Non-heroic heroes, making their way through down narratives involving detours and uncertainties, contend with pathological repression and temptation, often in the presence of characters that are psychic doubles. The assertive visual style mixes expressionism with realism and frequently links POV structures to "a derangement, criminality, or alienation that is mysterious."[4] Vision itself can seem sinful, for looking at things one should not look at can awaken awful wishes, terrible violence. "God is testing you," a character says to *Hardcore*'s protagonist, Jake Van Dorn; whether or not God watches him, Jake denies the risk of seduction.

Jake van Dorn: Peeper and Theologian

Hardcore opens on Christmas Day in Grand Rapids, Michigan, the city where Paul Schrader grew up. The location shooting, with its montage of Dutch Reformed churches, highlights the Calvinist character of the city's southern and eastern neighborhoods. Jake (George C. Scott) is introduced at a Christmas dinner held at his sister's house, where he sits at the head of the table and leads the family in blessing the gathering. Jake is a respected member of this community: a single father, an active church member, and a businessman whose successful manufacturing company has no apparent creditors. Likewise, Jake sees himself as a man whose spiritual accounts are balanced; as he states later, "I am a man who believes that he will be redeemed." On a trip to a youth Calvinist convention in California, his only child, the teenage Christine, vanishes, and her disappearance sets into motion the film's mystery plot. At the suggestion of the police, Jake hires a private investigator named Andy Mast (Peter Boyle) to locate Christine, and what Mast discovers unnerves and appalls her father. Christine has appeared in an explicit, "hard-core" adult film, a secret that Mast cruelly reveals by surprising Jake with footage of his daughter performing sex acts in an "eight-reeler" titled *Slave of Love*.

Becoming impatient with Mast, who is an unreliable detective, Jake determines to undertake the search for Christine himself. Mast has warned Jake that outside Grand Rapids, "there's a lot of strange things happening . . . things you don't want to know about. Doors that shouldn't be opened." Once Jake is in California, on a quest that will take him from Hollywood to San Diego to San Francisco, much of the film consists of Jake entering strange doors that take him deeper into private fantasy worlds advertised by neon-lit, carnivalesque exteriors. In these scenes, Jake becomes a version of a type of character that Schrader revisits in other films: "the Peeper," the cultural outsider with his face "frozen . . . against the window and passing judgment."[5] In addition to the sex trade, Jake is also flanked by the syncretic, fragmentary religious beliefs of the West Coast, post-counterculture. A representative of the zeitgeist is Niki (Season Hubley), a pornographic film actress and stripper who becomes Jake's native informant in San Francisco. While Jake marks his difference from her as a Calvinist, she describes herself as "a Venusian," a spiritual seeker. Like several other characters Jake meets, Niki is a consumer in the spiritual marketplace rather than a member of a closed religious society like the one he left behind.

At a loss to locate Christine, Jake goes undercover posing as an investor in adult movies, consulting LA's "porn mogul," Bill Ramada, and following leads to various adult film actors, vendors, and criminals. Resorting to violence to extort information and to vent his disgust with impurity, Jake displays an escalating capacity for rage, which he eventually turns against Niki. As the film approaches its bloody finale, Jake discovers that Christine has possibly fallen under the influence of a gangster and a producer of snuff movies named Ratan. After a confrontation results in Ratan's killing, Jake is reunited with Christine, who dispels one of her father's precious illusions. She was not kidnapped or coerced, as Jake has always believed of Christine's disappearance, but a willing runaway who hated and feared him and thought she was unloved. After rebuking himself for his "damnable pride," Jake persuades Christine to return to Grand Rapids, and the final long shot cranes over the nighttime streets of San Francisco.

With Christine's rescue and restoration, the film superficially seems to achieve narrative closure. However, working in the mode of film noir, Schrader actually destabilizes the viewer's allegiance to Jake by making him a type of the nonheroic noir hero. This type comes in several varieties, including the psychopath and the rogue cop. More commonly, he is a banal man whose capacity for sadism and madness is activated in an environment where guilt is metaphorically everywhere.[6] The big city, for example, is a noir topos for inducing a sense of moral vertigo and surprising the ostensibly ordinary fellow with his potential for evil. Jake Van Dorn is a novel example because his theology forewarns him of these potentials, identifying them as traits of the natural self. The sin of pride, for instance, of which he accuses himself, is the internal disposition that results in disobedience, from which all sin originates. In Calvinism, pride afflicts even the elect, a lesson that John Bunyan impresses through Christian's errors in *The Pilgrim's Progress*, a text that Shrader's vividly recalled from his childhood.[7] Yet, with the exception of Jake's self-rebuke in his daughter's presence, a story point to which I will return, he seems to rely on his theology to shield himself from Christian's trial of faith, becoming instead a questionable hero who justifies his vigilante acts and his aloof pity for the woman he enlists to assist his quest.

Jake explains his theology to Niki in the waiting area of the Las Vegas airport en route to San Diego. The scene is an interlude that does nothing to advance the mystery plot, but it does a great deal to explain Jake's self-perceptions, what he believes, and the utility of these beliefs. After identifying himself as Dutch Reformed, he proceeds to define the five classic tenets of orthodox Calvinism, followed by a matter-of-fact restatement of predestination.[8] Niki's reaction, "Then it's all *fixed*," elicits an affirmative nod from Jake—"Basically," he replies—before he returns to reading his paper. Jake's disinterest notwithstanding, Niki's remark speaks to *Hardcore*'s acerbically ironic play on the noir hero's moral atrophy. Jake's exposure to California's underbelly does confirm his sense of humankind's total depravity, but without himself feeling implicated in that common guilt. His certainty that he is one of the saints seems to psychologically preserve a distinction between his acting and his being. In his quest, Jake takes on the lingo and the look of the pornographer and criminal hustler. Within the logic of noir, this assumed "character" would be an exteriorization of some disowned aspect of himself, and, indeed, Jake becomes more feral and more ruthless once he adopts his alter ego. Yet Jake maintains that his pretense is strictly instrumental, even when his furious outbursts betray a loss of self-possession. In contrast to himself, he regards Niki as chaff adrift in secular culture; not a victim, a lamb stolen from the fold, as he imagines Christine, but as the fallen creature of a lost generation reared on television and movies. When Niki says that predestination deprives her of hope—"At least you get to Heaven. I don't get shit"—Jake does not contradict her, and, in fact, he stresses the irremediable difference between them, stating: "I'm a mystery to someone like you." As they travel together and converse—in the Vegas airport, dockside in San Diego, in the hotel room in San Francisco—Jake notably avoids making eye contact, a habit that he conspicuously breaks twice, each time in a manner that visually underscores Niki's

Otherness from him. The first is when he initially interviews her at a peep show, where he is separated from her by a glass wall and a descending metal shield. The second is the moment, near the climax, in which he closes the physical distance between them by choking her on the bed while drawing back his fist. In this latter case, Jake's stated motive is to extract information about Christine's whereabouts by all means necessary, but here, as elsewhere in the narrative when he seeks single-handedly to solve the mystery and save his daughter, the heroic archetype of the rescuing patriarch is spoiled by an excess that smacks of some deeper disturbance within the protagonist.

Noir Style Versus Transcendental Style

The visual style of *Hardcore* also owes to film noir and contributes to the viewer's evolving impression that Jake is not so clearly demarcated from life in the secular city as he imagines. Film noir, as Schrader defines it in a classic essay, is a mixed style, combining realism and expressionism to express a specific disillusionment with modern American life.[9] Disillusionment, in this formulation, is not a prelude to transcendence, and it points to darkness inward as well as outward. In expressionism, the object world takes on aspects of the projected ego, while in realism the object world reflects the inhuman impersonality of the cruel streets. Both contrast definitively with the reduced transcendental style that Schrader described in a book, *Transcendental Style in Film* (1972), which he published the same year as his film noir essay. In the book, Schrader delineates a form of visual and audio decluttering that removes impediments to sensing the sacred, or experiencing what Calvin called "the sensus divinitatis."[10] Transcendental style, being abstract and spare, creates stasis instead of identification with a human subject. The filmmaker minimizes or removes familiar narrative devices (POV structures, dialogue, verisimilar settings, melodic music, naturalistic acting) for engaging the viewer's emotions, as the protagonist inside the film is made to empty his so that he can receive holy truth.[11] *Hardcore*, in contrast, is designed to involve the viewer with Jake's psychological state, while rendering porous the boundaries between the character's interior, which he sees as divinely sanctified, and the external environment, which he sees as incidental to his soul. The mise-en-scène transforms with Jake's mood. After Christine's disappearance, the interiors in Grand Rapids suddenly become low-lit, and when Jake is present in Los Angeles, the look of the city alters. An earlier scene, in which Andy Mast, a native of the city, insinuates himself onto the set of an adult movie production, is distinctly bright, matching the scene's satiric tone; the director, a student wearing a UCLA Film School T-shirt, keeps fretting about the lighting and the angles. Once Jake appears, however, the city becomes a lurid nightscape of furtive voyeurism. The city darkens before Jake's gaze because its sights are being processed through his sensibility. In Jake's logic of moral equivalence, there is little difference between the movie capital, its *Star Wars* movies and adult film companies, and men like Ratan, who kill captive girls on camera. They are all aspects of the same fallen world, far from Grand Rapids, that maddens him the longer he must tarry in it. As the narration triggers shifts from scenes on location, as in West Hollywood or San Francisco's Tenderloin, to the interiors of buildings facing onto the streets, the narration's frequent attaching of the camera's angle, position, and motion to Jake's apparent optical perspective creates a symmetry between his subjectivity and the sights he discovers. *Hardcore*'s realism frames Jake against a material (and materialistic) world that he does not transcend, and its expressionism creates an ambiguous link between the city and Jake's subjectivity, which implicates him in what he perceives however much he would disavow it.[12]

Doubting the Elect: Seeing with and Beyond Jake's Gaze

What looks through this gaze that casts itself aggressively, probingly onto what it disdains? What does this gaze not apprehend? Theologically speaking, proper Calvinists are always *meant* to be looking at themselves, examining their inclinations for signs of grace as well as the tincture of sin. This notion that the justified self must supervise the natural self results in a parallel to the subject-object diremption: "The mind must monitor itself through the mechanism of conscience, and this is the point at which the dialect of the split self has sprung into being."[13] The purpose of this internal splitting into self-scrutiny is to reveal the Christian's inadequacy in order to better give glory to God for His unmerited mercy. The activity of self-surveillance must be rigorously maintained to keep alive the hope of salvation.[14] A trait of Jake, and one that he shares with the noir protagonist in spite of his theology, is that he does not seem to examine himself enough or to tremble enough at the mystery of his motivations. To Niki, Jake explains that God is omniscient—"He already knows who you are"—and therefore predestination is just. On the one hand, Jake is correct; Calvinism posits that the most important thing about ourselves is truly known only to God. On the other hand, Jake seems to chronically look past himself in the assurance that his name is among the elect, and it is this assurance that *Hardcore*'s narration undermines. In a fashion analogous to limited omniscience in literary fiction, *Hardcore*'s narration constructs a viewer that is more than Jake and less than God. Observing the protagonist, this viewing subject is not prompted to try to balance Jake's spiritual debts and credits, a balance that Jake has already decided in his favor, but to take note of Jake's alarming contradictions while holding final moral judgments in suspension. The rest of this essay considers three ways that *Hardcore* engages the viewer in a flow of sympathy, dissociation, and fear with regard to Jake: distanciation effects during scenes of violence, mirror motifs and deviant POV shots (which are noir earmarks), and the telling omission of the noir femme fatale despite atmospherics that would seem to conjure her up.

Formally, once the plot shifts to California, the narration switches back and forth between depicting Jake as a propulsive figure of forward motion, with whom the viewer is spatially aligned, and Jake as an object whose emotional volatility and explosive actions interrupt that alignment at crucial moments. These episodes trouble the sympathetic allegiance that is crafted by the narration's almost exclusive focalization to the character. One example is a shot that occurs in the midst of a chase sequence through an adult S&M site that Jake ransacks, bursting through successive interior walls in pursuit of Todd, an actor and affiliate of Ratan. After the tearing down of the last wall, Schrader introduces a jarring shot in which Jake seems about to break through the "fourth wall," the imaginary but transparent boundary separating on-screen from off-screen space. A second, even more striking example occurs earlier during Jake's assault on the porn actor Jim Slade, whom he drags into the shower of his hotel room. From a high angle vantage, perhaps paying homage to a similar shot in Hitchcock's *Psycho*, the viewer looks down into the shower as Jake throttles Jim in a headlock after having broken the actor's nose. The perspective is nonhuman, aligned with no subjectivity; the high angle, which could be taken to connote divine vision in a different kind of narrative, seems simultaneously cramped and alien. Thus, the narration establishes a visual norm, having Jake's POV generally aligned with the camera's field as it enters new venues and walks foreign paths, but this norm is shaken at significant moments when Jake is making someone the object of violence.

As in expressionism, mirrors in film noir are devices for suggesting alter egos, or *Doppelgängers*. In *Hardcore*, they are used to split Jake visually within shots, suggesting an internal disunity that he ignores. The first significant mirroring occurs when Jake is alone in Christine's bedroom after her disappearance. As he stands by her dresser, skimming the contents of the top drawer for clues, he looks up and catches his reflection in a medium-close shot that frames his head and shoulders within the frame of the mirror. In this lone instance, Jake looks at himself. Subsequently, shots of mirrors, occasionally combined with deviant POV shots, will create images of doubles that Jake does not see. After Andy Mast surprises Jake with footage of Christine in *Slave of Love*, Jake passes through black curtains from the theater auditorium into the lobby, where a surveillance mirror captures his image, which is grotesquely bent by the convex surface. Jake's identity as a revered father and spiritual leader of his household has just been challenged by the visual recording of his teenage daughter's sexual knowledge,

Figure 20.2 Schrader introduces a jarring shot in which Jake seems about to break through the "fourth wall" separating on-screen from off-screen space.
DVD screen capture, fair use

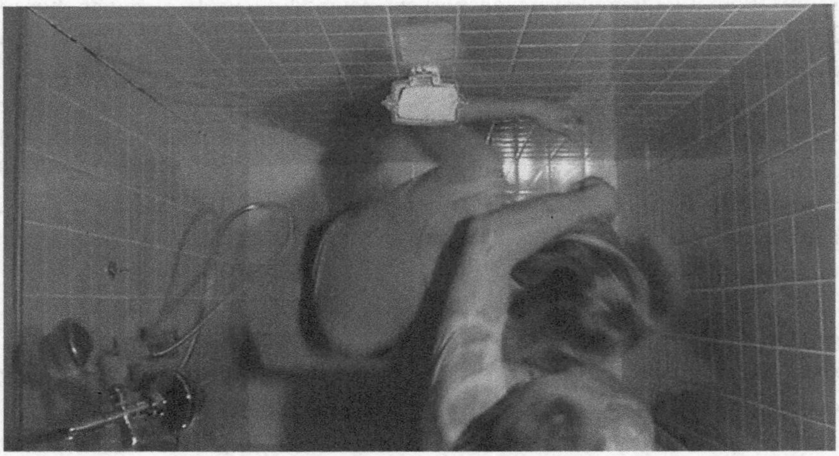

Figure 20.3 Nonhuman POV: from a high angle vantage, the viewer looks down into the shower as Jake throttles Jim in a headlock.
DVD screen capture, fair use

and he is imbalanced. As the scene ends, with Andy Mast warning Jake of the metaphorical "doors" that he should not try to open, the shot of the surveillance mirror recurs, as the camera zooms extremely close, eclipsing the edges of the glass and showing Jake's reflection growing grainy, stretched, slanted, and wavy.

The surveillance mirror not only underlines the viewer's act of looking at Jake but also implies the disruption in Jake that he will try to overcome by storming actual doors on the West Coast. A later deviant POV shot in Jake's Hollywood hotel room creates a sense of doubling without resort to a glass mirror. As he lies on the bed, listening to a choir on TV, the camera begins to pan across his room, apparently following the direction of Jake's gaze as it takes in the sights outside the window; suddenly, without a cut to signal any spatial discontinuity, the panning camera stops to reveal Jake, once again inside the shot, but standing on the opposite side of the room and in reverse profile to his position on the bed at the shot's start. Tellingly, the very next shot unveils him in his pornographer's disguise, under the alias Jack DeVries, standing in front of a *Hustler* magazine banner. To Jake, this alter ego has no connection to his essence, but an even more arresting instance of the mirror motif points up the blindness of his denial. When his brother-in-law Wes (Dick Sargent) visits Jake to persuade him to return to Grand Rapids, Jake sends him from the motel room. The scene closes on a shot within the black borders of a mirror, its reflection showing Wes depart as the viewer hears the words "Go home, go away." Jake, off-camera, appears to be speaking this farewell from behind a corner (its edge to the right of the mirror), but his voice seems oddly disembodied, as if it is floating above the soundscape as opposed to emitting from the character's location in space. Schrader, moreover, frames the shot asymmetrically, so that a gulf of empty space lies to the left of Wes's reflection, making Jake's absence from the mirror glaring. The eerie invisibility of the protagonist here suggests that Jake, as he would like to imagine himself and have others perceive him, is becoming effaced. His single-minded focus on the quest for his daughter helps him to look away from the dark recesses of himself, but *Hardcore*'s narrative devices cue the viewer to query Jake and the intensity of his disavowals, not just the city.

Hardcore's adult emporiums hawk fantasies of phallic pleasure using displays with titles like "Garden of Eden" and brim with fetishistic, leering imagery, but from this carnival of sexual wares no femme fatale steps forward. The classic type in film noir is both "destroying flesh" and "destroyed flesh," the Eve-like temptress luring to their ruination men who must be punished, usually with death.[15] As feminist criticism has demonstrated, the femme fatale generally functions to displace blame for prodigal desire away from the male narrative subject and to justify any retaliatory measures that the hero takes to protect himself from symbolic castration or contamination with taboo.[16] Occasionally a noir will lay bare the displacement, as in *The Night of the Hunter* (1955). When a psychopathic evangelist, Preacher, goes to a strip club to simmer over the evils of womanflesh, his vantage of the dancer onstage is expressionistically lit to evoke looking through a keyhole. A cut to a close-up shows his left hand, on which fingers are tattooed with letters spelling out H-A-T-E, clenching into a fist and reaching into

Figure 20.4 Mirroring motif: Jake steps from the X-rated theater auditorium into the lobby, where a surveillance mirror captures his image, which is grotesquely bent by the convex surface.
DVD screen capture, fair use

the pocket of his suit coat to grip something. After a second shot of the dancer onstage, a second cut to a close-up of the coat pocket shows the erect point of a suddenly clicked-open switchblade piercing the fabric from the inside in an obscene association linking male voyeurism, arousal, and sadism. Like *The Night of the Hunter*, *Hardcore* lacks a femme fatale to absorb the onus for the libidinal fantasies being merchandized in its narrative universe. Moreover, Jake's apparent sexual estrangement falls on himself—his own psychic maladies—and, in a broader respect, the pathology of the male gaze. In this last regard, Jake is symptomatic of a volatile mingling of eros, guilt, and aggression common to the masculine subject of noir; his Calvinist beliefs may be less to blame for causing his feelings than for blinkering him to their existence within his person.

Jake makes a point of being sexually disinterested and sermonizes to Niki about her generation's undue fixation on sex, of which it has made a kind of religion. But the viewer is left to wonder whether Jake's abstinence is purely a matter of prioritizing the right values. Jake's early interaction with a female design consultant, whom he has contracted to create a new logo for his company, is oddly tense, as he uses their meeting to try to rattle her confidence in her taste and acumen. The camera notably adopts the woman's line of sight as well as Jake's, and pans to signify the movement of her eyes in relation to Jake as he complains of her work in a fashion that diverts from the fact that he is clearly attracted to her. He uses the adjective "overpowering" to describe her design, but when she

Figure 20.5 In *The Night of the Hunter* (1955), a psychopathic evangelist, Preacher, goes to a strip club to simmer over the evils of woman-flesh.
DVD screen capture, fair use

Figure 20.6 His vantage of the dancer onstage is expressionistically lit to evoke a looking through a keyhole.
DVD screen capture, fair use

repeats it again, at the end of the conversation while looking at Jake, it carries a different subtext. There is also the curious detail that while Jake is searching for Christine, he gives her a pseudonym, "Joanna," the name of his first wife, Christine's mother. We learn late in the film that Joanna also ran away from home, a fact that Jake has denied, saying instead that she died. Could her reasons for running away have been similar to her daughter's? And is there any clue in the fact that when Jake is finally reunited with Christine, her first response is to cringe from him in a corner? Most portentously, Jake's horrified reactions to pornographic film footage are belied by his violence. When Jake sees the footage of Christine engaging in sex acts on-screen, a series of continuing POV shots show his face and body contorting into disbelief, outrage, frenzy, and grief as he shouts "Turn it off! *Turn it off!*" Later, when he views one of Ratan's snuff films with an all-male audience, the viewer is again given partial views of what Jake sees as well as his shocked reaction to it. The victim on camera is trussed in leather and clamps that obscure all of her face except for her eyes, which stare directly into the camera, which stands in for the assaultive gaze of the male audience. Just before her throat is slit, the camera cuts to Jake covering his eyes, the horror on-screen illuminating for him Christine's possible fate if she remains with Ratan. However, immediately following this moment in which he averts his gaze from sadism, Jake returns to his motel room for the terrifying exhibition of force against Niki. As he pins her to the bed by the throat, a close-up approximating Jake's assaultive gaze shows Niki's face struggling for breath, followed by a reverse close-up of Jake's snarling face from an angle and position that approximate Niki's visual orientation on the mattress where she has been pressed. Once again, Jake is defamiliarized during an act of violence, but the effect is layered here by the juxtaposition with the footage of the captive young woman being murdered in the snuff film. Incongruously, Jake caps this attack by raising up Niki and giving her a paternal kiss on the forehead. Surely this moment adds ominous implications to the first words that Christine speaks to Jake when he finds her, the first words that the daughter says to her father in the entire film: "Don't hurt me."

Conclusion: Calvinist Insight Confided in the Viewer

Superficially, Jake Van Dorn succeeds in his quest; he retrieves his daughter and takes her home. Yet the noir protagonist himself remains ambiguous, and the future—in Grand Rapids—disquietingly uncertain. Jake is too assured to doubt himself, too quick to rationalize violence in a fallen world, too convinced of his ultimate destiny to see that the evil he smites has correspondences in himself. Despite the admission of his pride, tearfully wrung from him by Christine's rejection, it is unclear whether Jake has achieved any lasting insight from his sojourn outside the sacred enclaves of home. The experience may be more instructive for the viewers than the protagonist, and the demons loosed on the quest may be only suppressed back in Grand Rapids, where doors are discreetly shut. For all its skepticism toward its protagonist's interpretation of his faith, in its profound representation of self-deception and false humility *Hardcore* ultimately makes a very Calvinist point.

Figure 21.1 Aslan and Edmund depicted in Walden Media's blockbuster adaptation of C. S. Lewis's *The Chronicles of Narnia: The Lion, The Witch, and the Wardrobe*.
PictureLux/The Hollywood Archive/Alamy Stock Photo

21

Lost in Adaptation: Aslan's Divinity and the Purpose of Real Pain in *Narnia* Versus Fantasy Film

Devin Brown

Near the beginning of *The Great Divorce*, C. S. Lewis's speculative novel about the afterlife, one of the inhabitants of hell is asked whether the others there like it. "As much as they'd like anything," he replies. "They've got cinemas and fish and chip shops and advertisements and all the sorts of things they want."[1] In a similar vein in *The Lion, the Witch and the Wardrobe*, as Edmund trudges through the snow on his way to betray his siblings to the White Witch, Lewis's narrator reports that his mind is filled with thinking about "what sort of palace he would have and how many cars and all about his private cinema."[2]

Despite these negative associations, C. S. Lewis (1898–1963) was not anti-cinema any more than he was anti–fish and chips. Though he was not an avid film-goer and there is no way to say how many films he attended, we do know that he went to a number of movies and at least in part enjoyed them. In 1933 Lewis went with his brother Warnie to see *King Kong* and sometime later wrote a friend, "I thought parts of 'King Kong' (especially where the natives make a stand after he's broken the gate) magnificent."[3] In 1937 he again went to the cinema with his brother, this time to see the Disney adaptation of *Snow White and the Seven Dwarfs*. Afterward Lewis wrote a correspondent that despite several elements he felt were poorly done, he thought "all the terrifying bits were good, and the animals really most moving."[4] A decade later the brothers went to see another Disney film, and afterward Lewis told an American friend: "I have always heard of the beauty of your 'fall,' and the other day I was much impressed by its loveliness on the screen: having paid one of my rare visits to the cinema to see 'Bambi.' "[5]

Despite a tradition stemming back to the Puritans for Protestantism—which Lewis, as a devout member of the Church of England, was part of—to view the theater and motion pictures with a certain measure of distrust, Lewis made it clear that he found nothing morally wrong with the cinema

Devin Brown, *Lost in Adaptation: Aslan's Divinity and the Purpose of Real Pain in* Narnia *Versus Fantasy Film*
In: *Protestants on Screen.* Edited by: Gastón Espinosa, Erik Redling and Jason Stevens, Oxford University Press.
 DOI: 10.1093/oso/9780190058906.003.0022

per se. He makes this point in the following passage from *Mere Christianity* where he writes:

> One of the marks of certain type of bad man is that he cannot give up a thing himself without wanting everyone else to give it up. That is not the Christian way. An individual Christian may see fit to give up all sorts of things for special reasons—marriage, or meat, or beer, or the cinema; but the moment he starts saying the things are bad in themselves, or looking down his nose at other people who do use them, he has taken the wrong turning.[6]

Given that he was not particularly drawn to films, it is no surprise Lewis said relatively little about them—positive or negative—in the writings he has left us. The one notable exception can be found in his essay "On Stories," where Lewis takes issue with the changes filmmakers made to the ending of the 1937 film adaptation of the H. Rider Haggard novel *King Solomon's Mines*. "Of its many sins . . . only one here concerns us," Lewis writes. "At the end of Haggard's book, as everyone remembers, the heroes are awaiting death entombed in a rock chamber and surrounded by the mummified kings of that land. The maker of the film version, however, apparently thought this tame. He substituted a subterranean volcanic eruption, and then went one better by adding an earthquake."[7] Perhaps, Lewis continues, the filmmaker was correct in thinking that "by the canons of his own art" the scene in the original was not "cinematic" enough. But in that case, Lewis concludes, "it would have been better not to have chosen in the first place a story which could be adapted to the screen only by being ruined. Ruined, at least for me." And in this final sentence, Lewis acknowledges the fact that the success or failure of any modification between the original and a screen adaptation can be highly subjective: a change one viewer fully approves of, another may detest.

Much has been written about the changes made to Lewis's originals in the three major motion picture adaptations of *The Lion, the Witch and the Wardrobe* (2005), *Prince Caspian* (2008), and *The Voyage of the Dawn Treader* (2010). While most reviewers acknowledge that some changes must be made in a cinematic adaptation of any book, many of their comments seem to focus on whether, in their opinion, the films were enhanced or ruined by the filmmakers' modifications. Because Lewis died long before the films were released, what he himself might have said about the three movies must remain speculation, but there can be speculation based on statements he made on matters that relate to the films. Two areas where the films can be evaluated in light of Lewis's statements are their depiction of Aslan and their portrayal of pain. The recent film adaptations portray Aslan as a somewhat less divine or Christlike figure than Lewis as a layman in the Anglican Church did, and they present a less disturbing, less genuine form of pain than Lewis included in his original stories—pain that Protestant doctrine sees as part of the redemptive process and life in a fallen world.

Depicting Aslan

One concern that Lewis had about any future film adaptations of his Narnia books was whether the screen representation of Aslan, the great Christlike lion, would do justice to his divine character. In May 1954, Jane Douglas wrote Lewis and his publisher about the possibility of producing a television series of the Narnia stories. Lewis replied, "I am sure you understand that Aslan is a divine figure, and anything remotely approaching the comic (above all anything in the Disney line) would be to me simple blasphemy."[8]

This did not mean Lewis was completely opposed to television versions of the stories, only that they would have to be done properly and would need to meet his approval—conditions that he doubted would be acceptable to the producers. As he explained to his publisher a short time later: "I wrote Miss Douglass emphasizing the fact that Aslan is a divine figure and I should regard any comic element in the treatment of him as blasphemous. For the rest, I left it to you. I feel we should allow it only under safeguards which the T.V. people will almost certainly not give us: i.e., specimen photos of the characters and a full script with a right of veto on our part."[9]

In 1959 Lewis wrote a BBC producer with whom he had collaborated on a radio version of *The Magician's Nephew* (during Lewis's day the sixth book in the Narnia series) to say that while he approved of the radio adaptation, he was "absolutely opposed" to a television adaptation because of the difficulty—at least then—of properly portraying the talking animals, especially Aslan. That Lewis was not opposed to a screen adaptation if it could succeed in portraying Aslan as he needed to be is made clear as Lewis goes on to say that while a human actor dressed up to play Aslan would be blasphemy, "cartoons (if only Disney did not combine so much vulgarity with his genius!) would be another matter."[10]

A brief glimpse into the limitations that special effects had in Lewis's day can be found in his description of the painting of the Narnian ship that comes to life early in *The Voyage of the Dawn Treader*. In seeking to explain to readers what Lucy, Edmund, and Eustace witness, Lewis writes: "What they were seeing may be hard to believe when you read it in print, but it was almost as hard to believe when you saw it happening. The things in the picture were moving. It didn't look at all like a cinema either; the colors were too real and clean and out-of-doors for that."[11] By the time of the recent film adaptations, special effects had advanced so far since Lewis's time that there were few if any concerns raised about the manner in which the majestic Aslan was visually portrayed.

Aslan, as Lewis has Mr. Beaver explain to the children in *The Lion, the Witch and the Wardrobe*, is "the King of the wood and the son of the great Emperor-beyond-the-Sea."[12] Beyond rare statements like these, Lewis is careful to leave the question of Aslan's divinity a veiled implication within the books themselves. At the end of *The Voyage of the Dawn Treader*, Aslan tells Lucy that he is present in her world as well, not just in Narnia. Then he explains—in a passage that has become a favorite among Narnia fans: "There I have another name. You must learn to know me by that name. This was the very reason why you were brought to Narnia, that by knowing me here for a little, you may know me better there."[13]

In his other writings, Lewis was somewhat more explicit about Aslan's religious connection. In one essay he described his motivation for the Narnia stories this way: "I thought I saw how stories of this kind could steal past a certain inhibition which had paralyzed much of my own religion in childhood. . . . But supposing that by casting all these things into an imaginary world, stripping them of their stained-glass and Sunday school associations, one could make them for the first time appear in their real potency."[14]

In a letter to a young fan, Lewis pointed out Aslan's origins more even directly as he addressed her question about the other name that Aslan refers to in his statement to Lucy. "As to Aslan's other name, well I want you to guess," Lewis wrote. "Has there never been anyone in *this* world who (1.) Arrived at the same time as Father Christmas. (2.) Said he was the son of the Great Emperor. (3.) Gave himself up for someone else's fault to be jeered at and killed by wicked people. (4.) Came to life again. (5.) Is sometimes spoken of as a Lamb (see the end of the Dawn Treader). Don't you really know His name in this world?"[15]

Through several minor omissions or additions, the filmmakers took small steps to veil the connection between Aslan and Christ slightly more than Lewis did—presumably to appeal beyond the Christian film audience to the broader fantasy film audience. For example, in the first scene mentioned above, Mr. Beaver says nothing about Aslan's being the son of the great Emperor-beyond-the-Sea. In another omission, Aslan's appearance as a lamb is entirely left out of the film version of *The Voyage of the Dawn Treader*. In the second scene discussed above, when Lucy asks a question not found in the book, "Will you visit us in our world?" the film Aslan replies only that he will be "watching" her when she is back in her own world—not that he is present there. Then Aslan goes on to make the same statement from the book about having another name and the reason she was brought to Narnia, but then the filmmakers have Lucy ask if they will meet again, another question not asked in Lewis's original. Aslan answers her, "Yes, Dear One, one day"—an answer that may seem to point more toward their Narnian reunion at the end of *The Last Battle* rather than to Lucy developing an ongoing relationship with Christ back in England within the Protestant tradition, as Lewis himself had.

Figure 21.2 Though Aslan sacrifices himself and is resurrected, the filmmakers veil his connection to Christ slightly more than Lewis did in the novel.
DVD screen capture, fair use

Two Kinds of Pain

Besides his concerns about a non-blasphemous depiction of Aslan, a second concern Lewis may have had about the films (and certainly he would have had had others that were more literary rather than theological) is that they might give viewers—particularly those who consumed a steady diet of fantasy films—a distorted position on various aspects of life, as viewers may form beliefs based not on life itself but on the misleading depictions of life they see on the screen.

One place where Lewis warns about this condition can be found in *Mere Christianity*, where he challenges those who disagree with his position on marriage to make sure that their ideas are not really coming from misrepresentations in movies and other popular forms of romance. Lewis writes: "If you disagree with me, of course, you will say, 'He knows nothing about it, he is not married.' You may quite possibly be right. But before you say that make quite sure that you are judging me by what you really know from your own experience and from watching the lives of your friends, and not by ideas you have derived from novels and films."[16] Lewis goes on to warn that "it takes patience and skill to disentangle the things we have really learned from life" from ideas and opinions that are based on unrealistic films we have seen or overly romantic novels we have read.[17]

One of these mistaken beliefs about life that viewers may form from a steady diet of fantasy films involves the nature of pain. While Lewis's own Protestant view was that pain in this earthly life is common to all people and is often quite disturbing and includes real suffering, the kind of pain found in fantasy films is frequently quite superficial, very brief, and, in fact, not all that painful.

Before turning to the way pain is represented in the recent Narnia films, we need to first look at what Lewis, a lay Protestant, had to say about life's pains and to explore two instances where he depicts this pain in the Narnia books.

In his highly respected work *Companion to Narnia*, Paul Ford points out that despite some who want to picture Lewis as living comfortably isolated from the real world in the ivory towers of Oxford, Lewis was well acquainted with life's pain. Ford notes that Lewis was wounded in World War I and suffered much from aging and disability. "Lewis also experienced emotional pain," Ford continues, "perhaps the greatest of which was at the death of his mother from cancer when he was nine."[18] Further misery followed as Lewis endured years of boarding school, where he was abused by schoolmasters and bullied by schoolmates.

That Lewis thought long and deeply about the pain of life and how it can be reconciled with Protestant beliefs is evidenced by his 1940 book *The Problem of Pain*—published originally by the Centenary Press as part of its Christian Challenge series. Here Lewis explores the question of how a God who is all-good and all-powerful can allow pain, and the evil that causes it, to exist in the world. Lewis analyzes various facets of this problem through chapters on divine omnipotence, divine goodness, human wickedness, human pain, and animal pain. Two aspects that are relevant in comparing the pain in the books and the pain in the films are (1) the manner in which Lewis believed pain can be a means to shatter our illusion of self-sufficiency and prevent us from being satisfied with our moral imperfections, or as he puts it, how pain can be God's "megaphone to rouse a deaf world," and (2) the Christian doctrine of believers coming to share in Christ's sufferings.[19] We can see an example of the first aspect in the physical pain Eustace experiences in *The Voyage of the Dawn Treader*. We find an example of the second in the emotional pain Susan and Lucy undergo at Aslan's execution in *The Lion, the Witch and the Wardrobe*.

In the book version of *The Voyage of the Dawn Treader*, Eustace gives a first-hand account of the agonizing pain he experienced as Aslan tore off his dragon skin and transformed him back into a boy. "The very first tear he made was so deep that I thought it had gone right into my heart," he tells Edmund. "And when he began pulling the skin off, it hurt worse than anything I've ever felt."[20] Here in Lewis's original we find the megaphone kind of pain, the kind that needs to be taken seriously. In *The Problem of Pain*, Lewis explains, "I am not arguing that pain is not painful. Pain hurts. . . . I am only trying to show that the old Christian doctrine of being made 'perfect through suffering' is not incredible."[21]

Lewis makes a similar statement in the chapter appropriately titled "Counting the Cost" from *Mere Christianity*, his most famous book about Christian doctrines. There Lewis describes the pain that transformation like the one Eustace undergoes will involve. Lewis explains:

> That is why He warned people to "count the cost" before becoming Christians. "Make no mistake," He says, "if you let me, I will make you perfect. The moment you put yourself in My hands, that is what you are in for. Nothing less, or other, than that. You have free will, and if you choose, you can push Me away. But if you do not push Me away, understand that I am going to see this job through. Whatever suffering it may cost you in your earthly life, whatever inconceivable purification it may cost you after death, whatever it costs Me, I will never rest, nor let you rest, until you are literally perfect—until my Father can say without reservation that He is well pleased with you. . . . This I can do and will do. But I will not do anything less."[22]

If the doctrine of being made perfect through suffering is present in the film version of *The Voyage of the Dawn Treader*, it is present to a much lesser degree, if at all, simply because in the film the pain Eustace undergoes is present to a much lesser degree. In the scene where he sheds his dragon skin, the film Eustace scratches a bit at his scales before Aslan scratches three times in the sand and then roars—actions that cause a great golden wind to lift Eustace into the air, where his dragon form simply dissolves in a glorious light. Then Eustace, returned to his boy form, gently floats to the ground, where he falls prostrate. Moments later we see him racing to Aslan's Table with the sword he has found. Later when asked what being changed back by Aslan was like, the film Eustace reports that the pain was not the kind we need to take seriously. "It sort of hurt," he explains with a shrug. "But it was a good pain, like when you pull a thorn from your foot."

In the book version of *The Lion, the Witch and the Wardrobe*, Lewis has Susan and Lucy undergo emotional pain as agonizing as Eustace's physical pain in the scene where they witness Aslan's death. After the Witch and her forces leave, Susan and Lucy crawl out from their hiding place and approach Aslan's body. Then readers are told, "And down they both knelt in the wet grass and kissed his cold face and stroked his beautiful fur—what was left of it—and cried till they could cry no more."[23] With difficulty they remove the muzzle the Witch had placed on Aslan, and Lewis's narrator reports, "And when they saw his face without it they burst out crying again and kissed it and fondled it and wiped away the blood and foam as well as they could. And it was all more lonely and hopeless and horrid than I know how to describe."[24] Susan and Lucy try to loosen the tight cords wound around Aslan but are unsuccessful. Then the narrator adds this final description of the pain the girls have experienced—as good a description of real grief as readers are likely to find anywhere: "I hope no one who reads this book has been quite as miserable as Susan and Lucy were that night; but if you have been—if you've been up all night and cried till you have no more tears left in you—you will know that there comes in the end a sort of quietness. You feel as if nothing was ever going to happen again."[25]

Figure 21.3 In the film version of *The Voyage of the Dawn Treader*, Eustace as the dragon undergoes much less suffering.
DVD screen capture, fair use

In this scene, Lewis may be drawing from the Protestant doctrine that claims that believers somehow spiritually and emotionally will share in the agonies of Christ's passion, much as Susan and Lucy share in the pains of Aslan's death here. In *The Book of Common Prayer*, used in the services at the Anglican church Lewis attended each Sunday, we find this prayer to be used on Palm Sunday that refers to this doctrine: "Almighty and everliving God, in your tender love for the human race you sent your Son our Savior Jesus Christ to take upon him our nature, and to suffer death upon the cross, giving us the example of his great humility: Mercifully grant that we may walk in the way of his suffering, and also share in his resurrection; through Jesus Christ our Lord, who lives and reigns with you and the Holy Spirit, one God, for ever and ever. Amen."[26]

Whether Lewis was seeking to depict what sharing in Christ's sufferings might feel like or simply to depict real pain, we find a sharp contrast between Lewis's portrait of the girls' grief and what is portrayed on-screen. Rather than crying until they can cry no more, the filmic Susan and Lucy mostly seem to be fighting back tears. In addition, rather than spending all night crying until there are no more tears left in them, Susan interrupts their somewhat short time of grieving by announcing to Lucy, "We must tell the others."

In his essay titled "On Three Ways of Writing for Children," Lewis considered the viewpoint that some critics put forth that fairy tales, such as the ones he himself wrote, should not frighten the child who reads them—and by this, Lewis explains, critics mean that "we must try to keep of out of his mind the knowledge that he is born into a world of death, violence, wounds, adventure, heroism and cowardice, good and evil."[27] Lewis goes on to argue that the pain and suffering of life should not be hidden from young readers as though it does not exist. "Since it so likely that they will meet cruel enemies," Lewis continues, "let them at least have heard of brave knights and heroic courage. . . . Let there be wicked kings and beheadings, battles and dungeons, giants and dragons, and let villains be soundly killed at the end of the book." J. R. R. Tolkien, Lewis's close friend and a fellow member of their writing group the Inklings, took a similar stance on the need for fairy tales to faithfully include life's pain. When asked about the dark or difficult parts of *The Hobbit*, parts that might trouble a young reader, Tolkien stated: "The presence (even if only on the borders) of the terrible is, I believe, what gives this imagined world its verisimilitude. A safe fairyland is untrue to all worlds."[28]

Lewis once described the kind of restrictions the fairy tale genre imposed upon him in writing the Narnia stories. "I fell in love with the form itself," he writes. "Its brevity, its severe restraints on description, its flexible traditionalism, its inflexible hostility to all analysis, digress, reflections and 'gas.' . . Its very limitations of vocabulary became an attraction; as the hardness of the stone pleases the sculptor or the difficulty of the sonnet delights the sonneteer."[29] Notably missing from Lewis's list of limitations is any mention of the need to omit any serious pain or real suffering.

Just as the fairy tale genre imposed certain limits on Lewis, it could be argued that the fantasy film genre and the expectations of the fantasy film audience in a globalized market imposed certain limits on the makers of the Narnia films, including limitations as to how much and what kind of pain could be shown—namely, the kind that is not particularly disturbing. On November 18, 1956—just eight months after *The Last Battle*, the seventh and final installment of the Chronicles of Narnia, was released—Lewis's essay "Sometimes Fairy Stories May Say Best What's to Be Said" appeared in the *New York Times Book Review*. And if we are looking to find what Lewis had to say about pain as it is understood in Protestant doctrine, we might agree that sometimes fairy stories—and not fantasy films—do say it best.

Conclusion

Lewis once stated, "Nothing can be more disastrous than the view that the cinema can and should replace popular written fiction."[30] We can say that for those people who know the first three Chronicles of Narnia only as they are appear on film, something—some of the glimpses of Aslan's divinity and some of the real pain in Lewis's originals—has been lost in the translation.

Notes

Introduction

1. Colleen McDannell, ed., *Catholics in the Movies* (New York: Oxford University Press, 2008).
2. On Vera Farmiga's mixed religious background, see Kane, Chapter 14. DuVernay is Catholic; she references her Catholic school education in Stephen Galloway, "Ava DuVernay Wishes She'd Challenged 'Privileged, Pedestrian' Criticism of Selma," *Hollywood Reporter*, March 7, 2008; Duvall is a self-reported Christian Scientist, though in some instances he has said that his beliefs are private and only affirms that he is not an atheist or an agnostic. Jeffrey Hildner, "The Virginian," *Christian Science Journal*, December 2008.
3. Clint Eastwood's spiritual beliefs are undefined, though he comes from a Protestant background, and Mel Gibson is a devout Catholic. On Eastwood's upbringing, see Richard Schickel, *Clint Eastwood: A Biography* (New York: Vintage, 1997), 27, 42. Paul Schrader is now an Episcopalian (part of the Anglican Communion), but at the time he made his film noir *Hardcore* (1979), he was an ex-Calvinist grappling with his Dutch Reformed background; see Stevens, Chapter 19.
4. Donald Thompson's Mark IV Pictures and the evangelical cycle of apocalyptic horror are covered in Beal, Chapter 16, as well as Parts IV, V, and VI of this Introduction.
5. McDannell, *Catholics in the Movies*, 29. Craig Detweiler enforces the misconception that evangelicals simply withdrew from being active producers of film in his essay "Christianity," in *The Routledge Companion to Religion and Film*, ed. John Lynden (New York: Routledge, 2009), 121. See Part IV for a complete list of evangelical films and discussion.
6. On Aschultz and Walden Media, see Part VI of this Introduction and Chapter 2.
7. McDannell, *Catholics in the Movies*, 14.
8. For two classic studies that discuss how the Protestant tenet of the priesthood of all believers evolved in religion, society, and political ideology, see Nathan Hatch, *The Democratization of American Christianity* (New Haven, CT: Yale University Press, 1989) and Ernest Tuveson, *Redeemer Nation: The Idea of America's Millennial Role* (Chicago: University of Chicago Press, 1968), esp. chap. IV on manifest destiny. Though these texts focus on the United States, they also discuss the European theological origins and contexts of the tenet.
9. McDannell, *Catholics in the Movies*, 29. Though our book focuses on film in the United States and Europe, we acknowledge that there is also vibrant Protestant filmmaking in Third Cinema. The Pentecostal video market has transformed the West African film industry. See Birgit Meyer, "Religious Re-mediations: Pentecostal Views

in Ghanian Video Movies," and Mitchell Joylon, "Towards an Understanding of the Popularity of West African Video Film," both in *The Religion and Film Reader*, ed. S. Brent Plate (New York: Routledge, 2007), 95–102 and 103–112. Former minister of culture Lee Chang-dong's *Secret Sunshine* (2007) calls attention to South Korea's large evangelical population in its story of an atheist's conversion and deconversion. In *Silent Light* (2007), about a contemporary Mennonite community in Chihuahua, director Carlos Reygadas made one of the most acclaimed Mexican feature films of the twenty-fist century. The "extraordinary mushrooming of [Brazil's] Protestant population over the past 30 years—the majority of whom are evangelical or Pentecostal" is reflected in the box office success of films such as *Os Dez Mandamentos* [The 10 Commandments] (2016), a life of Moses, and 2018's *Nada a Perder* [Nothing to Lose] (2018), a biopic about Bishop Edir Macedo, who founded the evangelical Universal Church of the Kingdom of God (UKCG) in the 1970s. *Os Dez Mandamentos* was originally produced in several episodes for Brazilian television by the UKCG. *Nada a Perder* was produced by the Brazilian company Paris Entretenimento but heavily promoted by the UKCG across its media platforms. See Phil Hoad, "Taking Cinema to the Pulpit: Brazil's Evangelical Film," *Al Jazeera*, March 19, 2016; Associated Press, "Biopic of Brazil Evangelical Bishop Breaks Box Office Record," *VOA News*, May 11, 2018. There are dissenting views. The ultra-conservative ideology of Brazil's Evangelical Christian Social Party is satirized in writer-director Gabriel Mascaro's dystopian film *Divino Amor* [Divine Love] (2019), in which the country is transforming into a futuristic theocracy.

10. Kathryn Reklis summarizes these positions in her "Introduction" to Kathryn Reklis and Sarah Covington, eds., *Protestant Aesthetics and the Arts (* New York: Routledge, 2020), 56 and nn. 15–19. See also Tracy Fessenden, *Culture and Redemption: Religion, the Secular, and American Literature* (Princeton, NJ: Princeton University Press, 2007).
11. H. Richard Niebuhr, *Christ and Culture* (New York: Harper & Row, 1951). John Lyden summarizes each of Niebuhr's five types in *Film as Religion: Myths, Morals, Rituals* (New York: New York University Press, 2003), 18–22.
12. Max. Weber, *The Protestant Ethic and the Spirit of Capitalism*, trans. Talcott Parsons (Crows Nest: Allen & Unwin, 1930 [1905]). Reklis summarizes Weber's problematic theory and also Counter-Reformation polemics in her "Introduction," *Protestant Aesthetics and the Arts*, 4–5.
13. See, for example, McDannell's dismissive claims in *Catholics and the Movies*, 12–14, 29.
14. David Morgan, *The Embodied Eye: Religious Visual Culture and the Social Life of Feeling* (Berkeley: University of California Press, 2012), 163–173.
15. "Religion," *Merriam-Webster Online Dictionary,* September 14, 2020.
16. Rodney Stark, *The Triump of Faith: Why the World is More Religious Than Ever*. Wilmington: ISI Books, 2015. Bryon R. Johnson and Jeff Levin, "Religion is Dying? Don't Believe It. Many of the 'Nones' Aren't Secular: They Belong to Minority Fiaths. The Problem is How to Count Them." *Wall Street Journal*, July 28, 2022. https://www.wsj.com/articles/religion-is-dying-dont-believe-it-nones-others-surveys-faith-institutions-atheists-agnostics-practice-minority-11659017037 Accessed June 13, 2023.

17. Pew Research Center, "The Changing Global Religious Landscape," April 5, 2017: https://www.pewresearch.org/religion/2017/04/05/the-changing-global-religious-landscape/ Pew Research Center, "Global Christianity—A Report on the Size and Distribution of the World's Christian Population," Religion and Public Life: Demographic Study, December 19, 2011, 1–6; Philip Jenkins, *The Next Christendom: The Coming of Global Christianity* (New York: Oxford University Press, 2002).
18. Jeffrey M. Jones, "How Religious Are Americans?" Gallup News, December 23, 2021: https://news.gallup.com/poll/358364/religious-americans.aspx Accessed June 13, 2023.. See Pew Research Center, "Global Christianity."
19. Annie Mueller, "Why Movies Cost So Much to Make," *Investopedia*, June 25, 2019.
20. Joseph Campbell, *The Hero with a Thousand Faces* (Princeton, NJ: Princeton University Press, 1973). Also see "Monomyth," *Lexico* (collaboration between Oxford University Press and Dictionary.com).
21. Reflecting on Campbell's influence on his own story telling, Lucas stated: "It was very eerie because in reading *The Hero with a Thousand Faces* I began to realize that my first draft of *Star Wars* was following classic motifs. . . . So I modified my next draft according to what I'd been learning about classical motifs and made it a little bit more consistent. . . . I went on to read 'The Masks of God' and many other books." Stephen Larsen and Robin Larsen, *Joseph Campbell: A Fire in the Mind: The Authorized Biography* (New York: Simon & Schuster, 2002).
22. Christopher Vogler, *The Writer's Journey: Mythic Structure for Writers*, 2nd ed. (Studio City, CA: Michael Wiese Productions, 1998). Vogler has had a significant influence in Hollywood, having worked in the development departments for Disney, Warner Brothers, and Fox 2000. For further examples of screenwriting craft, see Robert Kernen, *Building Better Plots* (Cincinnati, OH: Writer's Digest Books, 1999); David Howard and Edward Mabley, *The Tools of Screenwriting: A Writer's Guide to the Craft and Elements of a Screenplay* (New York: St. Martin's Griffin, 1993).
23. For the definition of Protestantism, see "Protestant," *Merriam-Webster Dictionary*, accessed September 14, 2020.
24. George Marsden, *Fundamentalism and American Culture* (New York: Oxford University Press, 2006).
25. Marsden, *Fundamentalism and American Culture*.
26. For the roots of Pentecostalism, see Donald Dayton, *Theological Roots of Pentecostalism* (Grand Rapids, MI: Baker Academic Press, 1987); Grant Wacker, *Heaven Below: Early Pentecostals and American Culture* (Cambridge, MA: Harvard University Press, 2003); Edith Blumhofer, *Assemblies of God: A Chapter in the Story of American Protestantism*, Vol. 1 (Springfield, MO: Gospel Publishing House, 1989); James Goff, *Fields White unto Harvest: Charles F. Parham and the Missionary Origins of Pentecostalism* (Little Rock: University of Arkansas Press, 1988); Gastón Espinosa, *William J. Seymour and the Origins of Global Pentecostalism: A Biography and Documentary History* (Durham, NC: Duke University Press, 2014); Gastón Espinosa, *Latino Pentecostals in America: Faith and Politics in Action* (Cambridge, MA: Harvard University Press, 2014).

27. See Espinosa, *William J. Seymour and the Origins of Global Pentecostalism*, 2–6.
28. Lary F. May, *Screening Out the Past: The Birth of Mass Culture and the Motion Picture Industry* (Chicago: University of Chicago Press, 1980), 250–251, 65–66, 94. May uses "Protestant" to refer to those of Protestant faith as well as those raised in the Reformed tradition who have "secularized" Weber's Protestant ethic. Thomas Edison is an example of the second. His mother was a Baptist and daughter of a minister, but her son grew up to be a freethinker. See Matthew Josephson, *Edison: A Biography* (New York: McGraw-Hill, 1959).
29. David Morgan, *Protestants and Pictures: Religion, Visual Culture, and the Age of American Mass Production* (New York: Oxford University Press, 1999).
30. Terry Lindvall, *Sanctuary Cinema: Origins of the Christian Film Industry* (New York: New York University Press, 2007), 41, 59–65, 74.
31. May, *Screening Out the Past*, 60–61. On the National Board of Review's founding, see 54–57.
32. Richard Wightman Fox, "The Culture of Liberal Protestant Progressivism, 1875–1925," *Journal of Interdisciplinary History* 23, no. 3 (Winter 1993): 639–660; R. Laurence Moore, *Selling God: American Religion in the Marketplace of Culture* (New York: Oxford University Press, 1994), esp. 146–237; May, *Screening Out the Past*, 3–22.
33. The Federal Council of Churches, a national body representing mainline Protestantism, lodged complaints against the "humiliating" treatment of ministers in movies that led in 1921 to the creation of an industry prohibition against ridiculing clergy. Compliance with the rule was at the discretion of studios, but eventually the rule made it into the 1930 Production Code, which was enforced by the Breen Office. Anne Morey, "Gendering Ministry and Reform: Griffith and the Plight of Protestant Uplift," in *A Companion to D. W. Griffith*, ed. Charles Keil (Oxford: Wiley-Blackwell, 2018), 374.
34. Terry Lindvall, "Silent Cinema and Religion: An Overview," in *The Routledge Companion to Religion and Film*, ed. John Lynden (New York: Routledge, 2009), 15–19.
35. On Griffith, see May, *Screening Out the Past*, 60–95; Lyden, *Film as Religion*, 15–16; Linda Williams, "Melodrama Re-Visited," in *Refiguring American Film Genres*, ed. Nick Browne (Berkeley: University of California Press, 1998), 42–88; Ben Singer, "Griffith's Moral Profile," in *A Companion to D. W. Griffith*, ed. Charles Keil (Oxford: Wiley-Blackwell, 2018), 34–73.
36. Morey, "Gendering Ministry and Reform," 376–377.
37. Martin F. Norden, *Lois Weber: Interviews* (Jackson: University Press of Mississippi, 2019), xxv.
38. Shelley Stamp, *Lois Weber in Early Hollywood* (Oakland: University of California Press, 2015). For a chronology of Weber's life, see Norden, *Lois Weber: Interviews*, xxv–xxxiv.
39. Apart from *Judith of Bethulia* (1914), Griffith's only other venture into the biblical epic was the Babylonian sequence of *Intolerance* (1916).
40. *King of Kings* had Protestant, Catholic, and Jewish consultants. On DeMille's liberal Protestant leanings and his use of the Bible, see Susan Craig, "Skin and Redemption: Theology in Silent Films, 1902–1927," *CUNY Academic Works*, 2010.

41. The Jewish community heavily criticized the film, especially for its portrayal of Caiaphas, played by Jewish actor Rudolph Schildkraut. See Richard Maltby, "*King of Kings* and the Czar of All of the Rushes: The Propriety of the Christ Story," in *Controlling Hollywood: Censorship and Regulation in the Studio Era*, ed. Matthew Bernstein (New Brunswick, NJ: Rutgers University Press, 1999), 60–86; Simon Louvish, *Cecil B. DeMille: A Life in Art* (New York: St. Martin's Press, 2007), 258–271; Scott Eyman, *Empire of Dreams: The Epic Life of Cecil B. DeMille* (New York: Simon & Schuster, 2010), 244–249.
42. Neal Gabler tells this history comprehensively in Neal Gabler, *An Empire of Their Own: How the Jews Invented Hollywood* (New York: Anchor Books, 1989). See also May, *Screening Out the Past*, 167–199.
43. Judith Weisenfeld. *Hollywood Be Thy Name: African American Religion in American Film, 1929–1949* (Berkeley: University of California Press, 2007), 120.
44. William D. Romanowski, *Reforming Hollywood: How Protestants Fought for Freedom at the Movies* (New York: Oxford University Press, 2012). The phrase "theology of the arts," is qtd. from 158.
45. Anthony Burke Smith, "America's Favorite Priest," in Colleen McDannell, ed., *Catholics in the Movies* (New York: Oxford University Press, 2007), 123; see also 48–51. The ministers in Hollywood's *One Foot in Heaven* (1941), *Stars in My Crown* (1950), and *I'd Climb the Highest Mountain* (1951) all have small-town or country parishes. Westerns, with pictorial roots in the "evangelical sublime" of nineteenth century American landscape paintings, continued in the 1950s to cultivate the association between Protestant community and the country's rural past, when it was the Virgin Land. The term "evangelical sublime" is from David Morgan, *The Lure of Images: A History of Religion and Visual Media in America* (New York: Routledge, 2007), 234–261.
46. Sally M. Promey, "Taste Cultures: The Visual Practices of Liberal Protestantism, 1940–1965," in *Practicing Protestants: Histories of Christian Life in America, 1630–1965*, ed. Laura Maffley-Kipp, Leigh Schmidt, and Mark Valeri (Baltimore: Johns Hopkins University Press, 2006), 250–294. See also Colleen McDannell, *Material Christianity: Religion and Popular Culture in America* (New Haven, CT: Yale University Press, 1995), 10–11, 187–188; Jason Stevens, *God-Fearing and Free: A Spiritual History of America's Cold War* (Cambridge, MA: Harvard University Press, 2011), 150–151.
47. See Laura Wittern-Keller and Raymond J. Haberski Jr., *The Miracle Case: Film Censorship and the Supreme Court* (Lawrence: University Press of Kansas, 2008). On the Paramount Decree and its consequences, see Robert Sklar, *Movie-Made America: A Cultural History of American Movies* (New York: Random House, 1994), 170.
48. Qtd. from "The Production Code of the Motion Picture Industry (1930–1967)," 1930 and 1934 versions, *The Motion Picture Production Code*, accessed February 28, 2020. The 1945 version of the code kept the same restrictions, and the expanded 1949 version focused even more attention on attitudes toward religion; see Peter Munby, *Public Enemies/Public Heroes: Screening the Gangster from* Little Caesar *to* Touch of Evil (Chicago: University of Chicago Press, 1999), 174–180, 227–235.

49. Adapted from Robert Riskin and John Meehan's Broadway play *Bless You, Sister* (1927), itself heavily derived from episodes in Sinclair Lewis's novel *Elmer Gantry*, *The Miracle Woman* stars Barbara Stanwyck as Florence Fallon, whose career clearly alludes to McPherson's.
50. The film was granted approval despite strong complaints lodged by the BFC's conservative West Coast office. On the negotiations, see Romanowski, *Reforming Hollywood: How Protestants Fought for Freedom at the Movies*, 129, and Jeffrey Couchman, *The Night of the Hunter: A Biography of a Film* (Evanston, IL: Northwestern University Press, 2009) 144, 169.
51. Stevens covers the cultural and political background of these three films in his *God-Fearing and Free*, chaps. 4–6.
52. *Elmer Gantry* is adapted from Sinclair Lewis's Pulitzer Prize–winning 1927 novel, and *Inherit the Wind* from Jerome Lawrence and Robert E. Lee's long-running play. *Inherit the Wind* was nominated for four Oscars in major categories; *Elmer Gantry* was nominated for Best Picture and won Oscars for Best Actor (Burt Lancaster), Best Supporting Actress (Shirley Jones), and Best Adapted Screenplay.
53. Jason Stevens, "John Huston's Adaptation of *Wise Blood* and Hollywood's Response to the New South," *The Flannery O'Connor Review* 12 (2014): 99–116, esp. 102–104.
54. Robert Ellwood, *The Sixties Spiritual Awakening: American Religion Moving from Modern to Postmodern* (New Brunswick, NJ: Rutgers University Press, 1994).
55. The "bad acid trip" sequence in the Catholic cemetery, for example, is at once blasphemous and mystical.
56. Ken Curtis, "The Baptists Are Taking to the Screen to Spread the Word," *New York Times*, July 2, 1972. *The Cross and the Switchblade*, based on Wilkerson's autobiographical bestseller, was co-produced by Ken Curtis and Dick Ross, who partnered in founding the Billy Graham Evangelical Association's film company, World Wide Pictures. See Terry Lindvall and Andrew Quicke, *Celluloid Sermons: The Emergence of the Christian Film Industry, 1930–1986* (New York: New York University Press, 2011), 157, 159–161.
57. For a summary of the evangelical response to *The Last Temptation of Christ*, see Bryan Stone, "Modern Protestant Approaches to Film (1960–the Present)," in *The Routledge Companion to Religion and Film*, ed. John Lynden (New York: Routledge, 2009), 78–80. For an in-depth account of the fallout between Universal Pictures and evangelicals, see Larry W. Poland, *The Last Temptation of Hollywood* (Highland, CA: Mastermedia Int'l, 1988).
58. Randall Balmer, *Redeemer: The Life of Jimmy Carter* (New York: Basic Books, 2014) charts how Carter's political fortunes rose and fall with the upsurge of the religious right. "Year of the Evangelical" proclaimed in Kenneth L. Woodward, "Born Again!," *Newsweek*, October 25, 1976, 68–78, and Kenneth L. Woodward, "Back to That Old-Time Religion," *Time*, December 26, 1977, 52–58.
59. *Time* ran an April 15, 2013, front-page cover story, "The Latino Reformation," which spotlighted the meteoric rise of Latino evangelicalism by focusing on one Baptist (Luis Cortes) and two Pentecostal leaders (Samuel Rodriguez and Wilfredo de Jesus). In *Alambrista!*, Robert M. Young's landmark 1977 independent film about

undocumented Mexican migrant workers in California, there is a four-minute-long documentary-style segment at a Sunday evening revival meeting. The segment shows Black, white, and Latino Christians signing, worshiping, and ecstatically dancing. Reverend J. D. Hurt, billed as "Revival Preacher" in the credits sequence, leads the service. Young retained this sequence for the 2004 director's cut version of the film that was released as part of the Alambrista Multimedia Project. On the film's history and its influence on Latino cinema, see Nicholas J. Cull and Davíd Carrasco, eds., *"Alambrista" and the U.S.-Mexico Border* (Albuquerque: University of New Mexico Press, 2004).

60. "Heaven Is for Real," *Box Office Mojo*, March 4, 2020.
61. Jakes co-produced *Woman Thou Art Loosed*, an adaptation of his 1993 novel. Quotation from a review by Bill Beyrer, "Woman Thou Art Loosed," *CinemaBlend*, March 27, 2016.
62. Perry discusses his call to ministry in Leonardo Blair, "Tyler Perry Reveals He Was Once a Minister and Attended Seminary Before God Called Him to Film Industry in Message at Lakewood Church," *Black Christian News*, August 7, 2018.
63. CBN News, "'Faith Without Works Is Nothing': Denzel Washington Tells CBN How He Pursues God's Will," YouTube, November 10, 2017. Also, "Denzel Washington: 'I Don't Think There Is a System,'" *The Talks*, September 5, 2012.
64. CBN News, "'Faith Without Works Is Nothing'"; Michael Haney, "The GQA: Denzel Washington," *GQ*, September 18, 2012. See also the introduction to Denzel Washington and Daniel Paisner, *A Hand to Guide Me: Legends and Leaders Celebrate the People Who Shaped Their Lives* (Des Moines, IA: Meredith Books, 2006).
65. Oyelowo describes himself as a "born again Christian" who now attends a "non-denominational church." Adelle M. Banks, "Actor David Oyelowo: 'For Me, Jesus Is My Denomination,'" *Charlotte Observer*, September 23, 2015. Oyelowo has said that "it was God ordained" for him to play King. Sergio Mims, "A Conversation with Director Ava DuVernay and Actor David Oyelowo," RogerEbert.com, December 22, 2014
66. Youmans won the Founders Prize at the 2019 Tribeca Film Festival. Matt Fagerholm argues that Youmans's feature rebuts *War Room* (by the makers of *Fireproof*) in his review essay, "Burning Cane," RogerEbert.com, October 23, 2019.
67. From May 13 to November 5, 2017, the Luther Memorials Foundation of Saxony-Anhalt welcomed the public to the National Special Exhibition "Luther! 95 Treasures—95 People." The top floor of the exhibition was devoted to Luther and Protestantism in art and the movies, spotlighting Luther biopics, oeuvres of Ingmar Bergman and Carl Dreyer, and Gabriel Axel's *Babette's Feast*.
68. See, for example, *The White Ribbon* (Germany, 2009). Director Michael Haneke omits—as is typical for him—non-diegetic music, but the on-screen rendering of Luther's "A Mighty Fortress Is Our God," this "Hymn of the Reformation" (Heinrich Heine), at the film's end is an obvious reference to the theological background of the plot. Director Jean-Marie Straub's Bach biopic, *The Chronicle of Anna Magdalena Bach* (Germany, 1968), features Bach's "St. Matthew Passion," which underscores the close connection between the Lutheran composer, the Protestant spirit, and musical

beauty. Luther, who believed music was the art form closest to God, composed hymns and encouraged congregational singing. Georg Maas makes these connections in his paper "J. S. Bach Movie Star—Protestantism and Ideology in the Biopic," presented at the conference Protestantism on Screen: Religion, Politics, and Aesthetics in European and American Movies, Wittenberg University, June 24–27, 2015, sponsored by the Muhlenberg Center for American Studies and the Martin Luther University Halle-Wittenberg. Portions of Frank Cordell's score for *Cromwell* (UK, 1970) are styled after seventeenth-century (Stuart) hymns, psalms, and chorales. See John Mansell, "Cromwell," *Soundtrack: The Cinemascore and Soundtrack Archives*, accessed August 17, 2020.

69. Esther Wipfler is the leading authority on cinematic lives of Luther. See Esther Wipfler, *Martin Luther in Motion Pictures: History of a Metamorphosis* (Göttingen: Vandenhoeck & Ruprecht, 2011).
70. For an overview of the Protestant influence on European art cinema in its classic era (1940–1980), see Mark Le Fanu, *Believing in Film: Christianity and Classic European Cinema* (London: I. B. Tauris, 2019), 141–176.
71. Maaret Koskinen, "Foreword," in *The Demons of Modernity: Ingmar Bergman and European Cinema*, ed. John Orr (New York: Berghahn Books, 2014), 3.
72. Peter Cowie, *Ingmar Bergman: A Critical Biography* (New York: Scribner, 1982), 10.
73. The "God's silence" trilogy refers to a trio of films that Bergman made in the early sixties: *Through a Glass Darkly* (1961), *Winter Light* (1963), and *The Silence* (1963).
74. The Åkians (named for their founder, Åke Svensson) were religious dissidents in Lutheran parishes who "tried to copy the early Christian church and return to the ways of the apostles." Vilhelm Moberg, *The Emigrants* (St. Paul: Minnesota Historical Society Press, 1995 [1949]), xxxii–xxxiii.
75. See, for example, Metro-Goldwyn-Mayer's *Plymouth Adventure* (1952).
76. Tino Balio, *The Foreign Film Market on American Screens, 1946–1973* (Madison: University of Wisconsin Press, 2010).
77. Promey, "Taste Cultures," 251. *Time* ran the cover story "The God Is Dead Movement" in the October 22, 1965, issue. The 1966 follow-up cover story (April 8, 1966) asked the question "Is God Dead?"
78. "The New Hollywood" refers to two waves of transformation in Hollywood from 1967 through the late seventies: first, the experimentation, deconstruction, and subversion of classic Hollywood formulas and ideologies; second, conglomerate control of the industry and the rise of the blockbuster. We are referring here to the New Hollywood chiefly in the first sense. Geoff King distinguishes the two senses in *The New Hollywood: An Introduction* (London: I. B. Taurus, 2002), chaps. 1–2. See also David A. Cook, *Lost Illusions: American Cinema in the Shadow of Watergate and Vietnam, 1970–1979* (Berkeley: University of California Press, 2000).
79. Haneke addresses his nonbelief, his fascination with theology in film, his Protestant background in Austria, and his attitude toward Protestant churches in Alexander Horwarth, "Michael Haneke Interview: Uncut," *Film Comment*, November–December 2009.

80. Billy Graham's *The Restless Ones* (1965) is the first Protestant coming-of-age film, but fewer films have followed in its wake than was the case with *The Trouble with Angels* (1966), likely the first Catholic coming-of-age film. American Stephen Cone, a queer filmmaker and Southern Baptist preacher's son, is distinguished for making films about gay teens growing up in the Bible Belt; his young characters, like those of Carl Dreyer, one of his favorite directors, struggle to understand "where the body stops and the spirit starts." Brad S. Ross, "Interview with Stephen Cone," *Arts Comment*, January 4, 2018. Intriguingly, several of the Protestant coming-of-age movies have been directed by filmmakers who did not grow up in the religious groups represented in their films. Terence Davis is an ex-Catholic and atheist, and Wim Wenders is a former Catholic and Lutheran convert (see Chapter 10). Garth Jennings grew up next to a family of Plymouth Brethren, but his family was not a member of this sect; see Garth Jenningy, "The Son of Rambow Pressbook," Celluloid-Dreams.com, accessed August 23, 2020. Miriam von Arx has not publicly identified her personal religious beliefs, other than to say that they are opposed to the "fundamentalism" of the Wilson family in her film; see "Director's Statement." *Virgin Tales*, accessed August 23, 2020. Daniel Kokotajlo, who is now an agnostic, draws on his upbringing as a Jehovah's Witness for the story of *Apostasy*; Rachel Cooke, "*Apostasy* Director: 'It Was Liberating to Leave the Jehovah's Witnesses,'" *The Guardian*, July 15, 2018.
81. Reklis, "Introduction," 4.
82. Covington, "Conclusion," 283.
83. Reklis, 14.
84. Reklis, 14
85. See John 1:14 ("The Word became flesh, and dwelt among us"). Catholics tend to interpret this passage in the relation to the Eucharist, while Protestants more commonly understand it in relation to the literal meaning of the Bible, as it is carried out in their lives.
86. In nineteenth-century America particularly, the Scottish school of Theistic Common Sense revolutionized theological language and the methods and epistemological foundations of biblical interpretation; see Mark Noll, *America's God: From Jonathan Edwards to Abraham Lincoln* (New York: Oxford University Press, 2002), 93–113, 233–238.
87. The literal sense contained the Bible's own figurative language and Protestant exegetes' typological readings of the Bible, for these were considered part of the author's (the Holy Spirit's) intention.
88. Scorsese's *The Last Temptation of Christ* and Darren Aronowsky's *Noah* not only blatantly deviate from the literal biblical accounts but also incorporate dream states and surreal images that the viewer as well as the hero (Jesus, Noah) must decipher. Torry and Flesher, for example, analyze how *Last Temptation* cultivates uncertainty about the meaning of what is happening on-screen because the presentation of its story "does not allow the audience to distinguish between the film's reality, Jesus's visions, and the symbolism of both"; Paul V. M. Flesher and Robert Torry, *Religion and Film: An Introduction* (Nashville, TN: Abingdon Press, 2007), 146–150.

89. John Lyden, *Film as Religion: Myths, Morals, Rituals* (New York: New York University Press, 2003), 18–22. Lyden refers here to H. Richard Niebuhr, *Christ and Culture* (New York: Harper & Row, 1951) and Paul Tillich's 1919 essay "On the Idea of a Theology of Culture," elaborated across the fifteen essays in his *Theology of Culture*, ed. Robert C. Kimball (New York: Oxford University Press, 1959).
90. For a broader overview of how modern evangelicals have used film review and online dialogues to promote media literacy and exchange views on Hollywood films, see Stone, "Modern Protestant Approaches to Film," 76–78.
91. Leo Braudy, *The World in a Frame: What We See in Films* (Chicago: University of Chicago Press, 1976), 104.
92. Braudy, *The World in a Frame*, 111.
93. On the Puritan underpinnings of the Western, see Scott Simmon, *The Invention of the Western Film: A Cultural History of the Genre's First Half Century* (New York: Cambridge University Press, 2003), 124–128. Simmons notes the parallel between the endings of *Hell's Hinges* and *High Plains Drifter*, 128. For further discussion of W. S. Hart and silent Westerns as screen parables for Protestant audiences, see Lindvall, "Silent Cinema and Religion," 76–78.
94. Horror, of course, has some deep Protestant roots, but evangelicals have tended to avoid horror cinema because modern instances of the genre emphasize nihilism. On Protestant sources of horror, see Victor Sage, *Horror Fiction in the Protestant Tradition* (London: St. Martin's Press, 1988); Edward J. Ingebretsen, *Maps of Heaven, Maps of Hell: Religious Terror as Memory from the Puritans to Stephen King* (London: M. E. Sharpe, 1996).
95. Andrew Quicke discusses Walden Media and the Narnia series's production and distribution (Disney and 20th Century Fox) in his essay for this volume (Chapter 2). For a fuller account, see Nathalie Dupont, *Between Hollywood and Godlywood: The Case of Walden Media* (Bern: Peter Lang, 2015).
96. For an in-depth analysis of Walden Media's compromises with American film industry practices and global markets, see Dupont, *Between Hollywood and Godlywood.*

Chapter 1

1. See William D. Romanowski, "Freedom Safe-Guarded by Self-Discipline: Will H. Hays, Protestantism and Movie Censorship," *Fides et Historia* 49, no. 1 (Winter/Spring 2017): 47–64.
2. "Hot Film Ads Bring Hot Edict from Czar Hays," New York *Daily News*, July 12, 1932, folder 2, box 112, Will H. Hays Papers, Indiana State Library, Indianapolis.
3. The adage is widely attributed to Irish dramatist George Bernard Shaw.
4. Andrew Crisell, *An Introductory History of British Broadcasting* (London: Routledge, 2002), 18–19; John Aldred, *British Imperial and Foreign Policy, 1846–1980* (London: Heinemann, 2004), 132.

5. Samuel McCrea Cavert to Orrin G. Cocks, December 21, 1920, box 14, folder 24, Record Group 18, Presbyterian Historical Society, Philadelphia.
6. Neville March Hunnings, *Film Censors and the Law* (London: George Allen & Unwin, 1967), 103, 121; James C. Robertson, *The Hidden Cinema: British Film Censorship in Action, 1913–1975* (London: Routledge, 1989), 170; Peter Borsay, *A History of Leisure: The British Experience Since 1500* (New York: Palgrave Macmillan, 2006), 55.
7. Andrew Higson, *Waving the Flag: Constructing a National Cinema in Britain* (Oxford: Clarendon Press, 1997), 186–187.
8. Fred Eastman, "Introduction," in *Modern Religious Dramas*, ed. Fred Eastman (New York: Henry Holt, 1928), viii; Fred Eastman, "What Can We Do About the Movies?," *Christian Century*, June 14, 1933, 779.
9. T. P. O'Connor, a Roman Catholic and liberal member of Parliament, served as president of the British Board of Film Censors from 1916 to 1929. Based on the board's annual reports, O'Connor drew up a list of examples of material previously excised from movies, known as "O'Connor's 43," that provided guidance for film reviewers until World War II.
10. Geoffrey Macnab, *J. Arthur Rank and the British Film Industry* (London: Routledge, 1993), 1, 6; John Trumpbour, *Selling Hollywood to the World: U.S. and European Struggles for Mastery of the Global Film Industry, 1920–1950* (Cambridge: Cambridge University Press, 2002), 8.
11. Macnab, *J. Arthur Rank and the British Film Industry*, 111.
12. Macnab, *J. Arthur Rank and the British Film Industry*, 117; "Review: 'Black Narcissus,'" *Variety*, December 31, 1946; Trumpbour, *Selling Hollywood to the World*, 11.
13. See Martin Long, "Film Industry Slipping Out of the Big Money," *Sunday Herald*, January 1, 1950, 7.
14. See William D. Romanowski, *Reforming Hollywood: How American Protestants Fought for Freedom at the Movies* (New York: Oxford University Press, 2012).
15. "About the BBFC," British Board of Film Classification, https://www.bbfc.co.uk/about-us, accessed August 5, 2016.
16. Ben H. Bagdikian, *The New Media Monopoly* (Boston: Beacon Press, 2004), 16.
17. James M. Wall, "Fighting the Media's Eroticizing of Violence," *Christian Century*, October 3, 1984, 892.
18. Robert N. Bellah et al., eds., *Habits of the Heart: Individualism and Commitment in American Life* (Berkeley: University of California Press, 1985), 224.
19. Dick Rolfe, "Give Families Choice of Editing Movies," *Grand Rapids Press*, June 14, 1993, A11. See William D. Romanowski, *Cinematic Faith: A Christian Perspective on Movies and Meaning* (Grand Rapids: Baker Academic, 2019).

Chapter 2

1. "Christian Movies at the Box Office," BoxOfficeMojo.com, accessed September 20, 2018.

2. Terry Lindvall, *Sanctuary Cinema: Origins of the Christian Film Industry* (New York: New York University Press, 2011), 62.
3. *Reverend Hannibal Goodwin, Inventor of the Motion Picture Film* (New York: Dombey T.M., 1921), 3–11.
4. Lindvall, *Sanctuary Cinema*, 59–65.
5. Terry Lindvall and Andrew Quicke, *Celluloid Sermons: The Emergence of the Christian Film Industry, 1930–1986* (New York: New York University Press, 2011), 36.
6. Lindvall and Andrew Quicke, *Celluloid Sermons*, 26.
7. Lindvall and Andrew Quicke, *Celluloid Sermons*, 30.
8. Lindvall and Andrew Quicke, *Celluloid Sermons*, 34.
9. Harvey Marks, "A Brief History of Church Films," *Christian Film and Video Review*, January/February 1985, 4.
10. Lindvall and Quicke, *Celluloid Sermons*, 48.
11. "Jesus Film Project Statistics," *JesusFilm*, accessed November 2018.
12. "Jesus Film Project Statistics."
13. Chris Franzen, "Dobson Brings the Family into Focus," *Christian Film and Video Review*, Spring 1987, 7.
14. J. Ryan Parker, *Cinema as Pulpit: Sherwood Pictures and the Church Film Movement* (Jefferson, NC: McFarland, 2012), 34.
15. Its earnings were $4.22 million. "Left Behind (2001)," IMDb, accessed November 11, 2018.
16. Parker, *Cinema as Pulpit*, 34.
17. Parker, *Cinema as Pulpit*, 35.
18. Jeff Jensen, "The Family Business: Walden Breaks Out as a Hollywood Power Player," *Entertainment Weekly*, April 21, 2006.
19. Earnings were $291.71 million in the U.S. market, $760 million worldwide. "The Lion, The Witch & the Wardrobe (2005)," BoxOfficeMojo, accessed November 11, 2018.
20. It earned $141.62 million in the U.S. market. "Prince Caspian (2008)," BoxOfficeMojo, accessed November 11, 2018.
21. Earnings were $104.38 million in the U.S. market. "The Voyage of the Dawn Trader (2010)," BoxOfficeMojo, accessed November 11, 2018.
22. Earnings were $370.78 million in the U.S. market. "The Passion of the Christ (2004)," BoxOfficeMojo, accessed November 11, 2018.
23. Laura Coverson, "Fox Pursues the Flock," ABC News, September 21, 2006.
24. Mark Moring, "Fox Feeds the Flock," *Christianity Today*, October 3, 2006.
25. It earned $3.2 million in the U.S. market. "The Ultimate Gift (2007)," BoxOfficeMojo, accessed November 11, 2018.
26. Earnings were $13.39 million in the U.S. market. "One Night with the King (2006)," BoxOfficeMojo, accessed November 11, 2018.
27. Richard Rogers, "Special Assignment: Fireproof," WRDW.com, November 5, 2008.
28. Production costs were $2 million, and it earned $34.52 million in the U.S. market. "Courageous (2011)," BoxOfficeMojo, accessed November 11, 2018.
29. Film adaptation of Bishop T. D. Jakes's self-help novel, chronicling a woman's struggle to come to terms with her legacy of abuse, addiction, and poverty.

30. Earnings were $6.80 million in the U.S. market. "Woman Thou Art Loosed (2004)," BoxOfficeMojo, accessed November 11, 2018.
31. "Diary of a Mad Black Woman (2005)," BoxOfficeMojo, accessed November 11, 2018.
32. It earned $60.75 million in the U.S. market. "God's Not Dead (2014)," BoxOfficeMojo, accessed November 11, 2018.

Chapter 3

1. David Kelsey, *Imagining Redemption* (Louisville, KY: Westminster John Knox Press, 2005), 5–6.
2. These cognate terms include "salvation," "liberation," "freedom," "emancipation," "release," "justification"—and, by extension, "reconciliation," "forgiveness," and "sanctification."
3. Two different examples of studies of such material are Christopher Deacy, *Screen Christologies: Redemption and the Medium of Film* (Cardiff: University of Wales Press, 2001) on film noir, and Ian Bradley, *You've Got to Have a Dream: The Message of the Musical* (London: SCM Press, 2004), on musicals.
4. For more on the approach being followed here, see my *A Cultural Theology of Salvation* (Oxford: Oxford University Press, 2018), 29–55, esp. 36–47.
5. "Die Verurteilten (1994)," Internet Movie Database, accessed February 21, 2019.
6. I have included an abbreviated summary of the findings of this chapter in *A Cultural Theology of Salvation*, 85–94.
7. This summary of a Protestant perspective is my own and based on no single source, but for a helpful parallel summary, see Richard Lints, "Soteriology," in *Mapping Modern Theology: A Thematic and Historical Introduction*, ed. Kelly M. Kapic and Bruce L. McCormack (Grand Rapids, MI: Baker Academic, 2012), 259–291.
8. For a commentary on the many graphic portrayals of hell through the ages, see Alice K. Turner, *The History of Hell* (New York: Harcourt Brace, 1993). It is notable that the range of portrayals thins out in the later chapters.
9. Turner, *The History of Hell*, 145–157.
10. At least four main theories exist. See, for example, Paul S. Fiddes, *Past Event and Present Salvation: The Christian Idea of Atonement* (London: Darton Longman and Todd, 1989), chaps. 4–7.
11. This is wording from the back cover of the DVD case: *Crazy Heart* (20th Century Fox Home Entertainment, 2010).
12. "Works righteousness" is the term used to characterize human effort to please God—that is, to seek to earn salvation. Martin Luther's theology in particular—and all theological traditions influenced by the Reformation followed his lead—challenged the view that human effort made any contribution to the work and experience of salvation. Though good works were deemed to be part of a Christian life, they followed the acceptance of justification which God brought about in Jesus Christ, received by faith alone (*sola fide*), and were effected in the Christian disciple by the Holy

Spirit. Human activity thus allied itself with the will of God but did not bring salvation about. For a summary of Luther's theology, see Markus Wriedt, "Luther's Theology," in *The Cambridge Companion to Martin Luther*, ed. Donald K. McKim (Cambridge: Cambridge University Press, 2003), 86–119.

13. Thomas Cobb, *Crazy Heart* (London: Corsair, 2010), 39.
14. Cobb, *Crazy Heart*, 57.
15. Cobb, *Crazy Heart*, 66.
16. A joint Lutheran/Roman Catholic statement on the doctrine of justification from 1999 is a major landmark: *Joint Declaration on the Doctrine of Justification: The Lutheran World Federation and the Roman Catholic Church* (Grand Rapids, MI: Eerdmans, 2000).

Chapter 4

1. The phenomenon was discussed almost exclusively by German scholars with theological, church-historical, or historical backgrounds. The only American contribution was a case study that \remains unpublished (Robert Fryer, "A Guide to the History and Art of the 'Martin Luther' Film," MA thesis, Columbia University, 1964. The first monograph analyzing all the feature films about Martin Luther was Esther P. Wipfler, *Martin Luther in Motion Pictures: History of a Metamorphosis* (Göttingen: Vandenhoeck & Rupprecht, 2011); for the state of research, see 137n1.
2. Herfried Münkler, *Die Deutschen und ihre Mythen* (Berlin: Rowohlt, 200), 181–196.
3. See Esther P. Wipfler, "Papstesel contra Lutherischer Narr. Themen und Motive der illustrierten polemischen Druckgraphik der Reformationszeit," in *Luther und Tirol. Exhibition catalogue Schloss Tirol 01.07.2017—26.11.2017*, ed. Leo Andergassen (Tirol: Südtiroler Landesmuseum für Kultur- und Landesgeschichte Schloss Tirol, 2017).
4. See Heimo Reinitzer, *Biblia deutsch. Luthers Bibelübersetzung und ihre Tradition* (Wolfenbüttel: Herzog August Bibliothek, 1983), 13.
5. On this, see Thomas Kaufmann, "Die Bilderfrage im frühneuzeitlichen Luthertum," in *Macht und Ohnmacht der Bilder. Reformatorischer Bildersturm im Kontext der europäischen Geschichte*, ed. Peter Blickle (Munich: Oldenbourg, 2002), 407–451; Esther Wipfler, "Götzenbild oder Adiaphoron—Positionen protestantischen Bildverständnisses," in *Verbotene Bilder. Heiligenfiguren aus Russland*, ed. Marianne Stößl (Munich: Hirmer, 2006), 41–48.
6. An example of such a documentary is *Johannes Calvin—Berufen zum Reformator* (DVD: Hänssler Verlag, 2008, 60 min.).
7. Oliver Demont, "Grosser Kinospielfilm zu Zwingli geht in Produktion," Ref.ch, June 17, 2015. According to the initiators of this film project, Zwingli's life contained every aspect that is necessary for a great biopic: religion, power, lust, passion, violence, and strong convictions ("Bei Zwingli ist alles da, was grosses Kino ausmacht und Menschen heute angeht: Religion und Macht, Lust und Liebe, Gewalt und starke

Überzeugungen"; flyer distributed in 2014 at the Swiss Reformed Church in the canton of Zurich).

8. Heiner Schmitt, *Kirche und Film, Kirchliche Filmarbeit in Deutschland von ihren Anfängen bis 1945*, Schriften des Bundesarchivs vol. 26 (Boppard am Rhein: Boldt, 1979), 29.
9. See Richard Maltby, "*King of Kings* and the Czar of All of the Rushes: The Propriety of the Christ Story," in *Controlling Hollywood: Censorship and Regulation in the Studio Era*, ed. Matthew Bernstein (New Brunswick, NJ: Rutgers University Press, 1999), 60–86, esp. 63–64.
10. There is no doubt that Lucas Cranach the Elder initiated Luther's iconography with his portraits. See Martin Warnke, *Cranachs Luther: Entwürfe für ein Image* (Frankfurt am Main: Fischer Taschenbuch Verlag, 1984); Günter Schuchardt, ed., *Cranach, Luther und die Bildnisse* (Regensburg: Schnell & Steiner, 2015). On the use of this image in the propaganda for the Reformation, see Ilonka van Gülpen, *Der deutsche Humanismus und die frühe Reformations-Propaganda: 1520–1526. Das Lutherporträt im Dienst der Bildpublizistik*, Studien zur Kunstgeschichte vol. 144 (Hildesheim: Olms, 2002),
11. Martin Steffens, *Luthergedenkstätten im 19. Jahrhundert. Memoria—Repräsentation—Denkmalpflege* (Regensburg: Schnell & Steiner, 2008), 15–25, 32–58, 325–350 (review by Esther Wipfler: "Rezension," *Kunstchronik* 62, no. 5 [2009]: 224–229); Wolfgang Flügel, *Konfession und Jubiläum. Zur Institutionalisierung der lutherischen Gedenkkultur in Sachsen 1617–1830* (Leipzig: Leipziger Universitäts-Verlag, 2005).
12. Gerhard Bott, ed., *Martin Luther und die Reformation in Deutschland, Exhibition catalogue Nuremberg* (Frankfurt am Main: Insel-Verlag, 1983), 222. On this, see also Henrike Holsing, "Luther—Gottesmann und Nationalheld: sein Image in der deutschen Historienmalerei des 19. Jahrhunderts," diss., Cologne University, 2004, 19n41.
13. See Bernd Möller, "Thesenanschläge," in *Faszination Thesenanschlag—Faktum oder Fiktion*, ed. Joachim Ott and Martin Treu (Leipzig: EVA, 2008), 11.
14. Henry McKean Taylor, *Rolle des Lebens. Die Filmbiographie als narratives System*, Zürcher Filmstudien vol. 8 (Marburg: Schüren, 2002), 378.
15. Cf. Taylor, *Rolle des Lebens*, 93. The term "biopic" has been used for biographical film since 1951. The biopic had its classical period from 1927 to 1960; for that period Custen counted three hundred films. George F. Custen, *Bio/Pics: How Hollywood Constructed Public History* (New Brunswick, NJ: Rutgers University Press, 1992). For the latest tendencies, see Sigrid Nieberle, *Literarhistorische Filmbiographien: Autorschaft und Literaturgeschichte im Kino. Mit einer Filmographie 1909–2007*, Media and Cultural Memory/Medien und kulturelle Erinnerung vol. 7 (Berlin: De Gruyter, 2008).
16. See Taylor, *Rolle des Lebens*, 139, 167.
17. See, for instance, Armin Kohnle, "Luther vor Karl V. Die Wormser Szene in Text und Bild des 19. Jahrhunderts," in *Lutherinszenierung und Reformationserinnerung*, ed. Stefan Laube and Karl-Heinz Fix, Schriften der Stiftung Luthergedenkstätten in Sachsen-Anhalt vol. 2 (Leipzig: Evangelische Verlagsanstalt, 2002), 52–56.
18. On the issue of church as filmmaker, see Wipfler, *Martin Luther in Motion Pictures*, 79–129.

19. See Wipfler, *Martin Luther in Motion Pictures*, 54–56.
20. Stefan Rhein, "Luther im Museum: Kult, Gedenken und Erkenntnis," in *Der Reformator Martin Luther 2017: Eine wissenschaftliche und gedenkpolitische Bestandsaufnahme*, ed. Heinz Schilling (Berlin: De Gruyter Oldenbourg, 2014), 256.
21. "Sir Peter Ustinov. Ein Interview zu seinem neuen Film 'Luther,'" *Münchner Wochenblatt* 45 (2003): G5.
22. On his representation, see Esther Wipfler, "'Reformator wider Willen' und 'Melanchthon-Rap.' Der Lehrer Deutschlands in den modernen Medien—Ein Überblick mit Schwerpunkt auf dem Jubiläumsjahr 2010," in *Philipp Melanchthon zur populären Rezeption des Reformators*, ed. Stefan Rhein and Martin Treu, Schriften der Stiftung Luthergedenkstätten in Sachsen-Anhalt vol. 19 (Leipzig: Evangelische Verlagsanstalt, 2016), 167–179.
23. Thus the tenor in Diarmaid MacCulloch, *Reformation: Europe's House Divided 1490–1700* (New York: Viking, 2004), 127 (the German translation is Diarmaid MacCulloch, *Die Reformation 1490–1700* [Stuttgart: DVA, 2008], 186). MacCulloch's work has been criticized for ignoring most of German scholarship; for example, see Dorothea Wendebourg, "Der ganze Westen kann nicht anders," *Süddeutsche Zeitung*, October 13, 2008, Literatur 14.
24. On the history and interpretation of this process, see, for example, Heide Fehrenbach and Uta G. Poiger, eds., *Transactions, Transgressions, Transformations: American Culture in Western Europe and Japan* (New York: Berghahn, 2000) and Lars Koch, "Zwischen Kontinuität und Innovation: Der westdeutsche Spielfilm 1945–1960," in *Modernisierung als Amerikanisierung? Entwicklungslinien der westdeutschen Kultur*, ed. Lars Koch (Bielefeld: Transcript Verlag, 2007), 89–109.
25. Heide Fehrenbach, "Persistent Myths of Americanization: German Reconstruction and the Renationalization of Postwar Cinema, 1945–1960," in *Transactions, Transgressions, Transformations*, ed. Heide Fehrenbach and Uta G. Poigner (New York: Berghahn Books), 88.
26. For example, the pure documentary *Luther und die Juden* (ZDF, November 12, 1983). On this, see the comments by the author of the film: Paul Karalus, "Erstlich, dass man ihre Synagoge oder Schule mit Feuer anstecke . . . ," in *Martin Luther. Reformator—Ketzer—Nationalheld. Texte, Bilder, Dokumente in ARD und ZDF, Materialien zu Fernsehsendungen*, ed. Margret Trapmann and Fritz Hufen (Munich: Goldmann, 1983), 223–240. Only one documentary with feature film elements mentions Luther's hostility toward the Jews: the production commissioned by the MDR that was broadcast in 2003.
27. King's father changed his and his son's name from Michael to Martin Luther after his visit to Berlin in 1934. Nevertheless, this change came about gradually, according to research by Ralph E. Luker and Penny A. Russell. See *The Papers of Martin Luther King*, ed. Ralph E. Luker and Penny A. Russell (Berkeley: University of California Press), 1:31n98. King referred to Martin Luther in 1949 as fundamentalist (*Papers*, 240): "These men argued that there could be no compromise on the unchanging fundamentals of the Christian faith. To gain support for their stand, the fundamentalist claimed that they were reaffirming the faith as Luther, Calvin, Knox, and Wesley

held it. Of course, in that claim they were undoubtedly correct. It was the Protestant Reformation which enunciated the doctrines which are now called 'fundamentalist.'"

28. For example, William Naphy writes: "When Martin Luther nailed 95 criticisms of the Catholic Church to the door of his local church in 1517 he sparked not just a religious Reformation, but an unending cycle of political, social and economic change that continues to this day. By challenging the authority of the Pope, Luther inadvertently unleashed a revolutionary force: the power of the individual to determine his or her own thoughts and actions. Over four centuries later, the Protestant minister Martin Luther King Jr. was acting on the same revolutionary principle, when he rejected racial discrimination and spearheaded the US Civil Rights Movement." William Naphy, *The Protestant Revolution: From Martin Luther to Martin Luther King Jr.* (London: BBC Books, 2007), blurb.
29. Werner Schneider-Quindeau, "Der Reformator als Leinwandheld: Lutherfilme zwischen Geschichte und Ideologie," in *Handbuch Theologie und populärer Film*, ed. Thomas Bohrmann, Werner Veith, and Stephan Zöller (Paderborn: Ferdinand Schöningh, 2009), 2:195–196.
30. Wipfler, *Martin Luther in Motion Pictures*, 115–127.
31. Hermann Gerber, *Problematik des Religiösen Films* (Munich: Ev. Presseverband für Bayern, 1962), 7: "Daß ein gut Teil der Verkündigung von den Theologen auf die Laien übergangen ist."
32. See Albert J. Bergesen and Andrew M. Greeley, *God in the Movies* (New Brunswick, NJ: Transaction, 2000), 177.
33. "Gute Quoten für 'Katharina Luther.' Über sieben Millionen sehen den Fernsehspielfilm über Luthers Ehefrau Katharina von Bora," *Evangelisches Sonntagsblatt aus Bayern*, March 5, 2017, 10; Karoline Schuch performed the part of Katharina von Bora and Devid Striesow played Martin Luther. The screenplay was written by Christian Schnalke. The producer Mario Krebs (EIKON) explained that he wanted to break with the tradition of the Luther films; see Mario Krebs, "'Katharina' Spielfilm für die ARD," in *Luther vermitteln: Reformationsgeschichte zwischen Historisierung und Aktualisierung*, ed. Benjamin Hasselhorn (Leipzig: EVA, 2017),, 229.

Chapter 5

1. Claire Cross, *Church and People: England 1450–1660* (Malden, MA: Blackwell, 1999), 42–152.
2. Antonia Fraser, *Cromwell: The Lord Protector* (New York: Smithmark, 1996), 3–22; Barry Coward, *Cromwell: Profiles in Power* (Essex, UK: Person Education, 1991), 6–22;
3. Cross, *Church and People.*
4. Coward, *Cromwell*, 24–43.
5. Coward, *Cromwell*, 24–80.

6. C. V. Wedgwood, *Oliver Cromwell* (New York: Barnes & Noble, 1973), 81–95; Fraser, *Cromwell*.
7. Patrick Little, ed., *Oliver Cromwell: New Perspectives* (New York: Palgrave Macmillan, 2009), 1–17.
8. With the phrase "a vexed man," I argue that Hughes portrays Cromwell as a distressed and contradictory man—distressed over whether to execute the king for treason because he supported a plot to invite the Irish and Scots to invade England, and contradictory because while he supports the Parliament, religious and political liberty, and an end to the divine rights of kings, he also sides against the anti-monarchist Levellers, promoting a constitutional monarchy, and acting like a dictator by demanding that England largely conform to his vision of society.
9. Roger Ebert, "Cromwell," RogerEbert.com, February 16, 1971; Glenn Erickson, "Cromwell," DVD Talk, October 8, 2003.
10. The many historical and chronological problems in the film become apparent when comparing it to Fraser's excellent biography, *Cromwell*.
11. Ebert, "Cromwell."
12. Erickson, "Cromwell."
13. Tony Mastroianni, "'Cromwell' Is a Lavish Spectacle," *Cleveland Press*, February 19, 1971.
14. Andy Webb, "Cromwell: Rebel with a Cause," The Movie Scene, accessed January 16, 2020.

Chapter 6

1. David Pirie, *A Heritage of Horror: The English Gothic Cinema, 1946–1972* (London: Gordon Fraser Gallery, 1973), 151.
2. For explorations of the relation between the horror tradition and the religious background, including theological differences and propaganda wars, see V. Sage, *Horror Fiction in the Protestant Tradition* (London: Macmillan, 1988); Diane Long Hoeveler, *Gothic Riffs: Secularizing the Uncanny in the European Imaginary* (Columbus: Ohio State University Press, 2010); and Alison Milbank, *God and the Gothic* (Oxford: Oxford University Press, 2018).
3. All quotations from the Bible unless otherwise indicated are from *The Bible: Authorized King James Version with an Introduction and Notes by Robert Carroll and Stephen Prickett* (New York: Oxford University Press, 1997). Local variations will be indicated.
4. The omitted verses of the biblical text gloss the horseman mentioned, as follows:

> And I saw heaven opened, and beheld a white horse; and he that sat upon him was called Faithful and True, and in righteousness he doth judge and make war. His eyes were as a flame of fire, and on his head were many crowns; and he had a name written, that no man knew but he himself. And he was clothed with a vesture dipped in blood; and his name is called The Word of God. (Revelation 19:11–13)

5. See, for example, the passage in King James, *Daemonologie, 1597*, ed. G. B. Harrison (Edinburgh: Edinburgh University Press, 1966), 2:33. The film script condenses both the historical and the novelistic characters of the refined, ruthless sadist and would-be gentleman Matthew Hopkins, played with perfect restraint by Vincent Price, and the vulgar brute John Stearne, who carries out most of the dirty work. In fact, the real Matthew Hopkins was also a zealot, named after a gospel saint, who came from a Puritan family and, instead of going to Cambridge like his brothers, might well have been going to America. Stearne was also more literate than he appears in the film.
6. On their zeal, see Matthew Hopkins, ed., *The Discovery of Witches with an introduction by Montague Summers* (London: Cayme Press, 1928), introduction, 22–24.
7. I owe these points to Gaskill, *Witchfinders*. For comparison with the earlier trials of the Lancashire witches under James I, see G. B. Harrison, ed., *The Trial of the Lancashire Witches* (London: Peter Davies, 1929).
8. Ronald Bassett, *Witchfinder General* (London: Pan Books, 1966), 253, is probably following Baxter; see Hopkins, *Discovery of Witches*.
9. On the practices of "running" and "swimming" in the case of John Lowes, see Hopkins, *Discovery of Witches*, 34. Hopkins himself in this pamphlet cites King James's *Daemonologie* as an authority for "swimming" (56–57). For background, see Gaskill, *Witchfinders*.
10. Compare the pointed incident in Bassett's novel, when one Elizabeth Gurrey forgets in the same way, and, in a reflex of piety, makes the sign of the cross when Stearne tips his hat to her in the street: he immediately rounds up a mob and has her thrown into a ditch and "mercilessly thrashed with sticks." Bassett, *Witchfinder General*, 222.
11. The Scottish Epicopalian Bible also uses "covenant" (Gk. *klomenon*) for "testament" (*didomenon*) in the authorized text. These are culturally significant variations and relevant to the "control" of the ceremony of the Eucharist. Howie uses an archaic Old Testament variation, because in Scotland "covenant" is a highly charged term. In the seventeenth century, Puritans were asked to subscribe to the "Solemn League and Covenant," and these are also the terms used in the propaganda literature of the time to describe a pact (a "covenant") with the Devil.
12. The dialogue quoted below echoes, for example, Protestant curate Charles Maturin's accusation of cannibalism in an 1824 sermon on the Catholic doctrine of the Real Presence. Quoted in Sage, *Horror Fiction in the Protestant Tradition*, 1988, 49–50. For the origins of this propaganda tradition and its connections with a sexual register, see also Diane Long Hoeveler, *The Gothic Ideology* (Cardiff: University of Wales Press, 2014).
13. Robin Hardy and Anthony Shaffer, *The Wicker Man* (London: Pan Books, 2000), 202.
14. Hardy and Shaffer, *The Wicker Man*, 202.
15. Hardy and Shaffer, *The Wicker Man*, 204.
16. Melissa Smith, "Mister Punch as Sacrificial Victim in *The Wicker Man*," in *Constructing The Wicker Man: Film and Cultural Studies' Perspectives*, ed. Jonathan Murray et al. (Dumfries: University of Glasgow/Crichton Publications, 2005), 157–171. Note the connection on 159 with Frazer's *The Golden Bough*, the figure of Punch, the scapegoat figure, and the sacrificial victim. For the notion of "carnival"

and the active role of sexual register in it, see M. M. Bahktin, *Rabelais and His World* (Bloomington: Indiana University Press, 1984), introduction.

17. See Sage, *Horror Fiction in the Protestant Tradition*, 57–58 and 236n4 on 1 Corinthians 15 and 2 Corinthians 5:1–6. For a recent, more Anglican reading of St. Paul's Corinthians, see Milbank, *God and the Gothic*, 2018.
18. For a discussion of Goethe's ballad and the notion of blood sacrifice, see Hoeveler, *Gothic Riffs*, 180–181.
19. Hardy and Shaffer, *The Wicker Man*, 284.
20. Psalm 31: 8, 12.

Chapter 7

1. See Birgitta Steene, *Ingmar Bergman: A Reference Guide* (Amsterdam: Amsterdam University Press, 2005), and Astrid Söderbergh Widding, "What Should We Believe? Religious Motifs in Ingmar Bergman's Films," in *Ingmar Bergman Revisited: Performance, Cinema and the Arts*, ed. Maaret Koskinen (London: Wallflower Press, 2008).
2. See the epigraph to the published scripts in Ingmar Bergman, *A Film Trilogy*, trans. Paul Britten Austin (New York: Marion Boyars, 1993).
3. This translation can (except for one minor change by the author) be found in Charles B. Ketcham, *The Influence of Existentialism on Ingmar Bergman: An Analysis of the Theological Ideas Shaping a Filmmaker's Art* (Lewiston/Queenston: Edwin Mellen Press, 1986), 54.
4. Author's translation. Ingmar Bergman, "Såsom i en spegel [Through a Glass Darkly]," program note for SF/Svensk Filmindustri, dated October 16, 1961.
5. Translation in Paisley Livingston, *Ingmar Bergman and the Rituals of Art* (Ithaca, NY: Cornell University Press, 1982), 58.
6. Bergman, *A Film Trilogy*.
7. In Stig Björkman, Torsten Manns, and Jonas Sima, *Bergman on Bergman*, trans. Paul Britten Austin (New York: Simon & Schuster, 1986), 219.
8. See, for instance, Sven Nykvist, "A Passion for Light," *American Cinematographer* 53, no. 4 (1972): 380–381, 456.
9. Ingmar Bergman, *Images: My Life in Film*, trans. Marianne Ruuth (New York: Arcade, 1994), 30, 264.
10. In Torsten Bergmark, "Ingmar Bergman och den kristna baksmällan" [Ingmar Bergman and the Christian hangover], *Dagens Nyheter*, October 6, 1968.
11. In chapter 4 of her study *Gender and Representation in the Films of Ingmar Bergman* (Columbia, SC: Camden House, 1997), Marilyn Johns Blackwell makes a fine observation in pointing out the dynamic tension between the ever-talkative knight and the silent servant girl in *The Seventh Seal*.
12. Author's translation. Ingmar Bergman Foundation Archive, "Såsom i en spegel. Dagbok för Tapeten [Through a glass darkly. Diary for The Wallpaper], 1.1.60–22.4.60," March 22, 1960 (referring to the working title that Bergman gave *Through a Glass Darkly*), F:020:02.

In 1998 Ingmar Bergman asked me to "take a look at his hell of a mess," which he called his (then) private archive. At the time it was housed at his residence on the small island of Fårö in the Baltic, where Bergman shot many of his films in the 1960s, and where he lived until his death in 2007, at the age of eighty-nine. This eventually led to Bergman's donation of his archive and the formation of the Ingmar Bergman Foundation. See www.ingmarbergman.se.

13. Author's translation. Ingmar Bergman Foundation Archive, "Stora bilderboken" [The big picture book], January 2, 1962.
14. Ingmar Bergman Foundation Archive, "Stora bilderboken," December 27, 1961.
15. Ingmar Bergman Foundation Archive, "Stora bilderboken," March 17, 1962.
16. Ingmar Bergman Foundation Archive, "Stora bilderboken," January 1 and 22, 1962.
17. Interestingly, Carl Theodor Dreyer, the Danish film director often mentioned in the same breath as Bergman, seems to have regarded the relation between the written order and that which he considered to be the "filmic" order as a deeply antagonistic one or, as James Schamus has phrased it, a constant battle of wills "for narrative supremacy between text and image." So one might say that Bergman was, just like Dreyer, preoccupied with "the film director's role in the translation of word into image. Who . . . is the real author of the film, the screenwriter or the director? From where does the director, as an artist, derive his own authority?" See James Schamus, "Dreyer's Textual Realism," *Rites of Realism. Essays on Corporeal Cinema*, ed. Ivone Margulies (Durham, NC: Duke University Press, 2003), 315–324.
18. Author's translation. Ingmar Bergman Foundation Archive, "Jungfrukällan. En legend från 1200-talet efter folkvisan Töres dotter i Vänge" [Virgin spring: A legend from the 13th century after the ballad "Töre's daughter in Vänge"], manuscript by Ulla Isaksson, n.p., shooting script for *Virgin Spring*, handwritten entry dated May 2, 1959, B:009.
19. Author's translation. Ingmar Bergman Foundation Archive, "Stora bilderboken," September 12, 1961.
20. Ingmar Bergman Foundation Archive, "Stora bilderboken," March 14, 1962.
21. Bergman, *Images*, 54.
22. Author's translation. Ingmar Bergman Foundation Archive, "Stora bilderboken," March 11, 1962.
23. Ingmar Bergman, *Laterna Magica* (Stockholm: Norstedts, 1981), translated as Ingmar Bergman, *The Magic Lantern: An Autobiography* (New York: Viking, 1988).
24. Ingmar Bergman, *Private Confessions*. A Novel, trans. Joan Tate (New York: Arcade Publishing, 1997), 19.
25. *Private Confessions*, 19.
26. Ingmar Bergman, *Four Stories of Ingmar Bergman*, trans. Alan Blair (New York: Anchor Press, 1977), 75.
27. *Private Confessions*, 16.
28. *Private Confessions*, 32.
29. Author's translation. Interview by Tore Carlsson, "Operan hoppas på Bergman" [The opera has high hopes in Bergman], *Dagens Nyheter*, sec. "På Stan" [Around town], November 1, 1991.

Chapter 8

1. Maurice Drouzy, *Carl Th. Dreyer, né Nilsson* (Paris: Editions du Cerf, 1982), 105–106.
2. Among classic studies: H. R. Trevor-Roper, *The European Witch-Craze of the Sixteenth and Seventeenth Centuries* (New York: Harper & Row, 1967); Keith Thomas, *Religion and the Decline of Magic* (London: Weidenfeld and Nicolson, 1971); Norman Cohn, *Europe's Inner Demons* (Brighton: Sussex University Press and Heinemann Educational Books, 1975); Robin Briggs, *Witches and Neighbors: The Social and Cultural Context of European Witchcraft* (New York: Viking, 1996); Stuart Clark, *Thinking with Demons: The Idea of Witchcraft in Early Modern Europe* (Oxford: Oxford University Press, 1997); Mary Beth Norton, *In the Devil's Snare: The Salem Witchcraft Crisis of 1692* (New York: Knopf, 2002); Walter Stephens, *Demon Lovers: Witchcraft, Sex, and the Crisis of Belief* (Chicago: University of Chicago Press, 2006).
3. "The Cinematization of *The Word*," in *Dreyer in Double Reflection*, trans. and ed. Donald Skoller (New York: E. P. Dutton, 1973), 165.
4. Casper Tybjerg, "The Sense of *The Word*," in *Film Style and Story: A Tribute to Torben Grodal*, ed. Lennard Højbjerg and Peter Schepelern (Copenhagen: Museum Tusculanum Press, 2003), 171–213 (the *ligsynsmand* quotation can be found on page 194).
5. Guido Aristarco, "Venice Film Festival," *Film Culture* 1, no. 5-6 (1955): 23.
6. Dreyer, "Metaphysic of 'Ordet,'" *Film Culture* 2, no. 1 (1956): 24.
7. Tybjerg, "The Sense of *The Word*," 199.

Chapter 9

1. Peter Bradshaw, "Babette's Feast—Review," *The Guardian*, December 13, 2012.
2. "*Babette's Feast* by Dinesen," *Britannica*, accessed February 2, 2021. For the text of the story, see Isak Dinensen, *Babette's Feast and Other Stories* (London: Penguin Classics, 2015).
3. "Skæbne-Anekdote," Karen Blixen Museum, accessed February 2, 2021.
4. Axel also wrote the screenplay. "Babette's Feast (1987)," IMDb, accessed March 19, 2015. In Blixen's short story, the pastor's parish was situated at the northern tip of Norway, in the town of Berlevaag, but in Axel's film it has been relocated to a fishing village on the west coast of Jutland in Denmark. However, even if these two places geographically are separated by fifteen hundred miles, they might theologically be very similar.
5. "Babette's Feast (1987), Awards," IMDb, accessed February 2, 2021.
6. Priscilla Parkhurst Ferguson, "Babette's Feast: A Fable for Culinary France," in *Accounting for Taste: The Triumph of French Cuisine* (Chicago: University of Chicago Press, 2004).
7. Mary Elisabeth Podles stresses the visual effects in "Babette's Feast: Feasting with Lutherans," *Antioch Review* 50, no. 3 (1992).

8. See, for example, Niels Bjerre, "A Prayer Meeting" [also known as "Children of God"] (1897), Wikimedia, accessed February 2, 2021; Peder Severin Kroyer, "Fishermen at Skagen" (1894), WikiArt, accessed February 2, 2021.
9. See William McDonald, "Søren Kierkegaard," *Stanford Encyclopedia of Philosophy*, accessed February 2, 2021.
10. The originator of the Pietist movement in Lutheranism was German theologian Philipp Jakob Spener (1635-1705), who was influenced by Johann Arndt (1555-1621). Also, Spener's godson, Nikolaus Ludwig von Zinzendorf (1700-1770), became a leader of a revival of the Moravian Church, stressing the spiritual relationship between the believer and Jesus.
11. See Titus 2:11-12. The stress on simplicity has also been seen as an implicit critique of Renaissance Catholicism.
12. Queen Sophia is mentioned; this may refer to Sophia, married in 1857 to the hereditary prince Oscar, later Oscar II, king of Sweden (1872–1907) and Norway (1872–1905). An official union existed between the countries 1814–1905. Queen Sophia was a supporter of Lutheran revivalism.
13. Thus, he was not an (obscure) sect leader, as some commentators have proposed. For example, Wendy M. Wright refers to "the prophet's sect" in "Babette's Feast: A Religious Film," *Journal of Religion and Film* 1, no. 2 (1997).
14. In the novel, theologian and humanist d'Etaples is described as a Protestant. Actually he remained a Roman Catholic throughout his life, although critical in his views of his church. Jaqueline de Rouville, "Jaques Lefèvre d'Etaples (1450–1537)," Musée Protestant, accessed February 2, 2021.
15. Hanne Lauvstad, "Petter Dass," Store Norske Leksikon, accessed February 2, 2021.
16. Maybe Papin's somewhat anguished initial reflection on his life is seen in the light of the concluding chorus of the opera *Don Giovanni*.
17. Roy M. Anker, *Catching Light: Looking for God in the Movies* (Grand Rapids, MI: William B. Eerdmans, 2004), 205.
18. As mentioned, some connect Babette to a Christ figure—a foreigner serving those around her through unselfish sacrifice. Additionally, she serves the twelve (disciples) around the table, paralleling the Last Supper. However, her violent past has no parallels to Jesus. Jesus was a pacifist; Babette had been using violence as an insurgent, and seems to be proud of this fact.
19. Ferguson, "Babette's Feast."

Chapter 10

1. I draw on Brian Cummings's essay "Protestant Allegory" regarding Martin Luther's and Philipp Melanchthon's anti-allegorical viewpoint. Cummings continues to demonstrate that Luther had a complicated, ambiguous view of allegory; see Brian Cummings, "Protestant Allegory," in *The Cambridge Companion to Allegory*, ed. Rita

Copeland and Peter T. Struck (Cambridge: Cambridge University Press, 2010), 177–190, esp. 178–180.

2. *Dr. Martin Luthers Werke. Kritische Gesamtausgabe*, ed. Joachim Karl Friedrich Knaake (Weimar: Heinrich Böhlaus Nachfolger, 1883), 42: 173. Translation by author.
3. See, for example, the anonymous medieval scribe of the *Ovide Moralisé*, who first translates stories from Ovid's *Metamorphoses* into Old French and then allegorizes them by establishing associative—even contradictory—metaphorical correspondences between the pagan stories and the Bible as well as the Catholic Church. He links, for instance, Phaeton's fall from the sky to Lucifer's fall from heaven, the chariot to the Christian doctrine, the four horses of the chariot to the four evangelists, and the driver of the chariot to the Pope; a few lines afterward, the medieval author correlates Phaeton with the Antichrist. See *Ovide Moralisé*, ed. Cornelis de Boer (Amsterdam: Muller, 1915–1938), 187–192. Luther has such imaginative-allegorical readings of literary texts and the Bible in mind when he denounces allegorical fantasies and advocates the return to strictly literal readings of the Bible.
4. Cummings, "Protestant Allegory," 177.
5. Qtd. in Cummings, "Protestant Allegory," 177.
6. Cummings, "Protestant Allegory," 177.
7. Qtd. in Cummings, "Protestant Allegory," 184.
8. Cummings, "Protestant Allegory," 185.
9. Thomas H. Luxon, *Literal Figures: Puritan Allegory and the Reformation Crisis in Representation* (Chicago: University of Chicago Press, 1995), x.
10. Cummings, "Protestant Allegory," 189.
11. For a brief history of allegory, see Jeremy Tambling's *Allegory* (London: Routledge, 2009) and the essay collection *Interpretation and Allegory: Antiquity to the Modern Period*, ed. Jon Whitman (Leiden: Brill, 2003). For recent studies on allegory and film, see David Melbye's *Landscape Allegory in Cinema: From Wilderness to Wasteland* (New York: Palgrave Macmillan, 2010), Tom Gunning's *The Films of Fritz Lang: Allegories of Vision and Modernity* (London: British Film Institute, 2000), and David E. James's *Allegories of Cinema: American Film in the Sixties* (Princeton: Princeton University Press, 1989). Michelle Langford touches upon the concept of an "allegorical mode" in cinema (and mentions Fletcher's work) in her study *Allegorical Images: Tableau, Time and Gesture in the Cinema of Werner Schroeter* (Bristol, UK: Intellect Books, 2006), but her main focus lies on what she terms an "allegorical image," that is, "a specific kind of time-image" (54), rather than on a "mode."
12. Angus Fletcher, *Allegory: The Theory of a Symbolic Mode* (Princeton: Princeton University Press, 2012), 2–3.
13. Fletcher, *Allegory*, 40, 25–26.
14. Fletcher, *Allegory*, 87.
15. Fletcher, *Allegory*, 87.
16. Fletcher, *Allegory*, 151.
17. Fletcher, *Allegory*, 151, 157.
18. Fletcher, *Allegory*, 221–247 (see 223–225 for Fletcher's definition and explanation of "theological dualism"), 247–254, 254–280.

19. See, for instance, Brenda Wineapple's biography *Nathaniel Hawthorne: A Life* (New York: Random House, 2004), 24, 35, and all the essays that trace the influence of Bunyan's *The Pilgrim's Progress* on Hawthorne's work, e.g., Stacy W. Johnson's "Hawthorne and *The Pilgrim's Progress*," *Journal of English and Germanic Philology* 50, no. 2 (April 1951): 156–166.
20. Fletcher, *Allegory*, 375.
21. Fletcher, *Allegory*, 376. Fletcher claims that "whenever allegory adopts the genre of Romance, it has already accepted a merging of the real and the ideal, the inside and the outside, and like Cervantes, Hawthorne uses Romance to introduce idealist perspectives into any merely realistic narratives." Hawthorne's allegorical mode, however, challenges the idealizing tendencies of his "anti-Romance."
22. Fletcher, *Allegory*, 368.
23. Fletcher, *Allegory*, 366n.
24. A Swedish émigré, Victor Sjöström had been a major force in his country's cinema. Ingmar Bergman knew and admired his work, especially another of Sjöström's silent films sporting the allegorical mode, *The Phantom Carriage* (1921). The film made a powerful impression on Bergman when he saw it as a child. Sjöström also plays the lead in one of Bergman's classic films, *Wild Strawberries* (1957), which uses allegorical images in its dream sequences; see Raphael Shargel, ed., *Ingmar Bergman: Interviews* (Jackson: University of Mississippi Press, 2007), 18–19; Peter Cowie, *Ingmar Bergman: A Critical Biography* (New York: Limelight Editions, 1992), 37–39, 156–157.
25. Fletcher, *Allegory*, 180.
26. Mark W. Estrin argues convincingly that "the very ambiguity with which Hawthorne imbues his novel . . . is entirely omitted from the [1926] film"; see Estrin's essay "'Triumphant Ignominy': *The Scarlet Letter* on Screen," *Literature/Film Quarterly* 2, no. 2 (Spring 1974): 110–122 (quote on 122)..
27. Spencer Lewerenz, "A View from Outside: An Interview with Wim Wenders," GodSpy, March 27. 2008. Wenders eventually converted from Catholicism to Lutheranism. He mentions his conversion in an interview with journalist Christiane Amanpour, "Amanpour: Joseph Yun and Wim Wenders," *Amanpour on PBS*, May 23, 2018.
28. Michael Dunne, "'The Scarlet Letter' on Film: Ninety Years of Revisioning," *Literature/Film Quarterly* 25, no. 1 (January 1997), 33.
29. There is one short sequence that could be read as expressing an allegorical impulse: the camera shows Hester and Pearl on top of a hill from a low angle. However, Wenders shuns a possible allegorical-spiritual interpretation of this image since he does not employ a vertical upward movement of the camera. Instead, the camera takes on the POV of a group of men who look upward to the strong, independent woman who is walking down the hill to meet them.
30. James M. Welsh and Richard C. Keenan, "Wim Wenders and Nathaniel Hawthorne: From *The Scarlet Letter* to *Der Scharlachrote Buchstabe*," *Literature/Film Quarterly* 6, no. 2 (Spring 1978): 176. Welsh and Keenan, however, point out that "Wender's invention springs from Hawthorne's Mistress Hibbins" and that "the character is consistent with Hawthorne's general design" (176).

31. Dunne, "'The Scarlet Letter' on Film," 33.
32. Welsh and Keenan, "Wim Wenders and Nathaniel Hawthorne," 178.
33. Sacvan Bercovitch, *The American Jeremiad* (Madison: University of Wisconsin Press, 1978).

Chapter 11

1. Alister E. McGrath, *Christian Theology: An Introduction* (Malden, MA: Wiley-Blackwell, 2011), 215–223.
2. See, for example, David Bentley Hart, *The Doors of the Sea: Where Was God in the Tsunami?* (Grand Rafspids, MI: William B. Eerdmans, 2005).
3. On the hiddenness of God, see Karl Barth, *Church Dogmatics II*, ed. G. W. Bromiley and T. F. Torrance (Edinburgh: T&T Clark, 1957), chap. V, §27.1, 179–204.
4. C. S. Lewis, *A Grief Observed* (New York: HarperOne, 2015), 5–6. See also C. S. Lewis, *The Problem of Pain* (New York: HarperOne 2001).
5. *The Tree of Life*, written and directed by Terrence Malick (New York: Criterion Collection, 2018), disc one, theatrical version, Blu-Ray.
6. In a rare moment of domestic tranquility, R.L. plays the guitar while his father accompanies him on the piano, a harmonious interlude that strikes me as a subtle tribute to Larry Malick (*The Tree of Life*, 1:07:34–1:08:06). Peter J. Leithart, *Shining Glory: Theological Reflections on Terrence Malick's* Tree of Life (Eugene, OR: Cascade Books, 2013), 3. Lawrence died in 1968, while Malick's other brother, Chris, died in 2008.
7. Malick's style has been characterized as philosophical, poetic, romantic, naturalistic, and transcendental. See Lloyd Michaels, *Terrence Malick* (Urbana: University of Illinois Press, 2009), 4–5, and Hannah Patterson, ed., *The Cinema of Terrence Malick: Poetic Visions of America* (New York: Wallflower Press, 2007), 2. For an overview of Malick and his films, see James Morrison and Thomas Schur, *The Films of Terrence Malick* (Westport, CT: Praeger, 2003).
8. This paper takes a religious studies methodological approach, which focuses on the religious dimension of the film, particularly its theological engagement with the problem of evil, as an "intellectual and academic" enterprise, rather than as an expression of faith. See, for methodological foundations, William R. Telford, "Through a Lens Darkly: Critical Approaches to Theology and Film," in *Cinéma Divinité: Religion, Theology and the Bible in Film*, ed. Eric S. Christianson, Peter Francis, and William R. Telford (London: SCM Press, 2005), 26. See also Clive Marsh and Gaye Ortiz, eds., *Explorations in Theology and Film* (Malden, MA: Blackwell, 1997).
9. On Malick's more philosophical engagement with the problem of evil in *The Thin Red Line*, see Mark S. M. Scott, "Light in the Darkness: The Problem of Evil in *The Thin Red Line*," in *Theology and the Films of Terrence Malick*, ed. Christopher B. Barnett and Clark J. Elliston (New York: Routledge, 2016).

10. McGrath, *Christian Theology*, 223–227; Leithart, *Shining Glory*, 15n7. "Is it correct, or helpful, to define *The Tree of Life* as a Christian film? I would prefer to say that it exemplifies and is animated and illuminated by grace, with a decidedly Christian tint" (Kent Jones, "Let the Wind Speak," insert with *The Tree of Life* [New York: Criterion Collection, 2018], 34).
11. For an extended analysis of the problem of evil and the major models and motifs in Christian theodicy, see Mark S. M. Scott, *Pathways in Theodicy: An Introduction to the Problem of Evil* (Minneapolis: Fortress Press, 2015).
12. John Hick, *Evil and the God of Love* (New York: Macmillan, 2007), 5.
13. Jürgen Moltmann, *The Trinity and the Kingdom: The Doctrine of God* (Minneapolis: Fortress Press, 1993), 47.
14. Peter van Inwagen, *The Problem of Evil* (New York: Oxford University Press, 2006), 15.
15. McGrath, *Christian Theology*, 224.
16. *The Tree of Life*, 7:37–7:50.
17. *The Tree of Life*, 47:42–47:45.
18. *The Tree of Life*, 8:47–9:24.
19. *The Tree of Life*, 9:32–9:38.
20. All Bible references (other than from the film) come from the NSRV, specifically Wayne A. Meeks, ed., *The HarperCollins Study Bible (New Revised Standard Version)* (New York: HarperCollins, 1993).
21. Nicholas Wolterstorff, *Lament for a Son* (Grand Rapids, MI: Eerdmans, 1987).
22. Wolterstorff, *Lament for a Son*, 5.
23. Wolterstorff, *Lament for a Son*, 67.
24. Wolterstorff, *Lament for a Son*, 67–68.
25. Leithart, *Shining Glory*, 3. Leithart views Jack as the film's Job figure: "Jack O'Brien is the Job of the film, *Jack* O'Brien, his very name (the only name given in the film) identifying him with the archetypal sufferer" (12).
26. *The Tree of Life*, 1:13:25–1:14:54.
27. Leithart, *Shining Glory*, 16: "Where was he when R.L. died? He will not say. He says only as he said to Job, 'I am love. Trust me, and love. Love every tree, every leaf, every drop of rain. Fall to the earth and embrace it. Love the world in all its ruin.'"
28. For a comprehensive commentary on the Book of Job, see Marvin H. Pope, *Job*, The Anchor Yale Bible vol. 15 (New Haven, CT: Yale University Press, 2008). On Job's engagement with the problem of evil, Pope comments: "It has been generally assumed that the purpose of the book is to give an answer to the issue with which it deals, the problem of divine justice or theodicy. . . . It must be admitted first and last that the Book of Job fails to give a clear and definitive answer to this question. . . . Of the various attitudes suggested in the different parts of the book, it is difficult to say which, if any, was intended to be decisive" (lxxiii). I argue that the divine speeches (Pope, *Job*, 38–41) are heuristically decisive to understanding the Book of Job's perspective on the problem of evil.
29. Leithart, *Shining Glory*, 12: "Job doesn't offer a theodicy, a philosophical solution to the problem of evil. Rather, the Book of Job points those who suffer undeservedly to

the Creator God and issues a call to faith. Job doesn't answer the problem of undeserved suffering. Its message is relevant precisely in the *absence* of explanations."

30. Marilyn McCord Adams, *Horrendous Evils and the Goodness of God* (Ithaca, NY: Cornell University Press, 1999), 149. She defines "horrendous evils" as "evils that participation in which (that is, the doing or suffering of which) constitutes prima facie reason to doubt whether the participant's life could (given their inclusion in it) be a great good to him/her on the whole" (26). On her subjective criterion for the defeat of evil, see also 28–29, 155, and 204.
31. *The Tree of Life*, 2:07:18–2:09:10. In his turn from cosmic to subjective symbolism at the end of *The Tree of Life*, his aesthetics and theology converge: "Malick seems a stubbornly romantic artist in depicting the isolated individual's desire for transcendence amidst established social institutions, the grandeur and untouched beauty of nature, the competing claims of instinct and reason, and the lure of the open road [or open future, in the case of this film]" (Michaels, *Terrence Malick*, 4). On eschatology, see McGrath, *Christian Theology*, 444–445, 461–464.
32. Hart, *The Doors of the Sea*, 6–7.
33. Friedrich Nietzsche, *Ecce Homo: How to Become What You Are*, trans. Duncan Large (New York: Oxford University Press, 2007), 25 (in German: "die einzige Entschuldigung Gottes ist, dass er nicht existirt"); Kallistos Ware, *The Orthodox Way* (Crestwood, NY: St. Vladimir's Seminary Press, 1995), 14.
34. I wish to thank my good friend Dr. Jason Stevens for his invaluable editorial assistance.

Chapter 12

1. Amy Taubin, "Bodies and Souls," *Village Voice*, December 23, 1997, 42, 51. Duvall alludes to New York City–based reviews in the DVD commentary: *The Apostle: Collector's Edition* (Universal Pictures Home Entertainment, 2002).
2. Duvall invested $5 million to make the film and $8 million to market it. After a buzzworthy debut at the Toronto Film Festival, it was picked up for distribution by October Films. The deal and its negotiation are covered in Peter Biskind, *Down and Dirty Pictures: Miramax, Sundance, and the Rise of Independent Film* (London: Bloomsbury, 2004), 301–307.
3. These details are covered in the DVD feature commentary with Robert Duvall and the bonus feature "The Apostle: The Making of the Film," in *The Apostle: Collector's Edition*. On J. Charles Jessup, see Randall Balmer, *Encyclopedia of Evangelicalism* (Waco: Baylor University Press, 2004), 363.
4. William L. Blizek and Ron Burke, "'The Apostle': An Interview with Robert Duvall," *Journal of Religion and Film* 2, no. 1 (April 1988): art. 2.
5. Some have argued that whites dress down on Sunday because they have to dress up in their white-collar suits all week at work, while Blacks, Latinxs, and others dress up on Sunday as a sign of respect to God and because they have to dress down all week in many menial jobs, where they are seen but not allowed to be heard. This is changing

as more minorities move into the middle-class and as religious institutions seek ways to reach younger families.

6. B. B. Warfield, *Counterfeit Miracles* (Carlisle, PA: Banner of Truth, 1996); John McArthur, *Charismatic Chaos* (Grand Rapids, MI: Zondervan, 1993); John McArthur, *Strange Fire: The Danger of Offending the Holy Spirit with Counterfeit Worship* (Nashville, TN: Thomas Nelson, 2013); Gastón Espinosa, *William J. Seymour and the Origins of Global Pentecostalism* (Durham, NC: Duke University Press, 2014), 4.
7. Espinosa, *William J. Seymour and the Origins of Global Pentecostalism*, 1–6.
8. Espinosa, *William J. Seymour and the Origins of Global Pentecostalism*, 41–68.
9. Espinosa, *William J. Seymour and the Origins of Global Pentecostalism*, 96–100.
10. Espinosa, *William J. Seymour and the Origins of Global Pentecostalism*, 1–8, 41–68.
11. While many Pentecostals were and remain apolitical, there have always been strands that have been politically involved. Grant Wacker, *Heaven Below: Early Pentecostals and American Culture* (Cambridge, MA: Harvard University Press, 2001), 217–250; Matthew Avery Sutton, *Aimee Semple McPherson and the Resurrection of Christian America* (Cambridge, MA: Harvard University Press, 2009), 212–260; Gastón Espinosa, *Latino Pentecostals in America: Faith and Politics in Action* (Cambridge, MA: Harvard University Press, 2014), 323–405.
12. W. J. Cash, *The Mind of the South* (New York: Vintage, 1991), 134–137. On the postwar shift in Hollywood representations of the South, see Jason Stevens, "John Huston's Adaptation of *Wise Blood* and Hollywood's Response to the New South," *Flannery O'Connor Review* 12 (2014): 99–117, esp. 96–98; James Kirby, *Media-Made Dixie* (Athens: University of Georgia Press, 1986), 91–110, 115–123; Chris Cagle, "The Postwar Cinematic South: Realism and the Politics of Liberal Consensus," in *American Cinema and the Southern Imaginary*, ed. Deborah E. Barker and Kathryn McKee (Athens: University of Georgia Press, 2011), 104–121.
13. For an extended analysis of Hollywood's *Elmer Gantry*, see Jason Stevens, "Introduction," in Sinclair Lewis, *Elmer Gantry: A New Edition* (New York: Signet Classics, 2008), xviii–xxiii, and Jason Stevens, *God-Fearing and Free* (Cambridge, MA: Harvard University Press, 2010), 170–181.
14. Peggy Dunn Bailey, "Coming Home to Scrabble Creek: Saving Grace, Serpent Handling, and the Realistic Southern Gothic," *Appalachian Journal* 38, no. 4 (Summer 2011): 424–439. First-time directors Britt Poulson and Dan Madison Savage's *Them That Follow* (2019), released by Amasia Entertainment, extends these tropes in a fictional narrative that unsuccessfully blends ethnographic detail and exploitation-thriller elements. Walter Goggins (Sammy in *The Apostle*) stars as the pastor of a Pentecostal snake-handling church.
15. Sarah Kernochan and Howard Smith's documentary was presented as an exposé of "holy roller" evangelicalism. See Sarah Kernochan, "Resurrecting *Marjoe*," *American Prospect*, January 26, 2006.
16. J. R. Jones, "Young Americans," *The Chicago Reader*, September 28, 2006.
17. Ralph Ellison, "Change the Joke and Slip the Yoke," in *Shadow and Act* (New York: Vintage, 1995), 45–59.

18. Roy M. Anker summarizes the film's mostly positive critical reception in *Beautiful Light: Religious Meaning in Films* (Grand Rapids: Wm. B. Eerdmans, 2017), 69n3.
19. Roger Ebert, "The Apostle Movie Review and Film Summary," RogerEbert.com, January 30, 1998.
20. Carl Greiner, "The Apostle: A Psychiatric Appraisal," *Journal of Religion and Film* 3, no. 2 (1999).
21. Ed Cohen, "Apostle E.F. and Saint Karla Faye: Robert Duvall's Exposure of the Ethics of Pentecostalism," *Humanist in Canada* 31, no. 3 (1998): 22–23, 31.
22. Mark Moring, "The 'Low'-Down on Robert Duvall," *Christianity Today*, July 27, 2010.
23. Taubin, "Bodies and Souls," 42, 51.
24. DVD feature commentary with Robert Duvall, *The Apostle: Collector's Edition.*
25. The "redneck" bigot has been played by a host of actors, including Tony Curtis, Telly Savalas, William Shatner, Kiefer Sutherland, Dennis Hopper, and James Woods.
26. DVD feature commentary with Robert Duvall, *The Apostle: Collector's Edition.*
27. The woman playing the evangelist in this segment is not a preacher but a renowned salsa dancer chosen for her dynamic physical presence. DVD feature commentary with Robert Duvall, *The Apostle: Collector's Edition.*
28. Harvey Cox, *Fire from Heaven: The Rise of Pentecostal Spirituality and the Reshaping of Religion in the Twenty-first Century* (Reading, MA: Addison-Wesley, 1995). Randall Balmer's bestselling *Mine Eyes Have Seen the Glory* (1989) and the Peabody-awarding PBS miniseries from his book also helped foster an intellectual climate more open to new scholarship.

Chapter 13

1. W. E. B. Du Bois, *The Souls of Black Folk*, ed. Herbert Aptheker (Millwood, NY: Kraus-Thomson, 1973), 189–206.
2. Taylor Branch, *Parting the Waters: America in the King Years, 1954–63* (New York: Simon & Schuster, 1989), 69–104.
3. Martin Luther King Jr., *Stride Toward Freedom: The Montgomery Story* (Boston: Beacon Press, 2010); Aldon D. Morris, *Origins of the Civil Rights Movement* (New York: Free Press, 1986); C. Vann Woodward, *The Strange Career of Jim Crow* (New York: Oxford University Press, 2001); A. J. Muste, *The Essays of A. J. Muste*, ed. Nat Hentoff (New York: Bobbs-Merrill, 1967). Many Black members of SNCC had been mentored in Christian activism by white Quaker A. J. Muste.
4. Albert J. Raboteau, Slave Religion: The "Invisible Institution" in the Antebellum South (New York: Oxford University Press, 2004), 139.

   Albert J. Raboteau, *Slave Religion: The "Invisible Institution" in the Antebellum South* (New York: Oxford University Press, 2004); Will B. Gravely, "The Rise of African Churches in America," in *African American Religion: Interpretive Essays in History and Culture*, ed. Timothy Fulop (New York: Routledge, 1997).

5. C. Eric Lincoln and Lawrence H. Mamiya, *The Black Church in the African American Experience* (Durham, NC: Duke University Press, 1990).
6. Martin Luther King Jr., *Strength to Love* (New York: Phoenix Press), 263.
7. Branch, *Parting the Waters*, 73–74, 95.
8. King, *Strength to Love*, 258; Branch, *Parting the Waters*, 84–87.
9. King, *Strength to Love*, 264–265; Branch, *Parting the Waters*, 207–208, 252–254.
10. Howard Thurman, *Jesus and the Disinherited* (Boston: Beacon Press, 1996); Branch, *Parting the Waters*, 6, 9, 124.
11. James Cone, *Martin and Malcolm and America: A Dream or a Nightmare* (New York: Orbis Books, 2012). Cone shows how much Martin Luther King Jr. and Malcolm X actually had in common philosophically, and how their positions began to move toward each other as King took up the Poor People's Campaign and began calling out imperialism.
12. James Baldwin, *Collected Essays* (New York: Library of America, 1998), 462, 474.
13. Michael A. Harris, *The Rise of the Gospel Blues: The Music of Thomas Dorsey in the Urban Church* (New York: Oxford University Press, 1992); *Say Amen, Somebody*, dir. George T. Nierenberg (1982).
14. Alex Cohen and Jacob Margolis, "The Music of 'Selma': Scoring the Civil Rights Movement," SCPR.org, January 9, 2015.
15. David Kaiser, "Why You Should Care That *Selma* Gets LBJ Wrong," *Time*, January 9, 2015.

Chapter 14

1. Judith Weisenfeld, *Hollywood Be Thy Name: African American Religion in American Film, 1929–1949* (Berkeley: University of California Press, 2007).
2. *Hallelujah*, directed by King Vidor, screenplay by Wanda Tuchok and Richard Schayer (MGM, 1929); *The Green Pastures*, directed by Marc Connelly, screenplay by Roark Bradford (Warner Bros., 1936).
3. *Sunday Sinners*, directed by Arthur Dreifuss, story by Wilson Frank, screenplay by Vincent Valentini (Goldberg Productions, 1941). Even Hollywood films featuring all-Black casts, such as *The Green Pastures*, project onto African American Christians a sentimentalizing innocence. The theme is magically conveyed in *The Green Pastures* by framing the entire film as the fanciful impressions of Black children at Sunday school as they listen to their teacher, Mr. Deshee (George Reed), retell Old Testament Bible stories.
4. *Pastor Jones: Preaching to the Choir* (video), directed by Albert Hartfield, screenplay by Peter Warren (Nu-Lite Entertainment, 2009); *Saving Grace* (video), directed by Anne Pratts, screenplay by Erin Davis (Nu-Lite Entertainment, 2011); *Walk by Faith: After the Honeymoon* (video), directed by Brett Stumpp, screenplay by Harmon Peter and Brett Stumpp (Nu-Lite Entertainment, 2010); *The Sins of Deacon*

Whyles (video), directed by Brendan Connor, screenplay by James Ward (Nu-Lite Entertainment, 2013).
5. Deleon Richards, *Move on Up the Mountain* (Myrrh Records, 1984); Eugene B. McCoy, *Climbing Up the Mountain: The Life and Times of a Musical Legend* (Nashville, TN: Sparrow Press, 1995); F. C. Barnes and Janice Brown, *Rough Side of The Mountain* (Atlanta International Records, 1984).
6. Mahalia Jackson, "Go Tell It on the Mountain," 1962 (this gospel music classic has been performed and recorded by a number of artists since 1962, including Dolly Parton in 1990 and Pentatonix in 2012); Martin Luther King Jr., "I See the Promised Land," Mason Temple, Memphis, TN, April 3, 1968, in *The Essential Writings and Speeches of Martin Luther King Jr.*, ed. James Washington (New York: Harper One, 1986), 279–286.
7. Luke 19; Luke 10; Mark 1:16; Mark 2:23; Matthew 5:7; Matthew 17:2.
8. Gastón Espinosa, *William J. Seymour and the Origins of Global Pentecostalism* (Durham, NC: Duke University Press, 2014), 53.
9. Exodus 33:19–34:7.
10. Isaiah 52:7.
11. Romans 10:15.
12. Matthew 5–7.
13. A Google search of "African American church name Mount" will produce a multiple-page list of churches with such names throughout the United States.
14. James Baldwin, *Go Tell It on the Mountain* (New York: Alfred A. Knopf, 1953).
15. Baldwin, *Go Tell It on the Mountain*, 207.
16. Carol Henderson, "Knee Bent, Body Bowed: Re-Memory's Prayer of Spiritual Re(new)al in Baldwin's *Go Tell It on the Mountain*," *Religion and Literature* 27, no. 1 (Spring 1995): 75–88.
17. All quotes from characters in this chapter are from *Why Did I Get Married?*
18. Stephanie Mitchem, *Introducing Womanist Theology* (Maryknoll, NY: Orbis Books, 2002), 48.
19. Jacquelyn Grant, "Womanist Jesus and the Mutual Struggle for Liberation," in *The Recovery of Black Presence*, ed. Randall C. Gailey and Jacquelyn Grant (Nashville, TN: Abingdon Press, 1995), 130.
20. King, "I See the Promised Land."
21. King, "I See the Promised Land."
22. Nat King Cole, "Every Time I Feel the Spirit," *Every Time I Feel the Spirit*, arrangements by Gordon Jenkins (Capitol Records, 1959; reissued 1966).
23. Mitchem, *Introducing Womanist Theology*, 11.
24. Jacquelyn Grant, "Womanist Theology: Black Woman's Experience as a Source for Doing Theology, with Special Reference to Christology," in *African American Religious Studies: An Interdisciplinary Anthology*, ed. Gayraud Wilmore (Durham, NC: Duke University Press, 1989), 219.
25. James T. Murphy Jr., *Defining Salvation in the Context of Black Theology* (Bloomington, IN: Xlibris, 2012), 112–113.
26. Murphy, *Defining Salvation in the Context of Black Theology*.

27. E. Patrick Johnson, "Madea's Big Scholarly Roundtable: Perspectives on the Media of Tyler Perry," panel discusion, Northwestern University, Evanston, IL, November 28, 2012.
28. Johnson, "Madea's Big Scholarly Roundtable."
29. Mona Faysal Sahyoun, "Black Cultural Heritage and the Subversion of Stereotypical Images of the Black Woman in Toni Morrison's *Sula*," *Spectra* 5, no. 1 (2016).
30. Tyler Perry, commencement speech at Tuskegee University, Tuskegee, AL, May 7, 2016.
31. L. Manigault-Bryant, T. Lomax, and C. Duncan, *Womanist and Black Feminist Responses* (New York: Palgrave Macmillan, 2014), 134.
32. Shayne Lee, *Tyler Perry's America: Inside His Films* (New York: Rowman and Littlefield, 2015), 127.

Chapter 15

1. The bestselling memoir of Elizabeth Gilbert, *Eat, Pray, Love* (New York: Penguin, 2006), traces her life after divorce, involving her quest for meaningfulness through a trip around the world that exposes her to different cultures, religions, and men. It struck a chord with many readers, inspiring similar quests for self-fulfillment. The film version, released in 2010, was appealing to audiences because it starred Julia Roberts, and was more escapist and romantic than the book.
2. In this regard, both Briggs's memoir and Farmiga's film duplicate research findings about conservative Protestant congregations—namely, that "it is common for rhetoric condoning patriarchal family patterns to permeate community life. As a result, noticeable signs of community favor accrue to women involved with these congregations who demonstrate their compliance with the familial ideal." Brenda E. Brasher, *Godly Women: Fundamentalism and Female Power* (New Brunswick, NJ: Rutgers University Press, 1998), 130.
3. Carolyn S. Briggs, *This Dark World: A Memoir of Salvation Found and Lost* (New York: Bloomsbury, 2002). Her subtitle suggests a dramatic connection to and a reversal of famous literary accounts of Christian salvation based upon the fall of Adam and Eve as described in the book of Genesis, such as Milton's narrative poem *Paradise Lost* (1667/1674) and its much briefer successor about the temptation of Christ, *Paradise Regained* (1671).
4. T. J. Jackson Lears, *No Place of Grace: Antimodernism and the Transformation of American Culture, 1880–1920* (New York: Pantheon Books, 1981) discusses the American preoccupation with locating the really real through intense experiences (associated with strong feelings induced by mysticism, exotic foreign cultures, or the medieval past) as a national quest among elites dating from the late nineteenth century and as a reaction against "overcivilization," industrialism, and positivism. Protestant fundamentalists represent the flip side of this movement: anti-intellectuals who look to first-century Christianity to escape the horrors of modernity in their

quest for literal truth in the Bible and to maintain traditional forms of social organization, notably patriarchy.

5. The 1954 novel is referenced in Briggs's memoir. William Golding's allegorical novel portrays the descent into savagery by a group of boys marooned on an island during a nuclear war. Their failure to govern themselves suggests the failure of moral and rational rules to structure society. The title is a biblical translation of Beelzebub, the Lord of the Flies.
6. Briggs, *This Dark World*, 1–4.
7. Briggs, *This Dark World*, 6.
8. Briggs, *This Dark World*, 22.
9. Briggs, *This Dark World*, 21.
10. Briggs, *This Dark World*, 23.
11. Briggs, *This Dark World*, 48–67.
12. Briggs, *This Dark World*, 68.
13. Briggs, *This Dark World*, 96.
14. Briggs, *This Dark World*, 87. Dispensational theology, unique to Protestants who read the Bible literally, emerged in the mid-1800s through the system devised by a self-taught Anglo-Irishman, John Nelson Darby (1800–1882). He interpreted human history as a succession of seven dispensations foreordained by God in which humans always fail the test of faithfulness and anxiously await God's final judgment at the end times. Darby's system, known as premillennial dispensationalism, regards the present era as the penultimate one, waiting for the final crisis to usher in the millennial age of Christ. Dispensationalism became popularized in the United States through the *Scofield Reference Bible* (1909), generated by another self-taught Bible student, Cyrus Scofield (1843–1921).
15. The song by Larry Norman is from 1969, and it was featured in Donald W. Thompson's low-budget dispensational/apocalyptic film about the post-rapture world, *A Thief in the Night*, released in 1972. It became the first of four films about the rapture that were widely circulated among American evangelical Protestants. For more on Thompson as an evangelical filmmaker and his impact upon Protestant youth, see Randall Balmer, *Mine Eyes Have Seen the Glory: Journey into the Evangelical Subculture in America* (New York: Oxford University Press, 2006), chap. 3.
16. Briggs, *This Dark World*, 118.
17. Briggs, *This Dark World*, 159.
18. Briggs, *This Dark World*, 178.
19. Briggs, *This Dark World*, 192. One episode not transferred to the film was Carolyn's conversion of Brianna, a Catholic friend; *This Dark World*, 198, 202–204.
20. Briggs, *This Dark World*, 254.
21. "The Substance of Things Hoped For: Making *Higher Ground*," interview included on the film DVD. On the family's religious changes, see Belinda Luscombe, "That's the Spirit," *Time*, August 29, 2011.
22. Amanda Fitzsimons, "Taissa Farmiga: It's All Relative," *Teen Vogue*, 7 August 2011.
23. "The Substance of Things Hoped For: Making *Higher Ground*," interview included on the film DVD.

24. The literature on the sixties is immense. One helpful place to begin is Robert Ellwood, *The Sixties Spiritual Awakening: American Religious Movements from Modern to Postmodern* (New Brunswick, NJ: Rutgers University Press, 1994).
25. "The Jesus Revolution," *Time*, June 21, 1971. Two recent histories of the mass movement are Larry Eskridge, *God's Forever Family: The Jesus People Movement in America* (New York: Oxford University Press, 2013) and Richard Bustraan, *The Jesus People Movement: A Story of Spiritual Revolution Among the Hippies* (Eugene, OR: Pickwick/ Wipf and Stock, 2014).
26. Rosemary Ruether, "An Unrealized Evolution," *Christianity and Crisis* 43 (1983): 399–404. On American Protestant women, in addition to Brasher, *Godly Women*, see Margret Lamberts Bendroth and Virginia Lieson Brereton, eds., *Women and Twentieth-Century Protestantism* (Urbana: University of Illinois Press, 2002); Pentecostal women are discussed in R. Marie Griffith, *God's Daughters: Evangelical Women and the Power of Submission* (Berkeley: University of California Press, 1997).
27. The phrase comes Ann Hornaday, "The Rise of Christian Movies for the Rest of Us," *Washington Post*, May 12, 2016.
28. Horton Foote's screenplay for *Tender Mercies* originally derived from his young nephew's experiences in the country music business but ultimately morphed into the salvation story of an old country singer and drunkard. Living in Texas, the singer Mac overcomes alcoholism and becomes a Christian, winning the love of Rosa Lee, through no merit of his own. Like *Higher Ground*, the film was favorably reviewed but never gained a mass audience.

Chapter 16

1. "Cosmic Christmas," CosmicChristmas.com, accessed July 2, 2020.
2. Quoted in William Romanowski, *Pop Culture Wars: Religion and the Role of Entertainment in American Life* (Westmont, IL: InterVarsity Press, 1996).
3. Richard Niebuhr, *Christ and Culture* (New York: Harper and Row, 1975).
4. Frank Walsh, *Sin and Censorship: The Catholic Church and the Motion Picture Industry* (New Haven, CT: Yale University Press, 1996).
5. William Romanowski, *Eyes Wide Open: Looking for God in Popular Culture* (Ada, MI: Brazos Press, 2004),12.
6. Romanowski, *Eyes Wide Open*, 13.
7. See, for example, Terry Lindvall, *Sanctuary Cinema: Origins of the Christian Film Industry* (New York: New York University Press, 2007).
8. Peter Biskind, *Easy Riders, Raging Bulls: How the Sex-Drugs-and-Rock 'n' Roll Generation Saved Hollywood* (New York: Simon and Schuster, 1998).
9. Richard G. Howe and Norman L. Geisler, *The Religion of the Force*, 2nd ed. (Arlington, TX: Bastion Books, 2015), 36.
10. Winkie Pratney, *Star Wars, Star Trek, and the 21st Century Christians* (Van Nuys, CA: Bible Voice, 1978), 11–12.

11. John Styll, "The Gospel of Lucas," *Contemporary Christian Magazine*, August 1983, 36.
12. Styll, "The Gospel of Lucas," 36.
13. Stephen Lawhead, "In a Galaxy Far, Far Away," *Contemporary Christian Magazine*, August 1983, 38.
14. Robert Marquand, "Preaching Gospel via Pop Culture," *Christian Science Monitor*, August 22, 1997.
15. Quentin James Schultze, *American Evangelicals and the Mass Media: Perspectives on the Relationship Between American Evangelicals and the Mass Media* (Grand Rapids, MI: Academie/Zondervan, 1992), 26, emphasis in original.
16. Richard Corliss, "The Gospel According to Spider-Man," *Time*, August 9, 2004.
17. Timothy Jones, *Finding God in a Galaxy Far, Far Away* (Sisters, OR: Multnomah, 2005); Bradley Hagan, *Star Wars Redeemed: Your Life-Transforming Journey with Jesus and the Jedi* (Liverpool: Big Mercury Press, 2015); Joshua Hays, *A True Hope: Jedi Perils and the Way of Jesus* (Macon, GA: Smyth and Helwys, 2015).
18. Dick Staub, *Christian Wisdom of the Jedi Masters* (San Francisco: Jossey-Bass, 2005), xix.
19. Staub, *Christian Wisdom of the Jedi Masters*, 47.
20. John C. McDowell, *The Gospel According to Star Wars: Faith, Hope and the Force* (Louisville, KY: Westminister John Knox Press, 2007).
21. Caleb Grimes, *Star Wars Jesus—A Spiritual Commentary on the Reality of the Force* (Emumclaw, WA: Winepress, 2007), 24.
22. Robert Velarde, "May the Force Bewitch You: Evaluating the Star Wars Worldview," Christian Research Institute, May 16, 2017.
23. Tal Brooke, "Creating a New Mystical Religion," *SCP Journal* 39, nos. 3–4 (2016): 4-23 (quote on 7). For further discussion of Campbell's direct influence on Lucas, see the Introduction.
24. Peter Jones, "Star Wars and the Ancient Religion," Ligonier Ministries, December 16, 2015.
25. Joshua Hays, "The Gospel of 'Star Wars,'" *Relevant*, December 17, 2015.
26. "Force for Good? How Star Wars Explores Big Questions About Faith, Power, and Morality," New Spring Church, accessed June 27, 2017.
27. Petey Bingham, "Functional Fulfillment," online video clip, Celebration Church, Vimeo, November 20, 2016.
28. The video has since been taken down from YouTube, but the URL was https://www.youtube.com/watch?v=VaK1FNR9CUI. At least one church attempted more than a movie trailer. Mark Jacobs's documentary film *Audience of One* (2007) follows a San Francisco–based Pentecostal church trying to make a *Star Wars*–inspired movie about the biblical Joseph (Genesis 37–50). The spiritual sci-fi epic, which was never finished, was to be titled *Gravity: The Shadow of Joseph*. The story is a curiosity, but it illustrates one of the most ambitious attempts that evangelicals have made to spread the gospel using Lucas's universe and the latest technology.
29. Mark Noll, "Mark Noll Extended Interview," *Religion and Ethics News Weekly* (PBS), April 4, 2004.

Chapter 17

1. A version of this chapter was originally published in Timothy Beal, *The Book of Revelation: A Biography* (Princeton, NJ: Princeton University Press, 2018).
2. For a fuller discussion of the evangelical dilemma of popularization and preservation versus the rise of Christian pop culture in the 1960s and 1970s, see Timothy Beal, *The Rise and Fall of the Bible: The Unexpected History of an Accidental Book* (New York: Houghton Mifflin Harcourt, 2011), 70–78, 10–18.
3. This historical overview is based primarily on Joel A. Carpenter, *Revive Us Again: The Reawakening of American Fundamentalism* (New York: Oxford University Press, 1997).
4. This history is thoroughly documented in Terry Lindvall, *Sanctuary Cinema: Origins of the Christian Film Industry* (New York: New York University Press, 2007), and Terry Lindvall and Andrew Quicke, *Celluloid Sermons: The Emergence of the Christian Film Industry, 1930–1986* (New York: New York University Press, 2011). My focus here is part of Lindvall and Quicke's second era in Christian independent filmmaking, the 16 mm sound era (40–46).
5. Doughten's estimate in his commentary on the DVD of *A Thief in the Night* was 100 million, but by the time of his death he was estimating 300 million. This higher number has been picked up in most articles and popular news media since.
6. Heather Hendershot, *Shaking the World for Jesus: Media and Conservative Evangelical Culture* (Chicago: University of Chicago Press, 2004), 188.
7. Hal Lindsey's bestselling books included *The Late, Great Planet Earth* (Grand Rapids, MI: Zondervan, 1970); see also his follow-up works, *Satan Is Alive and Well on Planet Earth*, with Carole C. Carlson (Grand Rapids, MI: Zondervan, 1972), and *There's a New World Coming: An In Depth Analysis of the Book of Revelation* (Eugene, OR: Harvest House, 1973), among others. Larry Norman's song "I Wish We'd All Been Ready" first appeared on his album *Upon the Rock* (Capitol, 1969). It was a staple in Christian youth group fellowship meetings and was covered many times by other Christian musicians over the next two decades.
8. E.g., Lindsey, *There's a New World Coming*, 8.
9. Lindvall and Quicke, *Celluloid Sermons*; Hendershot, *Shaking the World for Jesus*.
10. Thus these films adapt wholeheartedly to the familiar Hollywood mythos of the individual (almost always male) protagonist who must survive and overcome seemingly insurmountable obstacles, triumphing over evil not only by faith but also by courage and skill. On this Hollywood myth and the Christian film industry's conflicted relationship to it, see Lindvall, *Sanctuary Cinema*, 24.
11. As Kim Paffenroth points out in *The Gospel According to the Living Dead: George Romero's Vision of Hell on Earth* (Waco: Baylor University Press, 2006), zombies appear to be modeled on the image of the damned in Dante's *Inferno*, where he describes them as "the suffering race of souls who lost the good of intellect" (qtd. on 22) and, as Paffenroth puts it, "reduced just to appetite" (23).

Chapter 18

1. André Bazin, "The Western: or The American Film Par Excellence," in *What Is Cinema?*, ed. and trans. Hugh Gray (Berkeley: University of California Press, 2005), 2:140–148.
2. See, for instance, *Hell's Hinges* (William S. Hart, 1916), and the accompanying notes on the film (Scott Simmon, "Notes on *Hell's Hinges*," National Film Preservation Foundation, accessed January 27, 2021). Simmon notes that the film does not offer "the Western's standard theme of civilization's advance via America's westward progress" but rather anticipates Clint Eastwood's films *High Plains Drifter* (1973) and *Unforgiven* (1992), critical of the West.
3. The term "Manifest Destiny" was coined by John O'Sullivan in 1845. The annexation of Texas showed America's "manifest destiny to overspread and to possess the continent allotted by Providence for the free development of our yearly multiplying millions." John O' Sullivan, "Annexation," *United States Magazine and Democratic Review* 17, no. 1 (July–August1845): 5–10. For details on expansionism, see Robert Jewett and John Shelton Lawrence, *The Myth of the American Superhero* (Grand Rapids, MI: William B. Eerdmans, 2002), 58.
4. Richard Slotkin, *Regeneration Through Violence: The Mythology of the American Frontier, 1600–1860* (Middletown, CT: Wesleyan University Press, 1973), 6.
5. Slotkin, *Regeneration Through Violence*, 5.
6. Ernest Lee Tuveson, *Redeemer Nation: The Idea of America's Millennial Role* (Chicago: University of Chicago Press, 1968).
7. Increase Mather, *A Brief History of the War with the Indians in New England: An Online Electronic Text Edition*, ed. Paul Royster, 9–10, Digital Commons@University of Nebraska, accessed January 27, 2021.
8. The "city on the hill" mythology, Slotkin notes, "was the dream of an orderly, cleanly, symmetrical, Christian city . . . that from the beginning contrasted with the temptations of the Indian village in the tangled depths of the dark woods." See Slotkin, *Regeneration Through Violence*, 38–42. See also John Winthrop, "A Modell of Christian Charity (1630)," in *Settlements to Society 1607–1763: A Documentary History of Colonial America*, ed. Jack P. Greene (New York: McGraw-Hill, 1966), 68.
9. Max Weber, *The Protestant Ethic and the Spirit of Capitalism* (New York: Norton Critical Editions, 2009). Weber is discussed in André Biéler, *Calvin's Economic and Social Thought*, ed. Edward Dommen. trans. James Grieg (Geneva: World Alliance of Reformed Churches, 2006), chapter VI: "Calvinism and Capitalism," 423–436.
10. Scott Simmon also notes that the Western embraces "archaic Puritanism" in his *The Invention of the Western Film: A Cultural History of the Genre's First Half Century* (New York: Cambridge University Press, 2003), 124–128. Simmon contrasts this ethic with a "softer" religious tradition—"deist, Arminian, or Unitarian"—that is more ecumenical and takes a more reverent and sublime view of the wilderness (128–130).

11. Terry Lindvall, "God in the Saddle: Silent Western Films as Protestant Sermons," *Journal for the Academic Study of Religion* 21, no. 3 (2008): 318–344.
12. Kathryn Kalinak, *How the West Was Sung: Music in the Westerns of John Ford* (Berkeley: University of California Press, 2007), 81–82.
13. Kalinak, *How the West Was Sung*, 170–171.
14. Kent Jones, review of *Dead Man*, directed by Jim Jarmusch, *Cineaste* 22, no. 2 (Spring 1996): 45.
15. For an astute discussion of *The Searchers* and political morality, see Robert B. Pippin, *Hollywood Westerns and American Myth: The Importance of Howard Hawks and John Ford for Political Philosophy* (New Haven, CT: Yale University Press, 2010).
16. Kalinak, *How the West Was Sung*, 81–82.
17. David W. Blight, *Race and Reunion: The Civil War in American Memory* (Cambridge, MA: Belknap Press of Harvard University Press, 2001). See especially 211–300 on the twisting of historical memory into "Lost Cause" nostalgia, present in many Westerns but overt and problematic in *The Searchers*.
18. *A Fistful of Dollars* (1964), *For a Few Dollars More* (1965), *The Good, the Bad, and the Ugly* (1966). These movies made Clint Eastwood an international star.
19. See both versions of *3:10 to Yuma* (Delmer Daves, 1957; James Mangold, 2007), which dramatize one farmer's desperation due to drought.
20. Slotkin, *Regeneration Through Violence*, 411.
21. Anthony Mann's two movies in the fifties, *Winchester '73* and *The Man from Laramie*, questioned the premises of earlier Westerns: good man versus evil man, and the land as rightfully belonging to settlers. The films disturb, particularly as they tackle white settlers' prominent role in the tainted proliferation of guns. Yet the plots are confined to surface story worlds rather than laying bare the genre itself.
22. See Owen Wister, *The Virginian* (New York: Macmillan, 1922), a novel dedicated to Theodore Roosevelt that depicted the Wyoming territory during the brutal Johnson County War of 1889–1893, and the film adaptation (Victor Fleming, 1929), starring a young Gary Cooper, assigned a nameless, celibate gunman to rid the country of evil big ranchers, even by lynching.
23. Garry Wills, *John Wayne's America: The Politics of Celebrity* (New York: Simon & Schuster, 1997), 313.

Chapter 19

1. Alvin C. York received the Medal of Honor for his service in World War I, but unlike Doss, York carried a weapon in combat. In the Vietnam War, combat medics Thomas W. Bennett and Joseph G. LaPointe became the second and third conscientious objectors to receive (posthumously) the Medal of Honor.
2. Gibson's *The Passion of the Christ* also opens with a quote from Isaiah: "He was wounded for our transgressions; he was crushed because of our iniquities. By his stripes were we healed" (Isaiah 53:5).

3. Thinking of this (or any) film in this manner is admittedly simplistic and reductionist.
4. The film includes one stereotypical contrast between the Hebrew Bible and the New Testament. When the Army psychologist tells Doss that King David "was a warrior king and much loved by God," Doss replies, "That's the Old Testament! Jesus said, 'A new commandment I give unto you that you love one another.'"
5. See Matthew S. Rindge, "Dead Man Walking (1995)," in *Bible and Cinema: Fifty Key Films*, ed. Adele Reinhartz (New York: Routledge, 2012), 84–49. On the role of the Bible in *Hacksaw Ridge* and *Dead Man Walking*, see Rindge, *Bible and Film: The Basics* (London: Routledge, 2021), 127, 131-34, 138.
6. See the discussion of *Sergeant York* in Clayton R. Koppes and Gregory D. Black, *Hollywood Goes to War: How Politics, Profits and Propaganda Shaped WWII Movies* (Berkeley: University of California Press, 1990), 37–44.
7. It is unclear how Gibson might reconcile this elevation of personal authority with his own personal identify as a traditional Catholic.
8. On the "illusion of documentary" regarding Gibson's *The Passion of the Christ*, see Jack Miles, "The Art of *The Passion*," in *Mel Gibson's Bible: Religion, Popular Culture, and* The Passion of the Christ, ed. Timothy K. Beal and Tod Linafelt (Chicago: University of Chicago Press, 2006), 11.
9. The most attention the film gives in this regard is the curious scene of the Japanese military commander who commits seppuku and then is decapitated. I remain intrigued with the precise function of this scene and its relationship to the film's broader motifs. Is, for example, the act of suicide intended to be seen as a similar kind of honorable act as Doss's commitment to nonviolence and the help he provides to fallen soldiers?
10. See Kent Brintnall, *Ecce Homo: The Male-Body-in-Pain as Redemptive Figure* (Chicago: University of Chicago Press, 2011). For a discussion of the link between masochism and heroic masculinity, see Kent Brintnall and Mark Jordan, "Mel Gibson, Bride of Christ," in *Mel Gibson's Bible: Religion, Popular Culture, and* The Passion of the Christ, ed. Timothy K. Beal and Tod Linafelt (Chicago: University of Chicago Press, 2006), 81–90.
11. In addition to the *Mad Max* (1979, 1981, 1985) and *Lethal Weapon* (1987, 1989, 1992, 1998) series, see also *Payback* (directed by Brian Helgeland, 1999) and *The Patriot* (directed by Roland Emmerich, 2000).
12. See several of the essays in Steven Mintz and Randy Roberts, ed., *Hollywood's America: United States History Through its Films* (St. James, NY: Brandywine Press, 1993).
13. One might ask the same question about Clint Eastwood's film *Gran Torino* (2008).
14. On the pacifist nature of *The Passion of the Christ*, see Miles, "The Art of the Passion," 20. On *The Passion of the Christ* as a war film, see Susan Thistlethwaite, "Mel Makes a War Movie," in *Perspectives on* The Passion of the Christ: *Religious Thinkers and Writers Explore the Issues Raised by the Controversial Movie* (New York: Miramax Books/Hyperion, 2004), 127–145.
15. See Matthew S. Rindge, *Profane Parables: Film and the American Dream* (Waco, TX: Baylor University Press, 2016).

Chapter 20

1. Calvinism: "The developed and systematized teachings of John Calvin (1509–1564), which spread throughout Europe and internationally from the 16th century to the present day. It is also called the Reformed tradition. Calvinism embraces both theological beliefs and a way of life." Donald K. McKim, *Westminster Dictionary of Theological Terms* (Louisville, KY: Westminster John Knox Press, 1996), 36.
2. Schrader majored in theology at Calvin College and considered becoming a Reformed minister. On Schrader's Dutch Reformed background, see *Schrader on Schrader and Other Writings*, rev. ed., ed. Kevin Jackson (London: Faber and Faber, 2004), 1–10, 117, 140. Schrader now describes himself as Episcopalian. See Garry Wills, "Interview," in *Shouts and Whispers: Twenty-One Writers Speak About Their Writing and Their Faith*, ed. Jennifer Holberg (Grand Rapids, MI: William B. Eerdmans, 2006), 113–119.
3. On the film's influences, see Kevin Lincoln, "Let's Talk About the Ending of *First Reformed*," *Vulture*, June 5, 2018.
4. J. P. Telotte, *Voices in the Dark: The Narrative Patterns of Film Noir* (Urbana: University of Illinois Press, 1989), 118.
5. George Kouvaros, *Paul Schrader* (Chicago: University of Illinois Press, 2008), 122.
6. Last clause paraphrased from Dana Polan, *Power and Paranoia: History, Narrative, and the American Cinema 1940–1950* (New York: Columbia University Press, 1986), 243.
7. The original title of the film was to be *Pilgrim*, and twice in the narrative a character refers to Jake as "pilgrim." Schrader specifies this allusion in *Schrader on Schrader and Other Writings*, 153–156.
8. The five tenets are total depravity, unconditional election, limited atonement, irresistible grace, and perseverance of the saints. These tenets were adopted by the largely Dutch delegates at the Synod of Dordrecht in 1618. Predestination (in the Reformed tradition): "God's eternal decree by which all creatures are foreordained to eternal life or death" (McKim, *Westminster Dictionary of Theological Terms*, 217).
9. Paul Schrader, "Notes on Film Noir," *Film Comment*, Spring 1972, 8–13.
10. Paul Schrader, *Transcendental Style in Film: Ozu, Bresson, Dreyer* (Berkeley: University of California Press, 1972). Schrader describes his reasons for writing the book and references "the sensus divinitatis" in *Schrader on Schrader and Other Writings*, 27–29. Elsewhere Schrader states that he does not make transcendental films (Kouvaros, *Paul Schrader*, 14).
11. Schrader has identified *First Reformed* as the only one of his films that he has crafted in the "transcendental style." The ending, which can be interpreted as a supernatural miracle or an ecstatic vision, is both a disruption and a fulfillment of what has come before. On *First Reformed*'s ending and the film's relationship to the rest of his work, see Lincoln, "Let's Talk About the Ending of *First Reformed*"; Alissa Wilkinson, "Paul Schrader on *First Reformed*: 'This Is a Troubling Film About a Troubled Person,'" *Vox*, June 18, 2018.
12. *First Reformed*'s broken-spirited Calvinist plots to detonate his church in radical protest of its quiescence; *Hardcore*'s Calvinist leaves a closed church community that he

reveres to confront an outside world that he contemns for its fallenness. In the more recent film, humanity is ecologically and spiritually polluting the world while the modern megachurch, with its "Christ as culture" ideology, simply idles. *Hardcore* is much less concerned with the status of the church today than with the psychological vagaries of the righteous personality.

13. Victor Sage, *Horror Fiction and the Protestant Tradition* (New York: St. Martin's Press, 1988), 75.
14. Sage, *Horror Fiction and the Protestant Tradition*, 81.
15. Polan, *Power and Paranoia*, 242.
16. For an example of this interpretative approach to the femme fatale, see Frank Krutnik, *In a Lonely Street: Film Noir, Genre, Masculinity*. (New York: Routledge, 1991), 75–86.

Chapter 21

1. C. S. Lewis, *The Great Divorce* (New York: Touchstone, 1996), 16.
2. C. S. Lewis, *The Lion, the Witch and the Wardrobe* (New York: Harper Trophy, 1994), 91.
3. C. S. Lewis, *The Collected Letters of C. S. Lewis*, vol. 2, ed. Walter Hooper (New York: HarperSanFrancisco, 2004), 910.
4. Lewis, *Collected Letters*, 2:242.
5. Lewis, *Collected Letters*, 2:884.
6. C. S. Lewis, *Mere Christianity* (New York: HarperSanFrancisco, 2001), 78–79.
7. C. S. Lewis, "On Stories," *On Stories and Other Essays on Literature*, ed. Walter Hooper (New York: Harvest, 1982), 5.
8. C. S. Lewis, *The Collected Letters of C. S. Lewis*, vol. 3, ed. Walter Hooper (New York: HarperSanFrancisco, 2007), 491.
9. Lewis, *Collected Letters*, 3:492.
10. Lewis, *Collected Letters*, 3:1111.
11. C. S. Lewis, *The Voyage of the Dawn Treader* (New York: Harper Trophy, 1994), 9.
12. Lewis, *The Lion*, 79.
13. Lewis, *Dawn Treader*, 247.
14. C. S. Lewis, "Sometimes Fairy Stories May Say Best What's to Be Said," in *On Stories and Other Essays on Literature*, ed. Walter Hooper (New York: Harvest, 1982), 47.
15. C. S. Lewis, *Letters to Children*, ed. Lyle Dorsett and Marjorie Lamp Mead (New York: Touchstone, 1995), 32.
16. Lewis, *Mere Christianity*, 109–110.
17. Lewis, *Mere Christianity*, 110.
18. Paul Ford, *Companion to Narnia* (New York: HarperSanFrancisco, 2005), 324–325.
19. C. S. Lewis, *The Problem of Pain* (New York: Touchstone, 1996), 83.
20. Lewis, *Dawn Treader*, 109.
21. Lewis, *Problem of Pain*, 94.
22. Lewis, *Mere Christianity*, 202.
23. Lewis, *The Lion*, 157.

24. Lewis, *The Lion*, 158.
25. Lewis, *The Lion*, 158.
26. *The Book of Common Prayer* (New York: Church Publishing, 2016), 219.
27. C. S. Lewis, "On Three Ways of Writing for Children," in *On Stories and Other Essays on Literature*, ed. Walter Hooper (New York: Harvest, 1982), 39.
28. J. R. R. Tolkien, *The Letters of J. R. R. Tolkien*, ed. Humphrey Carpenter (New York: Houghton Mifflin, 2000), 24.
29. Lewis, "Sometimes," 46–47.
30. Lewis, "On Stories," 16.

Index

For the benefit of digital users, indexed terms that span two pages (e.g., 52–53) may, on occasion, appear on only one of those pages

16 mm film, 72, 73, 74, 77
35 mm film, 71–72, 73
21 Grams (film), 83–84
1960s cultural transformations, 18–19, 33–34, 52, 117, 137–38, 262–63, 268, 281–82. *See also* civil rights movement

Abbott, W. C., 113–14
Abernathy, Ralph, 225–26, 228, 229, 234–35
abortion issues, 203–4, 212, 256
Academy Awards. *See* awards for achievement
Adair, Peter, 211
Adams, Marilyn McCord, 199
Adam's Apples (film), 38
adaptations
  independent Protestant Films, 78, 79, 80
  Luther biopics, 105
  television adaptations, 337
  Babette's Feast, 167–76
  Chronicles of Narnia, 335–43
  Higher Ground, 253–64
  Left Behind movies, 287
  The Scarlett Letter, 187–90
advertising, 58–59, 268
Aerosmith, 281–82
aesthetics, 41–48
Africa, 10, 18–19, 76, 208–9
African Americans, 13, 17, 20, 34, 35, 51
  aesthetic crisis, beautiful Black people, 248
  call-and-response tradition, 227
  female stereotypes, 248–49
  independent Protestant films, 71, 80–81
  mountain motif, 240
  political capacity building, 224
  racial stereotyping, 20
  slavery, 172, 223–24, 240, 241, 295
  social movements of the 60s, 262–63
  white supremacy, 20, 208, 209–10, 213, 231
  "whites only"/Jim Crow segregation, 208–9, 221–23, 227–28
  Selma, 221–36
  Why Did I Get Married?, 239–50
African American churches, 34–35
  African Methodist Episcopal Church, 223–24
  African Methodist Episcopal Zion Church, 223–24
  Baptist churches, 223–24
  "Bluestone" Church, 223–24
  Church of God in Christ (COGIC), 224
  diversity within congregations, 203–4, 208–9, 211, 212, 213–14
  independence from white control and leadership, 223–24
  political capacity building, 224
  relationship with Christianity, 223
Ahlsen, Leopold, 100
Alambrista! (film), 33–34, 211
alcoholism/drunkenness, 87, 88–89, 206, 208, 255, 321
Alfred the Great (film), 117
allegory, 20–21, 46, 50–51
  defined, 181
  Protestant skepticism toward, 50–51, 179–90
  The Pilgrim's Progress, 261
  The Scarlet Letter, 179–90
  Star Wars, 270, 271
  See also symbolism
Allegory: The Theory of a Symbolic Mode (Fletcher), 181
Allen, Richard, 223–24
Allen, Woody, 142–43
"alternative" religious cults, 137–38
Amano, Yutaka, 269–70
AME (African Methodist Episcopal) Church, 223–24
American Film Theatre, 102
American Lutheran Film Associates, 101
American Mary (film), 289
Amish, 313–14
Anabaptists, 10–11, 15, 98
Anderson, Paul Thomas, 210
Andrews, George Reid, 98
Angel Baby (film), 51

Anglicanism/Church of England, 20–21, 37–38, 53, 109–11, 112, 130–31, 133, 335–37
Anne of the Thousand Days (film), 37–38
annihilationism, 208
Anschutz, Philip, 53, 78
antagonist (devil/evil/opponent) archetypal character, 8–9
Antichrist, 271, 288
antiheros, 27, 269
Antonioni, Michelangelo, 183
Antwone Fisher (film), 35
Apocalypse (film), 77
Apocalypse Now (film), 204–5, 316–17
apocalypticism/end of the world, 53, 77, 204–5, 255–56, 262–63, 300, 315–17
  end-times novels, 78
  horror films, 281–91
Apocalypto (film), 315–16
Apostasy (film), 41–42
The Apostle (film), 7–8, 33–34, 44–46, 91–92, 203–18, 224, 263–64
Apostolic Faith newspaper, 208–9
archetypes in films, 8–10
Areopagitica (Milton), 20–21
Arguinzoni, Sonny, 18–19
Aristarco, Guido, 164
Aristotle, 8–9
Armano, 270
Arminian Protestants, 13–14
Arminius, Jacob, 13
Aronofsky, Darren, 1–2
ARRAY, 36
art cinema
  Babette's Feast, 167–76
  The Communicants, 141, 142, 143–45, 150
  Ordet, 155–64
  The Scarlet Letter, 179–90
  The Seventh Seal, 141, 144–45
  Through a Glass Darkly, 141, 142, 143, 145, 149
Asia, evangelicals in, 76, 208–9
Assemblies of God, 17, 208–9
atheists, 7, 41–42, 193
atonement/repentence, 12, 13, 22, 85, 93, 183, 185
Audran, Stéphane, 166*f*
auteur/auteurism, 41, 50–51, 52, 73, 74, 127–28, 193
authenticity, 91, 97–98, 156, 205, 206–7, 215, 239, 254
autobiography, 253–64
Avatar (film), 6, 7, 9–10
awards for achievement, 37–38, 41, 143, 167, 209–10, 211, 217, 233–34, 309
awe and wonder, 45, 78, 159, 197–98, 199–200, 259, 263–64
Axel, Gabriel, 37, 167–76
Ayer, David, 309–10
Azusa Street Revival, 208–9, 215, 224

Babette's Feast (film), 37, 38, 45, 46, 167–76
Babettes Gestebud (Dinesen), 167
The Bacchae (film), 151
Bach, Johann Sebastian, 37, 45, 149, 150
Bailey, Julius H., 221–36
Baker, Ella, 222–23, 228
Baldung, Hans, 99
Baldwin, James, 224, 229–30, 241
Balmer, Randall, 285
Bancroft, Richard, 129–30
Bang, Herman, 156
banned films. *See* censorship
baptism, 12, 174–75, 210, 257
baptism in the Holy Spirit, 17, 208, 212
Baptista, Carlos, 73, 74, 287–88, 290
Baptists, 12–13, 22–23, 33–34, 36, 79–80, 89, 90, 209, 222, 223–24, 227, 229
Barabbas (film), 1–2
Barton, Bruce, 98
Basile, Frères, 98
Bass, Martha, 233–34
Bassett, Ronald, 131
Bavarian Lutheran Church, 98
Bazin, André, 293–305
Beal, Timothy, 281–91
Beasley, John, 205, 216*f*
Becket (film), 117
Ben-Hur (film), 32, 36–37, 45–46
Bennett, Dennis, 17–18
Beresford, Bruce, 91–92
Berger, Senta, 183, 188, 189*f*
Bergman, Ingmar, 38, 39–40, 45–46, 141–52, 183, 187, 321
Bergman on Bergman (Bjorkman), 142
Bevel, James, 225–26, 233–35
Beyond Good and Evil (Nietzsche), 283
Beza, Theodore, 12–13
Bible, 10, 12, 14
  allegorical exegesis, Catholic interpretations, 179–90
  assumed biblical literacy, 271–72
  as central source of authority, 226–27
  clutter of language, 145–51
  personal interpretation of biblical text, 313–15
  sola scriptura, 12, 176, 179, 310–13

Bible belt. *See* South/southern culture
Bible epics, 23, 50–51
  Ben-Hur, 32, 36–37, 45–46
  King of Kings, 2–3, 22–23, 27, 98
  The Passion of the Christ, 32, 34, 45–46, 53, 79, 310, 311–12, 315–16, 317
  The Ten Commandments, 22
The Bible (film), 36–37
Bible schools and study groups, 17, 208, 257, 263–64
"Big Eight" studios, 61
The Big Trail (film), 52
Bigelow, Kathryn, 316–17
Billy Graham Evangelistic Association, 75
Bingham, Ryan, 86
biopics (filmic biographies), 3–4, 26–27, 37–38
  John Lowes biopic, 131–33
  Martin Luther biopics, 97–106
  Neil Howey biopic, 134–35, 136–37
  Oliver Cromwell biopics, 109–25
The Birth of a Nation (film), 20
Biskind, Peter, 269
Bismarck, Otto von, 99–100
Bjerre, Paul, 168
Black Americans. *See* African Americans
Black Narcissus (film), 64–65
BlacKkKlansman (film), 20
Blade af Satans Bog [Leaves from Satan's Book] (film), 156
blasphemy, 127–38
Blixen, Karen, 167
The Blob (film), 282–83
blood revenge, 133, 304
blood sacrifice, horror films, 127–38
bloodthirst, zombies, 285, 288–91
Bodenstein, Andreas, 98
Bolt, Robert, 37–38
Bonnie Brae Street prayer group, 240
The Book of Common Prayer, 342
The Book of Eli (film), 35
Borat (film), 210
born-again experience, 7, 10, 15, 16, 17–19, 35–36
  U.S. demographics, 32
  in *The Apostle*, 207–9
Boulting, John, 38
Boulting, Roy, 38
Boyle, Peter, 322–23
Bradford, William, 294–95
Branch, Taylor, 226–27
Branch Davidians, 262–63
Brandes, Georg, 155–56
Braveheart (film), 315–16
Breaking the Waves (film), 38
Breen, Joseph, 62, 64
Breen Office, 26
Bresson, Robert, 41, 321
Bridges, Jeff, 82*f*–90*f*, 86
Brief History of the Warr with the Indians in New-England
  Mather, 294–95
Briggs, Carolyn S., 254–55
Britain
  British Israelism, 208
  censorship, British *versus* American, 58, 60, 61, 64–65, 66–67
  See also England; Scotland
British Board of Film Censors, 60, 66–67
Brooke, Tal, 275
Brooks, Richard, 209–10
Brown, Devin, 335–43
Brown v. Board of Education Supreme Court decision, 221–23
Bryan, William Jennings, 19–20
Bucer, Martin, 179–80
Buddhism, 7, 270–71, 275
Bunyan, John, 180–81, 261, 323–24
Burnett, Mark, 36–37
Burnett, Roma Downey, 36–37
Burnett, T Bone, 86
Burning Cane (film), 36
The Burning Hell (film), 283

Caesar and Cleopatra (film), 64
Cage, Nicolas, 287, 288
Calvin, John, 10–11, 13, 97–98, 110, 179–80
Calvinism, 12–13, 37, 324–25
  five classic tenets, 13, 324–25
  Hardcore, 321–33
Cambridge University, 112
camera angles/camera movement, 45–46, 214–15, 286, 299–300
  close-ups, 103, 104*f*, 156–58, 184, 188, 214–15, 258–59, 329–32
  plain camera style, 187–88
  Hard Core, 325–26, 327–29, 328*f*, 330–32
  The Scarlet Letter, 183–84, 187–88
Cameron, Kirk, 79–80
camp meetings, 208–9
Campbell, Joseph, 8–9, 10, 114–15, 275
Campolo, Tony, 16
Campus Crusade for Christ, 76, 281–82
Cape Fear (film), 7–8, 210, 310
capital punishment, 14, 311–12
Carlyle, Thomas, 113–14
Carmichael, Ralph, 284–85

Carnival of Souls (film), 285
Carrière, Mathieu, 102–3
Carroll, Lewis, 159
Carter, Jimmy, 32
Cash, June Carter, 205
Catholic Legion of Decency, 1–2, 61–62, 63–64
Catholicism, 12, 44–45
as largest Christian tradition, 7
allegorical exegesis in biblical interpretation, 179–90
censorship and restriction of films, 62–64
cinematics, Protestant *vs.* Catholic, 44–45
faith-based film market, 79
heretics, Catholics as, 133, 169–70
idolotry, 43, 100–1, 130–31
in Ireland. *See* Ireland/Irish Catholics
miracles, 159
Protestant Reformation propaganda films, 127–38
response in film, Church of England, 109–10
response in film, Lutheran, 98, 99–101, 102–3, 104
response in film, Puritan, 110–11
sola gratia, 176
and witchcraft, 130–31
cellphone technology, 77
censorship, 1–2, 57–68, 158
British *versus* American, 58, 60, 61, 64–65, 66–67
Catholic censorship, 60, 66
film classification system, 66
U.S. Supreme Court decision, 65
A Certain Nobleman (film), 73
cessationist theory, 16, 208
Chariots of Fire (film), 37
Charismatics, 17–19
Charismatic Catholics, 17–18, 208–9, 259
percentage of practitioners within world religions, 7
Charles I, 109–10, 112–13, 119, 130, 131–32
Charles II, 113
Charles O. Baptista's Scriptures Visualized Institute, 282
Cheatin' Hearts (film), 239
The Child of Bethlehem (film), 73
children
pregnancy and childbirth, 159–60, 255–56
suffering of, 194
Hardcore, 321–33
See also young people
the chosen/the elect, 13, 74, 253, 326–32
barriers between believers and outsiders, 254
Manifest Destiny, "redeemer nation", 293, 294, 295–96, 300
Christ. *See* Jesus Christ
"Christ against culture", 268–69, 277
Christ and Culture (Niebuhr), 268
Christ Fellowship megachurch, 276
Christensen, Emil Hass, 160
Christenson, Larry, 17–18
Christian films, defined, 71
The Christian Herald (magazine), 73
Christian Reformed Church, 321
Christian Science, 204–5
Christian Science Monitor, 271–72
Christian Wisdom of the Jedi Masters (Staub), 273
Christian Woodstock, 281–82
Christianity and the Social Crisis (Rauschenbush), 226–27
Christmas, 267, 277, 322–23
Christology, 22
The Chronicles of Narnia: The Lion, The Witch, and the Wardrobe, 7, 32, 46, 71, 78, 335–43
church films, 23, 71–81
history, 71–73
rental fees, 77
theaters, churches as, 71–72, 73
Church of England/Anglicanism, 20–21, 37–38, 53, 109–11, 112, 130–31, 133, 335–37
Church of God in Christ (COGIC), 224
Church of the Brethren, 313–14
Churchill, Winston, 113–14
Cilento, Diane, 134
Cinderella Man (film), 83–84
"Cinema for Christ" in Britain, 64–65
cinematic adaptations. *See* adaptations
Cinematograph Act, 60
civil rights movement, 31–32, 33–34, 35–36, 51, 105, 240
"Bloody Sunday", 223
Brown v. Board of Education Supreme Court decision, 221–23
Civil Rights Act of 1964, 227–28
Jim Crow segregation, 208–9, 221–23, 227–28
role of churches, 224
white violence during, 213, 230
Selma, 221–36
Civil War, 298, 299–300, 302
Clark, Jim, 225–26, 228–29
class issues, 7, 17, 20, 39, 51, 99, 105, 112, 113–14, 262–63
Evangelicals, shift to middle and higher classes, 32–34

"white trash", 210
The Apostle, 204, 206–7, 208–9, 210, 212–13
classical music, 149
Clavell, James, 37–38
Clay, Thomas, 41–42
Clementine (film), 296
close-ups, 103, 104*f*, 156–58, 184, 188, 214–15, 258–59, 329–32
Cloud Ten Pictures, 77, 78, 287, 288–90
Cobb, Thomas, 86
Coen brothers, 297
Cohen, Ed, 212
Cohen, Mickey, 75
Cohen, Sacha Baron, 210
Cold War, 36–37, 121, 290
propaganda, 101
Vietnam, 41, 52–53, 269, 290
Cole, William Atlas, 205
collective unconscious, 275
colonialism, 121
The Color Purple (film), 248
Colored Methodist Episcopal Church, 223–24
Comcast, 68
comedies/comic elements, 26–27, 29–30, 34–35, 51, 80, 156, 248, 337
Common (rapper), 233–34
The Communicants [U.S. title *Winter Light*] (film), 38, 39–40, 141, 142, 143–45, 144*f*, 150
Companion to Narnia (Ford), 340
Cone, Stephen, 41–42
confession, 10–11, 13–14, 136–37, 150, 189–90, 206
The Confirmation (film), 263–64
conflict, central to Protestant spiritual narratives, 261
Congregationalism, 98, 295
Congress for Racial Equality (CORE), 235
Connelly, Marc, 239
Connor, "Bull", 228–29
conscience *versus* church authority, obedience to, 64
conscientious objection, 307–18
conservative evangelicalism, 253–64
conservative politics, rise of the religious right, 259
consolidation of media outlets, 1–2, 67–68
Contemporary Christian Magazine, 270–71
Contemporary Christian music (CCM), 268–69
Convicts (film), 204–5
Cooper, Annie Lee, 228–29, 235
Cooper, Gary, 309
Cooper, Scott, 86, 91–92
Coppola, Francis Ford, 310, 316–17
Corliss, Richard, 272
cosmos/questions of existence, 198–99
imagery, 181–84, 274*f*
Star Wars, 270, 274*f*
Cotton, John, 294–95
counterculture, 32, 41, 122, 258–59, 262
country music, 89, 90–91
Courageous (film), 32, 79–80
Covington, Sarah, 42–43
Cox, Harvey, 217, 218
Coyle, John, 73
Cramner, Thomas, 110–11
Crash (film), 83–84
Crazy Heart (film), 83–93
Cries and Whispers (film), 39–40, 144, 149, 150
Crisell, Andrew, 58–59
Cromwell, Oliver, 109–25, 131–32
Cromwell, Richard, 113
Cromwell (film), 7–8, 37–38, 44–46, 109–25
Cronenberg, David, 289, 316–17
The Cross and The Switchblade (film), 33–34
Cru (Campus Crusade for Christ), 76
The Crucible (play), 157–58
Crucifixion/crucifix, 22, 23, 90, 170–71, 241, 316
Cruz, Nicky, 33–34
Cry of the Banshee (film), 37–38
cult, art as, 141–42
cults, 137–38, 262–63
Cummings, Brian, 179–80

The Da Vinci Code (film), 6
Daddy's Little Girls (film), 34–35, 248
"daemonic agency", 181–82
Dalton, Timothy, 109
Danish cinema
Babette's Feast, 167–76
The Communicants, 141, 142, 143–45, 150
Ordet, 155–64
The Seventh Seal, 141, 144–45
Through a Glass Darkly, 141, 142, 143, 145, 149
Dannelly, Brian, 41–42
Danno, Paul, 210
The Dark Knight (film), 83–84
Dass, Petter, 170–71
Davies, Rupert, 131–32
Davies, Terence, 41–42
Day-Lewis, Daniel, 210
Day of Wrath (film), 39, 157–58, 159–60
de Gastyne, Marco, 156–57

De Niro, Robert, 210
De Sica, Vittorio, 41
Deacon, Brian, 70*f*
Dead Hooker in a Trunk (film), 289
Dead Man (film), 297
Dead Man Walking (film), 311–12
"death of God" movement, 41
death penalty, 14, 311–12
Decency, League of, 73
Delannoy, Jean, 38
Delilah, Sister, 205
DeMille, Cecil B., 22, 36–37, 98
Democratic Party, 209, 212–13, 217
the demonic. *See* the Devil and diabolic possession
Dench, Judi, 102
Der arme Mann Luther [Poor Man Luther] (film), 100
Der Scharlachrote Buchstabe (film), 180–81, 187–90
Derrida, Jacques, 179
d'Etaples, Jacques, 169–70
determinism, 301–3
the Devil/diabolic possession, 208, 286–87, 288
  antagonist, archetypal character, 8–9, 271
  "daemonic agency", 181, 182–83
  exorcism, 130–31
  hell, 283, 335
  See also witches/witchcraft
Diary of a Mad Black Woman (film), 80
Diary of a Mad Housewife (film), 239–40
Diet of Worms, 100, 102*f*
Dinesen, Isak, 167, 171–72
The Dirty Dozen (film), 210
Dirty Harry (film), 302
Disney, 78–79, 274, 335
dispensational theology, 208, 255–56. *See also* apocalypticism/end of the world
A Distant Thunder (film), 283
Dobson, James, 16, 77
documentaries, 32, 41–42, 61
  newsreel style, 282
  quasi-documentaries, 315–16
  semi-documentaries, 205–6, 211
Döhring, Bruno, 100–1
domestic abuse, 241–42, 243–44, 245–46, 248, 249
Domińczyk, Dagmara, 252*f*
Domingo, Colman, 229
Don Giovanni (opera), 168, 170–71
Dorsey, Thomas A., 233–34
Doss, Desmond T., 307–18
Doughten, Russell S. Jr., 282–84
Douglas, Jane, 337
Dowsing, William, 130–31
dress codes in Protestant culture, 263–64
Dreyer, Carl, 39, 155–64, 321
Drouzy, Maurice, 155–56
drug abuse, 256
Du skal ære din Hustru [Master of the House] (film), 156
DuBois, W. E. B., 221
Duke Frederick III, 12
Dunkirk (film), 309–10
Dunne, Michael, 187–88
Dutch Reformed churches, 12–13, 321, 322–23, 324–25
Duvall, Robert, 33–34, 91–92, 203–18
DuVernay, Ava, 35–36, 221, 230–31
DVD technology, 77

Eastern religions, 7, 51, 274–76
Eastman, George, 72
Eastwood, Clint, 52, 293–305, 315
Eat, Pray, Love (film), 253, 260–61
Ebert, Roger, 114–15, 117, 212
ecumenism, 22, 174, 275–76
Edenic motif, 257
Edison Trust, 19–20
education/evangelism *versus* entertainment in film, 73–74, 75, 78, 97–98, 267, 276
  preaching as objective, 22, 71, 72, 73, 276
  Sermons from Science series, 74
  universal language of movies, 22
Edward VI, 110–11
Edwards, Ethan, 301
Eggers, Robert, 41–42
eighth-day creationism, 208
Eisenhower, Dwight D., 222–23
Elementa rhetorices (Melanchthon), 179–80
Eleutherius, 99
Elizabeth I, 110–11
Ellison, Ralph, 211
Elmer Gantry (film), 38, 51, 209–10, 217
The Emigrants (film), 40–41
end-times. *See* apocalypticism/end of the world
Engels, Friedrich, 113–14
England
  birth of Empire, 113, 125
  Church of England/Anglicanism, 20–21, 37–38, 53, 109–11, 112, 130–31, 133, 335–37
  Cromwell, Oliver, 109–25, 131–32
  English literature and rise of allegory, 180
  Reformation and Civil War, 41–42, 109–25
Episcopalian Protestantism, 134, 136–37

Episode I: A New Hope (film), 270, 273
Episode III: Revenge of the Sith (film), 273
Episode VII: The Force Awakens (film), 267, 274, 276
Erickson, Glenn, 114–15, 117
Espinosa, Gastón, 109–25, 203–18
Essek, Rudolf, 98–99
Eucharist, 134, 136
  Catholic Eucharist, 134–35
  reconciling conflicts of spirit and flesh, 174–75
  as sacrifice, 134–35
  Babette's Feast, 167–76
  The Communicants, 142
Euripides, 151
Evangelicalism, 15–16, 32–34, 50–51
  "browning" of evangelicalism, 33–34
  independent films, targeting evangelical Christians, 79–80
  and Pentecostalism, 207–8, 212–13
  percentage of practitioners within world religions, 7
  youth culture of 60s and 70s, 281
  Hardcore, 253–64
  Star Wars, 267–77
evil, 51, 193–201
  antagonist, archetypal character, 8–9
  clarity of demarcations between good and evil, 269
  mystery of, 193–94
  personal subjective restoration, 199–200
  soul's struggle, 321–22
  See also theodicy
Ewald, Carl, 155–56
Ewing, Heidi, 211
Exodus (film), 1–2
exorcism, 130–31
expressionism, 325–26
"extreme religion", 254
Eyes on the Prize series, 35–36

Facing the Giants (film), 32, 79–80
Fairfax, Thomas, 116
The Fairie Queene (poem), 180
fairy tale genre, 342–43
faith and doubt, 50, 51, 53, 141, 142–43
  as classic Protestant theme, 53
  contrast of faith with aesthetic, 168
  cultural, historical, and personal matter, belief as, 164
  sola fide, 12, 176, 179
faith-based films, 1–2
  box office profits, 77–80
  history, 71–77
faith healing, 207–8, 212, 213, 259, 308
Falconetti, Renée, 39, 156–57
Falwell, Jerry, 209
The Family That Preys (film), 34–35
Fanny Lye Deliver'd (film), 41–42
fantasy films, 53, 335–43
Farmiga, Taissa, 256–57
Farmiga, Vera, 252*f*, 253–54, 256–57, 263–64
Fawcett, Farrah, 206
Federal Communications Commission, 268
Federal Council of Churches, 65–66, 98
Federspiel, Birgitte, 159–60
Fehrensbach, Heide, 104–5
Fellini, Federico, 183
feminism, social movement of the 60s, 262–63
Ferguson, Priscilla Parkhurst, 167
fertility rite, 134
A Field in England (film), 41–42
Fiennes, Joseph, 102–3, 105–6
The Fighting Temptations (film), 41–42
Film as Religion (Lyden), 48–49
film noir, 45, 52–53, 325–27
  history of, 322
  versus transcendental style, 325–26
  Hardcore, 321–33
Finding God in a Galaxy Far, Far Away (Jones), 273
Finney, Charles G., 268
Fire from Heaven (Cox), 217
Fireproof (film), 32, 79–80
First Reformed (film), 263–64, 321
Firth, Jonathan, 102–3
Fisher, Becky, 211
The Fisher King (film), 85
The Fishmarket Combo, 283–84, 285–86
"Fistful" trilogy of spaghetti Westerns (film), 297
Flaherty, Micheal, 78
flashbacks, 169–70, 286
Fleischer, Richard, 1–2
flesh and spirit dichotomy, 170, 172, 173, 174–76
Fletch (film), 210
Fletcher, Angus, 180–81, 183
Flywheel (film), 79–80
Focus on the Family (film), 77
the Force, metaphysical concept, 269, 270–71, 273
Ford, John, 52, 295, 296–97, 302
Ford, Paul, 340
forgiveness and reconciliation, 172–73, 174, 175, 239–40
  "radical forgiveness", 52
  Unforgiven, radical forgiveness in, 293–305

Forman, James, 225–26, 231
Fort Apache (film), 296, 297
Fox Corporation, 78–79
Fox Faith, 32, 79
Francke, August Hermann, 169
freedom of religion, 4–5, 112, 113, 123–24
freedom of speech, 57, 262–63
French Catholics, 117, 121, 123–24
French cuisine, 172–74, 176
Friedkin, William, 41
Friedrich, James, 73–74
fundamentalism, 16, 51
  distinct from Pentecostalism, 204, 207–8, 212–13
  militant fundamentalism, 211
Fury (film), 309–10

Gandhi, Mahatma, 222, 226–27
Ganz, Bruno, 102–3
Garfield, Andrew, 306*f*, 307
Gateway Films, 75
gaze, 137–38, 185, 188, 273, 288
  assaultive gaze, 326–32
  self-examination, 326–27
Geisler, Norman, 269–70
gender issues, 51
  Black women's experiences, 235, 242–43, 244
  clergy, women as, 16, 39, 212, 217
  feminist movement of the 60s, 262–63
  femme fatale character, 329–30
  homosexuality, 241, 256
  masculine authority and patriarchy, 116–17, 253–64
  self-culture and gender assertion, 253
  sexual violence, 133
  sisterhood and female friendship, 259–62
  transformation of women, 239–50
  womanist theology, 249–50
  The Apostle, 208–9, 212–13, 215
  Higher Ground, 253–64
  The Scarlet Letter, 182–83, 187–89
  Why Did I Get Married?, 239–50
Gener8Xion Entertainment, 78
Genesis Productions, 76
Genevois, Simone, 156–57
genre
  explained, 51, 53
  fairy tales, 342–43
  fantasy, 335–43
  film noir, 321–33
  horror films, 281–91
  spiritual autobiographies, 253–64
  war films, 307–18
  Westerns, 293–305
Gerber, Hermann, 105–6
Germany
  German Protestant League, 100–1
  Nazi era, 38, 41–42, 101, 104–5, 158
  Weimar era, 37–38, 99–100, 104–5
Gertrud (film), 156
Ghosts of Mississippi (film), 213, 234–35
Gibson, Mel, 34, 79, 307–18
Gide, André, 38
Gilbert, Elizabeth, 260–61
Gish, Lillian, 183–84, 186*f*
Gnosticism, 275
Go Tell It on the Mountain (Baldwin), 241
God
  cosmic drama of God's salvation in Jesus Christ, 270
  as personal being and transcendent Creator, 269–70
The Godfather (film), 204–5, 310
The Godfather II (film), 310
God's Not Dead (film), 32, 80
Godspell (musical), 33–34, 259
Goggins, Walter, 215
Goldberg, Whoopi, 248
The Good, the Bad, and the Ugly (film), 302
Good News for Modern Man (book), 76
The Good Samaritan (film), 73
Good Will Hunting (film), 83–84, 85
Goodwin, Hannibal, 72
The Gospel According to Star Wars: Faith, Hope and the Force (McDowell), 273
gospel music, 45, 233–34
Gospels, 159, 240, 310. *See also* Bible
grace
  compassion, 239–40
  earthly means, 174–75
  operating through broken vessels, 215
  sola gratia, 12, 176, 179
  Babette's Feast, 167–76
Grady, Rachel, 211
Graham, Billy, 16, 75, 76*f*, 212, 259, 281
Gran Torino (film), 83–84
Granat, Cary, 78
Grant, Jacquelyn, 246
Great Commission, 76, 241
The Great Divorce (film), 335
The Great Santini (film), 204–5
The Great Train Robbery (film), 293–94
Green, Guy, 102
The Green Mile (film), 83–84
The Green Pastures (film), 239

Grenier, Carl, 212
Gresham, Douglas, 78
grief
 within theodicy, 193, 195
 The Tree of Life, 193–201
Grierson, John, 61
Griffith, D. W., 20, 22, 156
Griffiths, Rachel, 307–8
The Grim Reaper (film), 283
Grime, Caleb, 273
Groundhog Day (film), 85
growth, central to Protestant spiritual narratives, 261
Grudem, Wayne, 16
Grundtvig, N. F. S., 155–56, 158
Guinness, Alec, 109
Gyllenhaal, Maggie, 87

Hacksaw Ridge (film), 44–45, 307–18
Haggard, H. Rider, 336
Hallelujah (film), 239
Hamel, Lambert, 98–99
Haneke, Michael, 37, 41–42, 45–46
"happy endings", 64–65, 85–86, 87, 198–99, 249–50, 296–97
Hardcore (film), 44–45, 321–33
Hardy, Robin, 37–38, 134
Harper, Tess, 91–92
Harpo Studios, 35–36
Harris, Richard, 109, 117, 120
Hart, William S., 52
Hawke, Ethan, 321
Hawkey, Renn, 258–59
Hawks, Howard, 297, 309
Hawthorne, Nathaniel, 180–81
Hays, Will, 57, 62, 63*f*
healing, 207–8, 212, 213, 259, 308
Heaven Is for Real (film), 34, 80
Hell's Hinges (film), 52
Henderson, Carol, 241–42
Henrietta, Queen, 116–17, 119, 120
Henry Gamble's Birthday Party (film), 41–42
Henry VIII, 37–38, 110
A Heritage of Horror: The English Gothic Cinema 1946–1972 (film), 127
hero
 archetypal character, 8–10
 conscientious objectors, 309–10
 Luther as, 37–38
 nonheroic heros, 323–25
The Hero with a Thousand Faces (Campbell), 8, 275
Herrmann, Bernard, 284–85
Heyman, John, 76
Hick, John, 194
Hicklin standards, 65
Hickman, Daniel, 205, 206
High Noon (film), 295
High Plains Drifter (film), 52, 297
Higher Ground (film), 45, 46, 253–64
Higson, Andrew, 61
Hiller, Wendy, 39
Hinduism, 7, 275
hippie culture, 258–59, 262
history
 of Protestant films, 48–53, 71–73
 sola historica sententia, 179
History Channel miniseries, 36–37
A History of Violence (film), 316–17
Hitchcock, Alfred, 284–85, 322, 327
The Hobbit (Tolkien), 342–43
holiness, classic Protestant theme, 53
Holiness-Pentecostal movement, 206–7
Hollywood Be Thy Name: African American Religion in American Film, 1929–1949 (Weisenfeld), 239
Hollywood studios. *See* studio system
Holy Communion. *See* Eucharist
Holy Ghost (Holy Spirit), 17, 35
 baptism in the Holy Spirit, 17, 208, 212
 The Apostle, 203–18
Holy Ghost People (film), 211
homosexuality, 241, 256
Hoover, J. Edgar, 225–26, 227–28, 230
Hopkins, Matthew, 129–30
horror films, 37, 41–42, 52, 127–38, 211, 281–91
 evangelical apocalyptic horror films, 281–91
 fusion of horror and humor, 137
 sacred violence, defined, 133
 shift from horror films to thrillers, 288
Houston Bible School, 208
Howe, Richard, 269–70
Hubley, Season, 323
Hudson, Hugh, 37
Hughes, Ken, 37–38, 109, 114–15
human sacrifice, horror films, 127–38
humor, 137, 172, 209–10, 257, 262, 276, 301. *See also* comedies/comic elements
Hunchback of Notre Dame (film), 7
The Hurt Locker (film), 316–17
Hyde, Edward, 113–14
hymns. *See* music
Hypocrites (film), 20–21

I Can Do Bad All Myself (film), 34–35
Iakovos, Archbishop, 231

Ibsen, Henrik, 155
iconoclasm, 5, 43, 46, 103, 130–31
idolotry, 43, 100–1, 129–31
Image of the Beast (film), 283
Images (Bergman), 143
immigrants/ethnic minorities, 7, 17, 36, 208–9, 212–13, 215, 256–57
In the Heat of the Night (film), 213
In Your Hands (film), 39
incarnation theology, 175–76
independent Protestant films, 48–49, 71–81
Indiana Jones and the Temple of Doom (film), 7
indigenous people, 294–95, 296–97, 298, 302
individualism, 272
indulgences, Catholic, 10–11, 12
infidelity, 230, 239, 241–42, 243–44
Inherit the Wind (film), 209–10, 217
initial evidence theory, 208
The Institutes of the Christian Religion (Calvin), 12–13
internet
  "best movies about redemption," websites, 83–84
  media consolidation, 68
  online video consumption, 77, 272, 276
Intolerance (film), 20, 156
Invictus (film), 83–84
Ireland/Irish Catholics, 109–10, 112–14, 116–17, 121, 123–24
  Cromwellian invasion, 121
  origins of conflict in Northern Ireland, 119–20
  stereotypes, 117
Islam, 7, 35, 234–35, 270–71

Jackson, Jimmie Lee, 229–30, 233–34
Jackson, Mahalia, 233–34
Jakes, T. D., 16, 34, 36, 80, 205, 211, 214–15
James, Robert, 37–38
James I, 129–31
Jarmusch, Jim, 297
Jarrott, Charles, 37–38
Jaws (film), 269
Jenkins, Jerry, 78, 287–88, 289–90
Jennings, Garth, 41–42
Jensen, Anders Thomas, 38
Jessup, J. Charles, 205
Jesus and the Disinherited (Thurman), 226–27
Jesus Camp (film), 211
Jesus Christ, 14, 269–70
  "Christ figures", 83–84, 335–43
  "Christ transforming culture", 268–69
  cosmic drama of God's salvation, 270
  Crucifixion, 22, 90, 241, 316
  in the Gospels, 159, 240, 310
  incarnation theology, 175–76
  miracles, 159
  personal conversion, 4, 7, 10, 53
  solo Christo, 12
  "true religion", 156
  virgin birth of, 14
Jesus Christ Superstar (rock opera), 33–34, 259
The Jesus Film (film), 76, 98
The Jesus Generation (Graham), 259
Jesus movement/"Jesus freaks", 33–34, 253–54, 255–56, 258–59, 262–63
Joffé, Roland, 312
Johnson, E. Patrick, 248
Johnson, Lyndon B., 221, 225–26, 227–28, 232–33, 235
Johnson, Melanie, 239–50
Johnson, Sister, 205
Jones, Jim, 206
Joof, Hella, 41–42
Judaism, 22, 270–71
  anti-Semitism, 311–12
  Luther's hostility, 101, 104–5, 106
  percentage of practitioners within world religions, 7
  slavery of Hebrews, 172, 241
Jump, Herbert, 19–20, 48–49, 72
Jumping the Broom (film), 34
Jurassic Park (film), 9–10
Just Like Home (film), 38
justice, classic Protestant theme, 53

Kane, Paula M. , 253–64
Karlstadt, Andreas, 98
Katharina Luther (film), 106
Keach, Stacy, 96*f*, 98–99, 102
Kelly, Gene, 209–10
Kelsey, David H., 83
Kendrick, Alex, 79–80
Kendrick brothers, 32, 36, 249–50
Kernochan, Sarah, 211
Keswick movement, 208
Kierkegaard, Søren, 159, 273
killing, 133, 206, 330–32
  justified killing, 308
  lynching, 20, 127–28, 129–30
  shoot-outs, 293–94, 300, 303–4
  "Thou shall not kill", 311
  See also capital punishment; war/violence
King: A Filmed Record … Montgomery to Memphis (film), 35–36, 234–35
King, Coretta Scott, 225, 229, 230–31, 233–34, 235

King, Martin Luther Jr., 35–36, 105, 221–36, 240, 244
lineage within Black Protestantism, 227, 235–36
speeches, paraphrasing in film, 232–33
spokesperson for civil rights movement, 221–22
King James Bible, 22, 76, 129–30, 134
King Kong (film), 335
King of Kings (film), 2–3, 22–23, 27, 98
King Solomon's Mines (Haggard), 336
Kirkegaard, Søren, 168
Klöpfer, Eugen, 98–99
Knox, John, 12–13, 37–38, 110
Knuth, Hans Christian, 105–6
Kokotajlo, Daniel, 41–42
Koskinen, Maaret, 141–52
Kramer, Stanley, 209–10
Krøyer, Peder Severin, 168
Ku Klux Klan, 20, 209–10, 213
Kurosawa, Akira, 41
Kyser, Hans, 99–100

La Merveilleuse Vie de Jeanne d'Arc (film), 156–57
La Passion de Jeanne d'Arc (film), 156–57
La passion du Christ (film), 98
La Symphonie Pastorale (film), 38
LaHaye, Tim, 78, 287–88, 289–90
Lalonde, Paul, 288–89
Lamar Smith, 229
Lament for a Son (Wolterstorff), 196–97
Lancaster, Burt, 217
Land of Plenty (film), 41–42
Landau, Ely, 102
The Last Battle (film), 338
Last Days in the Desert (film), 263–64
Last Supper/Holy Communion, 172–73
The Last Temptation of Christ (film), 1–2, 32, 46
The Last Valley (film), 37–38
The Late, Great Planet Earth (film), 290
The Late, Great Planet Earth (Lindsey), 255–56, 286
Latinx, 33–34, 204, 208–9, 214, 215
Laud, Archbishop, 130, 131–32
Lawhead, Stephen R., 271
Le Fanu, Marc, 155–64
League of Decency, 73
Leap of Faith (film), 210
Lease of Life (film), 38
Lee, Christopher, 134
Lee, George, 229
Lee, Herbert, 229
Lee, Spike, 20, 234–35
Left Behind series, 7–8, 44–45, 52, 78, 263–64, 287–89
Legend, John, 233–34
Legion of Decency, 61–62, 63–65
Leithart, Peter, 193
Lejon, Kjell O., 167–76
Leon: The Professional (film), 83–84
Leone, Sergio, 297, 302
Letters from Iwo Jima (film), 315
Levellers, 121, 122
Lewis, John, 222–23, 231–32
Lewis, Warnie, 335
Lewis C. S., 78–79, 193, 273, 335–43
liberation theology, 240, 241–42, 249–50
Liddell, Eric, 37
Liele, George, 223–24
The Life and Passion of Jesus Christ (film), 98
The Life of Pi (film), 7
Life of St. Paul (film), 74
lighting techniques, 45–46, 142–45, 160, 184–85, 301, 302, 325–26, 331*f*
LightWorkers Media, 32
Lilburne, John, 113–14
Lilies of the Field (film), 33–34
Lincoln (film), 234–35
Lincot, Bernard, 98–99
Lindsell, Harold, 290
Lindsey, Hal, 255–56, 286, 287
Lindvall, Terry, 71, 287, 295
The Lion, The Witch, and the Wardrobe, 7, 32, 46, 71, 78, 335–43
Liquid Church, 267, 277
literalism, 4, 45–46, 53
doctrine of literal sense, 179–80
interplay between literalism and symbolism, 46
"Protestant allegory" and "Protestant literalism", 180
Litt, Hermann, 98–99
Little Rock Nine, 222–23
Liuzzo, Viola, 231
The Living Christ (film), 74
Lockwood, Margaret, 64–65
Long, Eddie, 34–35
Lopez, Abundio, 215
Lopez, Rosa, 215
Lord of the Flies (Golding), 254, 255
Lowes, John, 131–33
Lowes, Sara, 131–32
Lucas, George, 8, 267–77
Luther, die Nachtigall von Wittenberg (stage play), 100

Luther: Ein Film der deutschen Reformation (film), 99–101
Luther, Martin, 10–11, 97–106
and allegory, 179–81
as Catholic monk, 10–11, 100
and confession, 150
filmic representation, 7–8, 37–38, 44–45, 97–106
Ludher, Martinus, ex Mansfeldt, 99
Ninety-five Theses, 100
origins of Puritan tradition, 110
Luther biopics (films), 7–8, 37–38, 44–45, 97–106
Lutheranism, 14, 37, 39, 50–51
example of a good Lutheran, 171
Babette's Feast, 167, 168–69, 171, 174–75, 176
Bergman films, 49, 141, 142, 150
Martin Luther biopics, 97, 100–1
Ordet, 155–56, 158
Luxon, Thomas, 180
Lyden, John, 48–49
lynching, 20, 127–28, 129–30
Lynn, Jonathan, 41–42

MacNutt, Francis, 17–18
MacPherson, Jeanie, 22
A Madea Family Funeral (film), 239–40
Madea's Big Scholarly Roundtable, 248
The Magician's Nephew (film), 337
mainline Protestantism, 14, 67
Major Barbara (film), 39
Malcolm X, 35, 227–28, 229
Malcolm X (film), 6, 234–35
Malick, Larry, 193
Malick, Terrence, 41, 193–201
A Man for All Seasons (film), 37–38, 117
The Man from Laramie (film), 296
The Man Nobody Knows (book), 98
Man on Fire (film), 35
The Man Who Shot Liberty Valance (film), 297
Manifest Destiny, 293, 294, 295–96, 300
Mann, Anthony, 296, 301
Manson, Marilyn, 283
Manual of Practical Anatomy, 308
Marjoe (film), 210, 211
Mark IV Pictures, 282–83
Mark of the Devil (film), 37–38
Marquand, Robert, 271–72
marriage
divorce and separation, 87, 255, 256, 261
marriage counseling, 260, 261–62
and popular forms of romance, 339
Why Did I Get Married? (film), 34–35, 45, 239–50
Marsh, Clive, 83–93
Marshall, Richard, 133
Martin Luther, oder Die Weihe der Kraft (stage play), 100
Martin Luther (film), 101
Marxism, 121, 122
Mary, mother of Jesus, 7–8, 12, 14, 100–1
Mary, Queen of Scots (film), 37–38
Mary I, 110–11
Mary Tudor, 130–31
Mason, Charles M., 224
Mastroianni, Tony, 117
Mather, Cotton, 294–95
Mather, Increase, 294, 301
The Matrix (film), 6, 7
Maxwell, Edwin, 73
McCannell, Colleen, 44–45
McDonnell, Kilian, 17–18
McGinnis, Niall, 98–99
McManus, Erwin, 272
McPherson, Aimee Semple, 39, 209–10
Mean Streets (film), 310
Medgar Evers, 229
media consolidation, 67–68
megachurches, 267, 271–72, 276, 277
Melanchthon, Philipp, 104, 179–81
melodrama, 20, 23, 50–51, 64–65, 183–84, 321
memoir, 253–64
"Memphis Miracle", 208–9
Mencken, H. L., 209–10
Mennonites, 313–14
mentor, archetypal character, 8–9
Mere Christianity (Lewis), 335–36, 339, 340
Methodism, 13, 14, 17–18, 22–23, 64, 223–24, 295
Micheaux, Oscar, 20
migrant farm camps, 215
Mikaël (film), 156
Miller, Arthur, 157–58
Milton, John, 20–21, 113–14, 180
The Miracle Woman (film), 51
miracles, 22, 155–64
in grace and reconciliation, 172–73
within Pentacostalism, 208, 211
Miracles from Heaven (film), 34
The Mission (film), 312
missionary work, 20–21, 72, 74, 76
Mississippi Burning (film), 213, 234–35
Mitchem, Stephanie, 245–46
Moberg, Vilhelm, 40–41
mockumentaries, 210

modernism, 14, 16, 26–27
aesthetics, 41, 42–43
art films, 39–41, 50–51
film noir, 322
Moltmann, Jürgen, 194
monomyths/monomyth framework, 8–10
monopolies
Britain, 64
Hollywood, 61
media consolidation, 67–68
Montgomery, march from. *See Selma* (film)
Montgomery bus boycott, 221–22, 226–27
Montgomery to Memphis (film), 35–36
Moody Institute of Science, 74
Moon, Irwin, 73, 74
"moral fables", 64–65
Moral Majority, 32, 209
Moral Man and Immoral Society (Niebuhr), 222, 226–27
moral relativism, 275
moralism/pietism, as classic Protestant theme, 53
Moravian groups, 168–69
More, Thomas, 37–38
Morey, Anne, 20
Morgan, Gertrude, 233–34
Morgan Freeman, 298
Moring, Mark, 212
Morley, Robert, 109
Motion Picture Association of America (MPAA), 66
Motion Picture Producers and Distributors of America (MPPDA), 57
mountains as motif, 239–50
Movin, Lisbeth, 157–58
Mozart, 168
MPAA rating system, 269
Mr. Texas (film), 75
Mrs. Miniver (film), 73
multiethnicity/diversity of congregations, 36, 203–4, 208–9, 211, 213–14
Munk, Kaj, 158–59, 163, 164
Müntzer, Thomas, 98
Murdoch, Rupert, 79
Murphy, James T. Jr., 247
music
associated with Protestantism, 37, 45, 170–71, 295, 296–97
Christian Woodstock, 281–82
country music, 86, 89, 90–91
independent Protestant sound films, 73
megachurches, 271–72
Pentecostalism, 205, 211, 216
reenchantment of the mundane, 45
spirituals and gospel music, 233–34
Westerns, 295, 300
Higher Ground, 256, 257–60, 263–64
Selma, 232–34
Star Wars, 268–69, 273
A Thief in the Night, 283–84
Why Did I Get Married?, 239–40
musicals, 19, 31–32, 41–42, 259
Muslim faith, 7, 35, 234–35, 270–71
My Darling Clementine (film), 295, 302
mysticism, 270, 275
myth, 275, 293–95, 297–98, 315

The Naked Spur (film), 301
Näktergalen i Wittenberg (stage play), 100
The Narnia Chronicles: The Lion, The Witch, and the Wardrobe, 7, 32, 46, 71, 78, 335–43
narration, 149, 321–22, 325–27
Nash, Diane, 222–23, 225–26, 228, 234–35
National Baptist Convention, 223–24
National Board of Censorship of Motion Pictures, 60
National Board of Review of Motion Pictures, 60
National Catholic Office for Motion Pictures (NCOMP), 66
National Council of Churches, 65–66, 67
National Council of Churches of Christ in USA, 14
native peoples, 294–95, 296–97, 298, 302
Nazi Germany, 38, 41–42, 101, 104–5, 158
Neimöller, Martin, 38
The Neon Bible (film), 41–42
New Age religious influences, 51
New American Bible, 311
New Hollywood, 3–4, 32, 36–41, 321
The New Land (film), 40–41
Newspring Church megachurch, 276
Nicolet, Clément, 155–56
Niebuhr, Reinhold, 222, 226–27
Niebuhr, Richard, 48–49, 268
Nielsen, Carl, 158–59
Nierenberg, George T., 233–34
Nietzsch, Friedrich, 283
The Night of the Hunter (film), 215–16, 329–30, 330*f*, 331*f*
Night of the Living Dead (film), 285, 290
Ninety-five Theses, 100
Noah (film), 1–2, 46
Nolan, Christopher, 309–10
Noll, Mark, 277
Norman, Larry, 283–84, 286

Not Easily Broken (film), 34
Nykvist, Sven, 142–43

obesity and body image, 248, 249
occultism/occult influences, 51, 269–70, 275
O'Connor, Edward, 17–18
O'Connor, Flannery, 210
Of Gods and Men (film), 263–64
Oh Happy Day (film), 41–42
Olesen, Annette K., 39
Olesen, Ole, 156
The Omega Code (film), 78
omnipotence/omnipresence, friction with suffering, 193–201, 240–41, 244, 245, 246, 247, 248, 250
On Christian Doctrine (Augustine), 268–69
One Hour with You (film), 57
One Is Business, the Other Crime (film), 20
One Night with the King (film), 79
online video consumption, 77, 272, 276
Orange, James, 225–26, 228, 234–35
Ordet (film), 39, 41, 45–46, 155–64
Ordet (stage play), 158
Ormond, June, 283
Ormond, Ron, 283
Osborne, John, 102, 105
Oscars. *See* awards for achievement
The Outlaw Josey Wales (film), 297
Oyelowo, David, 35–36, 220*f*, 225, 232–33, 233*f*
Ozu, Yasujiro, 41

pacifism, 222, 226–27, 228, 307–18
  antiwar movements of the 60s, 262–63
  See also war/violence
pagan heresies, 127–38
pain. *See* suffering and pain
Paisley, Ian, 119
Pale Rider (film), 302
Palmer, Teresa, 308
pantheism, 270–71, 275–76
"papists", 169–70. *See also* Catholicism
parables, 246, 248–50
Paradise Lost (film), 180
Parham, Charles, 17, 208
Parkhurst, Charles, 19–20
Parks, Rosa, 221–22
parodies, 137–38
Parting the Waters (Branch), 226–27
Pascal, Gabriel, 39
Passion of Anna (film), 144
The Passion of Joan of Arc (film), 39
The Passion of the Christ (film), 32, 34, 45–46, 53, 79, 310, 311–12, 315–16, 317
Passion plays, 22–23, 98
Pastor Hall (film), 38
Pastor Jones: Preaching to the Choir (film), 239
patriarchy, 248–49, 253–54, 262–63
  in Calvinism, 321, 324–25
  hierarchies, 255, 260
  patriarchal oppression, 249–50
Paul: Apostle of Christ (film), 45–46
penance, 10–11, 89, 92–93
Pentecostalism, 16, 17, 203–18
  as apolitical, 207, 209
  distinct from fundamentalism, 204, 207–8, 212–13
  diversity within congregations, 203–4, 208–9, 211, 212, 213–14
  versus fundamentalism, 204, 212–13
  history, 206–7, 240
  percentage of practitioners within world religions, 7
Perkins, William, 179–81
Perry, Tyler, 34–35, 36, 80, 211, 239–50
Persona (film), 149
personal conversion/personal redemption, classic Protestant theme, 53
personal interpretation of biblical text, 313–15
personal nature of relationship with God, 314
Pietism/Pietist groups, 168–69
piety
  as classic Protestant theme, 53
  movie regulation, pietist approach, 58, 62, 63, 64, 65–66
  "visual piety", 19–20
Pilgrims, 12–13
Pilgrim's Progress (Bunyan), 180, 181–83, 261, 323–24
Pirie, David, 127–28
plainness/simplicity, 45–46, 168–69, 170
  mundane, within Protestant aesthetic expression, 45
  Pentecostalism, simple folk, 209–10
  plain camera style, 180–81
  plain writing style, 187–88
  "reduction" or "decluttering", 5, 45–46, 142, 143, 145
pleasure, reconciling conflicts of spirit and flesh, 172–74
Plessy v. Ferguson Supreme Court decision, 222–23
Poitier, Sidney, 33–34
poor and working-class. *See* class issues
Poor People's Campaign, 224
pop culture, 268–73
popular musical style, 268–69, 271–72

pornography/X-rated films, 66–67, 283, 321–33
Porter, Edwin S., 293–94
POV (in narrative), 322, 325–26
POV shots, 188, 326–29, 328*f*, 330–32
Præsidenten [The President] (film), 156
Pratney, Winkie, 270
The Prayer Meeting (painting), 168
The Preacher's Wife (film), 35
preaching as objective of films, 22, 71, 72, 73, 276
predestination, 13–14, 324–25, 326–27
pregnancy and childbirth, 159–60, 255–56
Prejean, Helen, 311–12
premillennialism, 16, 208
Presbyterians, 12–13, 14, 17–18, 22–23
  megachurches, 271–72
  Scottish Presbyterians, 61, 119
Price, Vincent, 129
"pricking", 132
priests and priesthood, 10–11, 26, 65–66, 73, 111, 112–13, 128, 129, 215–16, 226–27
  as classic Protestant theme, 53
Prince Caspian (film), 78–79, 336–37
prison labor, 215
Private Confessions (film), 149, 150
The Problem of Pain (Lewis), 340
Prodigal Planet (film), 283
Production Codes, 62–67, 268, 269
propaganda
  against communism, 101
  Protestant Reformation propaganda films, 127–38
  wartime propaganda, 38
prostitution, 299–300, 303, 304
protestant aesthetic, 41–48
Protestant Aesthetics and the Arts (Covington and Reklis), 42–43
Protestant Reformation films, 49
  Martin Luther representations, 97–106
  Oliver Cromwell, 109–25
  propaganda films, 127–38
  witch hunt films, 127–38
Protestantism, 10–19
  Evangelicals, Pentecostals, and Fundamentalists, 15–16
  historical origins, 10–14
  influence on filmmaking, 1
  mainline, 14
  percentage of practitioners within world religions, 7
providence, classic Protestant theme, 53
Provident Films, 32
Psycho (film), 284–85, 327
The PTL Club (television show), 255–56
Pure Flix, 32, 80
purgatory, 10–11, 12
Puritanism, 12–13, 110–11
  idolotry and heresy, 127–28, 130–32
  in New England, 111, 112, 113, 190
  Oliver Cromwell, 109–25, 131–32
  Puritans for Protestantism, 335–36
  stereotypes, 321
  and Western films, 295, 296–97
  The Scarlet Letter, 183–87

Quakers, 295, 313–14
Quicke, Andrew, 48–49, 71–81, 83–93, 287

Rabid (film), 289
race issues, 36, 51, 117, 296–97
  interracial Pentecostalism, 203–4, 207, 208–9, 211, 212, 213–14, 217
  See also African Americans; civil rights movement
radical fundamentalism, 211
radio, 73, 337
Raging Bull (film), 310
Raiders of the Lost Ark (film), 6
Rain Man (film), 83–84
Rambling Rose (film), 204–5
Rank, Arthur, 56*f*, 64–65
ranker.com, 83–84
rapture and tribulation movies, 281–91
  "us *versus* them" dynamic, 290
  See also apocalypticism/end of the world
The Rapture (film), 282
Rauschenbusch, Walter, 222, 226–27
Reagan, Ronald, 67
realism, 44–45, 61, 159, 163, 190, 315, 322, 325–26
rebellion, spiritual growth through, 261
reconciliation, 160–61, 175–76
Red River (film), 297
redemption, 51, 53
  independent filmmakers, 79–80
  key elements in redemptive process, 93
  lighting technique, 143–44
  Protestant doctrine, 84–86, 92–93, 336–37
  redemptive violence, 307
  The Apostle, 203, 207, 217
  Crazy Heart, 86–89
  Unforgiven, 207, 217, 294, 301
Redling, Erik, 179–90
"reduction" or "decluttering" of aesthetic excess, 5, 45–46, 142, 143, 145
Reeb, James, 231

Reeves, Michael, 37–38, 127, 130–31
reform, as Protestant aesthetic expression, 43–44
the Reformation
  Ninety-five Theses, 12
  See also Protestant Reformation films
Regina v. Hicklin (English decision), 58
Reith, John, 58–59, 59*f*
Reklis, Kathryn, 42–43
Relevant magazine, 275
religion, defined, 5–6
The Religion of the Force (Geisler and Howe), 269–70
religious archetypes, 8–10
The Religious Possibilities of the Motion Picture (Jump), 19–20, 72
religious right. *See* right-wing politics
Remonstrance (Arminius), 13
repentence/atonement, 12, 13, 22, 85, 93, 183, 185
The Restless Ones (film), 75
resurrection, miracle of, 137–38, 158–64, 339*f*
Resurrection (film), 36–37
Return of the Jedi (film), 269–72
Revelation (film), 77
Revelation-related themes, 286–87. *See also* apocalypticism/end of the world
revenge, 133, 297–300
revisionist films, 296–97
revivalism, 208–9
Richardson, Miranda, 205–6
right-wing politics, 90–91, 209, 212
  conservative evangelicalism, 253–64
  rise of the religious right, 259
righteousness, classic Protestant theme, 53
Rindge, Matthew S., 307–18
Risen (film), 45–46, 263–64
ritual, 149, 150
  art as, 142
  Protestant *versus* Catholic cinematics, 44–45
  reductionism, 150
Robbins, Tim, 311–12
Robertson, Pat, 16
Robison, James, 212
Rocky (film), 269
Rode, Christian, 98–99
Romanowski, William, 48–49, 57–68, 268–69
Romero, George, 285
Rossellini, Roberto, 41
RottenTomatoes.com, 118
Ruether, Rosemary, 261–62
"running", 132
rural theology and worship, 209–10, 239, 256–57, 262–63
Rye, Preben Lerdorff, 159–60
Sabbath, holiness of, 37, 111, 184–85, 313–14
sacraments in Protestantism, 12
"sacred clutter", 50–51, 143
sacred violence, defined, 133
sacrifice
  Eucharist as sacrifice, 134–35
  horror films, human sacrifice, 127–38
  passion of Christ, sharing in, 339*f*, 342
sadism, 330–32
Sage, Victor, 127–38
Sahyoun, Mona, 248–49
saints
  archetypes, 8
  in Calvinism, 13
  in Catholicism, 12, 111, 156–57, 159
  hagiographies, 221
  and miracles, 159
  tribulation saints in the rapture, 286, 288, 289–90
salvation, 10, 12, 13–14
  within Catholicism, 104
  cosmic drama of God's salvation in Jesus Christ, 270
  salvation stories, 83–93, 203–18, 241, 245–46, 255–56
  See also redemption
Salvation Army, 39
sanctification, classic Protestant theme, 53
sarcophagus, 172
Sargent, Dick, 327–29
Satan. *See* the Devil/diabolic possession
savagery of God, 133
Savalas, Telly, 210
Saved! (film), 41–42
Saving Grace (film), 239
Saving Private Ryan (film), 309
Say Amen Somebody (film), 233–34
Scandinavia
  art films. *See* Danish cinema
  Lutheran Protestant reformation in, 168–69
The Scarlet Letter, 45–46, 179–90
  1926 film, 183–87
  1973 film, 187–90
  political meaning of the letter A, 189–90
Der Scharlachrote Buchstabe, 179–90
Scherfig, Lone, 38
Schierbeck, Poul, 158–59
Schneider-Quindeau, Werner, 105
Schrader, Paul, 41, 321–33
Schultze, Quentin, 271–72
Schwartz, Stephen, 259
science and faith, relationship, 74
Scofield Study Bible, 287–88

Scopes trial, 14, 209–10, 281
Scorsese, Martin, 1–2, 32, 41, 210, 310
Scotland, 109–10, 112–13, 121, 127–28, 134–35
Scottish Episcopalian Bible, 134
Scottish Presbyterians, 119, 123–24
Scott, George C., 320*f*
Scott, Mark S. M. , 193–201
Scott, Ridley, 1–2
screen adaptions. *See* adaptations
The Searchers (film), 296–97, 301
Second Great Awakening, 223
secular humanism, 230–31
secular liberalism, 155–56
secularism, 4–5, 26, 53, 89, 125, 155, 324–25
self-confidence/self-assertion, 262–63
self-deception, 332–33
self-expression, 263–64
self-help culture, 92, 93
self-liberation, 248, 249–50
self-repression, 259–62
self-sufficiency, illusion of, 340
self-surveillance, 321–33
self-worth/self-esteem/self-image, 241–44, 245–46, 247, 248, 249–50
Selma (film), 7–8, 35–36, 44–45, 221–36
separation of church and state, 4–5, 112, 113, 123–24
September 11th bombings, 290
Sergeant York (film), 73, 309, 312–13
Sermons from Science series, 74
Seven Pounds (film), 83–84
Seventh-day Adventists, 310, 313–14
The Seventh Seal (film), 39–40, 41, 141, 144–45
sex
  fornication, 128–29
  pornography and X-rated films, 66–67, 283, 321–33
  prostitution, 299–300, 303, 304
  rape, 133
  sexual liberation movement of the 60s, 262–63
  sexual register, 135
  sexual violence, 133
sexism. *See* gender issues
Seymour, William J., 17, 208–9, 224, 240
Shane (film), 302
Shaver, Billy Joe, 205
Shaw, George Bernard, 39
The Shawshank Redemption (film), 83–84
shot-reverse shot sequences, 286
Siegel, Don, 302
silence
  clutter of language, 145–49
  dualism between words and silence, 149
  translating images into words, 146–47, 148
Silence (film), 263–64, 310
The Silence (film), 39–40, 142, 145–49, 148*f*, 151
silent films, 48–49, 71–72, 180–81
Silver Bluff Baptist Church, 223–24
Simmons, Jean, 209–10
Simons, Menno, 10–11
simplicity. *See* plainness/simplicity
sin and depravity, classic Protestant theme, 53
Sinatra, Frank, 281–82
singing. *See* music
The Single Moms Club (film), 248, 249
The Sins of Deacon Whyles (film), 239
Skæbne-Anekdoter [Anecdotes of Destiny] (book), 167
slavery, 172, 223–24, 240, 241, 295
Sling Blade (film), 204–5
Slotkin, Richard, 293–94
Smith, Chuck, 18–19
Smith, Howard, 211
Snow White and the Seven Dwarfs (film), 335
Social Gospel theology, 20, 222, 226–27
sola fide, 179
sola gratia, 179
sola historica sententia, 179
sola scriptura, 12, 176, 179, 310–13
soli Deo gloria, 12
Son of God (film), 32, 36–37, 45–46
Son of Rambow (film), 41–42
Sønderby, Knud, 163
songs. *See* music
sorcery
  art as, 142
  See also witches/witchcraft
Soska, Jen, 289
Soska, Silvia, 289
sound/soundtrack. *See* music
South/southern culture
  Second Great Awakening, 223
  "whites only"/Jim Crow segregation, 208–9, 221–23, 227–28
  Crazy Heart, 83–93
  Selma, 221–36
  The Apostle, 203–18
  See also civil rights movement
Southern Baptists, 22–23, 36, 89
Southern Christian Leadership Conference (SCLC), 228, 229, 232–33
Sparkle (film), 34
special effects, 45–46, 272, 282, 337
Spenser, Edmund, 180

Spielberg, Stephen, 248
Spielberg, Steven, 309
spirit and flesh dichotomy, 175–76
spirit baptism, 17, 208, 212
spiritual growth potential, Protestant spiritual narrative, 261
spiritual memoirs, 253–64
Stagecoach (film), 296, 302
Star Wars (films), 6, 7, 8, 9–10, 267–77
  Episode I: A New Hope, 270, 273
  Episode III: Revenge of the Sith, 273
  Episodes IV-VI, 274
  Episode VII: The Force Awakens, 267, 274, 276
Star Wars, Star Trek, and the 21st Century Christian (Pratney), 270
Star Wars Jesus— A Spiritual Commentary on the Reality of the Force (Grime), 273
Star Wars Redeemed: Your Life-Transforming Journey with Jesus and the Jedi (Hagan), 273
Staub, Dick, 273
Stendhal, 199–200
Stevens, Jason, 203–18, 321–33
Strindberg, August, 100, 155
Strong, Jeremy, 231
structural approach to movie regulation, 58, 62, 66
struggle
  central to Protestant spiritual narratives, 261
  mountains as motif, 239–50
Student Nonviolent Coordinating Committee, 222–23, 228, 231–32
studio system, 65, 67
  versus independent nontheatrical films, 71–81
  monopolistic expansion, 61
  Production Code, 268, 269
Styll, John, 270–71
suffering and pain, 51, 335–43
  being made perfect, 340–41
  part of redemptive process, 336–37
  sharing in Christ's sufferings, 340, 342
  subjective experience of, 193–94
suicide, 193
Sunday, Billy, 19–20
Sunday school, 23, 72, 73, 74, 255, 338
Sunday Sinners (film), 239
supply-and-demand model of film production, 67–68
Sweden, 158
Swiss Reformed Church, 97–98
symbolism
  interplay between literalism and symbolism, 5, 46
  "symbolic action", 181–83
  Hardcore, 329–30
  The Apostle, 213, 215
  The Lion, the Witch and the Wardrobe, 337–38
  The Scarlet Letter, 181–83, 184, 187
  The Tree of Life, 198, 199–200
  Unforgiven, 293–94, 295
  Why Did I Get Married?, 242, 248, 250
  See also allegory
syncretism, 51, 275, 323

Taoism, 270–71, 275
Tarkovsky, Andrei, 321
Taubin, Amy, 212–13, 217
teaching. *See* education/evangelism *versus* entertainment in film
teens. *See* young people
television
  adaptation for, 337
  advertising, 58–59, 268
  history, 268, 272
  The PTL Club, 255–56
  rise of, 65
The Ten Commandments (film), 22
Tender Mercies (film), 91–92, 204–5, 263–64
terrorism, 290
Tetzel, Johann, 10–11
Tetzel, Johannes, 100–1
Thein, Ulrich, 98–99
"thematic effect", 181–83
theodicy, 195–98
  defined, 194
  subjective experience of suffering, 193–94
theology of culture, 48–49, 268–69
A Theology of the Social Gospel (Rauschenbusch), 222
There Will Be Blood (film), 210
A Thief in the Night (film), 45, 281–91
Thies, Alexander, 102–3
This Dark World: A Memoir of Salvation Found and Lost (Briggs), 254
This Far by Faith: African American Spiritual Journeys (film), 35–36
Thompson, Donald, 52, 263–64, 282–84
Thomson, Anna, 292*f*
Thornton, Billy Bob, 207, 213
threshold guardian, archetypal character, 8–9
thriller films, 52, 287–88
Through a Glass Darkly (film), 39–40, 141, 142, 143, 145, 149
Thulin, Ingrid, 140*f*
Thurman, Howard, 226–27
Till, Eric, 102–3

Tillich, Paul, 48–49, 72, 83
Tim Metcalfe, 254
Time magazine, 270–71, 272
A Time to Kill (film), 213, 234–35
Time Warner Cable, 68
To Kill a Mockingbird (film), 204–5, 213
Tobacco Road (film), 51
Tolkien, J. R. R., 342–43
Tomorrow (film), 204–5
tongues, 17–18, 208–9, 210, 257, 258*f*, 259
  divisions among Protestants, 257
  faking of, 211
  "Jesus people" or "Jesus freaks", 259
  xenolalia and glossolalia, 17
torture, 133, 315–16
transcendence, 39, 45, 46
  God as personal being and transcendent Creator, 269–70
  longing for, 171, 273, 277
  noir style *versus* transcendental style, 325–26
Transcendental Style in Film (Schrader), 325–26
transformation
  "Christ transforming culture", 277
  mountains as motif, 239–50
  potential for, 261
The Tree of Life (film), 45, 46, 193–201, 263–64
Tribulation (film), 77
tribulation saints in the rapture, 286, 288, 289–90
tribulation themes. *See* horror films
trickster, archetypal character, 8–9
Trinity Broadcasting Network, 78
Troell, Jan, 40–41
Trotsky, Leon, 113–14
True Grit (film), 297
A True Hope: Jedi Perils and the Way of Jesus (Hays), 273
Truman, Harry S., 307, 315
Truth, Sojourner, 246
Två Människor [Two People] (film), 156
Twins of Evil (film), 37–38
Tybjerg, 163, 164
Tybjerg, Casper, 163

Ullmann, Liv, 40–41, 140*f*, 150
The Ultimate Gift (film), 32, 79
Unforgiven (film), 44–45, 293–305
unjust suffering. *See* suffering and pain
Urban League, 235
Ustinov, Peter, 102–3

vampires, 136
Vampyr (film), 156
van Inwagen, Peter, 194
Vaughn, Vince, 308
Vaus, Jim, 75
Vaux, Sara Anson , 293–305
vegetarianism, 313–14
Velarde, Robert, 275
vengeance, 133, 297–300
Venice Film Festival, 164
vernacular language, 12, 150, 151
video screens in megachurches, 271–72
videocassette technology, 66–67, 72, 77, 272
Vidor, King, 239
Vietnam era, 41, 52–53, 269, 290
Villa Valdez, Susie, 215
Village Voice newspaper, 212
Vimeo and other online consumption, 77, 272, 276
virgin birth within theological doctrine, 14
The Virgin Spring (film), 39–40, 143
Virgin Tales (film), 41–42
Vivian, C. T., 225–26, 234–35
Vogler, Christopher, 8–10, 114–15
von Arx, Mirjam, 41–42
von Heinz, Julia, 106
Von Sydow, Max, 40–41
von Trier, Lars, 38, 143
voting rights/voting restrictions, 222–23, 224, 225–26, 228, 229
The Voyage of the Dawn Treader (film), 78–79, 336–37, 338, 340
voyeurism, 325–26, 329–30

Wainer, Alex, 267–77
Walden Media, 32, 78–79
Wallace, George, 225–26, 227–28, 232–33
Wallis, Jim, 16
Walsh, Frank, 268
Walsh, Raoul, 52
war film, 307–18
War Room (film), 32, 36
war/violence, 52–53, 307–18
  American culture of war, 316–18
  antiwar movements of the 60s, 262–63
  versus pacifism, 312, 317–18
  radical forgiveness, 305
  redemptive violence, 307
  "regeneration through violence", 294
  sacred violence, defined, 133
  sexual violence, 133
  wartime propaganda, 38
  World War I, 61, 309, 316–17, 340
  World War II, 65, 73, 282, 290, 307
  Hacksaw Ridge, 44–45, 307–18

Ware, Kallistos, 199–200
Warner Bros., 76
Warren, Rick, 16
Washington, Denzel, 35, 36, 211, 234–35
Washington, March on, 233–34
WASP nationalism, 20
Watergate scandal, 269
The Way, Calvary (film), 263–64
Way Down East (film), 20
Wayne, John, 296–97
Weaving, Hugo, 307–8
Webb, Andy, 117
Weber, Lois, 3, 5, 20–21, 22
Weisenfeld, Judith, 239
Welles, Orson, 322
Wenders, Wim, 41–42, 46, 187–90
Werner, Friedrich Ludwig Zacharias, 100
Wesley, Charles, 13
Wesley, John, 13
Westerns, 52
  and American Puritan tradition, 52
  and Protestantism, 293–97
  Unforgiven (film), 293–305
Wheatley, Ben, 41–42
The White Ribbon (film), 37, 41–42
The White Rose (film), 20
white supremacy, 208, 231
Why Did I Get Married? (film), 34–35, 45, 239–50
The Wicked Lady (film), 64–65
The Wicker Man (film), 37–38, 45, 127–28, 134–35
Wilkinson, Tom, 226
Williams, Hosea, 225–26, 234–35
Wills, Garry, 303–4
Wilson, Frank, 239
Wilson, Woodrow, 222–23
Wimber, John, 18–19
Winans, Marvin, 34–35
Winchester '73 (film), 296
Winfrey, Oprah, 35–36, 225
Winter Light (film), 32, 38, 39–40, 141, 142, 143–45, 144*f*, 150
Winthrop, John, 294–95
Wipfler, Esther, 97–106
The Wiretapper (film), 75
Wise Blood (film), 210
The Wise Kids (film), 41–42
witches/witchcraft, 127–38, 157–58
  witch-finders, Calvinist stereotype, 321
  The Lion, the Witch and the Wardrobe, 335, 341
  The Witch: A New-England Folktale, 41–42
  Witchfinder General, 7–8, 37–38, 45, 46–48, 127–38
Within Our Gates (film), 20
Wittenberger Nachtigall (film), 100
Wolterstorff, Nicholas, 196–97
Woman Thou Art Loosed (film), 34, 80
womanist theology, 249–50
women. *See* gender issues
wonder and awe, 45, 78, 159, 197–98, 199–200, 259, 263–64
Woodlawn (film), 36–37
Woodstock, Christian, 281–82
Woolrych, Austin, 113–14
Worden, Blair, 113–14
working class. *See* class issues
World War I, 61, 309, 316–17, 340
World War II, 65, 73, 282, 290, 307
World Wide Pictures, 75*f*, 75, 76*f*
worship, art as, 141–42
Worthington, Sam, 309–10
The Wrestler (film), 83–84
The Writer's Journey: Mythic Structure for Writers (Vogler), 8–9
Wüstenhagen, Karl, 98–99

X-rated/pornographic content, 66–67, 283, 321–33

York, Alvin C., 309
Youmans, Phillip, 36
Young, Andrew, 225–26, 228, 230–31, 234–35
Young, Robert M., 33–34, 211
The Young Messiah (film), 45–46
young people
  1960s youth culture, 258–59, 261–62, 281–82
  censorship for, 60, 61–62, 66
  in Christian youth group meetings, 287
  film strategies for, 282–83, 287
  Jesus movement/"Jesus freaks", 33–34, 253–54, 255–56, 258–59, 262–63
  rallies, 282
  teaching moral values, films for, 270–71
  Young Life organization, 281, 283–84
  Youth for Christ movement, 281
YouTube and other online consumption, 77, 272, 276

Zeidler, Hans Dieter, 98–99
Zinnemann, Fred, 295
zombies, 285, 288–91
Zwingli, Huldrych, 97–98, 179–80